☀️ INSIGHT GUIDES

asia's Best Hotels & Resorts

"A well-written and truly
useful guide"
— Qantas Magazine —

" ...a succulent book that would inspire travel,
rather than guide tourists around."
— South China Morning Post —

" a great compilation of all the must-go R&R spots...
Flipping through the pages will get you in a holiday
mood... It's a perfect gift for any travel-mad loved one!"
— Elle Magazine —

"No need to worry about where to stay.... Discerning
travellers will find the guide full of descriptions, pictures,
contact details, room rates and customer ratings."
— Holiday Asia —

APA PUBLICATIONS L
Part of the Langenscheidt Publishing Group

Editorial

Project Editor
Ed Peters
Managing Editor
Francis Dorai
Publisher
Jon Stonham

Distribution

UK & Ireland
GeoCenter International Ltd
The Viables Centre, Harrow Way
Basingstoke, Hants RG22 4BJ
Fax: (44) 1256-817988

United States
Langenscheidt Publishers, Inc.
36–36 33rd Street, 4th Floor
Long Island City, NY 11106
Fax: (1) 718 784-0640

Canada
Thomas Allen & Son Ltd
390 Steelcase Road East
Markham, Ontario L3R 1G2
Fax: (1) 905 475 6747

Australia
Universal Publishers
1 Waterloo Road
Macquarie Park, NSW 2113
Fax: (61) 2 9888 9074

New Zealand
Hema Maps New Zealand Ltd (HNZ)
Unit D, 24 Ra ORA Drive
East Tamaki, Auckland
Fax: (64) 9 273 6479

Worldwide
Apa Publications GmbH & Co.
Verlag KG (Singapore branch)
38 Joo Koon Road, Singapore 628990
Tel: (65) 6865-1600. Fax: (65) 6861-6438

Printing

Insight Print Services (Pte) Ltd
38 Joo Koon Road, Singapore 628990
Tel: (65) 6865-1600. Fax: (65) 6861-6438

©2005 Apa Publications GmbH & Co.
Verlag KG (Singapore branch)
All Rights Reserved
First Edition 2003
Second Edition 2005

CONTACTING THE EDITORS
We would appreciate it if readers
would alert us to errors or out-
dated information by writing to:
11/D Ho Lee Commercial Building
38-44 D'Aguilar Street
Central, Hong Kong
guidebook@hotelclub.com

www.insightguides.com
www.HotelClub.com

ABOUT THIS BOOK

So successful was the first edition of this unique guide book (which ran to two reprints) that we decided to make the second bigger and more detailed. As with the first publication, the hotels have been chosen by the ultimate critics – guests who have actually been there. We have certainly relished sifting through the 64,000 nominations for the best hotels, and selecting the crème de la crème. This year we have covered more destinations and added more countries. Such is the speed of change at the moment; our team of expert travel writers has revisited many of the properties over the last six months to ensure that our information is up-to-date and accurate. We apologise if we have not nailed this moving target totally.

The speed of change is just one of the problems travellers face in finding a hotel. Asia's tourism market is developing so quickly it is often difficult to keep up with all the new hotels and resorts, especially given the trend for more intimate boutique properties. At the same time, the more established hotels are investing heavily to keep up with the pack - spas are now considered obligatory, as are in-room broadband connections and Wi-Fi'd public areas. And the chains

are muscling in on a market that was previously dominated by independently run hotels. One thing is for sure - Asia's collection of already impressive properties is getting better - something driven mainly by the consumer. All this means that finding a hotel to suit one's needs - whether it's a casual two-star family joint on the beach or a city-centre business property bristling with the latest gadgets and resident techno butler - is ever more difficult. This guide aims to make it easier.

As with the first edition, the book is structured to make it simple for you to select a hotel. Grouped by country, each hotel has a short description which we hope captures its true essence, supported by photographs and a list of facilities. Unfortunately there is only so much room in a book, so if you require more information there are further details at HotelClub.com. Reservations can also be made through this website, and by way of incentive we have included a discount membership card with this book.

Ed Peters has continued in the role of lead editor, supported by **Bill Cranfield** and **Andrew Dembina**. Ed first set foot in Asia 25 years ago, and has been travelling the region ever since, variously disguised as a backpacker, Gurkha officer and more recently as journalist and travel writer. He has dossed down in a number of unusual venues when more regular accommodation proved unavailable, including on beaches, a police cell and in the bed of a most hospitable Nepalese manager (who slept on the floor, in case you are wondering) - however he is not averse to a little five-star

slumming from time to time. He is based in Hong Kong, but also maintains a home in Phuket; otherwise he can be found gallavanting around the region under the pretence of writing a story.

Thanks go to **Sophie McLaughlin** for sub-editing the book, **Harry Llufrio** and his wife **Mina** from gingerbreadman.net for again meticulously laying it out, **Vivian Wong** for her administrative skills, the content crew at asia-hotels.com and the team at Insight Guides for production and distribution. The photographs were principally supplied by the hotels, but have been supplemented by national tourist associations and various other sources.

The front cover photograph of this second edition is graced by the lovely Four Seasons Kuda Huraa in the Maldives. On 26th December 2004 this outstanding resort was significantly damaged by the tsunami that laid waste to vast swathes of Asia, from Aceh in Indonesia to Tamil Nadu in southern India. Over 300,000 lives were claimed by the tragedy and millions lost their loved ones, their homes and their possessions. As well as hotels and resorts in the Maldives, properties in Sri Lanka, Thailand, the Andaman Islands and Malaysia were also affected. The Kuda Huraa was fortunate that no guests or staff were harmed, but elsewhere many were not so lucky.

Whilst the tsunami was a tragedy, it also brought to light the spirit and heart of Asia. From offering up their homes to victims to helping search for the missing, Asian people have shown their true

warmth, hospitality and affection. It is qualities like these which make Asia the fastest-growing tourist destination in the world. True, the region is blessed with some of the planet's best beaches, cleanest seas, most diverse cuisine and consistent sun, but it is the open arms with which Asians routinely welcome guests that makes the region so popular. With the exception of a select band of "Editors' Picks", the vast majority of hotels and resorts in this second edition have been selected by guests, and whilst the properties themselves are often stunning, it is the professional and sincere service which leaves the more lasting impression.

I hope you enjoy this guide. It's a testament to the resilience and resourcefulness of the wonderful people I have had the pleasure of meeting in this part of the world that I call home. By way of a footnote, most of the damaged hotels are back in business, although a few are slated to start welcoming guests again over the summer. The Four Seasons Kuda Huraa will reopen its doors in November 2005.

Jon Stonham
Publisher

Maps

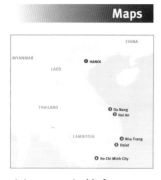

Picture credits

Front cover: *Four Seasons Resort Maldives
at Kuda Huraa (by Peter Mealin)*
Back cover: *Grand Hyatt Hong Kong,
Banyan Tree Bintan*
Page 1: *Sheraton Suzhou*
Page 4: *Taj Exotica Maldives*
Page 224: *Glyn Genin*
Page 92: *Club Bali Mirage*

The national tourism bodies of Australia
(page 8), Brunei by David Kirkland (page
26), Hong Kong (page 53), South Korea
(page 150), Macau (page 165), Malaysia
(page 169), New Zealand (page 230)
Philippines by George Tapan (page 240),
Singapore (page 254) Taiwan (page
283/284) and Thailand (page 292).

CONTENTS

Hotels by country

Indexes

About the ratings

As with the first edition, guests with first-hand experience essentially selected the hotels in this book. In 2004, asia-hotels.com, a subsidiary of HotelClub.com, polled its customers for their favourite hotels. Over 64,000 nominations were received, citing 3,732 hotels in 29 countries. Each hotel was rated on ten criteria using a scale of 1 - 10 (10 being best). This second edition has an additional rating of "Ambience", and the "Facilities" rating is now a combination of scores for business, leisure and room facilities. The "Overall rating" was calculated from the scores given using a HotelClub.com formula.

Our team of inspectors and independent travel writers then reviewed the ratings and number of votes to come up with 400 hotels, 100 more than the first edition, across the main destinations in the Asia-Pacific region. The team tried to select hotels in as many different locations as possible to improve the usefulness of the guide. However, to be considered for the book, hotels had to receive a minimum number of votes and excellent scores. A few "Editor's Pick" hotels were added to give the book an even broader coverage. These Picks are generally small hotels, or have opened in the

last two years and so are less well-known, or are in countries that do not receive so many visitors (e.g. Nepal). Although one of the team members has personally inspected each of these hotels, they have "n/a" for ratings.

The star rating has generally been supplied by the hotel, although in some cases we have adjusted them (always down) where the team felt the rating was misleading. A scale of five stars has been used, despite some hotels claiming six- or even seven-star classification. Where a hotel has not supplied a star rating, we have assessed it based on the experience of our inspections.

Room rates fluctuate dramatically - especially from high season to low season or when hotels experience strong or weak demand. We have given an indication of the amount you would expect to pay using a "$" scale - one "$" being at the budget end and "$$$$$" being seriously pricey!

Finally, while we do make every effort to get our facts right, hotels in Asia are changing quicker than ever. If there is a hotel you feel strongly should be included or if we have got something wrong, please do let us know.

Facilities

Baby Sitting

Beach

Business Centre

Casino

CNN

Disabled Facilities

Diving

Golf Course

Gymnasium

Kids' Club

In-room Computer Ports

Nightclub

Restaurant

Room Service

Satellite / Cable TV

Spa

Indoor Swimming Pool

Outdoor Swimming Pool

Tennis Court

Tourism Information

Water Sports

Price guide

$ - less than US$ 100
$$ - US$ 100 - US$ 200
$$$ - US$ 200 - US$ 300
$$$$ - US$ 300 - US$ 400
$$$$$ - Over US$ 400

Rates from: $$$$$
Star rating: ★ ★ ★ ★ ★
Overall rating: 🦢🦢🦢🦢🦢

Ambience :	1-10	Cleanliness:	1-10
Value:	1-10	Facilities:	1-10
Staff:	1-10	Restaurants:	1-10
Location:	1-10	Families:	1-10

For peace of mind, stay connected.

Stay at a CNN Partner Hotel.

In a world that never sleeps, you want access to the most up-to-date news coverage, 24-hours a day. CNN. It's reassuring to know that almost anywhere in the world, you can wake up in a comfortable room to a trusted and familiar voice.

For more information on CNN Partner Hotels and the latest travel news, please visit CNN.com/travel.

Be the first to know.

AUSTRALIA

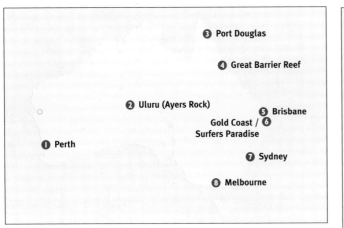

❸ Port Douglas

❹ Great Barrier Reef

❷ Uluru (Ayers Rock)

❺ Brisbane

Gold Coast / ❻
Surfers Paradise

❶ Perth

❼ Sydney

❽ Melbourne

Australia got the century off to a flying start by hosting a magnificent Olympic Games, shouldering aside the traditional image of a dinki-di Aussie - whether a gleaming, muscled Bondi lifesaver or laconic, bush-hatted sheep shearer - once and for all. Nowadays the iconic Aussie could easily be one of the prancing entrants in the annual Gay and Lesbian Mardi Gras parade. Or perhaps even one of the many recent Asian immigrants - from Vietnam, China or further afield - who have done much to add to the cosmopolitan mélange of the "Lucky Country". But the essence of Australia remains unchanged.

This vast continent (7,686,848 square kilometres) ranges between desert and tropical rainforest, sophisticated urban areas with sprawling suburbs and isolated townships in the bush, stunning mountains and lush pasture.

Australians enjoy a magnificent outdoor lifestyle, with a play-hard, work-hard (well, sometimes, mate) attitude that makes the most of its natural bounty. German immigrants planted the vineyards that have brought Barossa Valley wines world renown, the waves of Italian and Greek settlers did much to promote Australian cuisine beyond meat pies and beer, while Japanese finance helped to open up the Gold Coast. In other words, some of the best that the world has to offer is distilled into Australia.

With the possible exception of the purpose-built and rather soulless capital, Canberra, all the Antipodean cities exude their own character and allure to the casual visitor. Sydney is first port of call for many, and indeed where the first British convicts were dumped in the 18th century. The whole city is inspired and refreshed by its raison d'être, the harbour. Overlooked by the architectural masterpiece of the Opera House, and framed by the marvellous Harbour Bridge, it acts as a focal point for dining and relaxation, and is the centre of attention during major events such as the annual Sydney-Hobart yacht race. Melbourne has always seen itself as a rival, and while it lacks the spectacular location it has as much charm and sophistication, especially when it comes to theatre and cuisine, and is equally devoted to sports, horse-racing and "footy" to name but two. Adelaide, long known as the place for culture, has shaken off its previously staid image, and Brisbane, once derided as an overgrown country town, has become increasingly cosmopolitan after hosting a string of international events like the Commonwealth Games. Even Darwin, with a certain amount of cinematic assistance from *Crocodile Dundee*, has some claim

to "cool", although the weather is as hot as ever. Perth claims to be the sunniest of Australian cities, and even rain cannot damp its bright and breezy ethos. Cairns acts as the jumping-off point for most of northern Queensland, notably to the stunning beauties of the Great Barrier Reef and the rainforests of Cape Tribulation. Alice Springs, more or less in the centre of the continent, would probably not feature on any itinerary but for the proximity of Uluru, otherwise known as Ayers Rock - the outback's ultimate landmark and a sacred site for Australia's original inhabitants, the Aborigines. Mention should also be made of Australia's offshore islands, from the slightly other-worldly Tasmania to the hedonistic Hayman in the Whitsundays, which is also a prime venue for whale watching and scuba diving.

Most of Australia's 19 million inhabitants live in the coastal areas, so it follows that this is where the best hotels are. For location - right under the Harbour Bridge and looking on to the Opera House - it would be hard to better the Park Hyatt in Sydney, and up on the Gold Coast the Palazzo Versace is an intriguing jeu d'esprit of very modish accommodation. Head inland, and the main places to lay your head are bland motels or beery country pubs, where service echoes the old Australian ethos of "I'm as good as you are, mate". Between these two stellar stools is a range of decent resorts well placed to make the best of Down Under's natural assets of sun, sand and sea.

The weather varies immensely over such a vast continent, but all of Australia is hot in the summer between December and February, and the north is especially humid. It is best to time visits to the "Top End" during the cooler winter (June - August) and this is also when the snowfields of Victoria and New South Wales open up. In spring, large stretches of the outback are carpeted with wildflowers. Hotels are often booked solid over Easter, Christmas and other school holidays.

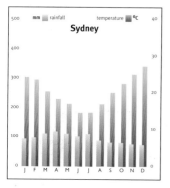

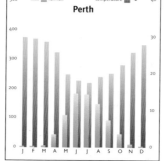

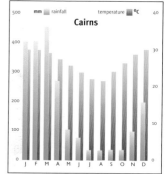

Burswood InterContinental Resort Perth

Great Eastern Highway, Burswood, WA 6100, Australia
T: +61 8 9362 7777 **F**: +61 8 9470 2553
www.HotelClub.com/Hotels/InterContinental_Burswood_Resort_Perth

Many visitors regard the 417-room Burswood as "Perth in a Packet". On the banks of the Swan River, it may not be everyone's idea of beautiful architecture, but it does offer just about all the fun and frolic that seems to be automatically associated with the capital of Western Australia. There are tennis courts and an 18-hole golf course right next to the resort; a spa, pools indoor and out, and a health and fitness centre; the wheels spin 24 hours in the casino, or you can bet on the TAB tote in Champions sports bar; some 11 other bars and restaurants offer international cuisine and wine, beer and spirits; rock your socks off in the Ruby Room nightclub, catch a play at the theatre or a concert in the Dome, which seats up to 20,000. Without doubt, this is a resort that fulfills the old saying about something for everyone.

One asset which few other hotels can match is the surroundings - 113 hectares of superbly landscaped gardens and parklands which comprise the magnificent Burswood Park. This makes for a perfect place to take a leisurely stroll, a bicycle ride or just to sit and relax. You can have a cook-out on the free electric barbecues, let your youngsters romp around the children's playground, or simply appreciate the abundant bird life.

Visitors who want to get to grips with Western Australia's past can follow the unique Heritage Trail with its bronze sculptures of historic figures, while friendly and experienced tour hosts conduct daily guided walking tours of the park.

For the energetic, there's a choice of three-, four- and seven-kilometre long cycle and jogging tracks, which form part of the extensive network of cycleways around Perth's waterways. Few hotels anywhere can offer such a wealth of space right on the doorstep.

Rates from: $$
Star rating: ★ ★ ★ ★ ★
Overall rating: ♌ ♌ ♌ ♌ ½

Ambience :	8.71	Cleanliness:	9.00
Value:	8.07	Facilities:	8.55
Staff:	8.19	Restaurants:	8.69
Location:	8.14	Families:	8.23

Crown Towers

8 Whiteman Street, Southbank, Melbourne, Victoria 3006, Australia
T: +61 3 9292 6888 **F:** +61 3 9292 6299
www.HotelClub.com/Hotels/Crown_Towers_Hotel_Melbourne

The banks of the Yarra River, Melbourne's central aquatic artery, have undergone a transformation in recent years. They are now distinguished by such landmarks as the Exhibition and Convention Centre, the city aquarium, the Southgate restaurant and gallery complex, Federation Square and the Victorian Arts Centre. Right in the middle, on the opposite bank to the central business district, is the Crown Entertainment Complex, home to the Crown Towers.

It is a somewhat unusual hotel, not least as on the doorstep is one of the country's largest 24-hour casinos (350 tables and 2,500 gaming machines), as well as a host of nightclubs, cinemas, virtual reality interactive game venues and a bowling alley. The fun continues within the hotel, with a 3,000-square-metre spa dispensing 60 different Eastern and Western health and beauty treatments, a 25-metre indoor heated pool, a high-tech gymnasium and two Rebound Ace championship tennis courts.

Fun, too, are the Crown's "villas" - not the bungalow plus garden that the name might lead you to expect, but penthouses with dining and living areas, a butler at your beck and call and a choice of up to three bedrooms. The hotel's other rooms and suites may not be so large, but they are all framed by richly toned fabrics and warm timbers, with a facsimile machine, private safe, separate dressing room and marble-lined bathroom. And if the entertainment in the surrounding complex seems insufficient, there are some 40 channels on the TV.

Equally appealing for leisure or business travellers (there are 26 meeting and function rooms), the Crown complex sports more than 40 different restaurants, bars and snack outlets. Of note are Breezes, serving a blend of Australian and Mediterranean cuisines, the Japanese Koko, Chinese at Silks and all-day dining at the Conservatory.

The Towers is complemented by its new sister hotel, the 465-room Crown Promenade, which opened next door in late 2003.

Rates from: $$$
Star rating: ★ ★ ★ ★ ★
Overall rating: ♣♣♣♣ ½

Ambience :	8.90	Cleanliness:	9.18
Value:	8.04	Facilities:	9.04
Staff:	8.49	Restaurants:	8.73
Location:	8.85	Families:	8.22

Four Seasons Hotel Sydney

199 George Street, Sydney, NSW 2000, Australia
T: +61 2 9238 0000 **F**: +61 2 9251 2851
www.HotelClub.com/Hotels/Four_Seasons_Hotel_Sydney

Adopting the not entirely absurd metaphor that the Four Seasons is an extensive, sunlit gourmet picnic, some of the morsels that the more sagacious might be inclined to savour would include: the 100 per cent Aussie view over The Rocks to the Opera House, Botanical Gardens and Harbour Bridge; the rich silks, exotic Honduras mahogany and Italian marble bathrooms in the 531 rooms and suites; the sweet onion-dusted Victorian beef tenderloin at Kable's restaurant, complemented by one of its cellar's boutique wines; Sydney rock oysters on the shell early one evening in the Bar; gently bronzing by a private cabana at the heated pool; and ingesting the aroma of a frangipani wrap in one of the spa's six soothing treatment rooms.

Delivered with the traditional Four Seasons service and style, it is not surprising many guests come back for more.

Rates from: $$$$
Star rating: ★ ★ ★ ★ ★
Overall rating: ♨ ♨ ♨ ♨ ½

Ambience :	8.68	Cleanliness:	9.08
Value:	7.95	Facilities:	8.47
Staff:	8.92	Restaurants:	8.29
Location:	9.41	Families:	7.17

Grand Hyatt Melbourne

123 Collins Street, Melbourne, Victoria 3000, Australia
T: +61 3 9657 1234 **F**: +61 3 9650 3491
www.HotelClub.com/Hotels/Grand_Hyatt_Melbourne

The Grand Hyatt is the point-and-click of hotels for corporate travellers. Its curved gold tower is right in the CBD, and the 549 rooms all have king-sized beds, window-side desks and the revolutionary Inter-touch Internet connection system. A techno butler stands ready to deal with set-ups, hang-ups and straightforward computer cock-ups round the clock, and there are two ballrooms and a host of function rooms for gatherings.

For corporate entertaining, the Plane Tree Café offers a stylish but casual buffet, while the Hyatt Food Court provides freshly made-to-order meals from around the globe. Evenings here tend to start with cocktails at Bar Deco, move on to one of the restaurants and finish at Monsoon's nightclub, with the R&B Thursdays proving especially popular. The usual roll-call of fitness facilities - pool, gym, tennis courts - is enlivened by the addition of a hotel nutritionist.

Rates from: $$
Star rating: ★ ★ ★ ★ ★
Overall rating: ♨ ♨ ♨ ♨

Ambience :	8.51	Cleanliness:	8.66
Value:	7.54	Facilities:	8.19
Staff:	8.10	Restaurants:	7.90
Location:	8.73	Families:	7.14

Hayman

Great Barrier Reef, Queensland 4801, Australia
T: +61 7 4940 1234 F: +61 7 4940 1567
www.HotelClub.com/Hotels/Hayman_Island_Resort

Hayman, the most northerly of the Whitsunday group, seems not so much a resort island as a mirage. It is also a sublime tribute to millennia of creation by the tiny coral polyp, which formed the Great Barrier Reef that runs for 2,300 kilometres along the east coast of Australia. Staggering in both its natural beauty and its extraordinarily diverse recreations, Hayman has few equals in the whole of the Asia Pacific.

Anyone landing here for the first time is beset by twin temptations. Do you just stay put on the 400-hectare island, rejoicing in the ice-block white crescented accommodation curving round the twin hexagonal "pools within a pool" by the beach - all embraced by 12 hectares of lush gardens, beyond which lie thick forests of Moreton Bay ash, hoop pine and Whitsunday kurrajong inhabited by white cockatoos, painted lorikeets and Bhraminy kites? From May to November, myriad butterflies swarm in gullies feasting on the nectar of eucalyptus blossom, and besides the main beach there are three others, two of which can only be reached by boat. As might be expected, there is a superlative spa here too.

Or, when Whitsunday wanderlust takes hold, do you plunge into that reality cliché - the wide blue yonder? A speedboat

can take you to an outlying island and drop you off for the day with a picnic - or just the evening for a champagne sunset. Drop in on the reef itself for a bit of diving or snorkelling, courtesy of the *Reef Goddess* cruiser, or get up close in the semi-submersible *Reef Dancer*. Romantics may prefer a trip out to Heart Reef, shaped by nature and Cupid, and yes, Hayman also handles weddings. The 12.5-metre *Sun Aura* has a spacious deck for easy access to tackle for game and bottom fishing trips. You can skim the waves behind a 225hp ski boat, or aboard a windsurfer or one of the resort's catamarans. Humpback whales can be spotted during their stately migration to the

Whitsundays between July and September. Seaplanes and helicopters handle flight-seeing trips year-round. Guests can also mix and match their excursions, for example, packing a helicopter ride to the world famous Whitehaven sands, a snorkelling trip to the inner reef and a slug of champers at sundown into a single seamless day. As the man said, three days here is good, a week better, a month - still not enough.

The choice of where to go and what to do around Hayman is mimicked in the resort, with the option of bedding down in anything from regular rooms (complete with balcony and breathtaking views) to the spiffy Beach Villa - with a private

infinity pool and outdoor entertainment area. Other options include the Retreat Rooms with their extended open patios and outdoor showers, and the Penthouses, which have varied themes including Greek, Oriental and English.

Hayman's restaurants are pretty international too, both in cuisine and outlook. La Fontaine is French and formal, La Trattoria rustic and Italian, the Beach Pavilion casual in the extreme with extremely good seafood.

Of course, Hayman is Utopia for children. A special crèche handles children from six weeks to five years, while kids up to 12 can be safely and entertainingly corralled at Hernando's Hideaway.

Intriguingly, Hayman also offers an etiquette class, teaching youngsters deportment, behaviour skills and the correct use of cutlery. If nothing else, the mere threat of being dispatched for an afternoon's P&Q-minding should be enough to keep even the most mischievous brat in line.

Rates from: $$$$$
Star rating: ★ ★ ★ ★ ★
Overall rating: ෆ ෆ ෆ ෆ ෆ

Ambience :	9.43	Cleanliness:	9.52
Value:	8.05	Facilities:	8.94
Staff:	9.19	Restaurants:	9.05
Location:	9.43	Families:	7.53

InterContinental Sydney

117 Macquarie Street, Sydney, NSW 2000, Australia
T: +61 2 9253 9000 **F:** +61 2 9240 1240
www.HotelClub.com/Hotels/InterContinental_Hotel_Sydney_1

There is no other word for it - the InterContinental is just so utterly Sydney. It incorporates the former Treasury Building - built in 1851 but now gorgeously renovated - and is backed by a modern state-of-the-art skyscraper. Stand on the open-air terrace of the Australia Suite (complete with grand piano and a bathroom more like a mini spa with Bang & Olufsen providing the background music) and the city and harbour are laid out below like a feast. The views from the other - somewhat smaller and less luxuriously appointed - 503 rooms may not be quite so evocative, but there is no denying this is an eminently comfortable hotel. The Cortile - a courtyard right in the heart of the original building - is a hugely popular meeting and eating venue, as is Café Opera with its seafood-laden buffets.

Unquestionably the most exciting venue though is 30 Something - unsurprisingly it is on the 31st floor and the views are quite mouth-watering (as is the Mediterranean cuisine).

Rates from: $$
Star rating: ★ ★ ★ ★ ★
Overall rating: 🌀🌀🌀🌀 ½

Ambience :	8.85	Cleanliness:	9.20
Value:	7.98	Facilities:	8.32
Staff:	8.43	Restaurants:	8.60
Location:	9.33	Families:	8.17

Langham Melbourne

1 Southgate Avenue, Southbank, Victoria 3006, Australia
T: +61 3 8696 8888   **F:** +61 3 9690 5889
www.HotelClub.com/Hotels/Langham_Hotel_Melbourne

If ever a hotel was ripe for adding to Great Eagle's upmarket Langham portfolio, it was the Sheraton.

Formerly part of the "Luxury Collection", it is at the hub of Australia's most Victorian city and was modelled with a Victorian mansion in mind. The Langham, after which the Hong Kong property giant's hotel arm was named, was a jewel of Victorian London.

The changeover could have accounted for a reported dip in service at one stage, but one can safely assume that the new management will be doing everything to inject stiffer imperial-style standards. Location-wise, it has everything going for it - atop the trendy Southgate shopping and restaurant complex, its 387 rooms overlook the Yarra River and historic Flinders Street.

On the understated side despite its plethora of gold and crystal, the Langham is ideally equipped for the business traveller: it is the only Melbourne hotel to offer videoconferencing, its covered lap pool is perfect for wind-down workouts, and the Melba Brasserie has picked up various local restaurant awards.

Rates from: $$$
Star rating: ★ ★ ★ ★ ★
Overall rating: 🌀🌀🌀🌀 ½

Ambience :	8.85	Cleanliness:	9.26
Value:	8.07	Facilities:	8.59
Staff:	8.44	Restaurants:	8.63
Location:	9.48	Families:	8.41

Longitude 131°

Via Yulara Drive, Ayers Rock, Northern Territory, Australia
T: +61 8 8957 7888 **F**: +61 8 8957 7474
www.HotelClub.com/Hotels/Longitude_131

You might well feel like a movie-star staying in the luxury of this African-safari-style collection of make-believe tents. Controversially plonked down just six miles from Aboriginal Australia's most sacred site (with minimal ecological interference, we are assured by Voyages Hotels & Resorts), Longitude 131° is a love-it-or-loathe-it experience, depending on your attitude to cultural voyeurism and theme-park tourism, however elevated.

The 15 "tents" are actually modernistic steel pods on stilts with flowing fabric canopies, and inside they are hotel rooms in all but

name, with sliding glass windows and touch-button electric blinds, solid wood furniture, separate showers and bathrooms, air-conditioning and sound systems.

Somewhat incongruously given their futuristic feel, each is named after a 19th-century Aussie explorer and there are black-and-white photos and faux artefacts on the wall to hammer home the theme. Wooden chests, of the sort pioneers used to lug around the Outback, abound.

Nearly completely destroyed in a bushfire a couple of years ago, the property has been enhanced in the re-building. A "Sounds Of Silence"

dining experience has been added to the refectory-table, three-course evening meals available at Dune House (where breakfast and lunch buffets are also served). Apart from grazing while you gaze at the stars, you will be serenaded by a didgeridoo player and entertained by a resident astrologer. The outstanding food is high-end Australian gourmet.

There is a small unheated pool and a comprehensive library with TV, and a variety of exotic activities are up for grabs, such as camel-riding or roaring across the red desert on a Harley-Davidson. The raison d'être for this whole experiment in ecotourism-without-tears is the 24/7 sight of Uluru, aka Ayers Rock, that it offers. You can catch it at sunset or sunrise, midnight or midday, up close as part of a base walk or from afar with G&T in hand - splendid.

Rates from: **$$$$$**
Star rating: ★ ★ ★ ★ ★
Overall rating: Editor's Pick

Ambience :	n/a	Cleanliness:	n/a
Value:	n/a	Facilities:	n/a
Staff:	n/a	Restaurants:	n/a
Location:	n/a	Families:	n/a

The Observatory

89-113 Kent Street, Sydney, NSW 2000, Australia
T: +61 2 9256 2222 F: +61 2 9256 2233
www.HotelClub.com/Hotels/Observatory_Hotel_Sydney_The

In the dozen years since it opened, The Observatory has rapidly become the pied-à-terre for Sydney insiders. Inspired by the historic 1850s Elizabeth Bay House, it glows with the warmth of a grand Australian home and its 100 rooms are luxuriously furnished with antiques, oil paintings and tapestries.

From the dome-shaped atrium of the entry foyer to the antique fireplace and polished walnut furniture of the guests' exclusive drawing room, there is much to admire here. Colonial-style sash windows and period balconies give the rooms a sense of history, while CD players, fax/modem facilities and four telephones bring them bang up to date. The 22 Junior and Executive Suites are each designed slightly differently, and some have four-poster beds and a private terrace.

Both the Globe Bar and Galileo restaurant are well worth repeat visits, the former for its voluminous library, the latter for its Italian-tinged modern Australian cuisine. But the Observatory spa is somewhere you could linger indefinitely, not least because of the amazing subterranean pool. Its roof is ingeniously lit by fibre optics, which turn it into a vast firmament of twinkling stars.

Perhaps the chief delight of the Observatory is its unending devotion to detail. There is a complimentary weekday city limousine service for starters. Beds are made up according to personal preferences - be it a particular sort of linen or non-allergenic pillows. The "specs box" contains a variety of reading glasses for the shortsighted who are also absent-minded. In-room companionship can be provided in the form of a goldfish or two. If you are feeling under the weather, staff deliver a get-well-soon kit - a bowl of broth, herbal teas and skin products together with a selection of CDs and magazines. And youngsters automatically receive a personalised choc-chip dinosaur and pint-sized bathrobes. After all, there is nothing like getting brand loyalty off to an early start.

Rates from: $$$
Star rating: ★★★★★
Overall rating: ½

Ambience :	9.14	Cleanliness:	9.57
Value:	7.57	Facilities:	8.71
Staff:	9.00	Restaurants:	8.30
Location:	8.71	Families:	7.10

Palazzo Versace

Main Beach, Gold Coast, Queensland 4217, Australia
T: +61 7 5509 8000 **F:** +61 7 5509 8888
www.HotelClub.com/Hotels/Palazzo_Versace_Gold_Coast

Mama mia! Las Vegas meets Old Europe in this deliciously over-the-top tribute by Donatella to her late brother Gianni. Kitsch, perhaps; tacky, never. Everything is genuine Italian, from the multi-coloured river-stones that line the approach-way to the giant chandelier in the lobby, that once hung in Milan's state library. And everything is genuine Versace, from the furniture and fabrics to the cutlery and crockery, to the artworks from Gianni's collection.

The Palazzo's 205 rooms and 72 condos look out onto ocean or marina views, while five palm-fringed, heated saltwater lagoons lap their surrounds. Staff are dressed all in Versace black and gold. The standard room/suite can accommodate three adults or two plus two children. They come equipped with all you would expect and more - a Sony PlayStation, for instance, and free Versace perfume and aftershave in the marbled bathrooms. Decor is mainly what

the fashionistas refer to as "timber tones", i.e. pale yellow and gold.

The restaurants are determinedly European - no token Japanese or Chinese outlets here. The signature Vanitas is about as haute as cuisine gets, Vie is built on a boardwalk overlooking the marina and includes a Cuban Cigar Room (none of your common Dutch or German panatellas here), Il Barocco offers "classic and contemporary" Italian dishes, and the conservatoire-style Le Jardin resembles somewhere swank in the Fifth Arrondissement.

The Latin-labelled Salus Per Aquum Spa features a splendid Roman bath of a pool and there is a Versace Boutique, where almost every item in this neo-classical fantasy world is for sale. But as you stroll among the palm trees and the gold leaf and the marble, it is not so much Michelangelo you expect to bump into as Tony Soprano.

Rates from: $$$
Star rating: ★ ★ ★ ★ ★
Overall rating: 🦢🦢🦢🦢½

Ambience :	9.17	Cleanliness:	9.30
Value:	8.57	Facilities:	8.89
Staff:	8.57	Restaurants:	8.80
Location:	8.48	Families:	7.47

Park Hyatt Melbourne

1 Parliament Square, Off Parliament Place, Melbourne, Victoria 3002, Australia
T: +61 3 9224 1234 **F:** +61 3 9224 1200
www.HotelClub.com/Hotels/Park_Hyatt_Melbourne

The interior designers obviously gave their imaginations free rein when it came to drawing up the plans for the Park Hyatt. It is modern, intriguing, stylish without being over the top or painfully trendy, and a lot of the time real fun as well.

A wall of vibrant blue, hand-sculptured glass signals your arrival at the art deco-themed, five-level radii restaurant and bar. The guestrooms also carry a hint of Art Deco, where the use of warm-toned fabrics blends together beautifully with walls panelled with Madroña wood and richly coloured soft furnishings. The domed ceiling and colonnaded sandstone interior of the indoor 25-metre, edgeless aquamarine pool is offset by a striking Grecian mural. And contemporary works of art from local and international artists are displayed throughout the hotel, with the attention to detail usually reserved for a private collection.

Not that style triumphs over substance - this is very much a hotel for executives with a job to do. All rooms enjoy dedicated high-speed Internet access and interactive television, while the studios on the club floor have a fetching open-plan design with king-size beds. The suites in particular have a distinctive design that captures the very essence of the city, with outstanding views of the historic cathedral, the enchanting gardens and century-old elm trees that surround the hotel.

Away from work, there is a great deal to enjoy at the Hyatt. Extensive health and spa facilities border the pool, including a personal training studio, a tennis court and a sun deck. While radii remains the hotel's chief dining and entertainment venue, right next door is Cuba, an exquisitely furnished cigar lounge hung with some arresting artworks. An open fire blazes here in winter in what is the only smoking venue in an otherwise "smoke-free" environment - very much a sign of the times.

Rates from: $$$
Star rating: ★ ★ ★ ★ ★
Overall rating: ♦ ♦ ♦ ♦ ½

Ambience :	9.25	Cleanliness:	9.50
Value:	8.34	Facilities:	8.68
Staff:	8.41	Restaurants:	8.27
Location:	8.97	Families:	6.83

Park Hyatt Sydney

7 Hickson Road, The Rocks, Sydney, NSW 2000, Australia
T: +61 2 9241 1234 **F:** +61 2 9256 1555
www.HotelClub.com/Hotels/Park_Hyatt_Hotel_Sydney

You cannot get more Sydney than The Rocks, and you cannot get more Rocks than the Park Hyatt, one of the city's most stunning boutique hotels. It is not simply the location - practically reflected in the sails of the Opera House and occasionally specked by waves from the harbour. There is a real sense of occasion here - it is not a hotel you drop into casually merely to get a night's rest or have a hurried lunch, but one that should be approached with mounting anticipation and glee.

The senses are indulged completely at this 158-room hotel - or should that be resort? - which is now preening itself in the wake of a stylish and contemporary makeover. The concept of a grand mansion by the water is expressly fulfilled, with personalised butler service for each guest, luxurious interior design and unique artworks. There is a choice of regular rooms, studios or suites, all with a private harbour-facing balcony and many with the premium view of Jorn Utzon's masterpiece of "frozen music". Each room is spacious, elegant and equipped with walk-in wardrobes, remote-control curtains, marble bathroom, CD player and Internet television access. There is also access to PlayStations, though much more imaginative entertainment is to be found elsewhere in the Park Hyatt.

This could be at the spa, where a petite rooftop pool is joined by a gym, sauna and steam rooms, and such exclusive treatments as the Vichy Shower, which deliciously combines high-pressure jets with a light rain effect. Similarly salubrious, the Harbourkitchen is a waterfront restaurant where a wood-fired oven, rotisserie and chargrill integrate the flavours of seasonal and mainly Australian produce. There is also a walkabout wine cellar containing over 600 mainly domestic wines. Drinking still ranks high on Sydney's list of favourite recreations. The Club Bar, with its wood-panelling, armchairs and fire warmth, serves rare malts and vodkas, while the Harbourbar is divided into three sections - Champagne, Draft Beer and Martini, the last with an impressive 60-item menu. But shortage of choice is never really an issue at the Park Hyatt.

Rates from: $$$$
Star rating: ★ ★ ★ ★ ★
Overall rating: 👍👍👍👍 ½

Ambience :	9.05	Cleanliness:	9.05
Value:	7.52	Facilities:	8.42
Staff:	8.41	Restaurants:	8.52
Location:	9.24	Families:	7.49

Shangri-la Hotel Sydney

176 Cumberland Street, The Rocks, Sydney, NSW 2000, Australia
T: +61 2 9250 6000 **F:** +61 2 9250 6250
www.HotelClub.com/Hotels/ShangriLa_Hotel_Sydney

For an instant Australian experience, this Antipodean outpost of the popular Asian group (for many years the ANA) can't be beat. Turn up before your room is ready and you can freshen up in the Arrivals Suite before feasting your eyes on the quintessential panorama of breathtaking harbour and iconic Opera House.

The hotel's spectacular views and fantastic Rocks location are undoubtedly the main selling points. On the debit side, its spacious rooms are nothing to write home about decor-wise, staff can be somewhat offhand and you have to climb a fairly steep hill to get to it.

Perhaps as a nod to the Shang's Oriental image, the accent seems to be more on Japanese food these days than the contemporary Aussie fare it used to favour. But with so many great restaurants just a walk away, this should be the least of your considerations. Finally, no prizes for guessing why the top-floor Blu Horizon bar got its name, or why the hordes hurtle there come dusk.

Rates from: $$$
Star rating: ★ ★ ★ ★ ★
Overall rating: ♪ ♪ ♪ ♪ ½

Ambience :	8.76	Cleanliness:	9.12
Value:	7.65	Facilities:	8.67
Staff:	8.69	Restaurants:	8.38
Location:	9.35	Families:	7.22

Sheraton Mirage Gold Coast

Sea World Drive, Main Beach, Gold Coast, Queensland 4217, Australia
T: +61 7 5591 1488 **F:** +61 7 5591 2299
www.HotelClub.com/Hotels/Sheraton_Mirage_Gold_Coast

Breakers Cocktail Lounge, but the party really gets going at weekends in Rolls, the hotel's swish nightclub. For those needing to venture out, Marina Mirage's boutiques and restaurants are adjacent to the hotel; Sea World is a gentle stroll away and Surfers Paradise a ten-minute walk up the beach.

Situated on the Gold Coast's Broadwater Peninsula, the Sheraton packs some of the very best of this holiday region into its 293 comfortable rooms and 16 hectares of lush palm gardens. Low-rise and well spread out, the resort features a one-hectare seawater lagoon pool, a spa and fitness facility, tennis courts and a unique beach-front location. The pick of the rooms are the Ocean Premiums with stunning sea vistas, and the 35 fully equipped home-style villas.

The restaurants make the most of Australian cuisine with the laid-back Oyster Bar in the garden, seafood buffet overlooking the pool and fine dining available in Horizons. There is live music in

Rates from: $$$
Star rating: ★ ★ ★ ★ ★
Overall rating: ♪ ♪ ♪ ♪ ½

Ambience :	9.24	Cleanliness:	9.08
Value:	7.60	Facilities:	8.79
Staff:	8.52	Restaurants:	8.32
Location:	9.04	Families:	8.36

Sheraton Mirage Port Douglas

Davidson Street, Port Douglas, Queensland 4877, Australia
T: +61 7 4099 5888   **F:** +61 7 4099 4424
www.HotelClub.com/Hotels/Sheraton_Mirage_Port_Douglas

With the celebrated Four Mile Beach on its doorstep, the Sheraton is fully justified in trumpeting that it is the "only international five-star beachfront resort in North Queensland". However, with so many other options on offer in this veritable village nestled in 120 hectares of rainforest, some guests probably don't even get their toes sandy. They are more likely to be playing the 18-hole golf course designed by Peter Thomson (remember him?), swimming in the saltwater pools that surround the hotel (in addition to freshwater and lap pools), or relaxing in their own jacuzzi if they're in one of the 101 villas that dot the property (these also all have two bathrooms). Self-contained is definitely the word for this pretty amazing resort, which also boasts its own shopping mall, a pillar-less, tent-like function facility called the Glade Pavilion and even a Las Vegas-style hitching post, the Crystal Wedding Chapel. For anyone feeling a tad isolated, a free shuttle service runs to the big city lights of Port Douglas.

Rates from: $$$
Star rating: ★ ★ ★ ★ ★
Overall rating: 👣 👣 👣 👣

Ambience :	8.92	Cleanliness:	8.96
Value:	7.58	Facilities:	8.42
Staff:	8.21	Restaurants:	8.13
Location:	8.79	Families:	8.00

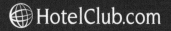

Sheraton On The Park

161 Elizabeth Street, Sydney, NSW 2000, Australia
T: +61 2 9286 6000 **F:** +61 2 9286 6668
www.HotelClub.com/Hotels/Sheraton_on_the_Park_Hotel_Sydney

One of the most satisfying activities offered by the Sheraton has the added inducement of being absolutely free. Slip into the top-floor heated pool first thing in the morning, and chances are that you will have it, and the view of the breaking dawn through the arched roof and eye-level windows, all to yourself. The pool's limpid surface and the general air of calm here allow a little time to reflect on the diverse attractions of the hotel beneath.

For starters, there are 510 rooms and 48 suites, smartly decorated, well up to speed with technical accoutrements, with roomy bathrooms and - in case anyone was wondering about the hotel's name - cracking views over Hyde Park, central Sydney's "lungs". Two floors are dedicated to the Sheraton's executive club.

Down on the first floor, the relaxed Botanica Brasserie is open seven days a week for breakfast, lunch and dinner, providing extensive buffets with extra-special seafood at the weekends. The Conservatory is an elegant lounge serving traditional high tea, snacks and cocktails, while Haris on the Park serves surf & turf with an all-Aussie wine list.

The Sheraton's meeting facilities include a grand ballroom that can hold up to 1,000, and a substantial array of smaller rooms suitable for banquets or conferences. An on-site event staging company can assist with audio-visual equipment, computer data display and sound and lighting as well as other expert techno back-up. Returning to the pool on the 22nd floor, the health club includes a fully equipped gym, massage rooms, saunas and steam rooms, a solarium and a team of personal trainers.

The Sheraton, apart from its obvious proximity to the park, is also only a short hop from downtown and has a covered walkway to the Monorail.

Rates from: $$$
Star rating: ★ ★ ★ ★ ★
Overall rating: ⬙⬙⬙⬙ ½

Ambience :	8.65	Cleanliness:	9.15
Value:	7.89	Facilities:	8.51
Staff:	8.74	Restaurants:	8.40
Location:	9.34	Families:	8.09

Sofitel Brisbane

249 Turbot Street, Brisbane, Queensland 4000, Australia
T: +61 7 3835 3535 **F**: +61 7 3835 4960
www.HotelClub.com/Hotels/Sofitel_Brisbane

Although it's now been in business since 1984 (refurbished in 2002 and recently switched to Sofitel), you'd be hard put to beat this Brisbane landmark for its superb amenities and CBD location - opposite the Brisbane River's South Bank, with both Parliament and the Old Government House nearby.

The 30-storey tower, atop Central Station, houses 410 cream-themed rooms flooded with light and all boasting great views and every convenience the business or vacationing traveller could need, including high-speed Internet access.

The Sidewalk Restaurant, which opens straight onto Anzac Square, does great buffets and the aptly named Whistlestop Bar & Bottleshop serves a fine range of beers on the station concourse. The only quibble would be with the small (but heated) pool, which is overlooked by surrounding offices; but then, centrality and seclusion don't often go together.

Rates from: $$
Star rating: ★ ★ ★ ★ ★
Overall rating: 🐾🐾🐾🐾

Ambience :	8.82	Cleanliness:	8.94
Value:	7.71	Facilities:	8.32
Staff:	8.41	Restaurants:	8.50
Location:	8.65	Families:	7.36

Sofitel Melbourne

25 Collins Street, Melbourne, Victoria 3000, Australia
T: +61 3 9653 0000 **F**: +61 3 9653 7733
www.HotelClub.com/Hotels/Hotel_Sofitel_Melbourne

Since its opening in 1981, the Sofitel has closely allied itself with Melbourne's arts scene, and the hotel's own consultant oversees the exhibitions that regularly grace the walls of Sofi's Piano Bar, the lobby, the Atrium on 35 and Café La. So there is a fair amount to look at inside the hotel, while the views are equally appealing across Melbourne and Port Phillip Bay from the 363 rooms and suites - which start on the building's 36th floor. The rooms, suspended around a stunning atrium, are conveniently set up with broadband and other business-friendly accessories, while meetings and conventions are covered by a pillar-less ballroom and an auditorium seating 380. Right in the centre of Melbourne on trendy Collins Street, the hotel is surrounded by stylish boutiques, restaurants and cafés, and is just a short tram ride from theatres, the Melbourne Cricket Ground and the beautiful Treasury Gardens.

Rates from: $$
Star rating: ★ ★ ★ ★ ★
Overall rating: 🐾🐾🐾🐾 ½

Ambience :	8.82	Cleanliness:	9.32
Value:	7.59	Facilities:	8.43
Staff:	8.86	Restaurants:	8.86
Location:	9.09	Families:	7.27

Surfers Paradise Marriott Resort

158 Ferny Avenue, Surfers Paradise, Queensland 4217, Australia
T: +61 7 5592 9800 **F**: +61 7 5592 9888
www.HotelClub.com/Hotels/Courtyard_by_Marriott_Surfers_Paradise_Resort

Towering 28 storeys with 330 rooms and suites, the highly aquatic Marriott is surrounded by lagoons, ponds and waterfalls, fronts the Nerang River and is a short stroll from the main beach. The theme here is very much to entertain yourself - sweat away in an aerobics class, pound around the floodlit tennis courts, or relax into a yoga session.

The al fresco Lagoon Restaurant offers informal buffet and an à la carte menu dripping with seafood, and there is also the Benihana Japanese Steakhouse inside. But the real "you beauty" of Surfers is its treasure trove of nearby attractions. The Marriott lies within easy reach of 27 golf courses, clay pigeon and rifle ranges, four-wheel drive circuits and bushwalks, horse riding, a performing arts centre and a bird sanctuary. And if it just happens to be raining there is always the nearby 24-hour casino.

Rates from: $$
Star rating: ★ ★ ★ ★ ★
Overall rating: 🐾🐾🐾🐾

Ambience :	8.33	Cleanliness:	8.70
Value:	8.07	Facilities:	8.32
Staff:	8.41	Restaurants:	7.81
Location:	8.67	Families:	8.59

W Sydney

6 Cowper Wharf Road, Woolloomooloo, NSW 2011, Australia
T: +61 2 9331 9000 **F**: +61 2 9331 9031
www.HotelClub.com/Hotels/W_Hotel_Sydney

Thoroughly, utterly, gloriously hip, W claims to be for the executive but it is hard to see how anybody could concentrate on work here - although the business centre is open 24 hours a day. The 104 sophisticated rooms are divided between nine different designs, ranging from Zs (no view but skylights instead) to Ultra Lofts with an unimpeded lookout from the downstairs lounge and a bedroom upstairs. Breakfast at the W Café, or wet your whistle at the Water Bar. Further choice of eating is available in the vicinity as W is part of the Wharf Woolloomooloo integrated retail complex. Oh, and W also stands for wellness of course, so you can sweat or swim or simply spa it at the Chakra where services are holistic - naturally. While the W is a little bit away from the centre this is a plus rather than a minus, and of course the Botanical Gardens are only a short walk away.

Rates from: $$$$
Star rating: ★ ★ ★ ★ ★
Overall rating: 🐾🐾🐾🐾

Ambience :	9.50	Cleanliness:	9.23
Value:	7.69	Facilities:	8.36
Staff:	8.48	Restaurants:	8.67
Location:	8.40	Families:	6.13

Westin Melbourne

205 Collins Street, Melbourne, Victoria 3000, Australia
T: +61 3 9635 2222 **F**: +61 3 9635 2333
www.HotelClub.com/Hotels/Westin_Hotel_Melbourne

At first blush, the modernistic Westin might seem to sit oddly with the redoubtable architecture of the nearby St Paul's Cathedral and city square. But in fact its grand public spaces and spacious balconied rooms have a timeless quality, plus a very Melbourne brio. The dedicated workstation in all 262 guestrooms - multi-function copier/printer/fax and ergonomic chair - means few headaches for executives, and the soft tones, timbers and classical furnishings have a soothing effect. Roving concierges are on hand to sort out any service problems, and you can relax over a glass or two at the elegant Martini Bar. Dining at Allegro is best done al fresco, weather permitting, with views down over cosmopolitan Collins Street, a shining emblem of millennium Melbourne. And even if gyms and suchlike make you shudder, drop into the basement wellness centre where the pool is a delirious exercise in Zen chic.

Rates from: $$$
Star rating: ★ ★ ★ ★ ★
Overall rating: ♦♦♦♦ ½

Ambience :	9.13	Cleanliness:	9.21
Value:	7.81	Facilities:	8.47
Staff:	8.74	Restaurants:	7.97
Location:	9.36	Families:	7.96

Westin Sydney

1 Martin Place, Sydney, NSW 2000, Australia
T: +61 2 8223 1111 **F**: +61 2 8223 1222
www.HotelClub.com/Hotels/Westin_Sydney_The

The Westin - a combination of 19th-century general post office and 20th-century tower block - is a delightful hotel that makes the most of its historical antecedents while ensuring guests do not want for modern conveniences. The old GPO's telegraph and telephone exchanges have been converted into a ballroom and health club, respectively, and the grand staircase leading up to the first floor under the landmark clock tower has been painstakingly restored. The 416 guestrooms - which reinterpret the classic designs of the 1950s - are split between old and new wings, the former with high ceilings and antique fittings and the latter with floor-to-ceiling windows. The public areas are concentrated in the old GPO, with a potpourri of upmarket restaurants (the steaks at Prime are superb), bars and cafés as well as a food emporium. Would that Australia had more buildings like this to convert into hotels. Even if you are not staying, drop by revel in the ambience; the suits fairly thunder in here for pre-drink drinks on a Friday night.

Rates from: $$$
Star rating: ★ ★ ★ ★ ★
Overall rating: ♦♦♦♦ ½

Ambience :	8.81	Cleanliness:	9.27
Value:	7.66	Facilities:	8.52
Staff:	8.53	Restaurants:	8.42
Location:	9.34	Families:	7.49

BRUNEI

BANDAR SERI BEGAWAN

MALAYSIA

The archetypal reason for climbing Mount Everest is said to be: "Because it's there." Brunei is about as un-Himalayan as it's possible to get, and the main reason - unless you happen to be on business - for going is that "Nobody else is there". The 5,765 square-kilometre Sultanate is the Bermuda Triangle of Asian tourism, squashed into two separate slices of Borneo, filthy rich and squeaky clean at the same time, and of all the destinations on Planet Earth, one of the more curious to drop by.

To dispense with one of the great myths of modern travel, Brunei is not dry. Visitors may import two litres of alcohol - either spirits or wine - and 12 cans of beer up to twice a day. These can either be brought into the country when you arrive or bought at any border at any time during your stay.

And the nearest border from the capital, Bandar Seri Begawan (BSB), is about half an hour by road at Limbang in neighbouring Sarawak. Not that anyone comes to tropical - think very hot and wet - - Brunei simply to scoot about its road system on bottle-runs. BSB, the only town of any size, is not exactly pulsating with life, but nearby Kampung Ayer is a higgledy-piggledy collection of water villages - home to around 30,000 people - built on stilts in the Brunei River.

By contrast, most of Brunei is well organised, efficiently run, home to some very charming natives, and - if it doesn't sound rude - ever so slightly dull.

Bandar's nightlife is non-existent and the streets are deserted at 9pm, but during the day folk head to Jerudong for the Playground, a giant fun fair cum amusement park with a host of rides, which is right next to Jerudong Beach. There are no "world-class" sights or Full Moon raves in Brunei, but pottering about the country you will find a number of interesting spots, and a corresponding lack of other tourists.

Away from the oil-fuelled wealth of the main towns, there are Iban villages, a smart beach or two and some spectacular rainforest in the interior, all of which are reasonably accessible.

Finally, on the subject of hotels, Brunei is home to the Liberace of Asian accommodation, a positively humungous pile called the Empire Hotel & Country Club. Not so much over-the-top as headed for orbit, it's worth a goggle even if you don't fancy checking in. Apart from this, the country's hotel inventory is what you might call sparse.

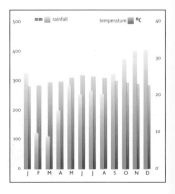

Empire Hotel and Country Club

Kampong Jerudong BG 3122, Negara Brunei Darussalam, Brunei
T: +673 241 8888 **F**: +673 241 8999
www.HotelClub.com/Hotels/Empire_Hotel_and_Golf_Club

This colossal property is without peer anywhere else in Asia - an effulgent hymn to top-dollar investment. On the beach, within driving range of an 18-hole Jack Nicklaus-designed championship golf course, and striking distance of one of the oldest rainforests in the region, the resort - which is surrounded by a 180-hectare tropical garden - goes beyond the merely palatial. Its 360 rooms are topped by 63 lavish suites and villas and the cuisines of the world are laid out in half a dozen restaurants. Naturally, the Empire suggests itself as a conference venue, but it's an equally feasible leisure option - the crisp and innovative spa being a case in point. Like much of the region's best accommodation, the Empire owes much to the personality of its general manager, in this case the dynamic English rose, Anne Busfield. The hotel's address could very well be "No. 1 Borneo".

Rates from: $$
Star rating: ★★★★★
Overall rating: 4½

Ambience :	9.22	Cleanliness:	9.34
Value:	8.39	Facilities:	9.21
Staff:	8.42	Restaurants:	8.82
Location:	8.05	Families:	9.03

Sheraton Utama Hotel

Jl Tasek, Bandar Seri Begawan BS 8674, Brunei
T: +673 224 4272 **F**: +673 222 1579
www.HotelClub.com/Hotels/Sheraton_Utama_Hotel

The Sheraton is probably the best hotel in downtown Bandar - although admittedly the choice is not overly large - and as such emblematic of the Bruneian capital. Everything in its 149 rooms and 10 suites (named for local flora and fauna) is very much as a road warrior or more off-the-beaten track tourist might hope for. The (complimentary) health club was recently spruced up, the Tagz Lounge allows BYO booze and should you so wish you could drive a car straight into the ground-level ballroom à la James Bond to get your conference off to a flying start. The excellent food in the Tasek Brasserie is only surpassed by the fare in the Sheraton's signature restaurant Deals. The largely expatriate staff are extremely efficient and helpful, while the limited delights of the capital are all only a short stroll away. No complaints here, but not too much to shout about either.

Rates from: $$
Star rating: ★★★★★
Overall rating: 4

Ambience :	8.33	Cleanliness:	8.67
Value:	8.33	Facilities:	8.08
Staff:	8.89	Restaurants:	8.44
Location:	8.11	Families:	8.43

CAMBODIA

THAILAND

❶ Siem Reap

❷ PHNOM PENH

VIETNAM

Cambodia is a small country, yet it has incredible depth. While easily overlooked on the map, it is a land of extremes and one that is far from anonymous. One glorious extreme is the historic ruined city of Angkor at Siem Reap. The ancient Khmer remains form one of the most incredible sites on the planet. This great civilisation reached its flamboyant zenith between the 9th and 14th centuries, with architectural feats culminating in the magnificent Angkor Wat, deservedly one of the wonders of the world. Some 100 temples survive and are generally being sensitively restored, although recently concerns have been voiced about the damage tourism is inflicting. Still, without doubt Angkor is the defining reason to go to Cambodia.

But Cambodia has known more sinister extremes. Regional instability in the 1970s saw civil war sweep Pol Pot's Khmer Rouge to power and his introduction of an ultra-Maoist policy. After inaugurating "Year Zero", he intended to wipe out the existing Cambodian way of life and start afresh, but ultimately the end result was appalling genocide. More than two million died amid atrocities of unimaginable cruelty, and the educated classes were almost entirely lost.

The Vietnamese forced out the Khmer Rouge. Political chaos continued until the late 1990s, when some stability returned and saw the battered country finally getting back on its feet, although it is still a long way from prosperity.

A stroll around Phnom Penh reveals a poor but lively city with Buddhist temples and French architecture. Reminders of the recent savage past are clearly visible - the Killing Fields and the Genocide Museum have become ghoulish yet compulsive tourist attractions. Today Cambodia wrestles with some big modern problems below its remarkably cheerful surface. The sex trade is massive, with grim statistics for AIDS and paedophilia. And you realise just where Cambodia is today when recreational activities available to tourists include hurling grenades into ponds, or for US$200 you can fire a rocket launcher and blow up a live cow.

The recent relative stability has led to a tourist boom and some very good hotels are springing up, as well as some pretty bad ones! The infrastructure is evolving and Cambodia is easier now than it has ever been. Siem Reap and Phnom Penh remain the most popular places to visit, although the beaches around Sihanoukville may emerge soon, as there is a good strip of coastline. Temperatures remain fairly constant and typically nudge 30°C, with the dry season running from December to April.

At other times of the year it can be uncomfortably humid - not the best time for clambering around the awesome but slippery temples.

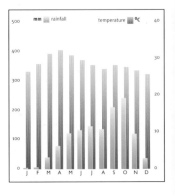

Amansara

Road to Angkor, Siem Reap, Cambodia
T: +855 63 760 333 **F**: +855 63 760 335
www.HotelClub.com/Hotels/Amansara_Hotel_Siem_Reap

Formerly a Siem Reap holiday villa for Cambodia's one-time king, long-reigning Norodom Sihanouk, this property was given the Aman signature sleek hotel treatment in 2002.

Much of the renovation was kept true to French architect Laurant Mondant's original structures and materials, and most of the 12 suites are set around a grass courtyard. One end is occupied by a compact swimming pool, about which guests may conjure images of Jackie Kennedy, Peter O'Toole or Charles de Gaulle - all of whom enjoyed royal hospitality here in the 1960s - disporting themselves in what used to be called gay abandon.

The pool's black and navy-blue tiles and its clean-lined cream loungers mirror the architecture: stark but not austere. Rooms follow suit, appearing in monochrome by day, but looking cosier at night with the effect of warm lighting. All bathrooms have a large soaking tub, separate shower and twin vanity basins. In-room mini-bars contain complimentary healthy herbal drinks, as well as the usual favourites.

Aside from the pool terrace, a roof garden, shaded by trees, is set about with low-slung tables and cushioned seating where outdoor lunch and sundowners are served. More dramatic is the circular restaurant, with its seven-metre-high ceilings and adjoining bar, where in-house guests are offered gratis cocktails every evening. A common area contains a small library of books and international journals, as well as Internet access and a few board games.

Amansara is one of the closest hotels to the main sites of Angkor. Its private fleet of custom-built moped trishaws - painted black, and with cream canopies, naturally - can access some of the best-known ruins in minutes. Complimentary house outings depart daily, with itineraries announced the night before.

As a final fillip, the resort's therapists can dish up traditional Khmer and international varieties of massage in a choice of locations within the compound. The Amansara Foot Cooler is popular with those who have overdone the temple trekking.

Rates from: $$$$$
Star rating: ★ ★ ★ ★ ★
Overall rating: ♦ ♦ ♦ ♦ ♦

Ambience :	9.67	Cleanliness:	9.00
Value:	8.00	Facilities:	9.00
Staff:	9.00	Restaurants:	8.67
Location:	8.67	Families:	9.00

Angkor Village Resort

Wat Bo Road, Siem Reap, Cambodia
T: +855 63 965 561 **F:** +855 63 963 363
www.HotelClub.com/Hotels/Angkor_Village_Resort

This is no chain hotel, so the facilities are also simple and in keeping with both nature and the local character. This is a polite way of saying that they are basic, but again the property's personality seems only to be enhanced by this. The Angkor Village has succeeded in incorporating Khmer culture through the pleasant restaurant, which is better described as enhanced home cooking rather than fancy international dining, and through traditional dance shows in the small theatre over the road. The bar is also a wonderful oasis in which to unwind over an Angkor Beer, the local brew. The pool has recently been improved but is still very modest. The quaint resort also has a nearby elephant farm offering treks through the temples. Service is friendly and warm but occasionally just a tad innocent. But the deficiencies are forgivable and with the hotel being a gentle stroll into the local town, it makes an excellent base for seeing Siem Reap and its main attractions.

The intimate Angkor Village is an architectural pioneer in Cambodia and has influenced other hotel projects in the area. Designed and built in 1995 by owner and French-trained architect Olivier Piot, the aim was to introduce guests to aspects of Khmer culture on as many levels as possible. The structure is built predominantly from teak, and Mr Piot and Vattho Tep, his equally talented Cambodian wife, have incorporated mainly local products in the construction and finish. The result is one of Siem Reap's most enjoyable and characteristic boutique hotels.

Set on 1.5 hectares of lush green gardens, the hotel is an assortment of wooden bungalows nestled among tropical ponds and gardens that help elevate the relaxed but slightly exotic mood, and a high, surrounding red-brick wall offers seclusion from the street hustle and bustle. The two-storey bungalows are connected by raised wooden walkways and incorporate 52 rooms. The Standard Rooms are somewhat basic apart from the wooden surrounds, whereas the Deluxe Rooms, being twice the size, are a perfect retreat from the heat after a hard day's temple trekking. This recommended category features glossy polished floors you can skate on in your socks, and large windows that flood the rooms with light. Simple yet cosy interiors include bamboo fittings and local fabrics; clean polished white-tiled bathrooms with simple lines and chrome fittings complete the picture.

Rates from: $
Star rating: ★ ★ ★ ★
Overall rating: 🦢🦢🦢🦢 ½

Ambience :	9.41	Cleanliness:	9.38
Value:	8.85	Facilities:	8.19
Staff:	9.21	Restaurants:	8.18
Location:	9.26	Families:	8.48

FCC Phnom Penh

363 Sisowath Quay, Phnom Penh, Cambodia
T: +855 23 210 142   **F**: +855 23 427 758
www.HotelClub.com/Hotels/FCC_Phnom_Penh

The Foreign Correspondents' Club in Phnom Penh - which is not a club at all; the name was dreamed up just over a decade ago to tease the much more august members-only FCC in Hong Kong - is an ersatz classic. More Graham Greene than Somerset Maugham, its view from the open-fronted bar (real-life hangout for local journos) of the confluence of the Tonlé Sap and Mekong Rivers is out of this world.

With a sundowner in hand at dusk, eavesdropping on some of the most informed gossip in town, you're the world-weary star of your own Hollywood Indo-China movie. The menu is eclectically hearty - fajitas, tapas, pizzas, curry and noodles - and incredibly popular. The FCC also embraces a good selection of quick-backgrounder books, newspapers and magazines in the ground-floor shop which doubles as a gourmet deli.

The seven rooms in this three-storey French Colonial building are romantically basic, though they do have Internet connections and cable TV. Best of all are the moto drivers parked permanently outside - US$1 will take you anywhere in town.

Rates from: $	
Star rating: ★ ★	
Overall rating: 🖐🖐🖐🖐 ½	
Ambience : 9.25	Cleanliness: 8.88
Value: 8.50	Facilities: 7.89
Staff: 8.50	Restaurants: 9.13
Location: 9.63	Families: 6.80

La Résidence d'Angkor

River Road, Siem Reap, Cambodia
T: +855 63 963 390   **F**: +855 63 963 391
www.HotelClub.com/Hotels/La_Residence_dAngkor

Angkor Wat is one of the fastest-growing tourist destinations in the world, so Siem Reap has gone from war-ravaged one-horse town to one-horse-town with hotels coming out of its ears in no time. But this place, previously known as the Pansea Angkor (it is owned by the Pansea Orient-Express group), is one of the best bases for embarking on the ultimate Indiana Jones experience.

Bang in the middle of town on the banks of the Siem Reap River, its main attraction is a pool set amid lush tropical foliage and built to the specifications of the typical "tanks", or artificial lakes, attached to many of the nearby temples. It is composed of 45,000 tiles in every shade of green imaginable.

The Résidence's 55 open-plan rooms are all cotton and silk, wood and bamboo, and feature enormous bathtubs. The food is a blend of French and Khmer, served al fresco in the colonial-style bar-lounge. Relatively unpretentious for a luxury hotel, it has the charm of the multitude of "guesthouses" that have sprung up in every back street of this former strategic prize among the Killing Fields, but without the inconveniences.

Rates from: $$	
Star rating: ★ ★ ★ ★ ★	
Overall rating: 🖐🖐🖐🖐 ½	
Ambience : 9.63	Cleanliness: 9.63
Value: 8.21	Facilities: 8.73
Staff: 9.11	Restaurants: 7.71
Location: 8.95	Families: 8.33

Raffles Grand Hotel D'Angkor

1 Vithei Charles De Gaulle, Khum Svay Dang Kum, Siem Reap, Cambodia
T: +855 63 963 888 **F**: +855 63 963 168
www.HotelClub.com/Hotels/Raffles_Grand_Hotel_DAngkor

Owned and run by the Raffles Group, the Grand Hotel D'Angkor is the finest hotel in Siem Reap. Originally built in 1928, black and white photographs reveal it was once very grand indeed. As the century passed, the building slowly faded into obscurity and malaise. It was finally rescued in the late 1990s by the Raffles salvage team and beautifully restored. The property is now grand again in many ways, the broad and proud château-like façade sitting majestically before 60,000 square metres of gardens. The property's plush colonial roots have been rediscovered and augmented and are clearly visible throughout.

On entering the wonderfully aloof lobby you come face to face with a beautiful original fitting, the antique cage elevator. A descending spiral staircase leads to the renowned Elephant Bar, a sophisticated cocktail bar with iron railings, wicker furniture, huge tusks and a pool table - crucially colonial. The dining choices are all luxurious and refined, although some are more casual than others. The candlelit Restaurant Le Grand offers Khmer flavours and fine dining in regal surrounds. The Café D'Angkor and Poolside Terrace share similar urbane themes with delicious international selections, but if there were to be a criticism it would be that there is not quite enough variety on the menu.

The hotel's new wing houses the State Rooms and Cabana Rooms. The rooms are modestly proportioned but decorated in homely European style with ample half-tester beds. They offer a choice of garden views or the infinitely preferable pool views. Landmark Rooms and Suites lie in the old wing and are larger and steeped in history. Interior features include free-standing cast iron baths and a fine selection of Cambodian art and memorabilia. Remarkably, next to the pool, you will find two luxurious private villas for those who really want to push the boat out, right down to the private wine cellar and 24-hour valet service.

For those worn-out temple gazers, the spa at the Grand provides a wonderful respite while the 35-metre lap pool, modelled on the ancient royal bathing pools of Angkor Thom, is a refreshing escape from the heat.

The hotel is expensive, immensely so if you consider the local economy. But it is the centrepiece of Siem Reap and lies a little closer than most to the thrills of ancient Angkor.

Rates from: $$
Star rating: ★ ★ ★ ★ ★
Overall rating: ♦ ♦ ♦ ♦ ½

Ambience:	9.28	Cleanliness:	9.16
Value:	8.07	Facilities:	8.48
Staff:	9.29	Restaurants:	8.64
Location:	9.12	Families:	8.66

Raffles Hotel Le Royal

92 Rukhak Vithei Daun Penh, Sangkat Wat Phnom, Phnom Penh, Cambodia
T: +855 23 981 888 **F**: +855 23 981 128
www.HotelClub.com/Hotels/Raffles_Hotel_Le_Royal_Phnom_Penh

For many, Le Royal is the top address in Phnom Penh. The sister to the Grand Hotel D'Angkor in Siem Reap and in the same elite class, Le Royal is probably the better of the two overall, although there are some obvious advantages to the Grand, primarily its proximity to Angkor Wat. Phnom Penh seems an unlikely setting for such an opulent property. Being in the centre of this rough and ready city is a double-edged sword - the location is wonderfully convenient for tourists or business travellers but it is besieged by the surrounding moped madness. Stepping inside provides a refreshing upper-crust respite. This classy hotel feels every inch a proud colonial heirloom from 1929, despite the upheavals the building has witnessed. After sliding into decay the building was respectfully restored and its 208 rooms were reopened in 1997.

The interior is majestic in both elegance and proportion, the historic grace radiating through the dignified chequered tiled corridors, robust European archways and cigar rooms. The three connecting wings of the hotel cover a complete city block and enclose an attractive and leafy pool. State Rooms revisit the historic theme and are set in the newer courtyard wings. In the original main building, splendid Landmark Rooms and Suites sumptuously present old-world charm with touches of Khmer art and original antiques. Personality Suites are dedicated to the distinguished figures with close links to Le Royal, such as the novelist Somerset Maugham.

The eight restaurants and bars never stray from the grand theme, Restaurant Le Royal offering a rich Khmer experience both for the eyes and palate, while the al fresco Café Monivong dishes out more casual Asian and continental fare. Service is courteous throughout the hotel and the Amrita Spa is a perfect place to shut out Phnom Penh and take in the sauna, jacuzzi or therapeutic massage treatments. The property has a capable business centre and good meeting rooms, and the regal ballroom is certainly fit for royalty. Being a Raffles property though, this is not really a business hotel - Le Royal is really an experience.

Rates from: $$
Star rating: ★ ★ ★ ★ ★
Overall rating: ❀ ❀ ❀ ❀ ½

Ambience:	9.48	Cleanliness:	9.00
Value:	7.95	Facilities:	8.40
Staff:	8.83	Restaurants:	8.26
Location:	8.58	Families:	8.32

Sofitel Royal Angkor

Vithei Charles de Gaulle, Khum Svay Dang Kum, Siem Reap, Cambodia
T: +855 63 964 600 **F:** +855 63 964 610
www.HotelClub.com/Hotels/Sofitel_Royal_Angkor

Opened in late 2000, the Sofitel Royal Angkor made a splendid addition to Siem Reap and a very welcome one for travellers. It is an excellent five-star hotel snapping at the heels of the previously untouchable Grand Hotel D'Angkor. Siem Reap still has plenty of rough edges but this hotel has all the trappings of modern international comfort. Spread liberally over large and immaculately trimmed gardens, there is an orderly and sedate contrast here to the lovable chaos of the country.

The calm, red-tiled resort keeps a low profile in height terms with its trim two-storey layout. The three wings are connected by covered boardwalks in case the heavens open, meandering past kept lawns and ponds. The interior, however, certainly does not keep a low profile - it is smart, stylish and feels every bit a top hotel. The decor incorporates subtle French and Khmer influences and is airy and bright throughout. Plenty of mock bas-reliefs and statues remind you exactly where you are - just a few kilometres from the stunning temples of Angkor and almost as close as any hotel is permitted to be.

Facilities again fly in the face of what you would expect from a hotel in Siem Reap. The three restaurants are astutely captained by overseas chefs and put out food well above the rather mediocre standards offered in many other parts of town. The Sofitel Royal Angkor certainly has a credible claim for offering the best international buffet in Cambodia. Mouhot's Dream, named after the French botanist explorer and stilted on Sala Lake, offers fine dining with matching wine list and choice cigars, all with a view. The hotel also has a fine lagoon pool, which can make all the difference to a trip out here. The pool is an enticing alternative to sweaty temple trekking, whether or not you are templed out. And the spa's eight treatments rooms refresh those weary limbs with a wide selection of massages and treatments.

The 238 light and spacious rooms are thoughtfully designed and a pleasure to return to. The teak floors and uplifting continental bathrooms are inspired by the French, and there are local flecks such as reproduction Khmer stone artistry. In a land of ancient splendour, the Sofitel Royal Angkor delivers modern five-star comfort and relaxation with style.

Rates from: $$
Star rating: ★ ★ ★ ★ ★
Overall rating: ♦♦♦♦ ½

Ambience:	9.14	Cleanliness:	9.35
Value:	8.27	Facilities:	8.65
Staff:	8.94	Restaurants:	8.40
Location:	8.88	Families:	8.74

CHINA

Lauded for its progress since its establishment in 1949, courted for its economic potential, excoriated for its human rights record, the People's Republic of China is Asia's waking giant - the world's most populous country (1.29 billion and counting) but still one that has a fair way to go before it takes its true place on the international stage.

Perhaps this will change in 2008 with the arrival of the Olympic flame.

The prodigious leaps from feudalist to communist to capitalist have greatly enhanced the PRC, and for much of the past quarter-century, China has been the world's fastest-growing economy. Yet it remains poor in many parts - there

are sharp divisions between rural areas and the cities, the rich coast and the poor interior, and schisms within the political elite. But just as staging the Olympics in Seoul catapulted South Korea to prominence, so the next Olympics should give Beijing the necessary fillip to show that it too can host the planet's most prestigious sporting event with requisite efficiency and panache.

As might be expected from a country with 9,561,000 square kilometres at its disposal, there is an enormous amount to see and do in China (too much to mention in detail here), whether showcasing thousands of years of culture or something that was only built last year. Beijing's attractions lie not merely in trophy sights like the Great Wall, the Forbidden City and Tiananmen Square, but also in its "hutongs", the maze of residential streets just out of the centre that are gradually being swept away in the name of development. Tianjin, to the east of the capital, is a former treaty port and hosts one of the country's more intriguing antique markets. A former German concession, Qingdao was Mao Zedong's favourite seaside holiday spot, and Chinese still flock to its beaches - backed by statuesque and very Germanic mansions - every summer. Shanghai is widely touted as China's "Next Big Thing", a hotchpotch of new energetic capitalism and construction, with an exotic and varied nightlife. Slightly inland, Hangzhou caught Marco Polo's eye when he passed through in the 13th century ("one of the most splendid cities in the world") and, despite the onslaught of tourism, its lakes and temples are

still utterly picturesque.

Shenzhen, on the border with Hong Kong, has gone from 99 per cent paddy fields to 99 per cent concrete in the space of 20 years, a Special Economic Zone that could be a metaphor for the new China. Inland, there are panoramic vistas in Guilin, the Terracotta Warriors in Xi'an, Tibetan highs in Lhasa and seemingly a different country altogether in the far-western city of Urumqi.

Gone are the days of staying in grubby, Soviet-style dormitories, an alarming prospect that greeted China's first foreign visitors when the country started to open up in the late 1970s. True, some of its lesser hotels lag behind when it comes to basic requirements like hot water and clean sheets, but nowadays all the major cities host a crop of five-star - or at least some very acceptable four-star - properties. Boutique hotels are making their first appearance around Beijing, and properties like the Grand Hyatt Shanghai (the highest hotel in the world) are setting a trend that other cities can only hope to emulate.

Gone too are the days of foreign visitors being stared at as if they were on day release from some anthropological zoo. You are likely to attract some attention at tourist spots - if only to be included in a friendly souvenir photograph - and if you wander off the beaten track you can expect to be quizzed enthusiastically. Many young Chinese are keen to practise their English and other languages, and Beijing is determined to hang the "world class" moniker at its gates.

China's borders embrace sub-tropical islands and frozen deserts, so it is difficult to recommend precise times to visit. The best rule of thumb is to avoid the sticky summers and chilly winters if possible. Spring, from March to April, and autumn (September to October) are more climatically welcoming. Lunar New Year, which falls in late January or early February, sees much of the populace uprooting and returning home for family celebrations, so expect hotel beds and rail and air tickets to be in short supply.

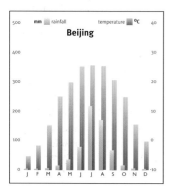

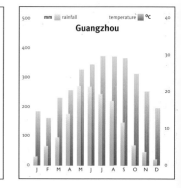

China World Hotel

1 Jianguomenwai Avenue, Beijing 100004, China
T: +86 10 6505 2266 **F:** +86 10 6505 0828
www.HotelClub.com/Hotels/China_World_Hotel

This is primarily a business hotel, not least because it sits in the heart of the diplomatic and business district, and right next to the China World Trade Centre with its two 38-storey office towers and extensive exhibition facilities. The hotel's 716 newly renovated rooms - in particular the 55-square-metre Premier Rooms - are spacious, designed to be somewhere you can sleep, work and relax without undue hassle, and of course electronic connectivity is a given. All are decorated with sleek fabric wall panels, luxurious furnishings and contemporary Asian art. Apart from its location, the China World's biggest plus is its exceptional sporting facilities. Squash and tennis courts, golf simulators, driving range and putting course and an aerobics studio all back up regulars such as the fitness centre and an indoor swimming pool. Very much a commanding address in the increasingly sophisticated Chinese capital, epitomised by the very slick gate-to-gate butler service.

Rates from: $$
Star rating: ★ ★ ★ ★ ★
Overall rating: ♨♨♨♨ ½

Ambience:	8.93	Cleanliness:	9.24
Value:	8.29	Facilities:	8.81
Staff:	8.70	Restaurants:	8.77
Location:	8.97	Families:	8.79

Four Seasons Hotel Shanghai

500 Weihai Road, Shanghai 200041, China
T: +86 21 6256 8888 **F:** +86 21 6256 5678
www.HotelClub.com/Hotels/Four_Seasons_Hotel_Shanghai

Sitting back with a fine Havana and a glass of aged Cognac in the cigar lounge of the Four Seasons' Jazz 37 and gazing at the panorama of the world's fastest-growing city spread out below - Pudong, the Oriental Pearl Tower and the Old French Concession as prominent as in a wide-screen travelogue - brings to mind Jimmy Cagney's immortal line before being immolated on celluloid: "Look at me, ma, top of the world!"

This hotel is nothing if not sophisticated, in keeping with the city's well-deserved reputation as the most cultured and cosmopolitan in China. The quality of its bed-linen is sans pareil, the demeanour of its personal butlers almost Wodehouse-ian, the efficiency of its housekeeping quite remarkable (send a shirt with a missing button to the laundry and it will come back with the item miraculously replaced).

Although aimed mainly at business travellers, accompanying spouses, friends and/or partners will appreciate the proximity to Shanghai Museum and Nanjing Road shopping - and a restorative cuppa in the garden-style setting of the atrium lobby lounge.

Rates from: $$$
Star rating: ★ ★ ★ ★ ★
Overall rating: ♨♨♨♨ ½

Ambience:	8.85	Cleanliness:	9.31
Value:	7.90	Facilities:	8.67
Staff:	8.85	Restaurants:	8.61
Location:	8.41	Families:	8.32

Garden Hotel Guangzhou

368 Huangshi East Road, Guangzhou 510064, China
T: +86 20 8333 8989 **F:** +86 20 8332 4535
www.HotelClub.com/Hotels/Garden_Hotel_Guangzhou

"Size doesn't matter" may be a sophisticated modern mantra, but in today's China, it matters hugely. And hotels don't come much bigger than Guangzhou's Garden, a Y-shaped, 1,000 room plus, 30-storey monolith in the northern business district of this born-again southern provincial capital.

The lobby alone claims to be the largest in Asia, though no-one has actually gone round measuring as far as we know. With massive murals on the walls, it enfolds a bar-lounge set in an ornamental pool. And there is, as the hotel's name implies, a rambling garden, complete with artificial hills and waterfalls and pavilions, as well as two tennis courts, squash courts, a bowling alley and a spa/sauna.

Genuine antiques and some excellent modern art line the walls and there is every amenity you can think of, including a children's playground and Wi-Fi Internet connection. The dozen restaurants and bars include the revolving Carousel and Lai Wan Market, whose traditional Cantonese specialities are popular with the spoiled-for-choice locals.

Rates from: $$
Star rating: ★ ★ ★ ★ ★
Overall rating: ♦♦♦♦

Ambience:	8.33	Cleanliness:	8.72
Value:	8.23	Facilities:	8.30
Staff:	8.26	Restaurants:	8.24
Location:	8.47	Families:	7.73

Grand Hyatt Beijing

Beijing Oriental Plaza, 1 East Chang An Avenue, Beijing 100738, China
T: +86 10 8518 1234 **F:** +86 10 8518 0000
www.HotelClub.com/Hotels/Grand_Hyatt_Beijing

One of the Grand Hyatt's most charismatic restaurants is called "Made in China" and - quite frankly - this could well be the hotel's motto, hallmark and theme song. Beijing lies right outside the front door - for all the confusion over which part of it can lay claim to being the city's true CBD, addresses don't come much more central than 1 East Chang An Avenue, on the corner of Wangfujing. The best shopping in Beijing (not forgetting Oriental Plaza itself, in which the hotel nestles), and just a short walk to the Forbidden City and Tiananmen Square: what more could you ask?

The hotel itself comprises 675 extremely comfortable rooms and suites, and apart from the previously-mentioned pan-Chinese cuisine there's also a notable Italian restaurant. Take a squint at the tropical island themed indoor pool - at its most jaw-dropping during winter months. Oh, and did we mention the music in the Redmoon Bar? Contemporary tunes on traditional Chinese instruments. Kinda interesting.

Rates from: $$
Star rating: ★ ★ ★ ★
Overall rating: ♦♦♦♦ ½

Ambience:	8.78	Cleanliness:	9.06
Value:	7.97	Facilities:	8.58
Staff:	8.53	Restaurants:	8.45
Location:	8.95	Families:	8.24

Grand Hyatt Shanghai

Jin Mao Tower, 88 Century Boulevard, Pudong, Shanghai 200121, China
T: +86 21 5049 1234 **F**: +86 21 5049 1111
www.HotelClub.com/Hotels/Grand_Hyatt_Hotel_Shanghai

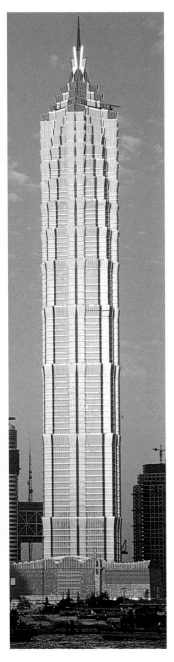

The Grand Hyatt is more than just a hotel. It is a glistening emblem of modern-day Shanghai - innovative, technologically advanced, ultra-luxurious and shaping the way forward for the new China. The entire structure is a catalogue of superlatives. Set in Pudong between the 53rd and 87th floors of the 421-metre, pagoda-like, US$540 million Jin Mao Tower (currently mainland China's tallest building), the views over the city are stupendous, whatever the weather. The atrium soars a neck-craning 31 storeys, the 555 rooms average 40 square metres making them some of the largest in the city, and the Sky Lounge bar, fitness centre and the hotel itself are all rated as the highest on the planet.

The hotel sits above 52 floors of offices and is capped by an observatory on the 88th floor, traditionally an exceptionally lucky number in China. While the building's foundations are sunk deep into the ground, strong winds can sway its pinnacle by as much as 75 centimetres. Wandering the Hyatt's Art Deco-style floors is like exploring a space ship. Blast off from the ground floor via the elevators, and once your ears have popped a couple of times the public areas unfurl themselves like a blossoming flower. The hotel is always a hive of activity with diners crowding the tables, smartly suited executives scurrying to and from meetings, awed holidaymakers treading gingerly along the corridors and fashionably dressed emissaries from Shanghainese society lingering over drinks and the latest titbits of metropolitan gossip.

There are 12 restaurants and bars, and their gourmet sophistication and ambience is summed up by On Fifty Six, which embraces Japanese, wood-fired pizza, a grill room and the atrium lounge. Elsewhere the Grand Café's show kitchen is a tempting array of haute cuisine sights and aromas, Club Jin Mao enjoys a well-deserved reputation as the city's most exclusive Shanghainese restaurant and Food Live is an innovative concept offering favourite dishes from nine different Asian and Chinese food stalls.

Mention should also be made of PU-J's, the ever-popular nightclub, which is divided into four different entertainment zones and whose name is not necessarily short for Pick Up, though such activity is not unknown. There is easy listening (and drinking) in the Music Room, a fair bit of bopping to a live band in the Dance Zone, a dramatic waterfall in the Wine Bar and eight private karaoke lounges - including one with a private terrace - all of which act as a magnet to Shanghai's jeunesse very-dorée partygoers.

The accommodation - if that is not too pedestrian a term - includes 45 suites (Executive, Diplomatic, Presidential and Chairman's) and the 73-room Grand Club with its own two-storey lounge. Individually decorated, the rooms would be hard to improve; all feature interactive TV, dimmable lighting, high-speed modem lines, electronic sensor reading lamps, double-sided wardrobes that can be accessed from bed or bathroom, a tower shower with three showerheads and a heated mirror that will not mist up. While the Hyatt was designed by an American company, enormous care was taken to include Chinese elements. The hotel's furniture was all locally made, from the ceramic ice buckets to the carpets and the artwork that decorates the walls.

As an endnote, the high-tech Jin Mao's car park has space for 2,000 bicycles, still the primary mode of transport in China! There is, however, parking for 1,000 or so cars as well.

Rates from: $$$
Star rating: ★ ★ ★ ★ ★
Overall rating: 🐾 🐾 🐾 🐾 🐾

Ambience:	9.52	Cleanliness:	9.63
Value:	8.77	Facilities:	9.30
Staff:	9.21	Restaurants:	9.33
Location:	9.07	Families:	9.05

JW Marriott Hotel Shanghai

399 Nanjing West Road, Shanghai 200003, China
T: +86 21 5359 4969 **F**: +86 21 6375 5988
www.HotelClub.com/Hotels/JW_Marriott_Hotel_Shanghai

Tomorrow Square, which the JW overlooks, just about says it all. If not the shape of hotels to come, then this is certainly as state-of-the-art as they come right now. Opened auspiciously on October 1 (China's National Day) 2003, the Marriott flagship on the mainland forms part of a futuristic 60-storey, multi-use tower in downtown Puxi that bestrides the city's traditional heart at the top of Nanjing Road, next to People's Square, the Grand Theatre and the Shanghai Museum.

And what it doesn't have you probably won't get - anywhere in the world. Its 342 spacious rooms and 255 Marriott Executive Apartments start from the 38th-floor lobby (with a Bette Davis-style sweeping staircase) and all have the most stunning 360-degree cityscape views, plus high-speed Internet access and cordless phones. Not to mention incredibly comfortable beds, showers with hydraulic massage, a choice of soaps in the bathroom, and tasteful decor in autumnal hues.

The dedicated lifts are programmed not to stop for any Tom, Dick or Chen who presses the button while you're ascending or descending, and the welcoming, mood-lit corridors are lined with tasteful art. You want to send out for some groceries while you luxuriate in the classy spa, or swim in the outdoor or indoor pool, depending on the prevailing climate? Or maybe you're busy hosting a confab in one of the 13 cream leather and teak meeting rooms. Can do.

When work is done, there's a choice of some very contemporary restaurants, including the off-white and orange JW's California Grill, the ultra-modern Wan Hao (great Shanghainese cuisine - reckoned by many connoisseurs to be the best of China's regional offerings), the all-day Marriott Café with its huge open kitchen, or JW's Lounge. This

includes the "decadent" 8-9-8 Cigar Bar, where they can come up with 50 different varieties of martini. Staying in this place will leave you stirred if not shaken.

Rates from: $$$
Star rating: ★ ★ ★ ★ ★
Overall rating: ♕ ♕ ♕ ♕ ½

Ambience:	8.77	Cleanliness:	9.31
Value:	8.44	Facilities:	8.64
Staff:	8.71	Restaurants:	8.80
Location:	8.71	Families:	8.49

Lu Song Yuan Hotel Beijing

22 Banchang Lane, Kuanjie, Beijing 100009, China
T: +86 10 6404 0436 **F:** +86 10 6403 0418
www.HotelClub.com/Hotels/Lu_Song_Yuan_Hotel_Beijing

In a rapidly changing world there are few hotels left that provide a genuine snapshot of days gone by. Most heritage hotels across Asia have been swept aside and replaced by stereotype tower blocks as cities economically blossom with concrete and glass. Usually, only the luxury period pieces scrape through the metamorphoses, and even these undergo extensive restoration that can compromise their authenticity. The Lu Song Yuan is one of a dying breed - an affordable and unspoiled two-star hotel, straight from the residential neighbourhoods of the 19th century.

The term "hotel" can only be employed loosely here as while the Lu Song Yuan is one of the most characteristic properties in Beijing, it branched off from the evolution of hotels well before the advent of what today would be considered standard facilities. There is no pool, no gym, no doorman, a business centre of sorts (with Internet access) and a simple restaurant - but you can hire a bicycle.

Hidden away down a little alleyway among the capital's hutongs (Mongolian for "water well"), the hotel can be hard to track down among the maze of charming backstreets, but this lends an air of seclusion and secrecy, plus bags of personality. Built in traditional Chinese style, it remains basic. The 58 rooms are set in the low buildings flanking a series of courtyards and quadrangles. They are generally small and spartan, but decorated with memorable Ming-style

furnishings such as the hard yet ornate beds. Larger rooms, opening directly on to timeless courtyards, are especially popular making them difficult to book. The sweeping roofs, chunky red beams and pillars and lanterns are vaguely reminiscent of the Forbidden City just two kilometres south, but immeasurably more modest! It has to be said that the hotel is not built for comfort or for those in a rush. It is all about style and character and is a top pick for the more adventurous traveller wanting to experience a piece of China that is disappearing fast.

Rates from: $
Star rating: ★★
Overall rating: 👍👍👍👍

Ambience:	9.25	Cleanliness:	7.88
Value:	8.69	Facilities:	6.24
Staff:	8.69	Restaurants:	6.67
Location:	8.13	Families:	8.67

Peace Hotel Shanghai

20 Nanjing Road East, Shanghai 200002, China
T: +86 21 6321 6888 **F:** +86 21 6329 0300
www.HotelClub.com/Hotels/Peace_North_Hotel_Shanghai

Creaky though the service and facilities may be at this celebrated septuagenarian, it is difficult to confront the 12-storey Peace Hotel without a rush of affection. It has yet to be gobbled up and deluxed by an international chain, so what you get is pretty much China 1929. The "Gothic Chicago" exterior - with its hallmark 77-metre-high, copper-sheathed pyramid roof and milky yellow granite walls - would not cause founder Victor Sassoon to break step. Inside the portentous grand entrance, the chandeliers, marble floors and rather dimly lit corridors are similarly unaltered.

The Peace Hotel's claim to fame is its Jazz Bar, with a venerable, showy six-piece jazz band thumping out the hits of the 30s and 40s - numbers that were current when the musicians (yes, the very same ones) were in their teens. The bartenders make a mean Irish coffee, so this is an especially charismatic place to wind down after dinner. And for typically modern Shanghainese evening entertainment, there is the inevitable karaoke bar on the roof.

Far from disavowing its colonial past, the state-run Peace Hotel has - somewhat surprisingly - embraced it with a will. Of its 363 rooms, eight suites are decorated with international themes - Indian, British, French, Italian, American, Italian, German and Spanish, and Sassoon's Room, the one-time opium trader's old private bedroom, is now available for private banquets. The rooms are slightly eccentrically appointed - with SOS buttons and hydrotherapy tubs in the suites - but also make a gesture to the millennium with modem jacks and IDD phones.

While the cuisine at the Peace is acceptable, it is bettered by its locations. The Peace Banquet Hall is billed as a "typical British palace", and the private rooms in Nine Heaven Hall have magnificent views over the Bund, while the French menu at the Peace Grill is augmented by dark brown patterned walls and Lalique lamps that present a highly apposite, old-fashioned ambience, just like the hotel.

Rates from: $$
Star rating: ★ ★ ★
Overall rating: 🖐🖐🖐🖐

Ambience:	9.18	Cleanliness:	8.40
Value:	8.11	Facilities:	7.66
Staff:	8.16	Restaurants:	8.13
Location:	9.60	Families:	8.03

Peninsula Palace Hotel Beijing

8 Goldfish Lane, Wangfujing, Beijing, China
T: +86 10 8516 2888 **F**: +86 10 6510 6311
www.HotelClub.com/Hotels/Peninsula_Palace_Hotel_Beijing

The ancient city gate towers of Beijing were characterised by a massive base supporting a middle section and topped by a colourful penthouse under overhanging eaves. Their design is successfully replicated in Peninsula Group's Palace Hotel, which also features a podium for its restaurant and banquet facilities, a main body of guestrooms and special accommodations on the top floors. Such historical echoes fit extremely well in the Palace, one of Beijing's older five-stars set in the Forbidden City cultural district on the quaintly named Goldfish Lane.

But it would be a mistake to think that this hotel is a musty tribute to times gone by, given the recent US$27 million refit. Its 525 rooms and suites carry thoughtful details like mist-free mirrors in their marble bathrooms and computerised controls for lighting and air-conditioning. Naturally, residents of the three Palace Club floors can enjoy their own lounge, but there is also a satellite business centre. The Duplex Suites probably enjoy some of the hotel's best views, while the Wangfujing and Presidential Suites come with two bedrooms, a kitchen, butler, whirlpool bath and private lift.

And it would be difficult to get more contemporary than Jing, with glass-walled, walk-in wine cellars, open kitchens and two private dining areas where you can feast on Western cuisine with distinctive Asian overtones. More traditionally, you can eat Cantonese with Beijing specialities at Huang Ting, in a traditional-style Chinese courtyard.

On the recreation side, the health club includes a gym, steam rooms and saunas, and an indoor swimming pool surrounded by tinted glass as well as an outdoor sun terrace for the summer months. And even non-shoppers should take a gander at the Palace's three-floor shopping arcade, populated by fashion heavyweights such as Christian Dior, Hugo Boss, Bruno Magli and Louis Vuitton and heavily patronised by trendy local Beijingers, who once - it is hard to believe - all wore unisex Mao jackets.

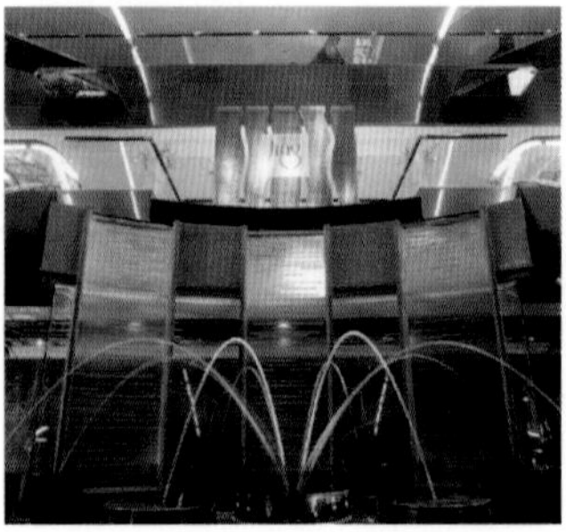

Rates from: $$
Star rating: ★★★★★
Overall rating: 👍👍👍👍👍

Ambience:	8.98	Cleanliness:	9.20
Value:	8.74	Facilities:	9.00
Staff:	9.19	Restaurants:	8.88
Location:	9.09	Families:	8.57

Portman Ritz-Carlton Shanghai

Shanghai Centre, 1376 Nanjing Road West, Shanghai 200040, China
T: +86 21 6279 8888 **F:** +86 21 6279 8800
www.HotelClub.com/Hotels/Portman_Ritz_Carlton_Hotel_Shanghai

The 578-room Portman Ritz-Carlton is like a city within a city within a city. As part of the Shanghai Centre on Nanjing Road West, it is in easy reach of a host of business and leisure facilities that augment what the hotel itself has to offer. This includes half a dozen restaurants and lounges; sporting facilities that embrace squash and racquetball courts as well the more regular gym and pool, and a 24-hour business centre. Small wonder the Ritz regularly hosts royalty and US presidents.

The latter naturally head up to the Portman's quartet of Presidential Suites, but there is a range of other accommodation here with fewer zeroes on the price tag.

All the rooms and suites are decorated with a traditional oriental motif but graced with a touch of modern flair, and they range in size from 37 to 69 square metres. Club-level guests can make free with five different servings of snacks and beverages throughout the day in the lounge, and also have a dedicated concierge. And guests in any of the hotel's rooms can enjoy little complimentary services that add a certain frisson to their stay - newspapers are delivered daily as a matter of course, shoes left out for cleaning come back glossily shined and the airport shuttle is free too.

Elsewhere in the hotel you can eat exceptionally well, and it is especially worth dropping in on the Tea Garden, particularly at Sunday brunchtime when the Moët & Chandon flows freely. And the Ritz-Carlton Bar has an exceptional range of cigars and malt whiskeys, a walk-in humidor with private lockers, and live jazz playing nightly.

Setting the seal on the Ritz-Carlton's exclusivity is its one-of-a-kind sightseeing tour. It is not exactly cheap, but where else in the world can you be piloted around the city aboard a limited-edition Chang Jiang 750cc motorcycle? Loyal guests get the trip for free on their 100th visit - plus the small matter of a Presidential Suite upgrade. Plus there is now the added fillip of boarding the hotel's partner luxury cruiser, the *Sheng Rong Guo Ji*, for a trip along the Huangpu River.

Rates from: $$$
Star rating: ★ ★ ★ ★ ★
Overall rating: 👍 👍 👍 👍 ½

Ambience:	8.82	Cleanliness:	9.20
Value:	8.15	Facilities:	8.69
Staff:	8.86	Restaurants:	8.59
Location:	8.97	Families:	8.63

Pudong Shangri-La Shanghai

33 Fu Cheng Road, Pudong, Shanghai 200120, China
T: +86 21 6882 8888 **F:** +86 21 6882 6688
www.HotelClub.com/Hotels/Pudong_Shangrila_Hotel_Shanghai

The executive-friendly Shangri-La is pretty much Pudong personified. Within spitting distance of the swizzle stick Orient Pearl TV Tower, it is also handy for the nearby Lujiazui commercial district while only a couple of minutes' ferry ride across the Huangpu River leads directly to the Bund.

The 606 rooms (soon to be 981 with the completion of Tower II) all come with a full-size writing desk, voicemail and Internet access, while the Horizon Club rooms are remarkably sleeper-friendly. The Grand Ballroom and function rooms have previously hosted such events as the World Economic and Fortune Global forums; and the business centre, IT support team, gym, laundry, hotel service centre, not to mention room service, all operate 24 hours a day, 365 days a year. Finally, to wind down, the basement entertainment centre BATS is a fun mix of Western cuisine and live music with private dining rooms also available. Throw in the traditional super Shang service and you are looking at a top-notch hotel.

Rates from: $$$
Star rating: ★ ★ ★ ★ ★
Overall rating: ♪♪♪♪ ½

Ambience:	8.80	Cleanliness:	9.03
Value:	8.04	Facilities:	8.50
Staff:	8.54	Restaurants:	8.37
Location:	8.37	Families:	8.14

Shangri-La Hotel Hangzhou

78 Beishan Road, Hangzhou 310007, China
T: +86 571 8797 7951 **F:** +86 571 8707 3545
www.HotelClub.com/Hotels/ShangriLa_Hotel_Hangzhou

warm and homely, and some of them have the bonus of balconies. The interior design, five restaurants and bars and facilities are certainly up to Shangri-La's high standards, especially the indoor swimming pool and sauna. In China, five-star can often be a gamble, but you certainly get the international interpretation here.

One of China's premier domestic tourist attractions is the scenic West Lake of Hangzhou. The best hotel in the area is no doubt the Shangri-La Hangzhou, the group's first property in China. Sitting pretty on the northern banks of the lake, the low-rise hotel is surrounded by 16 hectares of tranquil wooded countryside. Being five minutes from the centre of town, the setting is supreme and removed from the sometimes intrusive mass tourism, and the lake views can be sublime, especially around dawn and towards sunset. Spread over two wings, the 383 guestrooms are

Rates from: $$
Star rating: ★ ★ ★ ★ ★
Overall rating: ♪♪♪♪ ½

Ambience:	9.00	Cleanliness:	9.09
Value:	8.09	Facilities:	8.50
Staff:	8.79	Restaurants:	8.45
Location:	9.67	Families:	8.71

Shangri-La Hotel Shenzhen

East Side, Railway Station, 1002 Jianshe Road, Shenzhen 518001, China
T: +86 755 8233 0888 **F**: +86 755 8233 9878
www.HotelClub.com/Hotels/Shangrila_Hotel_Shenzhen

The artfully curved Shangri-La is one of the landmarks of the Hong Kong/China boundary line. Within sight of the Lo Wu immigration hall, the location is ideal for trans-border travellers doing business in Shenzhen's industrial economic zone, and also very handy for those on bargain-shopping expeditions. Having exercised the credit card, there are plenty of recreational facilities, including a decent pool and sauna, to recharge the batteries. No prizes for guessing why the top floor bar restaurant and lounge 360° - which got off to a flying start in January 2005 - got its name. By Shangri-La standards the 553 rooms are a tad ordinary but their service is well above the usually lacklustre local levels. The Shangri-La Shenzhen as a whole is not as good as other hotels of this stylish chain, but still deserves every one of its five stars.

Rates from: $$
Star rating: ★ ★ ★ ★ ★
Overall rating: ♙ ♙ ♙ ♙ ½

Ambience:	8.49	Cleanliness:	8.81
Value:	8.19	Facilities:	8.47
Staff:	8.58	Restaurants:	8.54
Location:	8.78	Families:	8.31

Sheraton Great Wall Hotel Beijing

10 North Dongsanhuan Road, Chaoyang, Beijing 100026, China
T: +86 10 6590 5566 **F**: +86 10 6590 5398
www.HotelClub.com/Hotels/The_Great_Wall_Sheraton_Hotel_Beijing

The first international luxury hotel to open in the Chinese capital (in 1984) and still one of the biggest with over 1,000 rooms, the Sheraton Great Wall both profits and suffers from its pioneer status. Many veteran business travellers have remained loyal, and it is also a popular rendezvous for the resident business community. But the years have taken their toll physically and in terms of trendiness.

At the end of the day, though, whether you choose to stay at this perfectly adequate but slightly faded five-star property will depend on whether your recreational tastes veer more towards nightlife than shopping and tourism. It is in Chaoyang and hence close to the renowned Sanlitun "bar street", and right next door to both the Hard Rock Café and the exhibition centre. But it is a cab ride to Tiananmen, the Forbidden City and Wanfujing. Live jazz in the ground floor Teahouse would also swing it for some with an aversion to tinkling lobby pianists:

Rates from: $$
Star rating: ★ ★ ★ ★ ★
Overall rating: ♙ ♙ ♙ ♙ ½

Ambience:	8.47	Cleanliness:	8.80
Value:	8.20	Facilities:	8.63
Staff:	8.59	Restaurants:	8.63
Location:	8.31	Families:	8.14

Sheraton Sanya Resort

Yalong Bay National Resort District, Sanya 572000, Hainan, China
T: +86 898 8855 8855 **F**: +86 898 8855 8866
www.HotelClub.com/Hotels/Sheraton_Sanya_Resort

There are two ways of looking at Hainan Island: you can be disappointed that it falls so far short of its claim to be "China's Hawaii" - or you can simply enjoy one of the most under-utilised holiday spots on the planet. And by whatever yardstick, this sprawling five-star resort is a bit of a lark.

Whether holding the "Miss World" beauty pageant here in 2004 was designed to boost the flagging flesh-show's fortunes or to kick-start Sanya's international appeal is a moot point, but in over-the-top terms, the pair certainly deserve each other. With its very own VIP lounge at Sanya Airport and a stretch-limo shuttle service, the Sheraton is indisputably queen of the bizarrely named Yalong Bay National Resort District.

The resort's Laguna Pool is pure Las Vegas and its 511 rooms boast rainforest showers and hypoallergenic pillows. But claims that its Samba Nightclub is the "hottest in Asia" rival those of the dreary stretch of local beach called "End of the Earth" for hyperbole. But when all is said and done, the hotel is well up to Sheraton's international standards.

Rates from: $$
Star rating: ★★★★★
Overall rating: ½

Ambience:	9.30	Cleanliness:	9.33
Value:	8.33	Facilities:	9.08
Staff:	8.85	Restaurants:	8.22
Location:	8.63	Families:	9.00

Sheraton Suzhou Hotel & Towers

259 Xin Shi Road, Suzhou 215007, Jiangsu, China
T: +86 512 6510 3388 **F**: +86 512 6510 0888
www.HotelClub.com/Hotels/Sheraton_Suzhou_Hotel_Tower

When so many hotels being raised in China nowadays are mere lumps of concrete and glass, it is a pleasure to discover one that takes its architectural cue from its 2,500-year-old surrounds. Only a couple of storeys high, the Sheraton is all local stone, winged roofs and canals, while the entrance is modelled on the nearby Panmen Gate, the last vestige of the walls that once surrounded the city. So the hotel is a sort of Suzhou in miniature, but without the crowds and the noise.

Ancient on the outside, the 400 rooms within are all acceptably modern, with voicemail, dataports and the like while the long-stay rooms incorporate a kitchen. If you are not self-catering, there is Cantonese at the Celestial Court, Asian and Western at the Garden Brasserie or wood-fired oven pizza at the very Art Deco Riva's.

Rates from: $$
Star rating: ★★★★★
Overall rating: ½

Ambience:	9.20	Cleanliness:	9.20
Value:	8.53	Facilities:	8.75
Staff:	8.87	Restaurants:	8.84
Location:	8.53	Families:	8.83

St Regis Beijing

21 Jianguomenwai Dajie, Beijing 100020, China
T: +86 10 6460 6688 **F**: +86 10 6460 3299
www.HotelClub.com/Hotels/The_St_Regis

It is pretty much the number one address in China's premier city and first choice for many local and visiting executives - so the St Regis definitely has its location right. The diplomatic district is in hailing distance and the main business quarter only a few minutes drive away. HQ for CEOs? For sure.

More than half of the St Regis' 273 rooms are suites; spacious, subtly lit, furnished with deep sofas, easy chairs, weighty beds and DVD players throughout. It is the sort of place, in short, you can settle into with consummate ease and set up a small business meeting, work alone or simply rest and relax, helped of course by the 24-hour butler service.

Elsewhere in the hotel there is a choice of nine places to eat and drink, including the Cigar Bar with its batteries of Monte Cristos and Cohibas and other first-class stogies. The Astor Grill is noted for fine dining, while the Garden Lounge is more of an intimate fireside dining affair, and the Celestial Court serves up faultless Chinese cuisine, drawing its dishes from all over the country. Keep your eyes peeled for long enough, and you will see a *Who's Who* of Beijing bent low over the menus and lingering over coffee and cognacs. Socialites should note that the Press Club Bar - patronised by a large number of professionals apart from journalists - is especially convivial.

In free moments, it is rewarding to take a dip in the 25-metre indoor pool, an impressive Romanesque affair with an adjacent fitness facility filled with the latest weights and the like. The range of treatments at the spa is equally inspiring, while the hotel bowling alley allows a window into one of Beijing's most popular indoor pastimes. It is not difficult to see why the city's upper echelons favour the St Regis. It is said that power is the greatest aphrodisiac, in which case this hotel is pretty damn sexy.

Rates from: **$$$**
Star rating: ★ ★ ★ ★ ★
Overall rating: 🐾🐾🐾🐾 ½

Ambience:	9.11	Cleanliness:	9.34
Value:	8.04	Facilities:	8.84
Staff:	8.94	Restaurants:	8.64
Location:	8.74	Families:	8.33

St Regis Shanghai

889 Dongfang Road, Pudong, Shanghai 200122, China
T: +86 21 5050 4567 **F:** +86 21 6875 6789
www.HotelClub.com/Hotels/The_St_Regis_Shanghai

Anyone travelling to Shanghai for the first time since the 1980s or before is in for a dose of culture shock when they hit the St Regis. Garbed in tail coats, a multi-lingual butler, savvy in the ways of the city and fluent in IT, will be waiting to escort you to your room. The gloomy dormitories of two decades back, watched over by harridans who regarded being asked to unlock your room as a personal affront, have long been demolished. In their place is the likes of the St Regis, whose standards of service and comfort should make similar establishments in London and New York look to their laurels.

The butlers, or butleresses even, remain on call 24 hours a day, happy to unpack luggage or advise on and make restaurant reservations. The 318 rooms, decorated with soft-toned rich fabrics, are at least 48 square metres - some of the most spacious in Shanghai. The desk chair is ergonomic, the bed is custom designed with a 900-coil mattress, Internet is broadband, the sound system is Bose and the TV is cable. Floris soap and shampoo are stacked on the shelf of the bathroom's rainforest shower. And all guests are automatically invited to evening "wind-down" cocktails in the Executive Lounge.

Cocktail downed, there is a medley of Chinese and Italian restaurants to sate the appetite. Danieli's rests on the top floor with

stunning views over the city complemented by an innovative, modern interior design and similar cuisine. Carrianna serves southern Chinese food, with the emphasis on fresh seasonal dishes, while Saints comes marching in all day with international fare.

Executives staying here - and the St Regis is very much positioned with them in mind - can also take advantage of the 600-seater Astor Ballroom and nine adjacent, if rather smaller, meeting rooms. It has been said that, even though it is in Pudong, the St Regis is a little remote, but with a hotel this good that is not really a valid criticism.

Rates from: $$$
Star rating: ★ ★ ★ ★ ★
Overall rating: 🌐🌐🌐🌐🌐

Ambience:	8.97	Cleanliness:	9.46
Value:	8.81	Facilities:	9.10
Staff:	9.19	Restaurants:	8.86
Location:	7.94	Families:	8.85

Westin Shanghai

Bund Centre, 88 Henan Central Road, Shanghai 200002, China
T: +86 21 6335 1888 **F**: +86 21 6335 2888
www.HotelClub.com/Hotels/The_Westin_Shanghai

Shanghai's fans are either Puxi people or Pudong people, and for those to whom this city will always be stuck in a 1920s time-warp - the Huangpu River ornamented by Victorian clock towers and banks reminiscent of Threadneedle Street - the Bund is the only place to be, for all its frantic modernisation.

Now they can enjoy the best of both worlds with some of the coolest accommodation in town just a five-minute walk from the fabled riverside boulevard (well, Giorgio Armani opted to stay here when he opened his first Shanghai boutique).

A little OTT for some, with its illuminated glass staircase and glitzily-clad door-girls (and F&B outlets with names such as Heavenlies, Bliss and Treats), but the guestrooms are eminently practical, with sliding doors to partition the sleeping area.

A Banyan Tree spa and a Rolls-Royce showroom are just two of the Westin's offshoots in a hotel that's a subtle blend of style, sophistication and location.

Rates from: $$$
Star rating: ★ ★ ★ ★ ★
Overall rating: ♦ ♦ ♦ ♦ ½

Ambience:	8.96	Cleanliness:	9.16
Value:	8.21	Facilities:	8.67
Staff:	8.58	Restaurants:	8.57
Location:	8.62	Families:	8.32

White Swan Hotel

1 Southern Shamian Street, Shamian Island, Guangzhou 510133, China
T: +86 20 8188 6968 **F**: +86 20 8186 1188
www.HotelClub.com/Hotels/White_Swan_Hotel_Guangzhou

The White Swan's bright lobby - with its high ceiling and cascading rockeries - gazes straight out on to the river and gives a grandness that sets the scene for the whole hotel, which is still undisputed champion of Shamian Island. The 843 spacious and well-maintained rooms and suites (half with river views) including two executive floors complete with broadband access and private lounge, a first-class business centre and extensive conference facilities, mean the business visitor is more than adequately catered for. These are complemented by an impressive array of leisure offerings from the two indoor and eight outdoor tennis courts, two squash courts, a golf driving range, two free-form swimming pools, health club and spa.

With nine restaurants and bars, the international range of food is broad to suit the hotel's clientele, from the French cuisine of the Silk Road Grill Room to the authentic sushi and teppanyaki of Hirata, from the Sichuan Provincial Restaurant to the elegant tea ceremonies and dim sum of the Jade River.

Rates from: $$
Star rating: ★ ★ ★ ★ ★
Overall rating: ♦ ♦ ♦ ♦ ½

Ambience:	8.83	Cleanliness:	9.09
Value:	8.17	Facilities:	8.51
Staff:	8.80	Restaurants:	8.77
Location:	8.63	Families:	8.64

HONG KONG

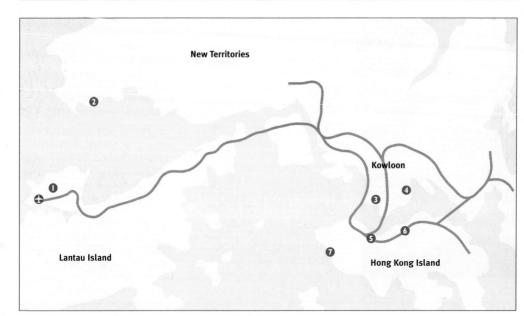

From the moment the harbour-side, 415-metre high International Finance Centre Two opened in 2004 it has symbolised the city - a place where the relentless crusade to make money in limited space rarely slackens. As the harbour shrinks amid a welter of reclamation, so the SAR's commercial offerings increase - most notably on the hotel front, as 2005 will witness the opening of both the water-front Four Seasons and the boutique Landmark as well as a major renovation of the redoubtable Mandarin Oriental.

Many Asian cities have developed along similar timescales to Hong Kong, encountered the same waves of growth and bust, and tend to resemble one another. Hong Kong had a head start on the rest of the region, with the former British colony booming as the only gateway to the vast, untapped resources of China. A motley crew of fishing junks and an assortment of paddy fields blossomed into one of the major cities of the Far East in the space of a few generations. Today, Hong Kong harbour bristles with sky-scraping success, and even with the economic wobbles of the 1997 handover and the pandemonium generated by SARS, the skyline changes by the month.

Hong Kong is tiny by international standards, a crowded and jumbled city with layer upon layer of development and urban clutter, mostly squashed around the harbour. In an effort to stop some of it falling in, land has been

everyone is at it. Where do Hong Kongers find room to stash it all in their compressed flats? For visitors, Tsim Sha Tsui is often the first port of call, but try diving into vibrant Causeway Bay for brand-name goods and shopping plazas. The malls of Central and Pacific Place in Admiralty are lined with fancy upmarket apparel. At the other end of the scale are the grungy street markets and bargains of counterfeit capital Mong Kok. For knick-knack types, the stalls of Cat Street on the Island offer a trove of kitsch.

When it comes to restaurants little needs to be said - the dining is predictably excellent. Yet it can also be very cheap and whatever your budget, the food is good. The Cantonese may be a tolerant bunch, but not when it comes to poor cuisine. Hotel restaurants are right up there, their menus bulging with world-class culinary indulgences. The hotels themselves are a reflection of Hong Kong - modern, compact, energetic and efficient - with service just a bit too rushed. Expect staff to be hurried and doing several things at once. Be warned that rooms in the territory tend to be half the size of those in other cities. Some can be comically small with not enough room to swing a spring roll, let alone a cat.

Hong Kong is a place that loses nothing with the seasons, but it

reclaimed. A patch only a few square metres across may hold office space, hotel rooms, a shopping plaza, a car park and an underground railway line, all stacked on top of each other. Given its history as a trading outpost it is not surprising that the territory remains an international business centre, and you will see plenty of suits nipping back and forth. But there is an optimistic spring in their steps, not the depressed plod you find elsewhere.

For tourists, Hong Kong is a major travel hub and it is a traditional jumping-off spot for shopaholics. There can be few places with more shops per square metre than Hong Kong - they are absolutely everywhere. And

can get uncomfortably humid in the summer months, and the monsoons between July and September can put a dampener on things. September through April is the time to come although it can get a tad chilly in January and February.

The touristy circuit is fairly limited but it is best to submerge yourself in the many enjoyable low-key diversions, all of which are close at hand. Museums are generally educational and presentable. Incense wafts through the temples that provide interesting pockets of culture among the modern progress. And then there is the pungent whiff of various unidentifiable shrivelled roots and creatures in the traditional medicine shops and wet markets. Hong Kong is an intriguing place to absorb.

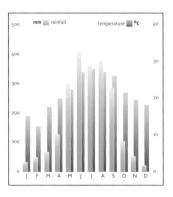

Conrad Hong Kong

Pacific Place, 88 Queensway, Hong Kong Island, Hong Kong
T: +852 2521 3838   **F**: +852 2521 3888
www.HotelClub.com/Hotels/Conrad_International_Hotel_Hong_Kong

If you subscribe to the view that Hong Kong is one big shopping mall, then you may as well stay in one. And they don't come any bigger or swisher than Pacific Place, of which the Conrad Hotel occupies floors 40 to 61.

Its 513 rooms are among Hong Kong's biggest at an average of 42 square metres and they come with everything you'd expect and then some - including umbrellas and ironing boards.

A late-night plunge in the heated outdoor pool is a surreal experience - you are up there swimming among the fabled skyscraper-scape, with the Peak and Victoria Harbour as a backdrop. The northern Italian fare in Nicholini's is consistently rated among the best of its kind in the world, while many locals reckon the English high-tea buffet in the Lobby Lounge offers great value for money. A baby-sitting service and access to a notary public sum up the Conrad's all-things-to-all-people approach.

Rates from: $$$
Star rating: ★ ★ ★ ★ ★
Overall rating: ♙ ♙ ♙ ♙ ½

Ambience:	8.85	Cleanliness:	9.24
Value:	7.87	Facilities:	8.69
Staff:	8.80	Restaurants:	8.66
Location:	9.13	Families:	8.40

Excelsior Hong Kong   *1994*

281 Gloucester Road, Causeway Bay, Hong Kong Island, Hong Kong
T: +852 2894 8888 **F**: +852 2895 6459
www.HotelClub.com/Hotels/Excelsior_Hotel_Hong_Kong_The

Into its fourth decade and going stronger than ever, the Excelsior provides a grandstand for all Hong Kong's most redoubtable icons. Look north from its 34 storeys, and there is Noël Coward's Noon Day Gun out in the midday sun, the (still) Royal Hong Kong Yacht Club, Victoria Harbour and the peaks of Kowloon in all their glory. A few steps from the back of the hotel leads straight into the manic heart of the island's busiest up-market retail district, so it is the perfect carrier-bag offloading point for the compulsive shopper.

Hong Kong's reputation for hyper-efficiency and good food is borne out in the accommodation and half-dozen restaurants. The 883 rooms and suites are mines of solid comfort, and perked up with broadband, voicemail and the like. The 270-degree views from the top-floor ToTT's Asian Bar and Grill are endlessly alluring, while the basement Dickens pub pulls a beer-swilling, sports-mad crowd, especially when big matches are on.

Rates from: $$
Star rating: ★ ★ ★ ★
Overall rating: ♙ ♙ ♙ ♙

Ambience:	8.42	Cleanliness:	8.76
Value:	8.12	Facilities:	8.16
Staff:	8.39	Restaurants:	8.47
Location:	9.23	Families:	8.22

Hong Kong Gold Coast Hotel

1 Castle Peak Road, Castle Peak Bay, New Territories, Hong Kong
T: +852 2452 8888 **F**: +852 2440 7368
www.HotelClub.com/Hotels/Gold_Coast_Hotel_Hong_Kong

This is not Australia. Nor yet Africa. Just another piece of clever Hong Kong nomenclature way up in the New Territories. Admittedly the beach is one of the better ones in the SAR, but even so it lies outside the hotel premises and is carpeted by the hordes, especially over summer weekends. So why come here? Well, five-star resorts are few and far between in a city that enjoys one of the highest population densities in the world, and very often a good proportion of guests actually live just down the road. The Gold Coast's alter ego is a conference centre, headed by a ballroom and seven versatile function rooms. A large - by local standards - garden can also be used for cocktail parties and similar events, and it's by no means unusual to find wedding groups posing in front of the topiary.

With 450 rooms (including ten suites) stacked up so each gets a seaview, this is one of the larger out-of-town hotels; it's not likely to win any awards for its interiors any time soon, but the decor is serviceable if a little worn in parts. Sports fans should enjoy the facilities here, while a marina and mini mall lie within easy walking distance.

Of all the hotel's restaurants, Qi deserves a special mention. The staff are solicitous and eager to provide navigational tips on the menu, the wine list is both imaginative and catholic, and - best of all - the restaurant overlooks spreading lawns, palms and shrubs rather than concrete jungle. While the pink-hued decor tends to "Barren Rock baroque", it shouldn't detract from the dishes on offer - barbequed chicken liver and pork, braised mixed veg and seafood in a clay pot, - casserole of baked crabs with egg - which are all first-rate. All in all, the restaurant is an invigorating break from the big city. And you could pretty much say the same for the whole hotel.

Rates from: $$
Star rating: ★★★★
Overall rating: 👍👍👍👍

Ambience:	8.61	Cleanliness:	8.53
Value:	8.23	Facilities:	8.33
Staff:	8.29	Restaurants:	8.26
Location:	8.51	Families:	8.30

Grand Hyatt Hong Kong

1 Harbour Road, Wan Chai, Hong Kong Island, Hong Kong
T: +852 2588 1234 **F:** +852 2802 0677
www.HotelClub.com/Hotels/Grand_Hyatt_Hotel_Hong_Kong

The Grand Hyatt has always been a distinctive establishment, and it continues to reinvent itself with remarkable finesse and agility. The latest embellishment is a 7,200 square metre spa floor, dubbed Plateau, which after much ballyhooing and immoderate delay opened in 2004. The wait was worth it, for - uniquely among hotels in the city - guests can now avail themselves of 23 rooms actually within the spa where they can subject themselves to a host of body and facial treatments, as well as spend the night on custom-designed futons. A 50-metre heated pool is only steps away, together with fitness and exercise studios and a restaurant - The Grill - which concentrates on healthy cuisine. All in all, Hyatt has come up with a winner - given the current fetish for all things spa - and the competition must be gnashing its teeth in envy. Indeed, there was quite a bit to turn other hoteliers green in the first place.

The statuesque lobby, with its black marble, soaring columns and twin staircases has always been a head-turner, and remains one of the most operatic introductions to any hotel anywhere. Much has been written elsewhere about the Grand Hyatt's proximity to the Convention Centre, and its suitability for executives who find the wired-and-ready workstations in the 566 rooms and suites as comfortable as the beds.

Much has been made of the hotels restaurants, to wit: the bold authenticity of the Chinese cuisine at One Harbour Road, the louche ambience and dainty pastries of teatime at the Tiffin Lounge, or the merry abandon that emanates from the circular Champagne Bar to name but three. As a final fillip, consider hiring the hotel's 45-metre yacht *Grand Cru* for corporate meetings, a dinner party or a "slow-boat-to-China" airport transfer.

Rates from: $$$
Star rating: ★ ★ ★ ★ ★
Overall rating: ♫ ♫ ♫ ♫ ½

Ambience:	9.00	Cleanliness:	9.26
Value:	7.85	Facilities:	8.73
Staff:	8.75	Restaurants:	8.89
Location:	8.68	Families:	8.39

Harbour Plaza Hong Kong

20 Tak Fung Street, Whampoa Garden, Hunghom, Kowloon, Hong Kong
T: +852 2621 3188 **F:** +852 2621 3311
www.HotelClub.com/Hotels/Harbour_Plaza_Hong_Kong_Hotel

This shiny blue block jutting out into the harbour gives the impression of almost being afloat. Smooth and well appointed, the modern Harbour Plaza takes full advantage of its Kowloon-side position with bay windows flooding the interior with light - especially in the bright lobby with its point-blank harbour views, marble staircase and hint of Italian flair. There is space, a rare Hong Kong commodity, and the immediate neighbourhood emits an equally smart air rather than the usual frantic clutter. Spacious and smart harbour-view rooms comprise three quarters of the total, and the outstanding glass-walled rooftop pool is a beauty. Being 10 minutes' drive from Tsim Sha Tsui is considered a minor inconvenience in international terms, but well off the beaten track by local standards. First-rate dining includes the local novelty of a breezy al fresco cafe (an almost impossible feature in the heart of the city), the staunchly traditional Harbour Grill and the original Pit Stop Formula One bar. A brave and thoughtful Hong Kong hotel.

Rates from: $$
Star rating: ★ ★ ★ ★ ★
Overall rating: ♦ ♦ ♦

Ambience:	8.60	Cleanliness:	9.00
Value:	8.21	Facilities:	8.55
Staff:	8.40	Restaurants:	8.43
Location:	7.89	Families:	8.31

Holiday Inn Golden Mile Hong Kong

50 Nathan Road, Tsim Sha Tsui, Kowloon, Hong Kong
T: +852 2369 3111 **F:** +852 2369 0948
www.HotelClub.com/Hotels/Holiday_Inn_Golden_Mile_Hotel_Hong_Kong

vodkas in Hari's Bar are two other major pluses, while the rooftop health club and outdoor pool are A-grade oases. Opened in 1975 but well maintained, the Holiday Inn has always been owned by the Harilela family who regard it as a personal trophy. A lot of regular guests feel the same.

If Hong Kong ever needed acupuncture, the best place to stick one of the needles would be Nathan Road - the so-called "Golden Mile". The sheer energy and brio of this neon-swathed strip of shops, clubs and pubs can be mesmerising - so sidestepping into the Holiday Inn is an exercise in calm. The hotel is never going to win any awards for its views, but the 585 ultra family-friendly 28-square-metre rooms are among the larger in the city and are big enough to accommodate two double beds. The innovative European creations in the Avenue restaurant and the 18 flavoured

Rates from: $$
Star rating: ★ ★ ★ ★
Overall rating: ♦ ♦ ♦ ♦

Ambience:	8.37	Cleanliness:	8.73
Value:	8.00	Facilities:	8.24
Staff:	8.27	Restaurants:	8.53
Location:	9.10	Families:	8.24

InterContinental Hong Kong

18 Salisbury Road, Tsim Sha Tsui, Kowloon, Hong Kong
T: +852 2721 1211 **F**: +852 2739 4546
www.HotelClub.com/Hotels/Intercontinental_Hotel_Hong_Kong

This is a hotel that inspires an enormous swathe of admiration and affection in equal measure. It's a stalwart of the Hong Kong scene, and has been for much of the past quarter-century, but it has never been pompous or stuffy. So you might want to eat amid the elegant simplicity of Harbourside, or dine in Alain Ducasse's Spoon, arguably one of the finest restaurants in the world. You could join in the morning poolside Tai Chi session, lead naturally by a master of the craft. Or you could simply watch the class going through its paces from the bubbling security of the nearby jacuzzi which, incidentally, has few equals as a harbour-gazing spot. The nearby I-Spa, feng shui'd to the gills, is without doubt one of the best in the city, while the hotel's chief concierge, Louis Baleros, is a prime example of the gentlemanly omniscience of his breed.

Marvellous and manifest though all the hotel's accoutrements are, pride of place - as it was in the beginning, is now and forever shall be - belongs to

the neon-tinted aqueous optical illusion more pedantically referred to as a harbour view. This reaches its full force when a cruise liner steams past - seemingly close enough to touch and redolent of everything that has made Hong Kong one of the world's premier ports. Observing this from a double bed early in the morning or late at night triples the thrill. Naturally, all 514 rooms and suites are luxuriously fitted out, with Italian marble bathrooms, Internet TVs and sumptuous furnishing, while a one-stop service centre replaces those fiddly buttons that used to

decorate bedside phones. All of the Interconti's rooms are about to get a major interior decor makeover, which if the prototype is anything to go by will make them the talk of the town. Here's to the next 25 years.

Rates from: $$$
Star rating: ★ ★ ★ ★ ★
Overall rating: ♦♦♦♦ ½

Ambience:	9.01	Cleanliness:	9.27
Value:	7.99	Facilities:	8.86
Staff:	8.87	Restaurants:	8.99
Location:	9.08	Families:	8.46

Island Shangri-La Hong Kong

Pacific Place, Supreme Court Road, Central, Hong Kong Island, Hong Kong
T: +852 2877 3838 **F:** +852 2521 8742
www.HotelClub.com/Hotels/Island_Shangrila_Hotel_Hong_Kong

Anyone lucky enough to have stayed at the Island Shang over the past 15 years is in for a pleasant surprise next time they check in, as the hotel has been given an almost complete makeover, which reached a triumphant conclusion in the spring of 2005. The signature 51-metre *Great Motherland of China* silk painting still adorns the atrium, of course, but elsewhere pretty much everything else has been spruced up.

Expect much refreshed decor and menus in the still utterly Gallic Petrus, Nadaman (the Japanese) and the Lobster Bar and Grill. A new meeting space - the Harbour Room and Roof Garden - has been added to the top floor, the former bristling with high-tech accessories and the latter complete with retractable roof and built-in stage. The ballroom and library have also been given the once-over.

But while the public areas have been given a new lease of life, it is the 565 rooms and suites that have been totally transformed. Always popular with executives on the move - not least for the oversize desks at which you could actually work - all rooms now have broadband, concealed dataports and power sockets, dual-line phones, a DVD player, a four-in-one contraption that faxes, prints, copies and scans plus an LCD TV in the bathroom.

Those parts of the property that did not receive the full force of the renovation are in as good shape as ever. Both the 24-hour fitness centre and adjacent outdoor pool are more than pleasant, there's the option of neat add-ons like aromatherapy and reflexology, while Hong Kong Park - attracting a fair amount of outdoor theatre from tai chi schools to wedding photo posers - stands on the very doorstep.

Finally, for anyone not in the know, café TOO remains the open-kitchen blissful buffet of choice on the island.

Rates from: $$$
Star rating: ★ ★ ★ ★ ★
Overall rating: ◌ ◌ ◌ ◌ ½

Ambience:	9.00	Cleanliness:	9.25
Value:	7.93	Facilities:	8.74
Staff:	8.76	Restaurants:	8.91
Location:	9.12	Families:	8.41

JW Marriott Hotel Hong Kong

Pacific Place, 88 Queensway, Central, Hong Kong Island, Hong Kong
T: +852 2810 8366 **F:** +852 2845 5808
www.HotelClub.com/Hotels/J_W_Marriott_Hotel_Hong_Kong

Arguably the junior member of the triumvirate of five-stars that hangs above Pacific Place, the Marriott has always felt as if it was crammed into the site as an afterthought. However the hotel's new Fish Bar and rather unusual Lounge and Wine Bar - with 60 blended teas, a dozen different noodles, more than 200 wines and a raft of tapas - have certainly given it a much-needed spruce-up. Ride the lifts to the upper storeys, and you're confronted with 602 rooms and suites - dominated by high, almost throne-like beds - with views stretching harbour-wards or up the slopes of Hong Kong Island. The outdoor pool, while on the small side, is heated throughout the winter and the health club never closes. Wireless meeting rooms make the business side of things rather easier. Certainly not first choice in this part of town, but very acceptable in the general run of things.

Rates from: $$
Star rating: ★★★★★
Overall rating: 🐾🐾🐾🐾 ½

Ambience:	8.85	Cleanliness:	9.15
Value:	8.06	Facilities:	8.61
Staff:	8.75	Restaurants:	8.65
Location:	9.28	Families:	8.57

Kowloon Hotel

19-21 Nathan Road, Tsim Sha Tsui, Kowloon, Hong Kong
T: +852 2929 2888 **F:** +852 2739 9811
www.HotelClub.com/Hotels/Kowloon_Hotel_Hong_Kong_The

Right behind that grande old dame the Peninsula in the core of Tsim Sha Tsui, the Kowloon Hotel is the rather newer dame opened in 1986, and the accommodation of choice for the budget-minded single executive. This property is no longer in the Peninsula group fold, but you can still expect the same type of service, but without the history and with substantially lower room rates. Included in those rates in each of the Kowloon's 736 smart if cramped rooms is a tri-lingual, multi-functional computer-cum-satellite television that includes broadband connections and fax and print facilities. If you can drag yourself away from it, of the hotel's quartet of restaurants, the crowds of Hong Kongers feasting on Cantonese delicacies in Wan Loong Court are the best recommendation any chef could wish for. On the downside, the Kowloon lacks exercise facilities, but entrance to the YMCA gym just across the street is available for a nominal fee.

Rates from: $$
Star rating: ★★★★
Overall rating: 🐾🐾🐾🐾

Ambience:	8.03	Cleanliness:	8.79
Value:	8.10	Facilities:	7.86
Staff:	8.26	Restaurants:	8.13
Location:	9.33	Families:	8.18

Kowloon Shangri-La

64 Mody Road, Tsim Sha Tsui, Kowloon, Hong Kong
T: +852 2721 2111 **F:** +852 2723 8686
www.HotelClub.com/Hotels/Kowloon_ShangriLa_Hotel_Hong_Kong

inch a world-class open-kitchen buffet, alive with mouth-watering smells, sights, sounds and tastes and staffed by enthusiastic professionals who give the impression they simply love their work. Eat here at least once during your stay, or call in if you happen to be staying somewhere else. The adjacent Deli is rather fun too.

Tempting though it is to regard this as a junior cousin to the higher-profile Island Shang, it enjoys far superior harbour views as it looks out over the water directly at the Manhattan-like skyscrapers to the south. The new railway construction immediately outside is finally finished and there are now subway links practically to the doorstep. And so it simply remains to enjoy this very smart 700-room (all refurbished in 2004) property, the doyenne of eastern Tsim Sha Tsui.

It's not straying into hyperbole to say that the hotel could be summed up by Café Kool - every

Rates from: $$
Star rating: ★ ★ ★ ★ ★
Overall rating: 🏵🏵🏵🏵 ½

Ambience:	8.99	Cleanliness:	9.21
Value:	8.09	Facilities:	8.70
Staff:	8.82	Restaurants:	8.83
Location:	8.79	Families:	8.29

Langham Hotel Hong Kong

8 Peking Road, Tsim Sha Tsui, Kowloon, Hong Kong
T: +852 2375 1133 **F:** +852 2375 6611
www.HotelClub.com/Hotels/Langham_Hotel_Hong_Kong

Older travellers may recall the Great Eagle, one of the region's more quixotically named hotels, which sensibly hatched itself into the Langham. Apart from the name, very little seems to have changed for the inside. If you doubt the aphorism that Hong Kong's hotels epitomise the best of east and west, a short walk from the Main St Deli to T'ang Court provides ample proof. One of Asia's most genial hosts, the avuncular Nigel Roberts, presides over the entire establishment and its highly comfortable 488 rooms and suites.

Perhaps the only and very minor complaint is that the Langham can be a tad noisy at times due to the roads on either side of the property, which sits squarely in Tsim Sha Tsui. Not to be confused with the brand new Langham Place, aka Palace, a mile or so north, of which we expect to see quite a bit in next year's edition.

Rates from: $$
Star rating: ★ ★ ★ ★ ★
Overall rating: 🏵🏵🏵🏵 ½

Ambience:	8.78	Cleanliness:	9.15
Value:	8.15	Facilities:	8.46
Staff:	8.73	Restaurants:	8.84
Location:	9.24	Families:	8.15

Le Méridien Cyberport

100 Cyberport Road, Pok Fu Lam, Hong Kong Island, Hong Kong
T: +852 2980 7788 **F:** +852 2980 7888
www.HotelClub.com/Hotels/Le_Meridien_Cyberport_Hong_Kong

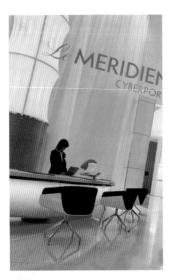

Hong Kong Island has a disconcerting habit of demolishing its more charismatic hotels - Repulse Bay, Hilton, Furama - so it's pleasing to report when a new one opens. More pleasing still when the establishment in question is a stylish ground-breaker. And so it is with Le Méridien, anchor accommodation for the government's somewhat controversial but nevertheless hi-tech futuristic business park west of Central.

It would be natural to start with the hotel's gizmos, but instead take a peek at the beds, all 173 of which are adorned with a supremely comfortable 14-inch mattress and Egyptian linen. From here you may gaze at the 42-inch plasma screen and jiggle with the wireless high-speed internet connection, with perhaps an occasional foray to the glass and chrome bathroom which is chock-a-block with Hermès gooeys. Don't bother looking for "Reception" when you arrive; one

of the smartly suited staff will check you in wherever you happen to be in the hotel - perhaps the chilled-out PSI bar or even, should time's winged chariot etc, while you're going up in the lift.

And similarly don't waste time seeking out the business centre, merely whistle up a laptop and set to work wherever you might find yourself sitting. It's difficult to recall when a hotel has been such - if this

doesn't seem to run contrary to what is essentially a business hostelry - sheer fun and where technology is properly harnessed to make life easier for one and all.

Innovative cuisine dominates all the hotels restaurants, with the wood-burning oven at Prompt and the tapas and cult wines in Podium leading the way.

As an endnote, Le Méridien Cyberport enjoys an energy and freshness of spirit that is present in no other hotel in Hong Kong. And don't let anyone tell you - with Central a mere 10 minutes distant by taxi - that it's "out of the way".

Rates from: **$$**
Star rating: ★ ★ ★ ★ ★
Overall rating: ♔ ♔ ♔ ♔

Ambience:	9.00	Cleanliness:	9.40
Value:	7.40	Facilities:	8.23
Staff:	8.60	Restaurants:	8.50
Location:	7.20	Families:	8.33

Mandarin Oriental Hong Kong

5 Connaught Road, Central, Hong Kong Island, Hong Kong
T: +852 2522 0111 **F:** +852 2810 6190
www.HotelClub.com/Hotels/Mandarin_Oriental_Hong_Kong

The Mandarin Oriental - it's difficult to write its name without adding "venerable" - is pungently characteristic of Hong Kong. When it first opened it was the city's tallest building, an accolade that now seems almost risible. Yet although it s now more than 40 years old and dwarfed by surrounding skyscrapers, its extraordinarily high standards of service ensure that it remains the doyenne of Hong Kong hotels, with a reputation that far exceeds the bounds of the SAR. The Mandarin successfully captures a classic and traditional air, liberally spread with such Chinese touches as intricately carved screens, bygone-era porcelain and robust furniture.

Equally adept at catering to both upper-echelon business and leisure travellers, the Mandarin is unique in Hong Kong in offering a balcony with almost all its 541 rooms, and harbour-view rooms come with binoculars. Extravagantly furnished, the rooms are particularly comfortable and care is taken to provide everything from designer toiletries to high-speed Internet access, while the suites include a mini business centre.

A manifold range of restaurants and bars wait to satisfy guests' appetites. The Chinnery is a cosy bar serving bangers and mash plus an exhaustive range of single-malt whiskies, while Vong is cutting-edge trendy Franco-Asian cuisine. Man Wah presents the acme of Chinese cuisine, and the menu at the Mandarin Grill comprises 300 dishes. The ground-floor Captain's Bar is wall-to-wall suits, with senior and junior captains of industry making free with the grain and the grape clinking glasses and pewter tankards with gusto. Breakfast at the Café is good opportunity to watch the myriad pedestrians scurrying the streets of Central, afternoon tea at the Clipper Lounge a time to relax with scones and the hotel's signature rose-petal jam.

Finally, the Health Centre comes as a minor surprise, with its centrepiece a pool in the style of a Roman spa with a domed roof and Doric columns. The hotel is due to undergo extensive renovations in December 2005, only a few months after a junior, sister, boutique - The Landmark - opens round the corner. So fans should watch this space. Avidly.

Rates from: $$$
Star rating: ★ ★ ★ ★ ★
Overall rating: ♭ ♭ ♭ ♭ ½

Ambience:	8.97	Cleanliness:	9.28
Value:	7.83	Facilities:	8.52
Staff:	9.08	Restaurants:	9.00
Location:	9.30	Families:	8.25

Marco Polo Hong Kong Hotel

3 Canton Road, Harbour City, Tsim Sha Tsui, Kowloon, Hong Kong
T: +852 2113 0088 **F:** +852 2113 0011
www.HotelClub.com/Hotels/Marco_Polo_Hongkong_Hotel_The

With a back door that opens straight out on to the Kowloon-side Star Ferry pier, this is the best of the three Marco Polos along Canton Road. The four-star hotel is cheek-by-jowl with a glittering branch of Lane Crawford, and it would not be too far-fetched to suggest a late breakfast at the very swish Café Marco, a couple of hours' shopping and then back in time for lunch.

The rooms are a major asset - giants by Hong Kong standards, and although they might seem a little old-fashioned to some, they are airy, welcoming and relaxing, and many enjoy unobstructed harbour views. A very decent outdoor pool is handy and the restaurants compete well with the countless others in the adjoining shopping centres of Harbour City and Ocean Terminal. Nice trimmings, a recently finished renovation, friendly and helpful staff, and a great stepping-off point for the ferries across the harbour or up to mainland China.

Rates from: $$
Star rating: ★ ★ ★ ★
Overall rating: ♦ ♦ ♦ ♦

Ambience:	8.42	Cleanliness:	8.75
Value:	8.22	Facilities:	8.31
Staff:	8.26	Restaurants:	8.28
Location:	9.12	Families:	8.27

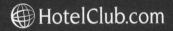

The Peninsula Hong Kong

Salisbury Road, Tsim Sha Tsui, Kowloon, Hong Kong
T: +852 2920 2888 **F:** +852 2722 4170
www.HotelClub.com/Hotels/Peninsula_Hotel_Hong_Kong

astonishment of some of the older members of the board - it opened the city's first discotheque ("Scene") in 1966.

The Peninsula underwent a spectacular renaissance in 1994, when a 30-storey tower was grafted on to the existing building. The Duke and Duchess of Kent flew in from Britain for the grand opening, where they were joined by thousands of Hong Kongers - quite of few of whom had actually been sent an invitation - desperate not to miss the party of the decade.

The Pen was built opposite what at the time was the main railway station, bringing passengers from as far away as Europe to its doorstep. Guests are more likely to arrive nowadays from the international airport in one of the hotel's 14 Rolls-Royces, although some land around the corner at Ocean Terminal at the end of a cruise. But the unique frisson of arrival at the Pen is the same even if you have just stepped off the MTR.

Wander where you will through the Peninsula and you always end up with the same conclusion: the term "five-star hotel" is a woefully inadequate description for your surroundings. You might be touching down on the rooftop helipad, peering majestically at the harbour through the telescope in the Marco Polo Suite, lingering over the signature braised veal shank in Gaddi's, day-dreaming while lazing in the Graeco-Roman pool, or simply taking a mildy cheeky air-conditioned short cut through the lobby where you will be greeted by a chorus of immaculate pageboys at the main door. Whether it is the Pen's style, service or downright sophistication, the oldest of Hong Kong's hotels is not so much a grande dame as a newly crowned empress.

The Pen celebrated its 75th anniversary two years ago, setting the seal on three quarters of a century of service. In peace and in war (a Japanese barber eavesdropped on British top brass while cutting their hair in the late 1930s) the Peninsula has always been a Hong Kong icon, a mine of tradition yet also a frequent innovator, like when - to the

Once inside the rarefied air of what one is tempted to describe as a caravanserai, there is a huge amount to discover. The

renovation gave the old hotel the space to expand its inventory to 300 rooms and suites, each decorously fitted out to be equally adaptable to the high-flying executive or high-class holidaymaker. The top of the new tower was made over to Felix, a restaurant that soon became equally celebrated for its eclectic cuisine and Philippe Starck design - to say nothing of the panorama of Kowloon from the gentlemen's bathroom. The spa grew as well, embracing a sun terrace and

grooming treatments under the eye of expert trichologist Wing Tan. But the cornerstone of the Pen has always been its lobby, with gilded pillars and an equally gilded air that lends itself naturally to an elegant high tea - delicate pastries and scones and a strainer by the silver pot - over titbits of the latest gossip. Very little has changed here since the Pen opened all those years ago - which is precisely why the vast majority of guests accord it a special place in their hearts.

Rates from: $$$$
Star rating: ★ ★ ★ ★ ★
Overall rating: 🐾🐾🐾🐾🐾

Ambience:	9.27	Cleanliness:	9.38
Value:	7.84	Facilities:	8.79
Staff:	8.93	Restaurants:	9.08
Location:	9.18	Families:	8.49

Regal Airport Hotel

9 Cheong Tat Road, Hong Kong International Airport, Chek Lap Kok, Lantau, Hong Kong
T: +852 2286 8888 **F:** +852 2286 8686
www.HotelClub.com/Hotels/Regal_Airport_Hotel_Hong_Kong

When they built the Regal Airport they cut a brand new template. Its airy, modern design makes it more like a resort than somewhere to spend a hurried night between flights. And many of the Regal's regular guests make it their Hong Kong base, using the express train service to commute into Central, 23 minutes away.

A short undercover trolley-push from Arrivals, the Regal's 1,100-plus rooms make it the largest hotel in Hong Kong. Yet there is no sense of being dwarfed by its 12 storeys, thanks largely to a crisp interior design. Combining a wealth of colour with chrome and plain wood finishes, the rooms - regular, suite or club floor - are universally habitable.

Double-glazing shuts out the whine of distant turbines, thick pile deadens passing footfalls, so this is somewhere you can sleep, work and rest in peace.

Note that guests focusing on food should head for Café Aficionado and its sumptuous 24-hour buffet. The new conference centre opening across the road in 2006 is likely to have some impact on room rates - and occupancy.

Rates from: $$
Star rating: ★ ★ ★ ★
Overall rating: ♭♭♭♭ ½

Ambience:	8.70	Cleanliness:	9.12
Value:	8.24	Facilities:	8.59
Staff:	8.52	Restaurants:	8.69
Location:	8.94	Families:	8.48

Ritz-Carlton Hong Kong

3 Connaught Road, Central, Hong Kong Island, Hong Kong
T: +852 2877 6666 **F:** +852 2877 6778
www.HotelClub.com/Hotels/Ritz_Carlton_Hotel_Hong_Kong

Amid the tearfully dull office blocks of Central, the Ritz-Carlton's bravely fought rearguard action is well worth commending. Blink and you could miss this shorter but perfectly formed building, blink again and you might not realise it's a hotel. Discreet and luxurious, it's a distinctly executive pied-à-terre, with the lobby almost an afterthought and the other public areas more akin to drawing-room than lounge. There is absolutely none of that minimalism nonsense that characterises some more modern accommodations - each of the 216 rooms is a big fluffy haven of comfort, ready for work if need be but much more attuned to relaxation. The more splendid of

the Ritz's restaurants naturally lend themselves to corporate dining – whether Italian in Toscana, Cantonese in Lai Kar Heen, or no-prizes-for-guessing at Shanghai-Shanghai. The Café and the Chater Lounge are rather more relaxed. Make sure you dally at the outside pool if time and weather permit.

Rates from: $$$
Star rating: ★ ★ ★ ★
Overall rating: ♭♭♭♭ ½

Ambience:	8.96	Cleanliness:	9.41
Value:	7.84	Facilities:	8.40
Staff:	9.02	Restaurants:	8.55
Location:	9.10	Families:	8.28

Sheraton Hong Kong Hotel and Towers

20 Nathan Road, Tsim Sha Tsui, Kowloon, Hong Kong
T: +852 2369 1111 **F**: +852 2739 8707
www.HotelClub.com/Hotels/Sheraton_Hotel_Hong_Kong

Calling this TST's "sleeper" might be a pun too far, but it is true that somewhere between the Peninsula and the InterContinental, the Sheraton tends to get lost in most travellers' mind map of Hong Kong hotels. Although it's stuffed with 782 rooms, the average guest should not feel overwhelmed, and the accommodation is thoughtfully kitted out with DVD players, 29" TVs, fax machines and all the other essentials of modern hotel life (charging for high-speed Internet access is a minus point, however). The Sheraton includes some inspiring bars and eateries, from the basement Someplace Else - a veteran American-style café - to the top floor Sky Lounge, where a sundowner or nightcap is imperative. There's also a branch of Morton's Steakhouse on the premises, which, while not managed by the hotel deserves a mention for its heroic martinis and equally remarkable sirloins and similar cuts. All in all, a very commendable and very Hong Kong hotel.

Rates from: $$
Star rating: ★ ★ ★ ★ ★
Overall rating: ♦♦♦♦ ½

Ambience:	8.66	Cleanliness:	8.92
Value:	8.10	Facilities:	8.52
Staff:	8.68	Restaurants:	8.55
Location:	9.18	Families:	8.42

YMCA - The Salisbury

41 Salisbury Road, Tsim Sha Tsui, Kowloon, Hong Kong
T: +852 2268 7000 **F**: +852 2739 9315
www.HotelClub.com/Hotels/Salisbury_YMCA_of_Hong_Kong_The

With a five-star location at peanuts prices, this quite admirable budget hotel is a world away from murky dormitories smelling of old socks. True, there are dorms here, but the bulk of the accommodation is indistinguishable from a regular hotel - and all for vastly less than guests are paying to lie with their eyes shut at the Peninsula next door! Likewise the facilities, whether you're talking about the dining rooms or the swimming pool and gym, which could belong to any three- going on four-star. Another boon is provided by the staff - chummy, efficient and proactive well beyond the dictates of much-bandied mission statements.

Being equidistant from historical, cultural, retail and entertainment attractions is the icing on this thoroughly tasty, if a little dowdy looking, cake.

Comparisons are odious, as the old saying goes, but not a few hotels around Asia could learn a thing or two from this particular Y.

Rates from: $$
Star rating: ★ ★ ★
Overall rating: ♦♦♦♦ ½

Ambience:	7.57	Cleanliness:	8.92
Value:	9.17	Facilities:	8.07
Staff:	8.58	Restaurants:	7.60
Location:	9.67	Families:	8.73

INDIA

India is one of the ultimate travel experiences. No other country possesses the diversity and depth of this mesmerising land. The engrossing culture is stunningly exotic and rich. The land varies wildly, from sweltering tropics to the unforgiving icy extremes of the mighty Himalaya. And the turbulent wake of ethnic variation, eventful history and political strife has led to an equally disparate people, filling every possible niche of human existence. India overflows with beauty and toil. The sights, sounds, smells and tastes will push your senses to their very limits.

India as we know it was born of the legacy of British colonial rule. Formerly a patchwork of feuding princely states, the subcontinent became the jewel in the crown of the British Empire. The independence movement led by world-shaker Mahatma Gandhi sounded the death knell for European colonialism around the globe, and the partition that accompanied the forced British withdrawal still drags on today.

The largest democracy on the planet is barely holding together a most complicated nation, and the traditional caste system, although formally outlawed, has ingrained itself in the social strata. The miniscule elite's vast wealth is contradicted by overwhelming poverty. Age-old religious tensions are fuelled by fundamentalism and irresponsible elements in the political arena.

Although immensely rewarding, travelling around India is hard-going. The nation grapples with widespread illiteracy, poor infrastructure and a distinct lack of services. Flying is the fastest way to traverse the subcontinent -

Hotel	Page	Hotel	Page
❶ New Delhi		**❻ Mumbai (Bombay)**	
Hyatt Regency Delhi	73	Grand Hyatt Mumbai	72
The Imperial	74	Grand Maratha ITC Sheraton	73
Maurya ITC Sheraton Hotel & Towers	77	JW Marriott Hotel Mumbai	75
Oberoi New Delhi	78	Oberoi Mumbai	79
Taj Mahal Hotel New Delhi	88	Taj Lands End Mumbai	85
Taj Palace Hotel New Delhi	88	Taj Mahal Palace & Tower Mumbai	87
❷ Agra		**❼ Goa**	
Amarvilas	71	Fort Aguada Beach Resort	72
❸ Jaipur		The Leela Goa	76
Rajvilas Jaipur	81	Park Hyatt Goa Resort & Spa	80
Rambagh Palace Hotel	83	**❽ Bangalore**	
❹ Jodhpur		Leela Palace Kempinski Bangalore	76
Umaid Bhawan Palace	90	Oberoi Bangalore	77
❺ Udaipur		Taj West End Bangalore	89
Shiv Niwas Palace	84	**❾ Kolkata (Calcutta)**	
Taj Lake Palace	86	Oberoi Grand Kolkata	78
Udaivilas	89	Taj Bengal	85

colonial structures. Spirituality courses through the nation's veins, not surprising as India gave rise to both Hinduism and Buddhism. Sprawling New Delhi and Mumbai (Bombay) are traditional gateways but both are worth escaping for the jewels that lie within. Agra hosts the exquisite white marble Taj Mahal, one of the planet's most striking destinations, and to the south are the amazing spires of Sri Meenakshi temple in Madurai. Goa's golden shores were first colonised by the Portuguese, then later by tousled hippies, and although it is slowly heading upmarket it retains much of its original appeal. Rajasthan, though, is most visitors' highlight - Jaipur, Jodphur, Jaiselmer, Udaipur and Puskar provide an enthralling variety of palaces, forts, havelis and bazaars.

and low-cost carriers are now setting the pace - but the rail network is highly developed and encompasses some memorable journeys and methods of transportation - the "Palace on Wheels" being the most immediate example. Going by car provides an acceptable alternative but take a driver, as the roads will test even the steeliest nerves.

With a population of more than a billion, India is second to China as the most populous country on earth. On the commercial front, outsourcing - notably of call centres and similar back-of-house operations - has had a dramatic effect on the economy, and the nation's contribution to IT and related fields has had world-wide significance. Yet business practices can still be frustrating, with corruption undermining what ought to be an industrial powerhouse. International hotel chains are heading back into the country, yet there is still a shortage of really smart properties. As a word of warning, star ratings are not always reliable and, relative to the rest of Asia, are typically inflated, so it pays to do your research before you check in. A few prominent chains are fittingly represented and India's better heritage hotels possess a magic that you just cannot get elsewhere.

Despite the challenges and head-scratching contradictions, the country is laden with wondrous sights to captivate the visitor. It is liberally dressed with incredible temples and forts and inspired

The Indian climate is as diverse as the country itself, from the searing heat of Chennai (Madras) to the cool hill stations of Shimla. The seasons are loosely divided into the hot (February to May), the wet (June to October) and the most temperate season, the cool (November to January). With a slice of humour, adventurous travellers who are willing to invest a little time and effort will find India to be one of the pinnacles of travel. And the gentle, unflappable Indians, with their alternative outlook on life have the innate ability to make you laugh, or at other times, cry.

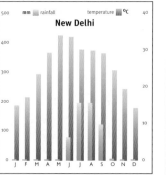

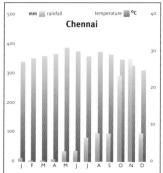

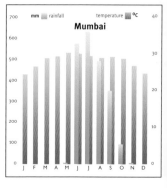

Amarvilas

Taj East Gate, Agra 282001, India
T: +91 562 223 1515   **F**: +91 562 223 1516
www.HotelClub.com/Hotels/Oberoi_Amarvilas_Hotel_Agra

Oberoi's Amarvilas is almost an outrageous concept - it has been built just 600 metres from the Taj Mahal. Naturally, there are views of the world's most wondrous monument to love from all of the 105 rooms and suites and most of its outlets (including The Spa, which for some reason employs Thai therapists to administer ancient Ayurvedic massage).

The argument for a luxury hotel in Agra is irresistible: the journey there and back from New Delhi can be hectic and the most famous shrine in the world surely merits more than just one look - it is worth savouring from dawn until dusk. Which you can do from your private terrace, your four-poster bed or the bar (preferably at night,

when the grounds of this three-storey, resort-style property come alive with lighted braziers set among the manicured lawns and sculpted fountains).

If you tire of the Taj (heresy!) there are chauffeur-driven cars to ferry you to nearby Fatehpur Sikri, the old Mughal capital, or Agra Fort. Or you can simply withdraw amid the opulent trappings of the hotel itself, all teak and antiques, marble and silk. There is alternative Asian and Mediterranean cuisine to soothe the palate after a surfeit of

fiery northern-Indian food in the Esphahan restaurant (brilliant raga background music), and you can luxuriate in the pool, which is heated in winter.

As always in India, there is the moral dilemma of whether one should be staying in such ostentatious surroundings while hemmed in on all sides by such dire human misery, but that is presumably a conundrum you will have solved long before you reach Amarvilas. Having concocted a rationale you are happy with, this is as good a place as any to put it to the test. One thing's for sure; the Taj Mahal's progenitor, Shah Jahan, would have approved.

Rates from: $$$$
Star rating: ★ ★ ★ ★ ★
Overall rating: 👍 👍 👍 👍 👍

Ambience:	9.62	Cleanliness:	9.85
Value:	8.08	Facilities:	8.65
Staff:	9.54	Restaurants:	8.46
Location:	9.46	Families:	8.36

Fort Aguada Beach Resort

Sinquerim, Bardez, Goa 403519, India
T: +91 832 564 5858 **F**: +91 832 564 5577
www.HotelClub.com/Hotels/Taj_Fort_Aguada_Beach_Resort_Hotel_Goa

Sfx is merrily laid-back) there are billiards and badminton, parasailing and golf (only five holes, mind you), squash courts, a swimming pool, an array of watersports and a spa.

So, in the light of all this, if you are still unsure whether the Aguada is for you, why not have a word with the hotel astrologer shortly after checking in?

Question: are you likely to enjoy your visit to the Aguada, which is built on the ramparts of a 16th century Portuguese fortress, part of an 35-hectare complex overlooking the Arabian Sea resting beneath the up-market mantle of the Taj group? Well, no matter whether you are staying in one of the regular rooms or suites or one of the cluster of cottages up on the hill, you can sally forth to indulge in this extremely enjoyable resort. To while away the hours between meals (Fish Tail's romantic gazebos and al fresco dining are all far too tempting, while

Rates from: $
Star rating: ★ ★ ★ ★ ★
Overall rating: ◊ ◊ ◊ ◊ ½

Ambience:	9.60	Cleanliness:	9.00
Value:	8.10	Facilities:	8.32
Staff:	8.80	Restaurants:	8.60
Location:	9.40	Families:	9.13

Grand Hyatt Mumbai

Off Western Express Highway, Santacruz (East), Mumbai 400055, India
T: +91 22 5676 1234 **F**: +91 22 5676 1235
www.HotelClub.com/Hotels/Grand_Hyatt_Mumbai

The Hyatt is way ahead of its time, as well as most of its competition. Dropped in what is best described as the up-and-probably-coming district of Santacruz just off the expressway connecting Mumbai's clogged south with its distant airport, the ultra-luxurious Grand is clearly currently out of keeping with its surroundings. Adorned with artwork curated by Rajeev Sethi, Wi-Fi'd and connected into the next century and serviced to Hyatt's usual impeccable standard, the 547 rooms and 147 serviced apartments are innovative and sophisticated beyond anything found in Mumbai. Four top-notch dining options - the tandoori grill at Soma is superb - a complete multi-level entertainment centre, fully pampering spa and adjacent Grand Hyatt Plaza shopping mall make this one of the lifestyle complexes of the city. Folly? Given the proximity of the fast expanding Bandra and Kurla business districts - more like inspirational foresight.

Rates from: $$
Star rating: ★ ★ ★ ★
Overall rating: ◊ ◊ ◊ ◊

Ambience:	8.75	Cleanliness:	9.00
Value:	8.00	Facilities:	8.67
Staff:	8.63	Restaurants:	9.00
Location:	8.00	Families:	7.57

Grand Maratha ITC Sheraton & Towers

Sahar Road, Mumbai 400099, India
T: +91 22 2830 30303 **F:** +91 22 2830 3131
www.HotelClub.com/Hotels/ITC_Hotel_Grand_Maratha_Sheraton_Towers

In booming Sahar, as part of the cluster of hotels that have sprung up not five minutes from the airport in northern Mumbai, the Sheraton's 386 well-appointed rooms make an obvious play for the business travel market, with all the requisite gadgetry including high-speed Internet and Wi-Fi access.

Indian food is a notable feature at the hotel, with North-West Frontier, South Indian and regional specialities to be had at the Peshawri, Dakshin and Dum Pukht restaurants, respectively. The centre-piece though is the 24-hour atrium Peshawa Pavillion with its pretty haveli style windows.

The predominantly low-rise Sheraton is built along classic colonial lines that blend nicely with its genteel surroundings. A preferred choice for conventioneers, press-conference organisers and pop singers (Bryan Adams and Enrique Iglesias have stayed), the Grand Maratha Sheraton would figure high on any traveller's list of stylish and practical accommodation in India's most frenetic city.

Rates from: $$$
Star rating: ★ ★ ★ ★ ★
Overall rating: 🏵🏵🏵🏵 ½

Ambience:	9.05	Cleanliness:	9.03
Value:	8.08	Facilities:	8.60
Staff:	9.05	Restaurants:	9.13
Location:	7.75	Families:	8.64

Hyatt Regency Delhi

Bhikaiji Cama Place, Ring Road, New Delhi 110066, India
T: +91 11 2679 1234 **F:** +91 11 2679 1122
www.HotelClub.com/Hotels/Hyatt_Regency_New_Delhi

Fashioned out of local sandstone in a style based on the Gupta period of Indian history, this ten-storey, 508-room Hirsch & Bedner-designed palatial pile rises iconically over one of New Delhi's chic-est districts, although it does look out over a patch of waste ground.

Built round a landscaped garden with pool (unheated), the rooms facing this are the ones to opt for. Although showing its age (now over 20) slightly, the design throughout - minimalist contemporary with ethnic touches - remains attractive.

La Piazza is generally reckoned to be the most authentic Italian eatery in town and Djinns "fun pub" has long been a starting point (and sometimes a finishing one, too) for the city's gilded youth and fast-rising execs out on the razz. The Polo Lounge, complete with cigar bar, is for the more mature set. Altogether, the place is a bit of an institution and provides a quick "in" to the lifestyle of the capital's elite.

Rates from: $$
Star rating: ★ ★ ★ ★ ★
Overall rating: 🏵🏵🏵🏵

Ambience:	8.72	Cleanliness:	8.77
Value:	7.77	Facilities:	8.42
Staff:	8.36	Restaurants:	8.54
Location:	7.95	Families:	8.10

The Imperial

Janpath, New Delhi 110001, India
T: +91 11 2334 1234 **F:** +91 11 2334 2255
www.HotelClub.com/Hotels/Imperial_Hotel_New_Delhi

The Imperial is a perfect blend of the nostalgic elegance of historic New Delhi and the modern requirements of today's hotels. Built in 1931 as part of Delhi's rejuvenation, the Art Deco hotel maintains much of its original aesthetics but constant restoration keeps it very functional (a new spa has just been added). Located centrally on Janpath, the Imperial is just a short stroll from the tourist heartland, Connaught Place. The area is somewhat chaotic but the hotel is intelligently set well back.

The Imperial is as stately and proud as its name would suggest, with plenty of historical throwbacks. Ceilings are high, paintings abound and little touches include brass fittings and historic photos. Spacious rooms split into four wings echo this colonial ambience, but have Internet ports to bring you up to date. One

striking aspect of the Imperial is the outstanding food. Restaurants are lavish and the food first-class - check out the wood-carved interior and menu of the Spice Route - it is no surprise the likes of Gandhi, Nehru and Kipling dined here. Suffice to say, the service is faultless throughout the hotel.

Indeed, while the dictates of political correctness spread their dreary tentacles around the rest of the world, the Imperial positively revels in its colonial past. Characterised as a "museum hotel" the Imperial was hosting art exhibitions as long ago as 1936, an event inaugurated by His Highness the Maharaja of Patiala, no less. It currently displays a priceless

collection of British art in India, including the works of great artists from the late 17th and early 18th centuries who produced lithographs, aquatints and mezzotints of the county's landscapes, architecture and daily life. One expo - Views of Lucknow - is even devoted to the mutiny (or revolt) of 1857. The Imperial is a marvellous character, dowager rather than grand dame, and a welcome sight amid the anonymous blandness that characterises far too many hotels nowadays.

Rates from: $$
Star rating: ★ ★ ★ ★ ★
Overall rating: ♕ ♕ ♕ ♕ ♕

Ambience:	9.47	Cleanliness:	9.02
Value:	8.29	Facilities:	8.42
Staff:	8.96	Restaurants:	9.07
Location:	8.80	Families:	8.85

JW Marriott Hotel Mumbai

Juhu Tara Road, Mumbai 400049, India
T: +91 22 5693 3000 **F:** +91 22 5693 3127
www.HotelClub.com/Hotels/JW_Marriott_Hotel_Mumbai

This hotel could be a set for one of those Bollywood extravaganzas they make just round the corner. Money-no-object luxury in an idyllic setting curved around the magnificent Juhu Beach combines with every conceivable facility for today's business travellers, who are increasingly using this upcoming northern district of Mumbai as a base in preference to the city's more traditional southern core.

Designed by Bill Bensley, the attractive five-storey building, housing 358 rooms and suites and with a dedicated executive floor, is surrounded (apart from the Arabian Sea on one side) by a tropical

garden with waterfalls and torch-lit pathways, lotus ponds and sandstone sculptures, and multiple swimming pools (including one for kids).

As might be expected, given its proximity to the studios, the Marriott is a haunt of the movie crowd and their hangers-on: they frequent the sprawling, conservatory-style coffee shop Lotus Café, the excellent Italian restaurant Mezzo Mezzo, the Indian Saffron and Southeast Asian Spices, and go for desserts to The Bombay Baking Company or a brandy and a cigar in the Club Lounge. But most of all they pack Enigma, one of the hottest nightspots in town.

From the moment you are picked up at the airport by the complimentary limo, presented with a bottle of ice-cold water and whisked on the 20-minute ride to the Marriott, you are treated as a VIP. If none of the eateries appeals, you have only to ask room service

and they will knock you up practically anything your heart desires or your stomach craves - and if you have to instruct them how to make it, they'll remember the recipe next time around.

The beds, as at most Marriotts, seem especially comfortable and the large work desks in the rooms are extremely user-friendly. There is a 350-square-metre spa and health club and you can hire a personal trainer. A dozen small but exclusive stores line the in-house shopping mall. A veritable self-contained resort - what more could you ask for while you work?

Rates from: $$
Star rating: ★ ★ ★ ★ ★
Overall rating: ♙ ♙ ♙ ♙ ½

Ambience:	9.03	Cleanliness:	9.03
Value:	8.03	Facilities:	8.69
Staff:	8.55	Restaurants:	8.90
Location:	8.35	Families:	8.68

The Leela Goa

Cavelossim, Mobor, Goa 403731, India
T:+91 832 287 1234 **F:** +91 832 287 1352
www.HotelClub.com/Hotels/Leela_Hotel_Goa

The Leela Palace encapsulates some of the very best that India has to offer - history, hedonism, gourmet dining, an intriguing menu of spa treatments, beautiful landscapes and luxury accommodation that is a blend of both ancient and modern.

Set on a peninsula wedged between the River Sal and the Indian Ocean, fringed by a 22-kilometre beach and set in 30 hectares of landscaped grounds, the Leela's centrepiece is an extensive artificial lagoon. Taking its architectural cue from Portuguese colonial days and the 13th-century Vijayanagara Palace, the resort's rooms, one- and two-bedroom suites are supremely comfortable, decorated with richly textured Indian fabrics and all come with spacious marbled bathrooms and balcony or private terrace. The more expensive accommodation includes a private pool.

The resort, of course, is not the popular Goa of hippiefied raves, but a much more rarefied locale. A 300-metre strip of beach is reserved for guests, who can also play a round on the 12-hole golf course.

Rates from: $$			
Star rating: ★ ★ ★ ★			
Overall rating: 🌿🌿🌿🌿🌿			
Ambience:	9.81	Cleanliness:	8.94
Value:	8.50	Facilities:	9.03
Staff:	8.88	Restaurants:	8.75
Location:	9.00	Families:	9.17

Leela Palace Kempinski Bangalore

23 Airport Road, Bangalore 560008, India
T: +91 80 2521 1234 **F:** +91 80 2521 2222
www.HotelClub.com/Hotels/Leela_Kempinski_Palace_Hotel_Bangalore

With palaces a rupee a dozen in the land of the rajahs, there are almost as many hotels modelled after them as there are restaurants with a Taj Mahal motif, but this one is a real stunner. The brainchild of C.P. Krishnan Nair, who named his deluxe group after his wife Leela, it is a pretty-in-pink Art Deco version of the palace at nearby Mysore. Its 256 rooms are set in 3.5 hectares of greenery, with waterfalls, rock gardens and a lagoon, at the end of a majestic palm-lined approach.

A renowned environmentalist, Nair has also ensured that the hotel's immediate surroundings are as green as its gardens. And Leela, apparently, grows the herbs that are used in the Citrus (a mix of

Mediterranean and Indian cuisine) and Zen restaurants - the latter offering a multi-ethnic smorgasbord of Japanese, Thai, Korean, Singaporean and Balinese dishes.

Russian president Vladimir Putin chose to stay here on a recent visit and you, too, can live like a potentate, with four-poster bed and private balcony. Adjacent to a golf course, a shopping mall and 20 minutes from Whitefields IT Park, it's no surprise the Leela is popular.

Rates from: $$$			
Star rating: ★ ★ ★ ★ ★			
Overall rating: 🌿🌿🌿🌿🌿			
Ambience:	9.45	Cleanliness:	9.25
Value:	8.43	Facilities:	8.95
Staff:	8.95	Restaurants:	9.05
Location:	9.00	Families:	8.96

Maurya ITC Sheraton Hotel & Towers

Diplomatic Enclave, New Delhi 110021, India
T: +91 11 2611 2233 **F**: +91 11 2611 3333
www.HotelClub.com/Hotels/ITC_Maurya_Sheraton_Hotel_Towers

India's five-stars can be hit and miss, but this one is certainly one of New Delhi's best and holds its own internationally. The location, halfway between the airport and city centre in the green diplomatic district, definitely helps to mellow the ambience of this rugged choking city. Opened in 1977 but well maintained, this spacious hotel is bright and open, with a large lobby. Of the 515 rooms, the new ITC One Wing is a class apart; pitched as "seven-star" by the hotel, it is aimed at the very top-end traveller with 76 private residence-style rooms including personal butler and exclusive lounge with a range of state-of-the-art facilities. It is not to be confused with the separately housed 107-room Tower Club or the 55 Executive Club rooms in the main hotel. Of the very good facilities, the North Indian restaurant Bukhara is perhaps the best-known, with many guests raving about its sensational menu and cosy setting.

Rates from: $$$
Star rating: ★ ★ ★ ★ ★
Overall rating: ◔◔◔◔ ½

Ambience:	9.00	Cleanliness:	9.02
Value:	8.16	Facilities:	8.44
Staff:	9.00	Restaurants:	9.11
Location:	8.22	Families:	8.56

Oberoi Bangalore

39 Mahatma Gandhi Road, Bangalore 560001, India
T: +91 80 2558 5858 **F**: +91 80 2558 5960
www.HotelClub.com/Hotels/Oberoi_Hotel_Bangalore

This is the proverbial oasis of tranquillity in an urban nightmare - once you get off Mahatma Gandhi Road (named for the karmic qualities you need to endure its screaming traffic jams) and onto the balcony of your room overlooking the lush pool and gardens in the "backyard" (beware kleptomaniac monkeys).

Though central in terms of shops and offices and only a short hop from the airport (accessed via free limo service), it can be a bit of a slog out to Electronics City in the rush-hour. Add a superb Banyan Tree-managed spa and bags of up-to-the-minute business services, as you would expect in the capital of India's Silicon Valley. And cable TV comes in English, French, German, Italian and Japanese.

The newish deluxe rooms boast TV in the bathroom and steam cubicles, DVD players, walk-in closets and 24-hour butler service. However, the place can be a bit dead at night. The food in the Szechwan Court restaurant may be authentic, but the spelling isn't.

Rates from: $$$
Star rating: ★ ★ ★ ★ ★
Overall rating: ◔◔◔◔ ½

Ambience:	8.86	Cleanliness:	8.76
Value:	8.14	Facilities:	8.35
Staff:	8.90	Restaurants:	8.83
Location:	8.52	Families:	8.74

Oberoi Grand Kolkata

15 Jawaharlal Nehru Road, Kolkata 700013, India
T: +91 33 2249 2323 **F:** +91 33 2249 1217
www.HotelClub.com/Hotels/Oberoi_Grand_Calcutta_Hotel_Kolkata

health club and spa. The Thai, Indian and international restaurants are certainly among the best in town, offering superb decor as well as tantalising flavours, with a wheelbarrow load of vegetarian options on each menu. Set in central Chowringhee district, the Oberoi Grand is well located for business or visiting the city's places of interest.

This classic property, built in the 1870s, is generally regarded as the best in Kolkata and, therefore by definition, eastern India. The Oberoi Grand is indeed grand in the flesh. The noble architecture and design draws on its Victorian past. The hotel's dignified marble lobby with green palms and leather sofas leads on to a healthy range of first-class facilities. In the 213 rooms, DVD are standard, as are voicemail and Internet. Outside, the 24-hour business centre and conference rooms are excellent. Leisure facilities include a fine courtyard pool and the local rarity of a genuinely inviting Banyan Tree-run

Rates from: $$
Star rating: ★ ★ ★ ★ ★
Overall rating: ♎ ♎ ♎ ♎ ½

Ambience:	8.92	Cleanliness:	8.42
Value:	8.00	Facilities:	8.32
Staff:	9.00	Restaurants:	8.67
Location:	8.67	Families:	8.67

Oberoi New Delhi

Dr. Zakir Hussain Marg, New Delhi 110003, India
T: +91 11 2436 3030 **F:** +91 11 2430 4082
www.HotelClub.com/Hotels/Oberoi_Hotel_New_Delhi

has fabulous city views. The Kandahar does top-notch Indian nosh and you can cool off after a fiery feast at Baan Thai with a plunge in the adjoining pool.

There have been complaints about the high telephone tariffs, but these are not likely to worry the likes of guests such as Mick Jagger or Nelson Mandela.

Opened 40 years ago as New Delhi's first international-standard luxury hotel, the Oberoi is still setting the city's benchmark, especially where service is concerned. Conveniently located yet exuding a tranquil, away-from-it-all feel, it overlooks the Delhi Golf Course on one side and the Humayan Tombs on the other.

Its 287 undemonstrative rooms (chintzy but modern - very Indian) all boast butler service and have interesting (and valuable) artwork on the walls. The higher you stay, obviously, the better the views.

The trendy new 360° complete with wine cellar is an exciting combo of world-class fare, whilst the slightly tired rooftop Taipan restaurant (Cantonese and Sichuan)

Rates from: $$$
Star rating: ★ ★ ★ ★ ★
Overall rating: ♎ ♎ ♎ ♎ ½

Ambience:	9.05	Cleanliness:	9.07
Value:	8.41	Facilities:	8.58
Staff:	9.02	Restaurants:	8.71
Location:	8.89	Families:	8.67

Oberoi Mumbai

Nariman Point, Mumbai 400021, India
T: +91 22 5632 5757 **F:** +91 22 5632 4142
www.HotelClub.com/Hotels/Oberoi_Hotel_Mumbai

The diamond in the Oberoi Mumbai's crown - and this is arguably the finest of this very fine chain of hotels - is the Kohinoor Suite. Whether you are a platinum-selling pop star or Joe Soap, the president of the USA or simply the president of your own one-man company, prior to your arrival the butler (repeat guests request their favourite by name) will be popping the champagne cork, making sure the piano is properly tuned, flicking a feather duster over the antiques, giving the gold-plated bathroom taps a final polish and making sure there is nothing obscuring the view of the Arabian Sea. Other luminaries who have stayed here include Richard Gere, Bill Gates and Rupert Murdoch, and the chances are that wherever they unpacked their bags at the Oberoi, they would have been more than moderately comfortable.

Anyone who knows the hotel of old but who has not visited lately should know that the adjacent block is now being run by Hilton, leaving the other 333 rooms safely in the Oberoi bosom. There is a great deal to enjoy here, specifically the spa, which is run by Banyan Tree. A sort of global village of pampering, Thai therapists provide a phalanx of holistic, non-clinical treatments and massages that incorporate Indian Ayurvedic principles, aromatherapy and western techniques. On the food front, TIFFIN is the latest arrival, the new all-day lobby restaurant that marries Pacific Rim and Indian cuisine in a warm and friendly ambience, while Kandahar

and Rotisserie continue as firm local favourites.

Pricey suites and prime eats aside, many loyal fans speak warmly of the Oberoi's staff. The housemaid who dropped off a phrasebook for the guest who mentioned wanting to learn Hindi, or her colleague who filled in as nurse for another client's elderly mother. This is natural hospitality, something you can't "train up" in a million years.

Rates from: $$
Star rating: ★ ★ ★ ★ ★
Overall rating: ♻ ♻ ♻ ♻

Ambience:	8.58	Cleanliness:	8.82
Value:	7.61	Facilities:	8.33
Staff:	8.66	Restaurants:	8.49
Location:	8.74	Families:	7.95

Park Hyatt Goa Resort and Spa

Arossim Beach, Cansaulim, South Goa 403712, India
T: +91 832 272 1234 **F:** +91 832 272 1235
www.HotelClub.com/Hotels/Hotel_Park_Hyatt_Goa

Would the hippies who flocked to Goa's beaches in the 1960s and so scandalised Indian society look askance at the deluxe, five-star Park Hyatt, a mini village on Arossim Beach? It is not overly stretching the imagination to state that a few decades on, bathed and balding, the former flower children could well be staying in one of the resort's 250 rooms (many with their own miniature and very private garden) which are housed in Indo-Portuguese pousadas set amidst glimmering waterways and lagoons and 18 hectares of lush landscaping.

There are no magic mushroom omelettes on the menu nowadays of course, though at the heart of the resort the chefs at a plaza full of restaurants will be delighted to whip you up authentic trattoria-style specialities, the freshest

seafood, tandoori and Goan dishes, or a variety of vegetarian dosas. An excellent selection of Spanish and Portuguese wines is backed up by a full range of premium whiskies, port and cigars. And nobody is sitting cross-legged on the beach any more hoping for a one-way ticket to Nirvana. It is far more likely these former offspring of the 60s have tucked their return business-class tickets securely in the room safe, and booked a couple of appointments at the Sereno Spa.

Here, indoor and outdoor pavilions are set around an inner courtyard and a holistic approach to health treatments is a central focus for both ancient and new-age therapies, which are offered by trained specialists and guided by an Ayurvedic doctor. One thing that has definitely not changed is the miles of blissfully white sandy beach, and the general allure of Goa as a centre of hedonism. But four decades on from the era whose mantra was "turn on, tune in and drop out", the Park Hyatt is somewhere exceptionally comfortable to do something approaching all three. Far out man.

Rates from: $$
Star rating: ★ ★ ★ ★ ★
Overall rating: ♦♦♦♦ ½

Ambience:	9.20	Cleanliness:	9.80
Value:	8.00	Facilities:	8.77
Staff:	9.20	Restaurants:	8.40
Location:	8.00	Families:	9.08

Rajvilas Jaipur

Goner Road, Jaipur 303012, India
T: +91 141 268 0101 **F:** +91 141 268 0202
www.HotelClub.com/Hotels/Oberoi_Rajvilas_Resort_Jaipur

At some stage or another just about everyone has fantasised about living in a palace, waited on hand and foot in opulent surrounds, the monarch of all they survey. Rajvilas turns the fantasy into reality, and even if the "king (and/or queen) for a day" has to check out and pay the bill sooner or later, the experience is unforgettable.

Rajasthan is India at its most exotic and colourful best, a one-

time cluster of principalities infused with a proud martial history and bedecked with ancient palaces. Rajvilas is just one such former stately home, converted into a conglomeration of four very different sorts of accommodation set in 12 hectares of beautifully manicured gardens. For the ultimate regal vision, you need to stay at one of the trio of villas, each with an outdoor dining

pavilion and a private swimming pool that is heated in winter.

Inside, four-poster beds draped with mosquito nets, metre-thick walls and latticed windows imbue a heartening feeling of security. The 1,143 luxury tents are rather more Rajasthan. Forget camping - these are fitted with teak floors, air-conditioning and beautifully appointed interiors, while the bathroom is centred around the magnificent colonial-style free-standing cast-iron tub. A combination of these two accommodations is provided by the single tented villa, which has a four-seater dining table and its own garden. However, the main body of Rajvilas' accommodation comes in the 54 Deluxe Rooms, clumped in groups of four or six around a central courtyard. There is a king-size bed, dressing room and walk-in closet, and the ensuite marble bathroom has a sunken tub as well as a separate shower overlooking a private walled garden. And steeped in history though Rajvilas may be, wherever you are staying in the hotel there is satellite TV, CD and laser disc players and connections for the Internet.

While Rajasthan waits outside Rajvilas' gates - be it rides in a horse-drawn buggy, watching polo matches or absorbing the palaces, forts and bazaars of the nearby Pink City of Jaipur - it is worth spending some time in the hotel simply to revel in the atmosphere. You can comfortably while away the hours in the Rajwada Library and Bar, where there are scores of books lined up on teak shelves, a white Italian marble fireplace and board games like chess and backgammon. Similarly, it would be a pity to rush meals in the Surya Mahal dining room, a study in Rajasthani decor with sculpted sandstone pillars, scalloped arches and handcrafted brass doors. Local culinary delights are served in silver thalis, but the

kitchen can also whip up light fusion cuisine with elements from Asia and Europe. You can also eat al fresco in the adjoining courtyard, with entertainment laid on by traditional folk dancers.

For active types, the Rajvilas has two floodlit tennis courts and an immaculate croquet lawn, as well as an outdoor swimming pool and jacuzzi. Just by the pool, the hotel's Banyan Tree-run spa is contained in a restored haveli whose walls are adorned with hand-painted frescoes and whose therapists are skilled in a wide range of holistic treatments. One of the most relaxing activities is to

take part in a yoga session in the precincts of a nearby centuries-old Shiva temple. This ancient philosophical exercise was devised in India, and it perfectly encapsulates the gracious recreation that is found everywhere at Rajvilas.

Rates from: $$$$		
Star rating: ★ ★ ★ ★ ★		
Overall rating: ◊ ◊ ◊ ◊ ½		
Ambience:	9.48	Cleanliness: 9.52
Value:	7.86	Facilities: 8.83
Staff:	9.34	Restaurants: 8.57
Location:	8.17	Families: 8.86

Rambagh Palace Jaipur

Bhawani Singh Road, Jaipur 302005, India
T: +91 141 221 1919 **F**: +91 141 238 5098
www.HotelClub.com/Hotels/Taj_Rambagh_Palace_Hotel_Jaipur

The Rambagh Palace is an Indian heritage hotel in the grandest and most palatial form. This distinctive property, which graces the Rajasthan capital of Jaipur and revels in the city's beautiful history and architecture, is impressive in both scale and presentation. Lying a few kilometres from the walled Pink City, it is built from white marble and sits in 20 hectares of manicured gardens abloom with ashoka, bougainvillea and lantana trees and preening peacocks.

The Rambagh started out as a subtle four-room pavilion built for Maharani Chandrawatji's lady-in-waiting back in 1835. It was expanded into a hunting lodge in 1887 and was officially named as a

palace in 1925 when Maharaja Sawai Man Singh II decided to move in. It became an elite hotel in 1957 when the prestigious Taj Group started to manage it in 1972. The graceful Rajasthan architecture was built in royal proportions and to lofty standards. The sweeping tiled floors, ornate columns and arches and regal domes took skill and craft to assemble.

Superior Rooms are comfy and themed, but quite spartan as far as luxury hotels go - but the suites are anything but standard. The four which formerly housed the royal family: the Prince's Suite, Maharani Suite and brace of Maharaja Suites are stunning in their grandeur and grace. Picture opulent Victorian wood-panelled rooms or elegant white marble chambers complete with a trickling fountain. The remaining Historical Suites and Luxury Rooms lie somewhere between these suites and the Superior Rooms, each is uniquely decorated and filled with character.

Service here is very idiosyncratic - most staff do a magnificent job but sometimes it is accompanied by an

outstretched hand. The facilities though can draw few complaints.

The grandeur of the Suvarna Mahal dining hall makes a wonderfully majestic dinner setting, the intricate decor of the Rajput Room 24-hour restaurant is equally pleasing to the eye and the palate and the Polo Bar is one of the most upmarket places to relax in Jaipur. Tennis, squash and an indoor pool (outdoor pool coming soon), with leaded windows, panelled walls and delicate carvings, are some of the recreational pursuits on offer. And in true Rajasthan tradition, horse riding can be arranged; or, having visited Jantar Mantar, the remarkable stone observatory in Jaipur, map your own destiny with the in-house astrologer.

Rates from: $$
Star rating: ★★★★★
Overall rating: ♙♙♙♙♙

Ambience:	9.92	Cleanliness:	9.38
Value:	8.15	Facilities:	9.19
Staff:	9.54	Restaurants:	8.75
Location:	8.38	Families:	8.57

Shiv Niwas Palace

The City Palace, Udaipur, 313001, India
T: +91 294 252 8016 **F:** +91 294 252 8006
www.HotelClub.com/Hotels/Shiv_Niwas_Palace_Udaipur

Palatial is a much-abused word in hotel parlance, but in Udaipur, most of the hotels actually are, or were, palaces. Ever since the late Maharana Bhagwat Singh decided to turn his amazing home into a hostelry, royalty has lived, if not quite cheek-by-jowl, then fairly close to paying guests of the cunningly named HRH - Historic Resort Hotels, now headed by his white-bearded but still polo-playing son Arvind, the 76th ruler of Mewar.

Shiv Niwas is part of a cluster of palaces on the shore and was once a royal guest-house (in every sense of the word - Queen Elizabeth II once stayed here, as, incidentally, did Roger Moore when playing James Bond in *Octopussy*). A crescent-shaped edifice built around a 19th-century marbled swimming pool, it consists of 17 suites and 19 Deluxe Rooms. The Terrace Suites, which have balconies overlooking the lake, are recommended (one of the Imperial Suites actually has a fountain in the bedroom, by the way).

Written off by some critics as resembling a wealthy aristocratic aunt's overstuffed sitting room, the accommodation is as quirky as the food and the service - romantics will love it, stuffed tigers, stuffy curries, friendly but frustrating old retainers and all. There is an air of authenticity about the place that more than makes up for any inadequacies in terms of up-to-the-minute facilities and amenities.

And what could be more evocative of a bygone regal lifestyle than to sit in the courtyard at dusk and listen to a bagpiper band salute the sunset? Or to enjoy a snifter in the swish Paneera Bar before repairing to the open-air restaurant where live sitar players will serenade you during dinner?

The Shiv Niwas didn't win a Heritage Award for nothing - and it is helping to keep a 1,400-year-old dynasty in the style to which it has always been accustomed.

Rates from: $$
Star rating: ★ ★ ★ ★
Overall rating: Editor's Pick

Ambience:	n/a	Cleanliness:	n/a
Value:	n/a	Facilities:	n/a
Staff:	n/a	Restaurants:	n/a
Location:	n/a	Families:	n/a

Taj Bengal

34 B Belvedere Road, Alipore, Kolkata 700027, India
T: +91 33 2223 3939 **F:** +91 33 2223 1766
www.HotelClub.com/Hotels/Taj_Bengal_Calcutta_Hotel_Kolkata

One of the best hotels in eastern India, the Taj Bengal sits comfortably in green surroundings a little south of the Maidan, and just a few kilometres from Kolkata's CBD. Though not particularly spectacular, the Taj remains a true respite in a mad city. The exterior is modest and angular, but inside is a trim and tidy luxury hotel with a striking 1,100-square-metre atrium lobby full of tall palms, marble floors and elegant chandeliers.

Business travellers frequent the hotel, attracted by the international-class facilities and services. The broad outdoor pool is perhaps the centrepiece, with a popular poolside barbecue sizzling away from November to March. The other restaurants offer quality, variety and in the case of the Hub, 24-hour flexibility. Incognito is one of the city's top discos. Rooms are fair with Internet access and dataports but the service levels are very high, as one would expect from the Taj Group.

Rates from: $
Star rating: ★ ★ ★ ★ ★
Overall rating: 🐾 🐾 🐾 🐾

Ambience:	9.00	Cleanliness:	8.80
Value:	7.87	Facilities:	8.37
Staff:	8.07	Restaurants:	9.00
Location:	8.00	Families:	8.31

Taj Lands End Mumbai

Bandstand, Bandra (West), Mumbai 400050, India
T: +91 22 5668 1234 **F:** +91 22 5699 4488
www.HotelClub.com/Hotels/Taj_Lands_End_Hotel_Mumbai

Incredibly, the original Taj Mahal hotel was built in what was then Bombay over 100 years ago, but the Tata Group's iconic brand is still leading the pack. This somewhat newer groundbreaker in the fashionable but far-flung suburb of Bandra began life as a Regent International property, but was taken over in 1999 and tweaked into yet another Taj success story.

Next to Mumbai's historic Portuguese fort and overlooking the Arabian Sea, it is a business hotel with a resort feel. Almost all of its 368 superbly equipped rooms have ocean views, and if you are soaking in the infinity pool, you could believe you were actually in the sea.

There are ladies-only, no-smoking and Taj Club floors, and all guests get a seated check-in and butler to pack and unpack. Indian and Chinese cuisine are on offer at the highly rated (and spiced!) Masala Bay and Ming Yang restaurants respectively, while the upmarket Churchill's Bar suggests nostalgic affection for rather than resentment of British colonialism.

Rates from: $$
Star rating: ★ ★ ★ ★ ★
Overall rating: 🐾 🐾 🐾 🐾

Ambience:	8.81	Cleanliness:	8.74
Value:	7.81	Facilities:	8.21
Staff:	8.28	Restaurants:	8.49
Location:	8.51	Families:	8.09

Taj Lake Palace

Udaipur 313001, India
T: +91 294 252 8800 **F:** +91 294 252 8700
www.HotelClub.com/Hotels/Taj_Lake_Palace_Hotel_Udaipur

The Taj Group's Lake Palace is one of the world's most celebrated concept hotels. The 17th-century pleasure retreat was originally built for royalty and is spectacularly set in the middle of Lake Pichola. Various Maharajas would impress their ladies here, and the old magic still works. The Lake Palace has a reputation that precedes it, and when drifting towards it on the hotel shuttle boat it is hard not to picture a majestic feast of Rajasthani indulgence.

To state that staying here is a once-in-a-lifetime experience is hardly an exaggeration. So it is difficult to sidestep the temptation to book the best sort of accommodation that your budget will allow. All 83 rooms and suites embrace opulent silks, richly coloured murals and ornately carved wood furniture that envelope guests in royal mystique. Something facing the lake is well nigh essential, and if you want to push the boat out a bit further, as it were, one of the suites - with clawfoot bathtub, 42-inch plasma TV, perhaps even a swing (which is certainly not intended as a child's plaything) - is the most amazing place to bed down in what is a really amazing hotel.

Despite the droughts that can shrink the lake, the location plus cultural depth makes this one of the most fascinating hotel experiences on the subcontinent. A romantic breakfast or dinner for two on the Pontoon is a highlight of most couples' stay - though Neel Kamal, facing the hotel's lily pond, excites many compliments on a regular basis. In between meals and general romping around the resort, a spa and swimming pool provide plenty of scope for diversion. The palace barge is perfect for parties - whether of a business or social nature. Oh, and make sure you hire the vintage Cadillac or Buick for at least one jaunt during your stay.

Rates from: $$$
Star rating: ★ ★ ★ ★ ★
Overall rating: ♌ ♌ ♌ ♌ ½

Ambience:	9.57	Cleanliness:	8.92
Value:	8.43	Facilities:	8.45
Staff:	8.76	Restaurants:	8.57
Location:	9.62	Families:	8.44

Taj Mahal Palace and Tower Mumbai

Apollo Bunder, Mumbai 400001, India
T: +91 22 5665 3366 **F:** +91 22 5665 0300
www.HotelClub.com/Hotels/Taj_Mahal_Hotel_Mumbai

Opened in 1903, the Taj Mahal Palace Mumbai is the grandest hotel in the city. The stunning Edwardian architecture is a distinctive landmark - the classic Mumbai postcard portrays the colonial Gateway of India archway aside this majestic hotel. It was built by local tycoon J.N. Tata who, so the story goes, indignant at being turned away from a top hotel on racist grounds, decided to build his own. True or not, the end result is a superb example of the architecture of the day, not to mention a fitting raspberry at the British Raj.

The Taj is gracious and distinguished inside and out. Some areas such as the lobby are sleek, businesslike and modern, offering contemporary luxury and comfort. Other areas bask in the glory of the Taj's portentous past - the beautifully ornate iron staircase is of particular note. Palatial yet tasteful banquet rooms could potentially mingle with the royal residences of Europe. The Harbour Bar is Mumbai's oldest licensed bar and offers a superior venue for a tipple, albeit with a stiff upper lip. Souk, the award winning Eastern Mediterranean rooftop restaurant, serves a mix of Lebanese, Greek and Moroccan with some fine views. With the exception of the more casual Shamiana, all the restaurants are elegant and highly refined. The Zodiac Grill with its domed astrological ceiling, full grand piano and white-gloved butler service is one of the city's more exclusive (and pricey) establishments.

The business and leisure facilities are world-class, but if one had to be picky the rooms are a tad below par in places (although many have been recently upgraded). The comfy Heritage rooms are all different with varying touches in decor and furniture, but feeling at times old rather than historical. The 1973 addition of the Tower Wing slightly blemished the exterior grace of the hotel, but the rooms within are more modern and many enjoy the same superb sea views as the original Heritage Wing.

There is no doubt that the illustrious Taj is one of the most characteristic hotels in India and goes a long way toward meeting its founder's objective of conceiving Bombay's (as it was then), if not Asia's, finest hotel.

Rates from: **$$$**
Star rating: ★ ★ ★ ★ ★
Overall rating: 🌐🌐🌐🌐 ½

Ambience:	8.98	Cleanliness:	8.65
Value:	7.92	Facilities:	8.34
Staff:	8.63	Restaurants:	8.60
Location:	8.82	Families:	8.32

Taj Mahal Hotel New Delhi

1 Mansingh Road, New Delhi 110011, India
T: +91 11 2302 6162 **F:** +91 11 2302 6070
www.HotelClub.com/Hotels/Taj_Mahal_Hotel

The well-established Taj Mahal is one of Delhi's best hotels. It is primarily aimed at business travellers, focusing on comfortable practicality. Hugely welcome is the fully equipped 24-hour business centre. All the predictable yet very presentable 300 or so rooms have dataports for modems and PCs, and in-room faxes. With roaming wireless connectivity and a cyber butler, you can be online just about anywhere in the hotel. The higher floor Taj Club offers additional perks including transfers, private check-in and further business facilities including valet service and meeting rooms. Celebrated restaurants are centred mainly on Indian and Chinese themes, but the 24-hour international outlet, Machan, is especially useful for the jet-lagged guest. The Taj also has the advantage of a central location near New Delhi's most famous landmark, India Gate, so is well positioned for tourists as well. For those taking time out, the hotel offers a decent fitness centre and a very generous outdoor pool.

Rates from: $$
Star rating: ★ ★ ★ ★ ★
Overall rating: 👍 👍 👍 👍 👍

Ambience:	9.83	Cleanliness:	9.50
Value:	9.00	Facilities:	8.94
Staff:	9.83	Restaurants:	8.83
Location:	9.17	Families:	8.50

Taj Palace Hotel New Delhi

2 Sardar Patel Marg, Diplomatic Enclave, New Delhi 110021, India
T: +91 11 2166 0202 **F:** +91 11 2611 0808
www.HotelClub.com/Hotels/Taj_Palace_Hotel_New_Delhi

An elder statesman of a hotel, aptly located in the city's diplomatic enclave and frequent host to visiting heads of state and multinational business bosses. Staid but impeccable, from its parquet-floored rooms to its Wi-Fi Internet connectivity, from its complimentary limo and free bottle of wine for Taj Club guests to its Moghul-liveried valets.

An uninspiring block of a building containing some 462 rooms and suites, it looks better from the inside looking out than vice versa, the view being a lovely garden with a large lawn and an inviting pool. There is a lot of greenery (2.5 hectares to be exact) and even a nine-hole putting green. Deluxe Suites have their own terraced gardens.

Service and food are of a consistently high standard - be it Mediterranean at Kafe Fontana, northern Indian at Masala Art or European Grand Tour at Orient Express. The Chinese cuisine at Teahouse Of August Moon, however, is about as confidence-inspiring as the fact that is has been named after a Marlon Brando movie set in Japan. Just My Kind Of Place nightclub is very much moneyed Delhi's kind of place.

Rates from: $$
Star rating: ★ ★ ★ ★
Overall rating: 👍 👍 👍 👍 ½

Ambience:	9.24	Cleanliness:	9.21
Value:	8.30	Facilities:	8.85
Staff:	8.88	Restaurants:	8.91
Location:	8.52	Families:	8.16

Taj West End Bangalore

25 Race Course Road, Bangalore 560001, India
T: +91 80 5660 5660   **F:** +91 80 5660 5700
www.HotelClub.com/Hotels/Taj_West_End_Hotel_Bangalore

Built in 1818, this is Bangalore before it became image-stamped as India's technological hot-spot, and may not therefore appeal to today's "just-do-it" business-travel mentality. The very address, Race Course Road, reeks of the Raj, of which this former Victorian boarding house, with its sloping, red-tiled roofs and centuries-old banyan trees, was once a prime specimen.

But it has been beautifully restored, with some stylishly tasteful touches, and, being Bangalore, everything Internet-related works like a digital dream. And it has laptops and mobiles for hire. The hip nomenclature of its restaurants is an indication of the sensitivities at work here - Blue Ginger for the Vietnamese eatery, Mynt for the coffee-shop.

The real glory of the place, however, is its wooded gardens (eight hectares of them), full of shady glades and winding pathways. Al fresco at Blue Bar is a must. The Taj Club Premium Rooms open onto private verandahs and the Heritage Wing features four-poster beds and sepia lithographs. Ideal for tuning out, after a frantic day in the silicon city.

Rates from: $$$
Star rating: ★ ★ ★ ★ ★
Overall rating: 🐾 🐾 🐾 🐾 🐾

Ambience:	9.30	Cleanliness:	9.41
Value:	8.90	Facilities:	8.95
Staff:	9.20	Restaurants:	9.10
Location:	9.20	Families:	8.33

Udaivilas

Haridasji Ki Majri, Udaipur 313001, India
T: +91 294 243 3300   **F:** +91 294 243 3200
www.HotelClub.com/Hotels/Udai_Villas_Udaipur

Step into that chauffeur-driven customised Ambassador limousine for the ride from the airport to the jetty. Putter across Lake Pichola in Udaivilas private launch. And then do the very best you can not to gape. The architecture of this awesome palace represents the rich heritage of the Rajasthan region, recreating a royal palace built in the grand Mewari style using traditional materials and construction techniques. From many of the rooms and public areas your gaze leads naturally out to panoramic views of the Aravelli mountains, the City Palace, two 17th-century island palaces and the Jag Mandir temple. Nothing has been spared to make the rooms supremely comfortable, which are decorated with exclusively designed, hand-crafted furniture, hand-knotted carpets and local works of art. There is a Banyan Tree spa, speciality restaurants (Indian of course) and conference facilities, though it is hard to imagine of any work getting done here. Nightly folk dances set the seal on a property that is nothing short of magnificent.

Rates from: $$$$
Star rating: ★ ★ ★ ★ ★
Overall rating: 🐾 🐾 🐾 🐾 ½

Ambience:	9.56	Cleanliness:	9.22
Value:	7.56	Facilities:	9.05
Staff:	9.33	Restaurants:	8.78
Location:	9.22	Families:	8.71

Umaid Bhawan Palace

Jodhpur 342006, India
T: +91 291 251 0101   **F:** +91 291 251 0100
www.HotelClub.com/Hotels/Umaid_Bhawan_Hotel

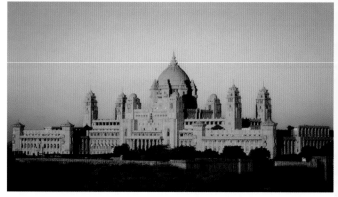

Little can the Maharaja of Jodhpur have known some 80 years ago when, in a bid to provide work for his famine-stricken subjects, he commissioned British architect H.V. Lanchester to build a 347-room palace opposite the Mehrangarh Fort, that it would one day play host to well-heeled travellers as one of India's major "palace-hotel" attractions.

It took 3,000 labourers 15 years to complete work on Lanchester's design - a humongous pink sandstone edifice centred around a cathedral-sized double dome and conceived as an aesthetic marriage between the best of Hindu architectural tradition and then-contemporary Western style.

The Maharaja's successor, polo-playing, Eton- and Oxford-educated Gaj Singh II, still lives there, a proud descendant of 13th-century Rajput warrior kings. But in 1972, following the abolition of royal privileges, he was forced to open about two-thirds of it to the public as a "heritage hotel". As such, it has housed a roll-call of the rich and famous, as well as many an everyday traveller happy to splash out to experience an Indian equivalent of Buckingham Palace or the White House.

The hotel is something of a hit-or-miss affair where the 70 rooms are concerned, given that none of them was actually designed as a hotel room (they originally housed the royal administrative staff).

Potential guests are advised to shop around and ask to see a few before deciding.

Some are veritable mini-suites, with private balconies and incredible views, others are less spectacular. Some of the suites boast sumptuous Art Deco furnishings and fittings worthy of a museum display. None is state-of-the-art by today's luxury-hotel standards: bathroom fixtures are like big-game-hunting guests of the Maharaja in the middle of the last century would have expected to find them, for example.

The main formal restaurant, Risala, used to be the family dining-room, but try the al fresco Pillars overlooking the gardens at the back of the palace, on the lawns of which peacocks strut their stuff. A truly regal touch.

Rates from: $$$
Star rating: ★ ★ ★ ★ ★
Overall rating: ✿ ✿ ✿ ✿

Ambience:	10.00	Cleanliness:	8.25
Value:	8.13	Facilities:	8.23
Staff:	7.50	Restaurants:	8.63
Location:	7.38	Families:	8.00

INDONESIA

The ebb and flow of troubles that have beset the Indonesian archipelago for much of the last decade reached their apogee when the earthquake struck Sumatra in 2004. In the wake of the financial crash of the late 1990s, governmental shenanigans and terrorist bombings in Bali and Jakarta, a natural disaster and horrific loss of life was the last thing the country needed.

Intermittent international advisories still warn that foreigners could be targeted by Indonesian terrorists, and the decision to visit remains very much a personal choice. That this is a source of regret cannot be overstated, as the country's 13,000-plus islands, strung between the Indian and Pacific oceans, make up one of the most fascinating and beautiful parts of Southeast Asia.

More than 1,000 years ago traders from as far away as China were sailing to the spice islands of Indonesia, and the same commodity drew Europeans as early as the 16th century. Dutch colonialists subsequently gained a strong foothold in the country, and - after the Japanese occupation during World War II - Indonesia finally achieved independence in 1949 after several years of armed struggle. The decades that followed were marked by a gradual increase in prosperity, interspersed with some domestic upheavals. Tourism only started to take off in the late 1960s, with Bali leading the way, as it has done ever since.

First port of call for many visitors is the capital, Jakarta, a maelstrom of a metropolis which acts as a magnet for Indonesians from all over the country who have come to look for work. Bandung, a lovely Art Deco city that the Dutch planned as an alternative capital, sits in the hills to the east, while further across Java are stunning man-made wonders like the 1,100-year old Buddhist temple of Borobudur and natural marvels like the dormant volcanic Mount Bromo. The Hindu enclave of Bali, most aptly described as "the morning of the world", remains the most picturesque and intriguing of all the Indonesian islands, while further east Lombok and Flores are less developed but still hold many attractions for more adventurous holidaymakers. Komodo is famed for its giant lizards, cunningly marketed as dragons, while divers tend to flock to Sulawesi, and in particular to Manado, where Bunaken Island is ranked as one of the top underwater sites in the world. More difficult to get to, the Bandas also have some superb coral reefs as well as a number of statuesque colonial forts. Sumatra, whose oil, rubber, pepper and coffee make substancial contributions to the Indonesian economy, has one of the country's most diverse ethnic populations. Irian Jaya remains very much the Wild East, however the trekking opportunities through the little-travelled hinterland cannot be matched.

With a wealth of culture, natural beauty and marine sporting facilities, Indonesia has all the potential to become one of the region's top tourist destinations. Families travelling here will find their children are greeted with especial warmth, providing an instant entrée to the local community.

The phrase "paradise resort" has been used so frequently it has almost lost its currency, but it really does apply to some of Indonesia's top-flight accommodation. Aman is the name that most obviously springs to mind, with three properties in Bali and two elsewhere, and the country's major destinations all host some very acceptable five-stars. Not that you always need to shell out a small fortune, as inexpensive labour leads to high staffing levels, and many of the intermediate hotels can be guaranteed to provide extremely comfortable stays. Perhaps the best value of all, Indonesia's guesthouses, or losmen, are often family-run, packed with charm and very hospitable.

Straddling the equator, Indonesia has two main seasons - wet between October and April, and dry for the rest of the year - with slight geographical variations. The wet season is by no means unbearable, as storms tend to come in sudden bursts and once they have subsided it will be dry for the rest of the day. The Christmas holiday season traditionally attracts a horde of visitors from Australia and the rest of the world. Despite all Indonesia's troubles, one can only hope that this continues to be the case.

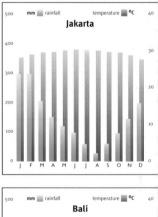

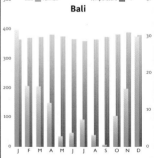

Alila Ubud

Desa Melinggih Kelod, Payangan, Gianyar 80572, Bali, Indonesia
T: +62 361 975 963 **F:** +62 361 975 968
www.HotelClub.com/Hotels/Alila_Ubud_Hotel_Bali

The Alila, which at one time was called the Chedi, has always been one of the most popular hotels in Bali's arts and culture capital. Whatever its name, very little changes at this stunning hotel, and its old friends (and they are many) would want it no other way. The approach could hardly be more charismatic. You wind your way through rice paddies and past stately banyan trees to get down to the hotel from the main road, an intermission between everyday life and the nigh delirious seclusion of the Alila. The swimming pool still looks like a slab of polished basalt perched above the forested slopes leading down to the Ayung River.

The 64 deluxe rooms and villas, clustered together like local village houses, still revel in panoramic views and intimate interiors, with a design that melds traditional Balinese with modern geometry: smooth plaster walls and concrete support thatched roofs, terrazzo tiles blend with gravel and crushed rock, wood meets glass. The brasserie-style Western, local and oriental dishes served up beneath the towering coconut pillars of the Restaurant are just as mouth-watering as ever they were. You can stand and be sluiced beneath the spa's waterfall showers that burst forth like a jungle cataract before and after an outdoor treatment. In sum, the Alila is the new face of an old friend.

Remarkably for a hotel in this day and age, guests will search their accommodation in vain for a television. The inference of course is that there is so much else to do here other than goggle, and that this is meant to be an escape from the intrusions of the modern world. Plus, you need only to look out of the window for a 24-hour entertainment channel.

Rates from: $$
Star rating: ★ ★ ★ ★ ★
Overall rating: ♫ ♫ ♫ ♫ ½

Ambience:	9.25	Cleanliness:	9.00
Value:	8.30	Facilities:	8.26
Staff:	9.28	Restaurants:	8.49
Location:	9.00	Families:	7.84

Amandari

Kedewatan, Ubud, Bali, Indonesia
T: +62 361 975 333 **F:** +62 361 975 335
www.HotelClub.com/Hotels/Amandari_Hotel_Bali

For as long as anyone in Kedewatan can remember, every six months the villagers have donned full temple dress and walked a sacred path that leads to the Ayung River gorge, where they pay their respects to the spirits that live there. The path leads straight through Amandari. While the resort's 30 free-standing suites and solitary stupendous villa were under construction, workmen uncovered a tiger carved in a rock. A copy of it was placed in the colonnaded courtyard across from Amandari's entrance. Shortly after, a night watchman swore he saw the stone tiger move, so now a temple-keeper places a canang - an offering of flowers and sandalwood incense - by the statue daily.

Ubud could almost be described as the soul of Bali, and Amandari - meaning "peaceful spirits" - is one of its most evocative locales. With its entrance designed like a wantilan, or community meeting place, it could really be just another earth-toned village, spread among the rice fields. Each suite has a private swimming pool or courtyard. They are connected by river-stone walkways and lined with high walls of soft volcanic rock. Only coconut and teak woods are used in the villas, which are redolent with the smell of natural thatch. The suites are delightfully polarised between bed and bath - the former a four-poster, and the latter the last word in al fresco, with a tub that is totally open to the sky, framed by stone planters. The Amandari Suite includes an outdoor dining bale surrounded by tropical gardens and a private swimming pool with views of the valley. Cream of the crop at Amandari is a single three-bedroom villa, set slightly apart in its own compound with a two-tier swimming pool and two staff on call.

Meals at Amandari are served at the Restaurant, a casual, double-decker affair set above the green-tiled pool, whose curving sweep mimics the rice terraces that tumble down towards the gorge. After dusk, gamelan players wearing bright red headcloths, called destar, strike up merging their rhythms with the night.

To work up something of an appetite here, guests can make use of the floodlit tennis court, or try out the fitness centre. For the less energetic, the library is crammed with newspapers, magazines and books. And to take the best advantage of the glorious surrounding countryside, Amandari has its own private *bale* across the gorge. A morning hike, plunging down to the river, crossing the swaying suspension bridge and then climbing up the other side, is an exhilarating way to start the day. And at the top, with cold towels and a continental breakfast, stands a waiter looking for all the world as if he was wafted across the ravine by magic. Which given the spiritual nature of Amandari, may just be possible.

Rates from: $$$$
Star rating: ★ ★ ★ ★ ★
Overall rating: ♌ ♌ ♌ ♌ ½

Ambience:	9.62	Cleanliness:	9.28
Value:	7.62	Facilities:	8.69
Staff:	9.23	Restaurants:	8.65
Location:	8.73	Families:	8.14

Amanjiwo

Borobudur, Central Java, Indonesia
T: +62 293 788 333 **F:** +62 293 788 355
www.HotelClub.com/Hotels/Amanjiwo_Resort_Java

To Amanjiwo's complement of butlers, chefs, managers and other virtuoso staff, add the Artist In Residence, whose studio is open to guests, who are welcome to make use of the easel and paints on hand. There is also a watercolour set in each suite, and regular guided expeditions to the countryside for a morning's charcoal sketching. This part of Java is regarded as the island's cultural and spiritual heart, so what better way to ease yourself into the surroundings than to dabble with a brush or pencil for a while?

There could scarcely be a more inspirational subject than the nearby landscape. Amanjiwo - "peaceful soul" - is cradled in a natural amphitheatre with the horizon punctuated by a quartet of volcanoes. And in the middle of the lush rice fields of the Kedu plain rises Borobudur, the largest Buddhist sanctuary in the world. At the resort's heart is a spherical limestone monolith centred by a soaring, bell-shaped rotunda; this is flanked by two crescents containing 36 free-standing suites, 15 of which have their own pool. All the suites include an outdoor kubuk, or pavilion, for private dining or lolling, and the interiors are characterised by typical Yogyakarta style - lofty ceilings, wooden screens, batik pillows and glass paintings - all concentrated around the centrepiece four-pillar bed set on a terrazzo platform.

Java is renowned for its age-old massage, called pijat, which is both hedonistic and healing, and Amanjiwo's therapists can also deliver facials, cream baths and beauty treatments within the privacy of your suite. Supper at Amanjiwo is usually taken to the strains of a gamelan orchestra in the antique-finished, silver-leaf ceilinged, theatre-like Dining Room which serves Indonesian and Western cuisine, or on the Terrace overlooking the Kedu plain. And the Bar - built about the rotunda which is the highest point of the resort - is the consummate place for a nightcap.

Rates from: $$$$$
Star rating: ★ ★ ★ ★ ★
Overall rating: ♦ ♦ ♦ ♦ ♦

Ambience:	9.85	Cleanliness:	9.62
Value:	7.54	Facilities:	9.19
Staff:	9.85	Restaurants:	9.31
Location:	9.54	Families:	9.2

Amankila

Manggis 80871, Bali, Indonesia
T: +62 363 41 333 **F:** +62 363 41 555
www.HotelClub.com/Hotels/Amankila_Resort

If you think you know Bali, and even if you have more than a passing acquaintance with Aman, this lovely oasis set well away from much of the mainstream tourist development relights the much-quoted but never-bettered phrase about the island being "the morning of the world". And the Emerald Isle. And the Island of the Gods. But it transports these aphorisms far away from being mere clichés.

Set on a cliff in the Karangasem Regency in the east of the island of Bali, Amankila's 33 free-standing suites with their alang-alang thatched roofs incorporate a series of inwardly curving shapes. The motif is visible right the way through the suites, from the paras-stone moulding around the entrance doors to the floor-to-ceiling mirror between the bedroom and the bathroom. Canopied, king-sized beds, deep soaking tubs, cozy [d]ivans, double terrazzo vanities and

seashell-finished taps complete the interior decor. Each suite has an outdoor terrace and nine have their own pool.

An elevated walkway leads from the suites to Amankila's heart, a trinity swimming pool that flows down toward the sea like a rice terrace. At the beach itself, reached by a winding stone pathway, a 45-metre turquoise-tiled lap pool lies secluded by a throng of coconut palms and shaded by a stately frangipani tree.

Here at the beach club crisply uniformed staff proffer snorkelling equipment, rig windsurfers, polish your boogie board or kayak prior to use or join you aboard a hobie-cat if you stand in need of a partner. Of course they are dab hands at instruction as well. And if the last thing you want is to engage in anything remotely sporty, there are eight lounging bales set in the sand, each secluded amongst the foliage for added privacy.

marvellously picturesque countryside not simply on the island but in the entire Indonesian archipelago. To take the best advantage of this, Amakila has cunningly sited a couple of mini lodges - Bale Tirta Sira and Ketug Bale - up in the hills where there are especially spectacular views of rice fields, banana trees and Amuk Bay. Head up here for a picnic, or stop over after a jeep tour, a trek or a cycle ride through the countryside. This is the stuff that Aman moments are made of.

Come evening, the Restaurant up by the main pool opens for dinner, but for the acme of private dining, book the single candlelit table on the flower-strewn sand. The menu performs a delicate minuet around the very best of western and Asian cuisine, and dishes are always served with more than a touch of élan. Supper is prepared and served by a dedicated chef and waiter, who discreetly retire at the end of the meal, leaving you to digest in the adjacent lounging *bale* fitted with cushions and bolsters, and lit by flaming bamboo torches. Such is the pace of life at the resort whose name means "peaceful hill".

Tempting as it is to settle here for the entire duration of your stay - and of course there is a sizeable contingent who say they never want to leave - the eastern end of Bali contains some of the most

Rates from: $$$$$
Star rating: ★★★★★
Overall rating: 🌛🌛🌛🌛🌛

Ambience:	9.53	Cleanliness:	9.38
Value:	8.19	Facilities:	8.76
Staff:	9.56	Restaurants:	8.84
Location:	8.69	Families:	8.68

Amanusa

Nusa Dua 80363, Bali, Indonesia
T: +62 361 772 333 **F**: +62 361 772 335
www.HotelClub.com/Hotels/Amannnusa_Villa_Bali

Sometimes, some people somehow feel the need to say that Amanusa is not quite as stellar as some of the other inhabitants of the Aman galaxy. Call it quibbling, but they insinuate that its 35 thatched-roof suites are merely an extension of the rest of Nusa Dua, rather than a mini palace in its own exclusive location. Not so.

Couples staying here (and to check in alone is an exercise in self-mortification) can take part in an exhilarating romp through all the inimitable diversions that are utterly - and there is no other word for it - Amanesque. Take, for example, the ride down to the Bali Golf and Country Club (with preferential tee times for guests, of course) or the adjacent beach, where Amanusa maintains nine private bales, each with its own pot of frangipani water to wash sandy feet. Your transport is an open-topped Volkswagen, which swoops and putters along the tree-hung lanes as if it were bearing visiting royalty. At the resort's pool, bordered by unglazed batik pots, the attendants offer bathers sweet orange slices in a bowl of ice. Pause between sets during a floodlit game of tennis on one of the hardcourts, and there is a pot of chilled chrysanthemum tea waiting to refresh you.

All Amanusa's suites embrace a four-poster bed and a mahogany desk and table for private dining. The light-filled bathroom is blessed with a marble-tiled tub enclosed in a glass wall recessed into a reflection pond. There is also an outside shower dripping with bougainvillea, and eight suites have private swimming pools.

Besides offering dining at the beach, Amanusa has two main restaurants - the Terrace with commanding views down toward the sea, and the Restaurant, an Italian extravaganza where you eat inside or out by the pool. Nusa Dua means "two islands"; Amanusa means "peaceful isle". You can not get more apposite than that.

Rates from: $$$$$
Star rating: ★ ★ ★ ★ ★
Overall rating: ♔♔♔♔ ½

Ambience:	9.42	Cleanliness:	9.17
Value:	7.54	Facilities:	8.67
Staff:	9.17	Restaurants:	8.54
Location:	8.75	Families:	8.43

Amanwana

Moyo Island, West Sumbawa, Indonesia
T: +62 371 22 233 **F**: +62 371 22 288
www.HotelClub.com/Hotels/Amanwana_Resort_Moyo_Island

This is possibly the most adventurous, spectacular, luxurious jungle resort in Asia, and falls outside the usual Aman format as it is largely comprised of tents and trees. Any association with Boy Scouts and/or Girl Guides is totally illusory, for this is one of the most exclusive camp sites imaginable. All 20 guest tents are air-conditioned, stretch over 58 square metres and contain hardwood floors, sofas, bouncy cushions, king-size beds and bathrooms fit for several queens. In fact, it is only the roof which is at all tent-like. The only real choice to make is whether you go for a jungle or - inevitably more pricey - ocean view.

Suggest to an "Aman junkie" (as the group's regulars are called) that all this sounds a tad pampered, and they'll simply shrug their shoulders and grin. This is one of the most beautiful and exclusive corners of the Indonesian archipelago, so why not enjoy it in the very best comfort?

Now in operation for over a dozen years, Amanwana lies east of Bali in a nature reserve on the island of Moyo, poised by the sheltered Saleh Bay. It is an ideal base for cruising and island-hopping. Other diversions include treks to a hidden waterfall in the forest or a massage beneath spreading tamarind trees behind the beach. The Music Pavilion suggests an afternoon stretched out listening to an entire symphony, the Boardwalk has a full array of watersports equipment, and of course the (non-tented) dining room and bar would not disgrace a five-star hotel anywhere else in the world, be they in the midst of an urban jungle or the ordinary sort.

With rates starting at US$650 plus US$75 a day for all food and laundry - not to mention tax and service - you cannot really say this is roughing it.

Rates from: $$$$$
Star rating: ★ ★ ★ ★ ★
Overall rating: ☾ ☾ ☾ ☾ ☾

Ambience:	9.25	Cleanliness:	9.00
Value:	8.55	Facilities:	9.00
Staff:	9.75	Restaurants:	8.75
Location:	9.75	Families:	8.25

Bagus Jati Health & Wellbeing Retreat

Banjar Jati, Sebatu, Kecamatan Tegallang 80572, Bali, Indonesia
T: +62 361 978 885 **F:** +62 361 974 666
www.HotelClub.com/Hotels/Bagus_Jati_Health_and_Well_Being_Retreat

What a gem! A good 30 minutes' drive north of Ubud, along winding ill-made roads, Bagus Jati repays the journey with interest. Roll back several decades and this is what the area must have been like when the very first foreign tourists started to wend their way inland. A mere eight villas are strung out along a spur, each thatched and shaped like an African rondavel, and containing a mammoth double bed, 160 degree windows, sunken baths and their own spa treatment room. A stiff climb will get you down to the riverside spa and pool, however you can cheat by hitching a lift on the shuttle. The jacuzzi here is at eye level with the cliff opposite, the treatment rooms' French windows open out directly onto nature, and the meditation sala is practically invisible behind thick clumps of mature bamboo. Some 20 staff labour year round in the resort's kitchen garden supplying the Surya restaurant, which concentrates on healthy and natural foods. Small wonder guests who can't stay here drive up especially to spa and dine.

Rates from: $$$$
Star rating: ★ ★ ★ ★ ★
Overall rating: Editor's Pick

Ambience:	n/a	Cleanliness:	n/a
Value:	n/a	Facilities:	n/a
Staff:	n/a	Restaurants:	n/a
Location:	n/a	Families:	n/a

The Balé

Jl Raya Nusa Dua Selatan, Nusa Dua 80363, Bali, Indonesia
T: +62 361 775 111 **F:** +62 361 775 222
www.HotelClub.com/Hotels/The_Bale_Bali

out, the menu at Faces restaurant is kept deliberately short as the emphasis is on freshness, while the range of spa treatments is rather longer and includes polarity therapy. A short walk from the beach, this is certainly one of the more imaginative of Bali's resorts, with the emphasis on eco-awareness as much as enjoyment. Bravo.

There's a simple rule at The Balé (rhymes with parlay): No under-16s. So the resort provides a tailor-made excuse for dumping the kids, chucking a few essentials in a bag and jetting to Nusa Dua.

Assuming a break at this ultra-sexy resort is to rekindle some dormant passion, you won't need to bring too many clothes. The high walls surrounding the 20 (eight more coming) very contemporary pavilions keep prying eyes away from the pool, verandah and the daybed in the secluded tropical garden, all of which seem to make skinny-dipping imperative. If you have a spare moment to venture

Rates from: $$$$$
Star rating: ★ ★ ★ ★ ★
Overall rating: ♦ ♦ ♦ ♦

Ambience:	9.08	Cleanliness:	9.08
Value:	7.50	Facilities:	7.87
Staff:	9.33	Restaurants:	8.00
Location:	7.42	Families:	7.55

Bali Dynasty Resort

Jl. Kartika,Tuban 80361, South Kuta, Bali, Indonesia
T: +62 361 752 403   **F:** +62 361 752 402
www.HotelClub.com/Hotels/Bali_Dynasty_Resort

If anywhere has got the synergy thing pretty much down to a T, it's the Dynasty. Walk off the street into Gracie Kelly's, and you're deluged with blarney, billiards, Guinness and Murphy's. Step through the pub's glazed doors into the hotel proper, and behold a craftsman sitting cross-legged on the floor carving a wooden water buffalo. The great thing is this all seems to fit perfectly, as do the Pokémon kids' suites (with bunk beds partitioned from the parents) and the slightly under-employed spa with its half-dozen treatment rooms and outdoor sala. Access to the beach is via an alleyway at the side of the hotel, however as this is lined with shops and their cheery owners it is hardly a hardship trek. Gracie's probably serves up the best food on the property, but the Chinese and Coffee Garden are quite satisfactory. Not one of Bali's classics, but still great fun.

Rates from: $	
Star rating: ★ ★ ★ ★	
Overall rating: 🌀🌀🌀🌀 ½	
Ambience: 8.23	Cleanliness: 9.40
Value: 9.01	Facilities: 8.98
Staff: 8.76	Restaurants: 8.22
Location: 8.94	Families: 9.44

Bali Hilton International

Ayodya

Nusa Dua 80363, Bali, Indonesia
T: +62 361 771 102   **F:** +62 361 771 616
www.HotelClub.com/Hotels/Bali_Hilton_International_Hotel

For the sake of argument, suppose you are part of the typical two plus 2.4 nuclear family, in search of a Balinese resort that encompasses some or all of the following: a kids' club with a daily happy hour on ice-cream prices; an 18-hole golf course in putting distance of the front gate; the choice of eating sushi or pizza or pub grub; free aquarobics at the free-form pool; scenic Balinese architecture as a backdrop; a private beach; a spa with a super selection of treatments and suites; rooms with all the fun stuff like balconies and spacious bathrooms - and so on and so forth. Well, the 537-room Hilton would probably fit the bill. As an extra fillip, though with an extra dollar or two attached, the Ayodya Palace wing acts as the resort's "last resort", with its own pool, lounge, and rather exclusive ambience. There are those who say that Nusa Dua is not quite the real Bali. Whatever your feelings on this, the Hilton would prompt few complaints.

Rates from: $$	
Star rating: ★ ★ ★ ★ ★	
Overall rating: 🌀🌀🌀🌀 ½	
Ambience: 9.20	Cleanliness: 9.03
Value: 8.41	Facilities: 8.67
Staff: 8.94	Restaurants: 8.50
Location: 8.93	Families: 8.67

Bali Hyatt

Jl Danau Tamblingan, Sanur, Bali, Indonesia
T: +62 361 281 234 **F:** +62 361 287 693
www.HotelClub.com/Hotels/Bali_Hyatt_Resort

Pretty much in the centre of Sanur Beach, the Bali Hyatt was built in 1973 (and renovated in 1994) and so the 600 different species of flowers and shrubs that grow in its 15 hectares have had time to mature into a stunning labyrinth of pathways full of tropical colour. The 390 rooms and suites with thatched roofs, natural wood finishes and batik trimmings, are divided between three courts - Hibiscus, Frangipani and Bougainvillea.

Given a few days or weeks here, there is plenty to keep just about anybody occupied. For entertainment, discover some of the more subtle nuances of pampering in the Balinese village-style spa. Push a ball about - be it tennis, ping pong, billiards or pitch and putt. Aquatic diversions include everything from deep-sea fishing to jacuzzis. There are loads of places to stoke up on energy for this highly active programme - Pizza Ria is especially popular, and the seafood at the Omang Omang Grill could have plopped straight out of the Indian Ocean.

Rates from: $
Star rating: ★ ★ ★ ★ ★
Overall rating: 🐧🐧🐧🐧 ½

Ambience:	9.21	Cleanliness:	8.93
Value:	8.25	Facilities:	8.54
Staff:	8.95	Restaurants:	8.67
Location:	8.75	Families:	8.89

Bali InterContinental

Jl Uluwatu 45, Jimbaran 80361, Bali, Indonesia
T: +62 361 701 888 **F:** +62 361 701 777
www.HotelClub.com/Hotels/Intercontinental_Resort_Bali

Is size important? By far the largest of the string of mainstream Jimbaran Bay beachfront hotels, the 425-room InterContinental (each with private balcony) is the sort of resort where a family can divert itself for an entire holiday without ever having to leave. A mammoth, fortress-like building split into six wings, the Interconti is beautifully decorated with fine artwork and handicrafts, and contains a comprehensive assortment of recreational and gustatory facilities, all by the edge of the sea and amid leafy tropical acres - a sort of "Bali on a plate" concept, but not one that feels in any way artificial. Yet, while the hotel is huge, the scale is balanced by intimate corners such as the Bale Bengong - a romantic private dining pavilion on a raised platform set back a little from the beach, dinners à deux here naturally lead to "The Question" being popped over coffee.

Rates from: $$
Star rating: ★ ★ ★ ★ ★
Overall rating: 🐧🐧🐧🐧 ½

Ambience:	9.12	Cleanliness:	8.90
Value:	8.26	Facilities:	8.63
Staff:	8.83	Restaurants:	8.56
Location:	8.45	Families:	8.93

Bali Nikko

Jl Raya Nusa Dua Selatan, Nusa Dua 80363, Bali, Indonesia
T: +62 361 773 377   **F**: +62 361 773 388
www.HotelClub.com/Hotels/Nikko_Bali_Resort_and_Spa

Shimmying down the 40-metre cliff face with the grace and élan of a Legang dancer, it is no surprise the Bali Nikko's Tower rooms have stunning views of the Indian Ocean. The clifftop ones in the North and South wings are not bad either. There are 390 rooms in total, including some stunning suites and a very select few right next to the lagoon pool, which is fringed with a man-made beach. The secluded cove at the cliff base incorporates a 30-metre water slide with free-form pool, an amphitheatre, a camel troop and a tidy little spa. The Bali Golf and Country Club is just around the corner.

Restaurants showcase Japanese, Chinese and Balinese and are rounded off by the onomatopoeic OoLooLoos Fun Pub and Karaoke. If you want a break from the bright lights, head to the top of the observation tower and point the telescope at the constellations spread out across the heavens. Free entertainment doesn't come any better.

Rates from: $$
Star rating: ★ ★ ★ ★ ★
Overall rating: ♢ ♢ ♢ ♢ ½

Ambience:	8.98	Cleanliness:	8.47
Value:	8.40	Facilities:	8.48
Staff:	8.60	Restaurants:	8.51
Location:	8.07	Families:	8.47

Bali Padma Hotel

Jl Padma 1, Legian 80361, Bali, Indonesia
T: +62 361 752 111 **F**: +62 361 752 140
www.HotelClub.com/Hotels/Padma_Hotel_Bali

While most people come to Bali to escape anything that remotely smacks of work and the office, it is also a popular destination for the business boondoggles more properly described as incentives and conventions. Smack on the beach in Legian, with 405 rooms running the gamut from the Presidential Suite down to specially equipped Family Rooms, each with private balcony, the Bali Padma is no slouch at hosting corporate events. Combining its exotic location with the richness of Balinese culture and a wide variety of cuisine, the hotel can serve up themed events from a Rijsttaffel dinner to a tropical beach party, with events varying from kampong village style to wild jungle raves. The 1,000-square-metre pool is a great draw whether you are staying for pleasure or a pleasurable sort of business, and all guests will appreciate the facilities which include water sports on the beach, a spa, squash, kids club and tennis courts.

Rates from: $
Star rating: ★ ★ ★ ★
Overall rating: ♢ ♢ ♢ ♢ ½

Ambience:	9.27	Cleanliness:	9.10
Value:	8.60	Facilities:	8.81
Staff:	9.17	Restaurants:	8.48
Location:	8.93	Families:	9.27

Banyan Tree Bintan

Site A4, Lagoi Bintan Island, Indonesia
T: +62 770 693 100 **F:** +62 770 693 200
www.HotelClub.com/Hotels/Banyan_Tree_Bintan

With not much going for it apart from its hotels, Bintan is in Indonesia, but only just. The island is 45 minutes by catamaran from Singapore, and a further 15-minute drive transports you to the picturesque Banyan Tree. On the peaceful northwest tip of this lush tropical island, the resort is big on luxurious ambience and leafy green tranquillity. It is spectacularly laid out and dramatically photogenic. A choice of 70 secluded luxury villas are perched at intervals among the wooded hillside, and march right down to the rocks by the sea. Each is spacious and airy with a private jacuzzi or pool and delightful verandahs with some quite amazing views of the thriving canopy, the sapphire bay or the sandy beach cove. Villa themes are closely linked to their environment and include Valley Villa, Seaview Pool Villa and Villa-on-the-Rocks.

A feeling of romance and the privacy is maintained throughout the resort. The Banyan Tree is renowned for its spas, and this one enjoys the added bonus of a hillside elevation and sweeping views. The restaurants offer a wonderful selection of Southeast Asian specialties at the Saffron, Mediterranean cuisine at the Cove or snacks and salads at Treetops, although prices are more in line with top Singapore hotels rather than top Indonesian ones.

Generally, facilities are low-key to keep the resort in that idyllic spa mode. Apart from the two tennis courts and various beach and water sport activities there are no energetic facilities such as a gym, and there is not even a bar. However, nearby is the Greg Norman-designed 18-hole Laguna Bintan Golf Course, one of three courses on Bintan.

As you would expect from Banyan Tree the staff really are a magnificent crew, and even with its top-end price tag the resort proves incredibly popular, and not just with weekending Singaporeans.

Rates from: $$$$
Star rating: ★ ★ ★ ★ ★
Overall rating: ♦♦♦♦ ½

Ambience:	9.29	Cleanliness:	8.81
Value:	7.66	Facilities:	8.40
Staff:	9.06	Restaurants:	8.19
Location:	8.51	Families:	8.19

Begawan Giri Estate

Banjar Beeawan, Desa Melinggih Kelod, Payanean, Ubud, Bali
T: +62 361 978 888   **F:** +62 361 978 889
www.HotelClub.com/Hotels/Begawan_Giri_Estate_Bali

Perfect is a word to be used with the utmost caution when applied to hotels, but there can be no other description for Begawan Giri. Some six years in the making, it occupies a ridge looking down over an outrageously picturesque part of the Ayung River gorge, its tranquil air only occasionally punctured by the eldritch cries of rafters far below. As an estate, Begawan Giri is made up of five residences, each named after a different element such as Water or Fire. Each is a self-contained haven with four or five double bedrooms, and a shared pool, dining and relaxation area as well as full kitchen facilities. They are perfect (that word again) for extended families or groups of friends, although the butler in overall charge of each residence is more than adept at ministering to the individual needs of guests who don't know each other. The details are not far short of (pleasant) shock and awe. Antique lavatory pans decorated with bunches of flowers, a pizza oven for in-house dining, a secret entrance to your pool - each of the residences features something witty and fun. Seven simple but stunning villas make up the rest of Begawan's unparalleled inventory. Elsewhere around the property an amphitheatre - decadently strewn with cushions on performance nights - occupies a small hillside, the Indonesian restaurant, Kudas House, is contained in a 150-year-old village house, while chef David King works his own particular brand of New World and Indonesian magic in Biji. The spa is a natural hymn to all things pampering, but you might enjoy yourself just as much by seeking out one of Begawan's several *bales*, tucking yourself up here and contemplating one of the most beautiful locations anywhere on the island.

As the manager, Matthew Taverner, admits with characteristic disarming charm: "It's very spiritual here - walking around I get goose bumps on a daily basis". Which - not to overuse to term - is as about as perfect as you can get.

Rates from: $$$$$
Star rating: ★ ★ ★ ★ ★
Overall rating: ♦ ♦ ♦ ♦ ½

Ambience:	9.76	Cleanliness:	9.29
Value:	6.95	Facilities:	8.45
Staff:	9.24	Restaurants:	8.24
Location:	9.05	Families:	7.88

The Dharmawangsa

Jl Brawijaya Raya 26, Kebayoran Baru, Jakarta 12160, Indonesia
T: +62 21 725 8181 **F:** +62 21 725 8383
www.HotelClub.com/Hotels/Dharmawangsa_Hotel_Jakarta_The

The highly exclusive Dharmawangsa experience starts at the international airport, with uniformed staff meeting you way before you get anywhere near Immigration. Chauffeur-driven BMWs speed guests to the hushed residential area of Kebayoran Baru. No-one ever checks in at the lobby.

Butlers pack, unpack, and pack a whole lot of other services into the 24-hour-a-day service. Exclusive? Answer that one with a multi-starred "yes". The Dharmawangsa's 64 rooms and 36 suites make up not so much a boutique hotel as a graceful Indonesian mansion, with the interiors reflecting the grace and beauty of the country's culture and heritage. The hotel's restaurants blend the finest elements of Indonesian and international cuisines. There are swimming pools (indoor and out), tennis and squash courts for the energetic and a supremely luxurious spa for the sybaritic. Expensive? Answer that one with a multi-dollar signed "yes" - certainly for Jakarta. But it is worth every cent.

Rates from: $$$
Star rating: ★ ★ ★ ★ ★
Overall rating: ♥♥♥♥ ½

Ambience:	9.55	Cleanliness:	9.36
Value:	8.34	Facilities:	8.75
Staff:	9.27	Restaurants:	8.55
Location:	8.32	Families:	8.47

Discovery Kartika Plaza Hotel

Jl Kartika Plaza, Tuban 80361, Bali, Indonesia
T: +62 361 751 067 **F:** +62 361 752 475
www.HotelClub.com/Hotels/Discovery_Kartika_Plaza_Hotel_Bali

One of the older hotels in Tuban, the Kartika's generous space allowance - be it the broad wooden balconies of its Ocean View rooms, the 1,000-seat ballroom, or the wide but still very private lawns of its six villas - is its trump card. That, and the fact that the architects stopped to think for a bit before putting pen to drawing board. So walk up the steps past the spectacular circular fountain and your eye is drawn through the cathedral-like lobby to the sea beyond. The beach is not that spectacular, but there is plenty to occupy you in the hotel itself, while the Bali Waterbom Park is just down the road and a gargantuan new shopping mall opened next to the Kartika in December 2004. La Cucina, the Italian restaurant, deserves a special mention, and there's rarely a seat free at the swim-up pool bar. First choice in the area for incentive groups, but it is pretty good for families too.

Rates from: $
Star rating: ★ ★ ★ ★
Overall rating: ♥♥♥♥ ½

Ambience:	9.24	Cleanliness:	9.24
Value:	8.94	Facilities:	8.93
Staff:	9.00	Restaurants:	8.42
Location:	9.41	Families:	8.93

Four Seasons Resort Bali at Jimbaran Bay

Kawasan Bukit Permai Jimbaran, Denpasar 80361, Bali, Indonesia
T: +62 361 701 010 **F**: +62 361 701 022
www.HotelClub.com/Hotels/Four_Seasons_Resort_Jimbaran_Bay_Bali

Bravura, forethought and attention to detail distinguish the Four Seasons. Other resorts have villas with plunge pools and thatched roofs, gamelan-toned dining under the stars and gentle, caster-footed staff with frangipanis tucked behind their ears. But here they pull it off with such subtle panache it is almost indiscernible. For example, it is rare for hotels to admit it is possible to eat anywhere but in their own restaurants, but Four Seasons leaves a list of the island's most popular bars and eateries in every villa to add to its own five offerings. And on the subject of food, the resort's specially designed cooking school embraces a holistic menu that includes the art of Balinese entertaining, Asian seasonings from the herb and spice garden and health-conscious spa cuisine.

And so to the resort proper. Four Seasons employed indigenous building materials and styles, and the vast majority of the coralline limestone rock used for many of the walls was quarried on site, individually chipped and put into place by hand. The result is 156

secluded walled villas, the majority with one bedroom, but there are also six doubles and two extra-large Royal Villas complete with staff quarters, sauna and jacuzzi. These are arranged in groups of approximately 20 around a village square with staff on duty around the clock. On top of the regular accommodation offerings, a short stretch down the road and opposite the Four Seasons' beachside restaurant Pantai Jimbaran (universally known as PJ's) stand the Private Estates. Comprising four-, three- and two-bedroomed villas, they beg to be filled with friends and family for a highly memorable celebration, wedding or party.

Finally, Four Seasons Jimbaran is

distinguished by an exceptional spa, with nine treatment rooms spread over 930 square metres, dispensing the likes of rain-shower and side-by-side massages. And for anyone in need of a little extra Balinese culture, the Ganesha Art Gallery presents four curated shows every year, with a revolving collection of additional work by local artists.

Rates from: $$$$$
Star rating: ★★★★★
Overall rating: ♦♦♦♦ ½

Ambience:	9.45	Cleanliness:	9.17
Value:	7.82	Facilities:	8.83
Staff:	9.19	Restaurants:	8.60
Location:	8.84	Families:	8.50

Four Seasons Resort Bali at Sayan

Sayan, Ubud 80571, Bali, Indonesia
T: +62 361 977 577 **F:** +62 361 977 588
www.HotelClub.com/Hotels/Four_Seasons_Resort_Sayan_Bali

Discard any ideas of conventional design and execution, all ye who enter here. For everything at Sayan conspires to startle and amaze. Starting at the entrance - a long teak platform bridging a roaring chasm that leads to the lobby - this is a resort that seems to have been turned on its head. The main building is no pseudo-Balinese thatchery, but a boldly contemporary circular structure that could almost be a flying saucer that has fortuitously landed in Ubud.

Pillars, ponds, hanging vines and a wealth of shrubs and trees help blend the Four Seasons into the surrounding rice terraces. Overall, it is an astonishing architectural achievement, and the 18 suites and 42 villas merely emphasise this. The bulk of the villas are within a few steps of the Ayung River, and are so compactly tucked into the hillside that each entrance is via stairs leading from the roof, which has its own deck and lotus garden. Down the circular stone stairway, there is a private plunge pool, a second deck, indoor and outdoor bathing facilities, handmade Indonesian furniture and a euphoric sense of peace and privacy.

At the very pinnacle of places to stay at Sayan, the Royal Villa's private terraces, sundecks and gardens stretch over 1,000 square metres. The villa's three bedrooms are approaching the last word in luxury, there's a dining room and kitchen for entertaining, while in addition to the plunge pool a private bale overlooks the river. It's a perfect bolthole, love nest and secluded pied-à-terre where you can shut yourself away secure in the knowledge that the entire staff is at your bidding only a phone call away.

The resort's all-embracing sense of peace is emphasised in the spa, with its 180-degree view of the valley and four treatment rooms, where rejuvenation programmes focus on using elements from the earth such as clay, mountain plants and warming spices.

Some of the more comprehensive treatments can occupy the best part of an entire day, starting with a steam shower that opens the pores, moving on to hot-stone therapy, an exfoliation, a body wrap, a massage and a long soak in a frangipani blossom bath - all of which is capped with a spa lunch. Anywhere else you might feel guilty about spending so much time on what - presumed health benefits aside - is little more than sheer indulgence. But at Sayan this simply seems to be the right way to go.

While the oval-shaped Ayung Terrace offers top-class dining with a view, there is also the option of eating at the Riverside Café, with its own wood-burning pizza oven.

However, the Four Seasons' triumph here is its pool, a two-tier affair almost within arm's reach of the river, perfectly melding human creation with nature. And on the subject of human creation, children are now actively encouraged to come here. Naturally the concierges are highly experienced at drawing up entertainment programmes for the whole family.

Rates from: $$$$$
Star rating: ★ ★ ★ ★ ★
Overall rating: 🐚🐚🐚🐚🐚

Ambience:	9.44	Cleanliness:	9.43
Value:	8.03	Facilities:	8.92
Staff:	9.11	Restaurants:	8.51
Location:	8.86	Families:	8.31

Gran Melia Jakarta

Jl HR Rasuna Said Kav. X-O, Kuningan, Jakarta 12950, Indonesia
T: +62 21 526 8080 **F:** +62 21 526 6060
www.HotelClub.com/Hotels/Gran_Melia_Jakarta

This is Sol Melia's Asian flagship and it shows. The architecture employed is distinctive and bold, the exterior being tiled in blue glaze and muscling in on the sky line. The impressive Wi-Fi'd lobby is cavernous and representative of the ambition of the hotel. Within the enormous atrium trickling water and a giant silver globe make a further grandiloquent statement - in such a crowded metropolis few hotels have a comparable luxury of space and scale.

The hotel has a total of 404 rooms and suites with extensive facilities to match. The European-style rooms are smooth, calm and well fitted. In keeping with the hotel's dimensions they are especially generous in size and business travellers will be pleased to find the desk is located sensibly next to the data and phone ports, rather than across the room as in other local hotels. The executive floor rooms are exceptional and the associated facilities especially well done. One memorable feature is the incredibly thick and rich carpets. You virtually need a combine harvester to carve through them. The restaurant choice is suitably wide following the expected Asian cuisine norms of local, Chinese and Japanese, with a sidestep to Southern European. The quality of food is high, from casual to fine dining. The business guest is catered to fully, and corporate

facilities include 11 meeting rooms and a giant pillarless ballroom with a capacity of 2,200. On the leisure side, there's a very pleasant outdoor pool, a 24-hour gym and a brace of tennis courts.

The location is not bull's-eye central, but it is convenient, being in the rapidly developing Golden Triangle area of Kuningan. The business district is ten minutes away and the immediate area is populated by embassies. Overall, this is a top five-star hotel with more than a dash of flair.

Rates from: $
Star rating: ★ ★ ★ ★ ★
Overall rating: ♪ ♪ ♪ ♪ ½

Ambience:	8.94	Cleanliness:	9.06
Value:	8.65	Facilities:	8.85
Staff:	8.85	Restaurants:	8.86
Location:	8.47	Families:	8.80

Grand Hyatt Bali

Kawasan Wisata Nusa Dua, Bali, Indonesia
T: +62 361 771 234 **F:** +62 361 772 038
www.HotelClub.com/Hotels/Grand_Hyatt_Resort_Bali

The humungous Grand Hyatt stretches along a substantial part of the beach on the eastern side of Nusa Dua, looking out toward the isolated promontory of Pura Bias Turgal and its solitary shrine. This is a mainstream tourist resort, for sure, embracing 653 rooms, villas and suites, yet the ambience is solidly Balinese. Designed along the lines of one of the island's traditional water palaces, the accommodation is grouped into four self-contained "villages" so guests are not overawed or disoriented by their surroundings, which are spread over 16 hectares.

Landscaped gardens, two free-form pools and a host of other water features connected by meandering pathways complete a picture that is near idyllic. Kids -

and this resort was built with them uppermost in mind - should love to hare around exploring. There is also the specially equipped Camp Nusa for three- to 13-year-olds to keep youngsters occupied in fun, hands-on activities that range from fish-feeding to squash clinics, from painting and pottery to kite-flying and cooking.

The Hyatt's rooms themselves might be air-conditioned and fitted with satellite television, but such modern accessories do not detract in any way from the decor - muted batik fabrics, graceful bamboo furnishings and Balinese handicrafts. And you only have to step outside to balcony or garden to admire the island's nature in the raw.

Although guests can tuck in at any of the resort's eight restaurants and bars, two - the Watercourt and the night market - especially ooze local character. The Watercourt is surrounded by statues of the Garuda, Vishnu's winged transport of Indonesian mythology, and serves Balinese cuisine in a courtyard overlooking a pond teeming with carp. And the Pasar Senggol market brings together a conglomeration of food stalls and dance performances while artisans create puppets and carve, weave or paint as they would in their home villages.

Rates from: $$
Star rating: ★ ★ ★ ★ ★
Overall rating: � ½

Ambience:	9.15	Cleanliness:	8.91
Value:	8.43	Facilities:	8.66
Staff:	8.98	Restaurants:	8.62
Location:	8.57	Families:	8.91

Grand Hyatt Jakarta

Jl MH Thamrin Kav 28-30, Jakarta 10230, Indonesia
T: +62 21 390 1234 **F**: +62 21 390 6426
www.HotelClub.com/Hotels/Grand_Hyatt_Hotel_Jakarta

The magnificent lobby of the Grand Hyatt makes a vigorous introduction to this hotel that is part executive headquarters, part retreat from the city and all pleasure. Sturdy columns soar three floors to the ceiling, and a double staircase and escalators lead down to ground level flanked by a series of ponds set about with palm trees and greenery. The whole harks back to Jakarta's boom years, while hinting that the Indonesian capital may well get on its financial feet again one day soon.

The 428 rooms are sumptuously decorated, smartly wired and considerately laid out. The inventory includes 22 suites (some with their own terrace and all with 24-hour butler service) and 15 apartments for long-staying guests, while the club floors enjoy their own lounge with a concierge and a host of other complimentary facilities.

The Hyatt's eateries and drinking holes are excellent both for entertaining clients and colleagues or simply entertaining yourself. The menu at the Grand Café - crispy salads, roast station and sashimi bar - changes daily, and the ice cream is home-made. C's Steak and Seafood serves prime US beef while its cellar holds 3,000 labels. There are four private rooms in the Sumire Japanese restaurant, and the poolside Seafood Terrace is transformed into a market-style buffet in the evenings with an open kitchen and fish tanks. After dinner, the burgundy lounge is usually full to the gills with socialites out to listen to one of the international bands and sample the extensive range of wines, spirits and cigars.

When it comes to recreation, the Hyatt surpasses itself. Fans of golf, tennis, squash, basketball and jogging all get their own putting green, courts or track. The lagoon swimming pool is 43 metres long, and the fitness centre fairly bulges with state-of-the-art equipment, jacuzzis, plunge baths and VIP massage rooms. Further off-duty entertainment is available right next door in Plaza Indonesia, a mammoth shopping complex that can be reached directly from the hotel and just goes to emphasise the hotel's top location. Note that construction of the Grand Hotel Indonesia and mega mall next door is likely to continue well into 2006 - assuming it doesn't stop for lack of funds first.

Rates from: $$
Star rating: ★ ★ ★ ★ ★
Overall rating: ♭ ♭ ♭ ♭ ½

Ambience:	8.97	Cleanliness:	8.94
Value:	8.19	Facilities:	8.73
Staff:	8.68	Restaurants:	8.64
Location:	8.85	Families:	8.39

Hard Rock Hotel Bali

Jl Pantai, Banjar Pande Mas, Kuta, Bali, Indonesia
T: +62 361 761 869 **F:** +62 361 461 868
www.HotelClub.com/Hotels/Hard_Rock_Hotel_Bali

the Hard Rock Café (although there are two other restaurants and three bars), there are scads of collectibles in the Mega Store, while the business centre contains a rock library and Centrestage triples as a lobby, bar and live venue. Hard Rock Bali is now one of eleven similar hotels around the world. Oh world.

Yes - a hotel for rock 'n' roll Peter Pans, where everything is always groovy. This is for the young, families with young(ish) children and the very young-at-heart. Some 418 rooms are mashed into this Technicolor-plus property on Kuta Beach that must be the last word in the science of branding. Never

mind the bright and breezy balconied rooms in six blocks themed blues, reggae etc. you can interact with Radio Wave 87.6 FM DJs, burn your own CD in the Boom Box recording studio or chill out in one of the cabanas by the pool where, of course, piped music is inescapable. Dining is naturally in

Rates from: $
Star rating: ★ ★ ★ ★
Overall rating: ◑ ◑ ◑ ◑ ½

Ambience:	8.77	Cleanliness:	8.60
Value:	8.11	Facilities:	8.38
Staff:	8.76	Restaurants:	8.57
Location:	8.97	Families:	8.75

Hilton International Jakarta

Jl Gatot Subroto, Jakarta 10002, Indonesia
T: +62 21 570 3600 **F:** +62 21 573 3055
www.HotelClub.com/Hotels/Hilton_International_Jakarta

largest hotel with 1,104 rooms, there's plenty of choice - the balconied suites probably ranking as the best. There's a similar wealth of opportunities in the ten restaurants and bars. The very modern spa may be confined to the basement, but is cheery and well-run. Twenty-nine-year-old dogs and new tricks and all that.

Oh, for the days three decades ago when accountants were a tad less voracious and building a five-star hotel involved spreading out in all directions rather than balancing every last square centimetre against potential revenue. The first block of the Hilton opened in 1976. It has since added two more towers forming a rough Y-shape, with the

whole site encompassing a swathe of tennis courts, a lagoon, a low-rise tiled bazaar and a lake-like swimming pool. Wandering the public areas is something of a journey through time, with the main lobby heavily Javanese and the two new wings contrastingly crisp and modern. Right next to the convention centre, as the country's

Rates from: $
Star rating: ★ ★ ★ ★
Overall rating: ◑ ◑ ◑ ◑

Ambience:	8.54	Cleanliness:	8.82
Value:	8.02	Facilities:	8.32
Staff:	8.43	Restaurants:	8.55
Location:	8.61	Families:	8.38

Holiday Inn Resort Lombok

Senggigi Beach, Lombok 83355, Indonesia
T: +62 370 693 444 **F:** +62 370 693 092
www.HotelClub.com/Hotels/Holiday_Inn_Resort_Lombok

Anyone expecting a run-of-the-mill outpost from the Holiday Inn chain is in for a very pleasant surprise here. Perched on the shoreline adjacent to Mangsit Village, the resort is a stunner. Built in 1995, it still feels quite new and the design successfully spreads the facilities around 15 hectares in an appealing way. Located some three kilometres from the low-key shops and bars of Senggigi Beach, the resort is well equipped with a handsome pool, tropical beach and satisfying restaurants. The standard rooms are trim, modern and comfy. But the bungalows are really worth the indulgence with their private gardens, outdoor bathrooms and direct access to the spotless beach. Families will love the Mangsit apartments with two bedrooms, lounge and dining area and fully-fitted kitchen. Staff are active and very helpful, arranging tours, diving and transport with ease. The relative isolation of the resort does not hurt and it is fantastic value for money.

Rates from: $
Star rating: ★ ★ ★ ★
Overall rating: ♻♻♻♻

Ambience:	8.63	Cleanliness:	8.46
Value:	8.46	Facilities:	8.32
Staff:	8.61	Restaurants:	8.18
Location:	8.20	Families:	8.84

Hyatt Regency Yogyakarta

Jl Palagan Tentara Pelajar, Yogyakarta 55581, Indonesia
T: +62 274 869 123 **F:** +62 274 869 588
www.HotelClub.com/Hotels/Hyatt_Regency_Hotel_Yogyakarta

Yogyakarta is the cultural and intellectual heart of Java, and the Hyatt Regency has done its best to reflect this. While its seven storeys are indubitably modern, its design incorporates many of the architectural details and the same axis as the renowned Borobudur temple, which stands just 42 kilometres away. The hotel is surrounded by 24 hectares of luxuriant gardens, Javanese thatching gives the public areas a village feel, and even the lifts are naturally lit via a glass rooftop stupa.

The well-appointed 260 rooms and suites are spread among four wings, either looking out over the nine-hole golf course or toward Mount Merapati. The health club and free-form swimming pool are both excellent venues in which to relax, children can be safely deposited at Camp Hyatt, and the hotel's facilities are completed by five restaurants and bars. Note that Bogey's Teras serves healthy drinks and snacks rather than what some schoolboys might suggest.

Rates from: $
Star rating: ★ ★ ★ ★ ★
Overall rating: ♻♻♻♻

Ambience:	8.88	Cleanliness:	8.56
Value:	8.31	Facilities:	8.25
Staff:	8.63	Restaurants:	8.33
Location:	8.38	Families:	8.71

JW Marriott Hotel Jakarta

Jl Lingkar Mega Kuningan Kav E12 No.1 &2, Mega Kuningan, Jakarta 12950, Indonesia
T: +62 21 5798 8888   **F**: +62 21 5798 8833
www.HotelClub.com/Hotels/JW_Marriott_Hotel_Jakarta

The JW Jakarta has the dubious distinction of being the only hotel in this book to have been bombed. The damage of 5th August 2003 has long been cleared away, and the 333-room property is now performing with gusto once again, though naturally with extra security in place. So damnation to all terrorists, and plaudits to owners, management and staff for getting back on track so speedily.

There is plenty to enjoy here, from the bright and bouncy open kitchen at Sailendra, to the compact spa with its city-view indoor plunge pools, to the floor-to-ceiling windows that are a feature of all the rooms and suites. The entire hotel runs seamlessly and with a very polished air. While it may be on the fringes of the centre, this is very much one of the up-and-coming areas of Jakarta.

Rates from: $$
Star rating: ★ ★ ★ ★ ★
Overall rating: ♦ ♦ ♦ ♦

Ambience:	8.47	Cleanliness:	8.61
Value:	8.31	Facilities:	8.33
Staff:	8.20	Restaurants:	8.50
Location:	7.86	Families:	8.63

JW Marriott Hotel Surabaya

Jl Embong Malang 85-89, Surabaya, East Java, Indonesia
T: +62 31 545 8888   **F**: +62 31 546 8888
www.HotelClub.com/Hotels/JW_Marriott_Surabaya

There are those who say Surabaya is nothing more than an industrial sprawl with a silicone chip on its shoulder. This might have been true in years past, but nowadays the city is catching up with its rival Jakarta. And the JW is a case in point. One of a number of hotels which sprang up during a construction boom in the 1990s, its 412 rooms include a mix of suites and apartments for long-staying guests, decorated with a blend of western and Oriental styling. There should be absolutely no complaints about the sushi at Imari or the clarity of the water in the outdoor pool, nor indeed about the standards of service here or any other aspect of the hotel. It has to be said the city is hardly a beauty spot, and given that most guests will be here on business, the Marriott provides a most welcome bolthole.

Rates from: $$
Star rating: ★ ★ ★ ★ ★
Overall rating: ♦ ♦ ♦ ♦

Ambience:	8.48	Cleanliness:	8.72
Value:	8.16	Facilities:	8.48
Staff:	8.64	Restaurants:	8.58
Location:	8.28	Families:	8.28

Komaneka Resort

Jl Monkey Forest, Ubud, Gianyar 80571, Bali, Indonesia
T: +62 361 976 090   **F**: +62 361 977 140
www.HotelClub.com/Hotels/Komaneka_Resort_and_Suite_Bali

Set back from the rather touristy Monkey Forest Road, the Komaneka is the sort of hotel everyone dreams of when they think of Ubud. And this is where they can come to turn their dreams into reality. As the management says: the actual hotel is not so important as the ambience, which they strive to make like a friend's house. Afternoon tea is one of the key, and most amicable, events of the day, stretching for several hours and entirely free to all guests.

The Komaneka is owned by the same family that runs the Neka Museum, and due emphasis is placed on both the arts and fitting into the surrounding environment. A gallery fronts the hotel's long, narrow site, which gives way to a pleasant semi-open-air restaurant and then the 20 rooms and villas. Welcoming roundels of freshly cut flowers decorate the double beds, which in some suites are at eye-level with the rice paddies immediately outside the windows. A full-size mirror by the sunken bath grants a similar vista. The resort's scenic rectangular pool looks directly onto a small stream and a group of picturesque local houses, and is only a short step away from the Komaneka spa, whose treatment rooms are also within plucking distance of the rice fields. One of the resort's most relaxing spaces occupies the spa's upper floor - a lounge-cum-library, where guests can come to sit and while away the hours in perfect peace, watch TV, read and chat.

Given its location, the Komaneka's guests can step straight out into the retail and café culture of central Ubud, yet be back in their own private space swiftly. The Komaneka's sister resort up the road at Kedawatan, containing 20 villas and suites, is equally pleasant but with a more remote feel to it.

Rates from: $$
Star rating: ★ ★ ★ ★
Overall rating: 🖑 🖑 🖑 🖑 ½

Ambience:	9.63	Cleanliness:	8.63
Value:	8.50	Facilities:	8.89
Staff:	9.25	Restaurants:	7.71
Location:	8.88	Families:	6.57

Le Méridien Nirwana Golf & Spa Resort Bali

Jl Raya Tanah Lot, Kidiri 82171, Tabanan, Bali, Indonesia
T: +62 361 815 900 **F:** +62 361 815 901
www.HotelClub.com/Hotels/Le_Meridien_Nirwana_Gold_Spa_Resort_Bali

You might as well call it "The Holy Trinity". Hectares of rice paddy provide the "rough" alongside a superb Greg Norman-designed 18-hole golf course. The spa offers a cornucopia of massage and other Balinese treatments. And the island's most photogenic temple, Tanah Lot, stands in full sight of this stunning hotel that is flecked by spray from the Indian Ocean.

While more than adequately catering to guests' sporting, physical and spiritual requirements by day, the discreetly landscaped Le Méridien also provides succour by night, with a combination of 278 rooms, suites and villas. It would be folly not to go for something with an ocean view here, and equally silly to miss out on at least one evening aperitif in the Sunset Lounge overlooking Tanah Lot. As the old saying goes - "a river runs through it" - so water is a principal feature of the resort and is found throughout the hotel's extensive gardens, waterfalls and ponds.

Rates from: $
Star rating: ★ ★ ★ ★ ★
Overall rating: ۵۵۵۵ ½

Ambience:	9.00	Cleanliness:	9.08
Value:	8.53	Facilities:	8.66
Staff:	8.93	Restaurants:	8.55
Location:	8.53	Families:	8.84

Legian Beach Hotel

Jl Melasti, Legian, Denpasar 80033, Bali, Indonesia
T: +62 361 751 711 **F:** +62 361 752 651
www.HotelClub.com/Hotels/Legian_Beach_Hotel_Bali

The footpaths of the Legian Beach Hotel resound each morning to the measured tread of its lean, bronzed resident surfing community, resolutely heading past the more sedate families and couples at breakfast with their eyes fixed firmly on the horizon and their minds transfixed by the prospect of the coming day's rollers. This is surfer country, make no mistake, though it is by no means compulsory and you can simply hang out rather than hang ten if you prefer. The spa is booked solid for much of the day, and there are usually a few couples putting the world to rights in the shallow end of the pool towards the end of the evening. Everybody else has hunkered down in one of the snug rooms in the main block, or in the Legian's thatched cottages, all of which are in the process of gradual renovation. Long-serving and especially matey staff round out this not exactly luxurious but very comfortable and popular property.

Rates from: $
Star rating: ★ ★ ★ ★
Overall rating: ۵۵۵۵ ½

Ambience:	9.08	Cleanliness:	9.17
Value:	8.27	Facilities:	8.38
Staff:	8.91	Restaurants:	8.08
Location:	9.00	Families:	8.04

Mandarin Oriental Majapahit

65 Jalan Tunjungan, Surabaya 60275, Indonesia
T: +62 31 545 4333 **F:** +62 31 545 4111
www.HotelClub.com/Hotels/Mandarin_Oriental_Hotel_Majapahit_Surabaya

Over the course of the last century, the hotel now known as the Majapahit has witnessed some truly historic events. Opened as the Oranje in 1910 by Lucas Sarkies (from the same family that created Raffles in Singapore and numerous other grand hotels), it has hosted Charlie Chaplin, Joseph Conrad and Prince Leopold of Belgium. The distinguished Art Deco lobby was added in 1936, and the Japanese used it variously as a prison camp and barracks during World War II. September 1945 witnessed the hotel's greatest red-letter day. Infuriated

by a Dutch flag that had been raised on the roof, a crowd of Indonesians stormed the hotel, ripped the blue part off the colonialists' tricolour and so launched the country's struggle for independence.

Renamed Hotel Merdeka ("liberty") it lapsed into obscurity for some years, until a dazzling renovation and relaunch in 1996 reinstated it as Surabaya's premier address. The Majapahit's graceful low-level design, colonnades, five garden courtyards and creamy white walls from Sarkies' time are still in place, but they have been augmented by the addition of an outdoor pool, tennis court and a comprehensive spa.

The hotel's assortment of accommodation is also highly impressive, with 110 suites and 40 rooms characterised by Asian carpets, polished floors, high ceilings and private balconies or terraces. Nine of the suites have their own theme; the Merdeka was once occupied by the Dutch politicos whose flag caused all the

fuss at the end of the war, and contains many contemporary captioned photos; the Sarkies Brothers commemorates the hotel's founding fathers; and the Wayang pays tribute to Indonesia's folk puppets. Completing the inventory, the Presidential Suite, at 800 square metres, is one of the largest in Asia.

Of the Majapahit's half-dozen restaurants and bars, quite the most intriguing is the Euro-Asian Indigo, with a spectacular show kitchen at one end and wide windows at the other, looking out on to the street where the traders and trishaw drivers dawdle past just as they must have done way back in 1910.

Rates from: $
Star rating: ★ ★ ★ ★ ★
Overall rating: ♔ ♔ ♔ ♔ ½

Ambience:	9.11	Cleanliness:	9.00
Value:	8.56	Facilities:	8.27
Staff:	8.50	Restaurants:	8.44
Location:	8.06	Families:	8.27

Mandarin Oriental Jakarta

Jl MH Thamrin, Jakarta 10310, Indonesia
T: +62 21 3983 8888 **F:** +62 21 3983 8889
www.HotelClub.com/Hotels/Mandarin_Oriental_Jakarta

The Mandarin is one of the well-established business hotels grouped around the Welcome Statue in downtown Jakarta in the heart of the financial and diplomatic district. Given the Indonesian capital's traffic problems, it certainly has the location right, and the interiors are similarly pertinent. The 404 rooms and suites are a mine of solid comfort backed up with the sort of amenities - high-speed Internet, laptop-friendly safes - that make life simpler for peripatetic executives, and are supported by a business centre that goes the extra mile with services like mobile phone hire and arranging appointments.

The hotel's eight restaurants and bars are highly favoured by local businessmen as venues to wine, dine and parley - especially the newly restored Kafe Kafe - while La Casa del Habano is frequently thick with the aroma of Punch or Churchills and fine cognacs. Not quite the same style and calibre as other hotels from this superior group, but certainly one of the best in Jakarta.

Rates from: $
Star rating: ★ ★ ★ ★ ★
Overall rating: ♦♦♦♦ ½

Ambience:	8.58	Cleanliness:	9.16
Value:	8.21	Facilities:	8.69
Staff:	9.13	Restaurants:	8.55
Location:	8.97	Families:	8.21

Maya Ubud Resort & Spa

Jl Gunung Sari Peliatan, Bali 80571, Indonesia
T: +62 361 977 888 **F:** +62 361 977 555
www.HotelClub.com/Hotels/Maya_Ubud_Resort_Spa_Bali

The largest hotel in Ubud, Maya makes a good job of disguising its 108 rooms by splitting them between a colourful double-winged, three-storey building and two ranks of villas on either side of a lawn which then plunges down the hillside to the spa, pool and restaurant. A lift eases the stress of getting down to this most popular corner of the resort. The Maya's interior designers were brave enough to step away from the traditional Balinese ethos, while nodding to its synchronicity. So tables and chairs may be made from recycled railway sleepers, but the wall by the beaten stainless-steel bathroom sink will be coloured a tasty orange. The blend of old and new appeals directly to Japanese visitors, who make up a good proportion of the clientele. Under the command of the redoubtable veteran Paul Blake, who brings three decades of experience to the property, it seems highly likely the Maya is set to prosper.

Rates from: $$
Star rating: ★ ★ ★ ★ ★
Overall rating: ♦♦♦♦ ½

Ambience:	9.60	Cleanliness:	9.13
Value:	8.33	Facilities:	8.72
Staff:	9.13	Restaurants:	8.29
Location:	8.40	Families:	8.45

Melia Bali Villas & Spa Resort

Jl Pratama, Nusa Dua 80363, Bali, Indonesia
T: +62 361 771 510 **F:** +62 361 771 360
www.HotelClub.com/Hotels/Melia_Bali_Villas_and_Spa_Resort

that provides a magnificent mix of Balinese and international dance one of the highlights.

However, guests can equally just sit back and relax, with the obvious place to do this - as the hotel's name suggests - the spa with its bank of both indoor and outdoor treatment rooms.

Unusually for a hotel in manicured Nusa Dua, none of the Melia's 495 rooms and suites has a view over the ocean. Instead, echoing the Balinese ethos of venerating the land rather than the sea, the hotel's prime lookout is over the luxuriant grounds and their free-range population of tame squirrels. This is essentially a family resort - girdled by a 3,000-metre jogging track - although couples may want to tuck themselves away in one of the wireless-connected villas that are surrounded by exceptionally large and shady gardens. There is a mind-boggling array of entertainments laid on each day, backed up by five restaurants and bars, with the thrice-weekly cabaret

Rates from: $
Star rating: ★ ★ ★ ★ ★
Overall rating: 🌙🌙🌙🌙 ½

Ambience:	8.72	Cleanliness:	9.03
Value:	8.36	Facilities:	8.66
Staff:	8.78	Restaurants:	8.28
Location:	8.56	Families:	8.70

Mulia Senayan

Jl Asia Afrika, Senayan, Jakarta 10270, Indonesia
T: +62 21 574 7777 **F:** +62 21 574 7888
www.HotelClub.com/Hotels/Mulia_Senayan_Hotel_Jakarta

which serves up innovative Indonesian fusion as well as Thai steamboats. What saves the Mulia from being yet another multi-storey bed-and-board monster is its extensive collection of sculptures, paintings, ceramics and glass art pieces, and an exceptionally well-attuned and helpful staff.

For fans of hotels that are big, bold and well appointed, first stop should be the Mulia Senayan. Opened in 1997 for the Southeast Asian Games, it is slightly removed from central Jakarta, and counts an inventory of 1,008 rooms, each of which is at least 48 square metres. The suites come with their own "mini-spa" - a shower capsule that combines a sauna, water massage and background music. The ballroom can pack in 4,000 people without too much of a push, and there are seven restaurants and bars, including the Samudra Suki,

Rates from: $$
Star rating: ★ ★ ★ ★ ★
Overall rating: 🌙🌙🌙🌙 ½

Ambience:	8.94	Cleanliness:	8.95
Value:	7.86	Facilities:	8.66
Staff:	8.77	Restaurants:	8.82
Location:	8.23	Families:	8.49

Novotel Coralia Benoa

Jl Pratama, Nusa Dua 80361, Bali, Indonesia
T: +62 361 772 239 **F:** +62 361 772 237
www.HotelClub.com/Hotels/Novotel_Coralia_Benoa_Bali

Standing towards the end of the Nusa Dua peninsula and bordering the fishing village of Tanjung Benoa, the Novotel has it just right. It is neither too big, nor too small. It is Balinese in decor and style, yet with all the necessary international accents. It is a gorgeous hideaway hangout but also fabulously family friendly.

Although the property is split by the main road, this really keeps the hotel to scale and makes it feel as if it is part of the community. The lobby maintains an environmentally amicable theme, being built mainly of wood, but with a bright blue background to the reception desk that makes it look like a fish tank. The complement of 187 rooms -

with subtle coconut-wood interiors - all have a private balcony or a small garden. Better still, the dozen set back thatched bungalows ranged along the pretty beach comprise lofty ceilings, dual basins and an inspirational outdoor tub that is large enough for a couple to lie side by side. And dozens of quaint fishing boats are drawn up on the sand right alongside jet-skis, dinghies and other watersports accessories.

Mediterranean-style lunch or dinner on the beach at Coco's is probably the most idyllic dining location, metres away from the sea

or the combined jacuzzi and pool. A second pool - Nirwana - lies on the other side of the road among the "villages", as the bulk of the Novotel's accommodation is called. Sunbathers are usually out here shortly after breakfast, and Nirwana's attractions continue well into the early hours, when it is not unknown for revellers to launch into an impromptu party. As well as offering tennis and other sports, the Novotel also runs a full-day entertainment programme, with indoor alternatives just in case it happens to be raining. Add to this a basic health spa and the Dolfi Kids' Club and it is clear the resort offers something for everyone.

Rates from: $
Star rating: ★ ★ ★ ★
Overall rating: ◔ ◔ ◔ ◔ ½

Ambience:	9.26	Cleanliness:	8.95
Value:	8.85	Facilities:	8.52
Staff:	8.97	Restaurants:	8.54
Location:	8.26	Families:	9.24

Novotel Coralia Lombok

Mandalika Resort, Pantai Putri Nyale, Lombok 83001, Indonesia
T: +62 370 653 333 **F:** +62 370 653 555
www.HotelClub.com/Hotels/Novotel_Coralia_Resort_Lombok

The island of Lombok, a short boat ride from Bali, remains happily secluded and underdeveloped. The Novotel - marooned towards the south of the island - is a good hour's drive from the capital Mataram. With virtually nothing in the surrounding areas other than quiet backpacking digs and simple rural villages, the main reason to head so far out is the amazing powdery white sands of Kuta Beach.

The resort itself is a superb shoreline collection of 100 bungalows and rooms built in the style of a traditional Sasak village. A cosy rustic feel is brought out by plenty of timber and locally inspired thatched roofs. Huge wooden rooms are great value, especially the cabanas. Facilities are perfectly adequate and include a simple spa, three swimming pools and a host of water sports. The two restaurants are fair, which is just as well given the isolated location. A beautiful setting, but best suited to more adventurous travellers.

Rates from: $
Star rating: ★ ★ ★ ★
Overall rating: ♙ ♙ ♙ ♙ ½

Ambience:	9.36	Cleanliness:	9.00
Value:	8.86	Facilities:	8.50
Staff:	8.93	Restaurants:	8.46
Location:	8.57	Families:	8.85

Nusa Dua Beach Hotel & Spa

Kawasan Pariwisata, Lot North 4, Nusa Dua, Bali, Indoonesia
T: +62 361 771 210 **F:** +62 361 771 229
www.HotelClub.com/Hotels/Nusa_Dua_Beach_Hotel_and_Spa_Bali

The Nusa Dua went the whole hog when it came to incorporating Balinese architecture, with practically every available surface carved and decorated. And for months after its opening in 1983 artisans came back to the hotel to show off their handiwork to friends and relations, to the minor bemusement of staff and guests.

A great deal of that pride and homespun civility lives on in the 381 rooms, from the three-bedroomed Residence complete with private pool, through the Palace Club rooms with private club lounge, to the more basic family and superior category. Each room incorporates the rich textures of Bali, from batik textiles to ornate panelled walls. The hotel has been given a thorough makeover in recent years, and to the extensive facilities and nine restaurants and bars, a deluxe spa has been added whose many accoutrements include a 25-metre lap pool that even broadcasts music under water.

Rates from: $
Star rating: ★ ★ ★ ★ ★
Overall rating: ♙ ♙ ♙ ♙ ½

Ambience:	9.26	Cleanliness:	8.93
Value:	8.47	Facilities:	8.74
Staff:	9.00	Restaurants:	8.69
Location:	8.68	Families:	8.84

Oberoi Bali

Seminyak Beach, Jl Laksmana, Bali, Indonesia
T: +62 361 730 361 **F**: +62 361 730 791
www.HotelClub.com/Hotels/The_Oberoi_Bali_Hotel

While many hotels in Bali nod towards the island's spiritual side, it really comes to the fore at the Oberoi. The resort fronts one of the holiest beaches on the western coast of the island, where every morning villagers walk on to the sand to lay offerings to placate the gods. Worshippers have flocked to the nearby temple of Pura Petitenget for the past 600 years. The trees in the Oberoi's six hectares of tropical gardens are believed to have a soothing effect on spiritual well-being. And the lotus pond at the resort's main entrance is dedicated to Dewi Laut, goddess of the sea, to whom staff pray before starting work. Little wonder, then, that the whole of the Oberoi is infused with an aura of peace and beauty.

Built almost 30 years ago as a private club (and only later converted to a resort), it retains a palpable feeling of exclusivity, from the 15 villas whose coral stone-walled courtyards (most with a private swimming pool) ensure absolute privacy to the 60 Lanai cottages - with their teak beds, softly toned furnishings and marble floors - which are set in clusters of four around a central lily pond.

Most days spent here are little short of idyllic, but the perfect evening might encompass stepping out of the beachside pool shortly before dusk, knotting a sarong around your waist and strolling over to the Frangipani Café. Peruse the menu for a while - perhaps some of the superb seafood, or one of the Balinese specialities - let the waiter light the candle on the table, and then sit back. The Frangipani overlooks not just the sea and the 200-metre beachfront but the resort's amphitheatre, and here - to the crash of a gamelan orchestra - dancers weave and swirl in an entrancing performance that is entirely magical. This is pure Bali, in one of the most heavenly locations on the whole island.

Rates from: $$
Star rating: ★ ★ ★ ★ ★
Overall rating: 🌸🌸🌸🌸 ½

Ambience:	9.41	Cleanliness:	9.08
Value:	7.87	Facilities:	8.52
Staff:	9.21	Restaurants:	8.13
Location:	8.97	Families:	7.96

Oberoi Lombok

Medana Beach, Tanjung, Lombok, Indonesia
T: +62 370 638 444 **F:** +62 370 632 496
www.HotelClub.com/Hotels/The_Oberoi_Lombok_Hotel

Even the most cursory inspection will tell you something about the Oberoi Lombok's aspirations. It trumpets itself as the best resort on the island, and architecturally that is unquestionably right. It is visually stunning; a beautiful piece of design that has been thoughtfully put together right down to the last detail. There is a peace and tranquillity to this isolated ten-hectare property, a wonderful serenity overlooking Medana Beach and its surrounding fishing villages and palm groves.

Even if the resort were absolutely full it would be hard to tell, as most guests staying in this exclusive retreat's 20 superb Luxury Villas have barely any reason to step out. Elegant and very spacious, traditional influences are successfully expressed in a contemporary fashion. Local artefacts such as wooden chests and stone statuettes help set the stylish tone and the villa amenities keep you comfortable and entertained. In

most cases their surrounding walls frame a private swimming pool, gardens, dining pavilion, courtyard and pond. The resort's 30 Terrace Pavilion Rooms are not quite in the same class of indulgence, but are still highly generous on space with plenty of soothing wood finishes. Each also has a private garden, a rather tempting sunken bath and modern amenities including video, CD player and, for some reason, a dedicated fax machine.

The resort's breezy lobby looks

out on to an arcing, cone-shaped swimming pool and reflective ornamental ponds leading to the small beach cove from where you can make out the golden beaches of the Gili Islands, 20 minutes' boat ride across the sea. The nearest town of Senggigi is 25 kilometres away and there are few taxis out here, so this means that you are pretty much resort-bound when it comes to meals. Not that this is much of a hardship - with a choice of an informal beachside café, fine dining at the Lumbung restaurant or a buffet and cultural performance at the amphitheatre. And in between breakfast, lunch and dinner there is a wealth of diversions, from activities like water sports and tennis to the far less strenuous pastime of indulging in the spa.

Rates from: $$
Star rating: ★ ★ ★ ★ ★
Overall rating: 👍 👍 👍 👍 ½

Ambience:	9.78	Cleanliness:	9.33
Value:	8.44	Facilities:	9.00
Staff:	9.22	Restaurants:	8.11
Location:	8.56	Families:	7.50

Pita Maha Resort & Spa

Jl Sanggingan, Ubud 80571, Bali, Indonesia
T: +62 361 974 330 **F:** +62 361 974 329
www.HotelClub.com/Hotels/Pita_Maha_A_Tjampuhan_Resort_Spa_Bali

Built less than ten years ago, Pitha Maha ("great shining") looks as if it has been around for centuries, so well do the expertly dressed stone walls and uniform thatching of its 24 villas blend into the hillside above the River Oos. Owned by the local branch of the Balinese royal family, the Pita Maha is a celebration of everything for which Ubud is famed. Perch by the edge of the restaurant and you look straight down onto the infinity pool, which is fed by a natural spring. Wander the resort's pathways and frog statues clad in *kamang saput* saris strike a humorous pose by every doorway. Despite the hotel's name, the spa - a villa at the lowest point of the property - can only host two guests at a time. But most of the villas have their own pool so you can do a bit of DIY spa-ing without it costing you a penny.

Rates from: $$$
Star rating: ★ ★ ★ ★ ★
Overall rating: ♙ ♙ ♙ ♙ ½

Ambience:	9.47	Cleanliness:	8.79
Value:	8.32	Facilities:	8.02
Staff:	9.05	Restaurants:	7.89
Location:	9.00	Families:	8.50

Poppies Bali

Gang Poppies 1/19, Jl Legian, Kuta 80361, Bali, Indonesia
T: +62 361 751 059 **F:** +62 361 752 364
www.HotelClub.com/Hotels/Poppies_Hotel_Bali

It is of course futile to speculate what Kuta might look like if development had followed the pattern so artfully set out by Poppies. The story is simple enough - late 1970s, trio of vacationing Americans, Balinese girl already running her own restaurant, some simple cottages get built, add some landscaping and a Kuta sunset or two and hey presto. Poppies excels when it comes to landscaping - the cottages are set fairly close together, and while comfortable are not really that spacious. But everything within is laid out precisely as you might want. Winding pathways draped with vegetation give the impression that the site is much larger than it really is. Sooner or later, everybody seems to find their way to the pool and its adjacent sun deck. You can eat at the pool bar, but most people choose to step across the lane to Poppies restaurant, which serves a happy blend of the best of Indonesian and international. Which just about sums up Poppies itself.

Rates from: $
Star rating: ★ ★ ★
Overall rating: ♙ ♙ ♙ ♙ ½

Ambience:	9.55	Cleanliness:	8.60
Value:	8.55	Facilities:	8.37
Staff:	8.85	Restaurants:	8.56
Location:	8.55	Families:	8.44

Ritz-Carlton Bali

Jl Karang Mas, Sejahtera, Jimbaran 80364, Bali, Indonesia
T: +62 361 702 222 **F**: +62 361 702 455
www.HotelClub.com/Hotels/The_Ritz_Carlton_Hotel_Bali

It may seem odd to start with Kubu Beach, but there is a very good reason for doing so. Several hundred winding steps down a steep cliff lead to rolling breakers and a strip of sand that at first sight appears deserted. But discreetly located next to a placid lagoon at the rear of the beach stands the Ritz-Carlton's tented bar, with loungers, umbrellas and snacks. A few Balinese might be fishing off the rocks, but chances are you will have this place to yourself for much of the day.

Kubu's serendipity is reflected throughout the rest of the resort perched on a bluff in Jimbaran. From the lobby you look straight down across the infinity pool and out to the Indian Ocean. Beneath the pool, tropical fish swarm in the 42,000-litre saltwater aquarium. And all around the gardens and extensive spa facilities are thick with bougainvillea, monkey pod, banyan breadfruit and frangipani trees.

The resort's 375 rooms, villas and suites are heavily influenced by their surroundings, with alang-alang thatched and tile roofing, limestone carvings and Indonesian art and antiques. Slate, wood and marble floors are used throughout the public areas, guestrooms and even the 595-square-metre ballroom.

Of the resort's half-dozen wining and dining options, which include the outdoor seating pavilions of Padi that appear to float in a lily pond, and the Langit Theatre with its dinner dance performances, the most impressive is the Kisik Bar and Grill. This sand-floored restaurant and bar has been carved out of the cliff, and serves its signature dish of freshly grilled seafood on banana leaves. Savvy diners book days in advance to get the table closest to the ocean, so they can eat under the stars to the sound of the surf crashing on the rocks below.

Even if you're not staying here, try to wangle an appointment at the palatial spa, overlooking the Indian Ocean and with a 650-square-metre Aquatonic pool and some of the most amazing Balinese treatments on the island.

Rates from: $$
Star rating: ★ ★ ★ ★ ★
Overall rating: 🌙🌙🌙🌙 ½

Ambience:	9.32	Cleanliness:	9.17
Value:	8.26	Facilities:	8.77
Staff:	9.22	Restaurants:	8.73
Location:	8.51	Families:	8.73

Santika Beach Bali

Jl Kartika Plaza, Tuban, Bali, Indonesia
T: +62 361 751 267 **F**: +62 361 761 889
www.HotelClub.com/Hotels/Santika_Beach_Hotel_Bali

The Santika is an unusual hotel, with an odd conglomeration of 171 rooms, bungalows and suites that have been renovated several times since the property first opened in 1986. They can seem a little dark, almost cavernous, but are relieved by the lovely grounds which are bedecked with mature frangipani trees and gorgeous bunches of bougainvillea. Three pools keep things fresh, and the seaside restaurant is an ideal venue for starting the day, taking a break half way through, or rounding things off after sunset. It's no secret that a substantial proportion of the clientele checks in for months at a time, forming their own community within the hotel, chatting with the staff on first-name terms and generally as happy as sandboys and girls. Possibly one of the best recommendations (and revenue earners) any hotel could wish for. The string of 11 villa-like suites, which is set away from the main property and therefore semi-independent, rounds out the accommodation here.

Rates from: $
Star rating: ★ ★ ★ ★
Overall rating: ♦♦♦♦ ½

Ambience:	8.97	Cleanliness:	9.13
Value:	8.30	Facilities:	8.21
Staff:	9.03	Restaurants:	8.28
Location:	8.77	Families:	8.60

Shangri-La Hotel Jakarta

Kota BNI, Jl Jend Sudirman Kav 1, Jakarta 10220, Indonesia
T: +62 21 570 7440 **F**: +62 21 570 3530
www.HotelClub.com/Hotels/ShangriLa_Hotel_Jakarta

Jakarta can be a handful even for experienced visitors, so it is a relief to pitch up at the Shang. Although the hotel suffered an all-out strike a couple of years ago it is now back on form, a true city five-star setting high standards in every department.

Located centrally in the Golden Triangle at Kota BNI, it is bang in the middle of the business district and minutes from the World Trade Centre on Jalan Sudirman. Its 32 floors hold 668 first-class rooms and suites and the facilities match their refined mood. The restaurants are excellent in both ambience and flavours offering Chinese to quality French cuisine, international to teppanyaki Japanese, and a swish coffee shop that opened for business in 2004. The basement bar BATS is a lively part of Jakarta's nightlife, especially at weekends. With a surprisingly large outdoor pool and fully equipped health spa, the Shangri-La attracts business travellers and Jakarta residents alike.

Rates from: $$
Star rating: ★ ★ ★ ★ ★
Overall rating: ♦♦♦♦ ½

Ambience:	8.71	Cleanliness:	8.77
Value:	8.12	Facilities:	8.59
Staff:	8.84	Restaurants:	8.79
Location:	8.02	Families:	8.44

Shangri-La Hotel Surabaya

Jl Mayjen Sungkono 120, Surabaya 60256, Indonesia
T: +62 31 566 1550 **F:** +62 31 566 1570
www.HotelClub.com/Hotels/ShangriLa_Hotel_Surabaya

The Shangri-La is one of the best hotels in Indonesia's second city, and reinforced its position by opening a new spa in 2005. Its 389 rooms and suites are superbly equipped with every comfort one could reasonably hope for in a bustling metropolis. For business travellers the location is handy, being only ten minutes from the business district, close to the harbour and two golf courses. A competent business centre is accompanied by a full spread of meeting and banquet rooms, the largest of which holds up to 2,500 people. The hotel's well-appointed interior is smart yet subdued with the luxury decor typical of this chain. Rooms follow the theme and have little Javanese touches, and the hotel puts forward a truly international restaurant choice - local, Tex-Mex, Italian, Chinese and Japanese. Good leisure options and a slightly off-centre location help bring a more relaxed mood to this well-packaged property.

Rates from: $
Star rating: ★ ★ ★ ★ ★
Overall rating: ♎♎♎♎ ½

Ambience:	9.14	Cleanliness:	9.57
Value:	7.57	Facilities:	8.85
Staff:	9.14	Restaurants:	8.29
Location:	8.43	Families:	8.50

Sheraton Bandung Hotel & Towers

Jl Ir H Juanda 390, Bandung 40135, West Java, Indonesia
T: +62 22 250 0303 **F:** +62 22 250 0301
www.HotelClub.com/Hotels/Sheraton_Bandung_Hotel_and_Towers

Bandung is a picturesque but slightly faded garden city, set about with Art Deco buildings laid out by Dutch colonisers in the 1930s. Their plans to make it the new capital never came to fruition, and today Bandung largely acts as the prime getaway from the turmoil of Jakarta, more than two hours' drive away. The Sheraton is well placed as a resort - set six kilometres out of the town centre near the 18-hole Dago Endah golf course. It is not over-large, with only 152 rooms and suites, each with a private balcony or patio, kitchettes, a jacuzzi in the bathroom and masseurs on call or available in the spa. There are two outdoor pools (one for kids), Chinese, Indonesian and Italian restaurants, and the Samsara Lounge for live entertainment. The Sheraton is an excellent antidote to the hurly-burly of Jakarta, as well as a good base for exploring the rest of west Java.

Rates from: $
Star rating: ★ ★ ★ ★ ★
Overall rating: ♎♎♎♎ ½

Ambience:	8.89	Cleanliness:	8.33
Value:	8.89	Facilities:	8.46
Staff:	9.67	Restaurants:	8.00
Location:	7.78	Families:	9.00

Sheraton Laguna Nusa Dua

Kawasan BTDC Lot 2, Nusa Dua 80363, Bali, Indonesia
T: +62 361 771 327 **F:** +62 361 771 326
www.HotelClub.com/Hotels/Sheraton_Laguna_Nusa_Dua_Bali

The Sheraton is utterly Nusa Dua. The area was specifically designed as a tourist resort - a cluster of tailor-made, manicured, spick-and-span hotels enclosed in their own beachfront compounds. And at the very core is the Sheraton Laguna.

The U-shaped hotel is pointed towards the beach and built around a 5,000-square-metre series of swimmable lagoons. To take full advantage of the aquatic design, go for one of the 48 sea-level rooms. First thing in the morning you can just step on to the balcony and down the steps into the water, and breaststroke your way across to Café Lagoon for breakfast.

Naturally, all the Sheraton's 270 rooms and suites are eminently habitable, all the more so as they are distinguished by a butler who escorts you to the door on arrival and remains on call 24 hours a day. A pressing service is also at guests' disposal and the resort's chefs wheel out a complimentary afternoon tea in the lobby lounge as a matter of course. As well as scones and cakes, the Sheraton also does a fine line in fine dining, producing silver service to piano accompaniment at Mayang Sari, which is also in earshot of the resort's lovely waterfall. Beachside meals at the Ocean Terrace are rather more relaxed, and the Sapphire Bar by the lagoon comes with an aquatic touch.

The acme of the Sheraton's hospitality lies in the spa, where gym and hydrotherapy treatments are available for a nominal fee, or guests can choose to indulge in something more exotic like a Thalgo body gommage or micronised marine algae body wrap.

The Sheraton is a popular choice for families, but also for executives, who occasionally may be able to tear themselves away from the nearby 18-hole championship Bali Golf & Country Club to explore the delights of the International Convention Centre, which stands next to the hotel.

Rates from: $$
Star rating: ★ ★ ★ ★ ★
Overall rating: ♤ ♤ ♤ ♤ ½

Ambience:	9.07	Cleanliness:	8.94
Value:	8.44	Facilities:	8.62
Staff:	8.96	Restaurants:	8.35
Location:	8.75	Families:	8.78

Sheraton Senggigi Beach Resort

Jl Raya Senggigi Km 8, Senggigi, Mataram, Lombok, Indonesia
T:+62 370 693 333 **F:** +62 370 693 241
www.HotelClub.com/Hotels/Sheraton_Senggigi_Lombok

It is not overstating the case to say the Sheraton is the star attraction of lazy Senggigi Beach. Away from Bali, Indonesia's hotel standards can plunge dramatically, but the Sheraton is a true international-class resort. The wings are low-rise with all 154 rooms looking out over the Lombok Straits. Each features a balcony while the ground floor terrace rooms have patios that spill out into tropical gardens. With deep brown teak trimmings, the blinds and shutters contrast with the lighter interior shades and the colourful tropical views outside. The facilities are modern and luxurious, including the Laguna Beach Spa and a full selection of water sports. The food from the three restaurants matches the five-star ambience, but perhaps the option of private dining on one of several beaches would be the highlight for many. The pool gets singled out for special praise - stunningly designed and creative it is exactly what you want when on holiday, and is manned by the most courteous of staff.

Rates from: $$
Star rating: ★ ★ ★ ★ ★
Overall rating: 🦢🦢🦢🦢 ½

Ambience:	9.41	Cleanliness:	9.32
Value:	8.09	Facilities:	8.52
Staff:	9.05	Restaurants:	8.57
Location:	8.68	Families:	9.36

Tugu Bali

Canggu Beach, Bali 80361, Indonesia
T: +62 361 731 701 **F:** +62 361 731 704
www.HotelClub.com/Hotels/Tugu_Hotel_Bali

The Tugu is a remarkable hotel, practically unique in Asia and the result of one visionary individual's passion for Indonesia's heritage. Disenchanted with his medical studies, Anhar Setjadibrata turned to the law and from there to the hospitality industry which he was only too delighted to combine with his hobby of collecting antiques. Described as a "museum boutique" the Tugu (opened in 1997, but parts of which are centuries old) occupies a hushed corner of Canggu, near Tanah Lot, with its own little-used beach and rice fields for neighbours. Some 22 suites, no two of which are alike, are scattered around the property, whose focus is a magnificent lobby which is dominated by a 4.9-metre Garuda, the mythical transport for Lord Vishnu, which was carved from a single tree. Nothing is remotely casual about this entrancing hotel, whose every aspect is redolent of history and purpose. That said, there is no formal dining room as such, with guests encouraged to eat wherever, whatever and whenever they feel so inclined, be it a grand

Rijsteffel in the memorial room to the Balinese martyrs of the 1900s or a Peranakan dinner in a 300-year-old Kang Xi Buddhist temple (that had been scheduled for demolition, but which was saved at the last minute by Mr Setjadibrata).

The suites are a joy - intimate, characterful and defiantly sexy; two in particular stand out - the Walter Spies Pavilion, which was built in tribute to the renowned German painter for his great contribution to Balinese art, and Puri Le Mayeur, which is dedicated to the Belgian painter Jean and the beautiful Legong dancer Ni Polok, photographs of whose gorgeous undraped curves adorn the walls.

With imaginative simplicity as the watchword here, the Waroeng Djamoe Spa incorporates elixirs and potions made from plants and flowers grown in its own garden. And anyone who thinks this hotel might be a bit snooty need only pop into the Waroeng Tugu, a simple hut with rustic benches serving traditional Indonesian food - consumed using only your fingers, of course.

Rates from: $$$
Star rating: ★ ★ ★ ★ ★
Overall rating: ♦♦♦♦♦

Ambience:	9.44	Cleanliness:	9.68
Value:	8.88	Facilities:	8.48
Staff:	9.60	Restaurants:	8.88
Location:	8.72	Families:	9.33

Uma Ubud

Jl Raya Sanggingan Banjar Lungsiakan, Ubud 80571, Bali, Indonesia
T: +62 361 972 448 **F:** +62 361 972 449
www.HotelClub.com/Hotels/Uma_Ubud_Hotel_Bali

It is of course people rather than anything else who make a great hotel, and Uma Ubud is a case in point. Owned by the legendary Singaporean tycooness Christina Ong, Uma burst into life on the footprint of an old and rather tired resort overlooking the Tjampuhan valley. The Uma's 29 rooms and suites were designed by the Japanese architect Koichiro Ikebuchi. Australian chef Chris Miller champions the kitchen, Balinese Iga Nilawati is spa queen, and overseeing the whole enterprise is global villager and general manager Harry Apostolides. All are united with a sparkling personality and charm that could only belong to a really exclusive resort like this.

No matter whether you are staying in a terrace or garden room, or one of the five suites, the thrill of showering beneath the sky sandwiched between jet black walls can rarely be equalled. Likewise sitting in a statuesque tub swathed in a mosquito net. The decoration in the rooms is kept to a bare minimum, with occasional walks on the wild side, but otherwise it is all plain white woods, high-tech gadgetry, and thought-provoking ponds and gardens.

The Uma's bar, which is capped by a yoga room, looks out over the rectangular pool, and a nearby stream tumbles down past the restaurant. Sit here in the mornings when the sun is coming up and the setting could hardly be more Balinese. A few feet below, the spa - and the Japanese design elements come to the fore here - has its own special touch of Zen. A meditation pavilion marks the limit of the resort, and from here you can gaze down onto the rushing River Oos and watch as village women make stately progress up and down the path with burdens balanced delicately on their heads.

A few steps outside the resort leads to a host of galleries, some charismatic restaurants and bars and the broad green rice paddies for which Ubud is renowned. Step back inside and like Alice through the looking glass you enter the alternative world of Uma Ubud.

Rates from: $$
Star rating: ★ ★ ★ ★ ★
Overall rating: Editor's Pick

Ambience:	n/a	Cleanliness:	n/a
Value:	n/a	Facilities:	n/a
Staff:	n/a	Restaurants:	n/a
Location:	n/a	Families:	n/a

Watergarden Hotel

l Raya Candidasa, Karangasem 80851, Bali, Indonesia
T: +62 363 41 540   **F**: +62 363 41 164
www.HotelClub.com/Hotels/Watergarden_Hotel_Bali

Smaller hotels are starting to categorise themselves nowadays, and Watergarden falls neatly into the "romantic boutique" class. Here are a dozen quaint thatched cottages, streams and mini waterfalls and a luxuriant pool, all overseen by the most revered of Bali's volcanoes, Mount Agung.

The Watergarden - which was bought by a British couple in 2004 who have since put a substantial amount of time and effort into its renovation - marks a hopeful renaissance for Candidasa, an area happily removed from more mainstream vacation Bali. Sheer vandalism saw the town's lovely coral reef ground down for building materials in the 1970s and 80s, and the subsequent disappearance of its beach. A system of breakwaters has halted the environmental destruction, and Candi is now enjoying a second lease of life. As indeed is the Watergarden. One of its most enjoyable features is the private balcony attached to each cottage, with views over the nearby lily ponds whose resident Koi fish are incredibly tame. The gardens include a sawah, or miniature rice field, an emblem of Bali's natural bounty, which is echoed in the resort's cool, open-air restaurant. This too has undergone a determined makeover, moving upmarket from a rather pedestrian Mexican to a fresh and imaginative café that includes European and Asian dishes as well as vegetarian specialities and some exceptionally toothsome desserts.

Naturally the Watergarden is ideally placed for exploring the surrounding area, whether it's to skim out to sea in a glass-bottomed boat, taking a step back in time to the pre-Hindu weaving village of Tenganan, roaming the magnificent palace at Tirtha Gangga (and itself an inspiration for Watergarden) or visiting the bat cave at Goa Lawah. A good couple of hours drive from the international airport, Candi thankfully lies beyond the reach of the hordes that flock to the beaches and entertainment areas closer to the capital.

Rates from: $
Star rating: ★ ★
Overall rating: Editor's Pick

Ambience:	n/a	Cleanliness:	n/a
Value:	n/a	Facilities:	n/a
Staff:	n/a	Restaurants:	n/a
Location:	n/a	Families:	n/a

JAPAN

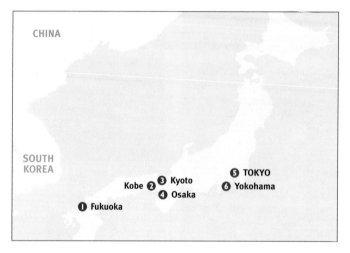

What is the quintessential Japanese hotel? One of the gargantuan world-class five-stars that dot Tokyo and other major cities, a traditional ryokan with sliding paper doors, futons and tatami mats, or one of the multi-themed, psychedelic love shacks that get rented out by the hour? Japan's gallimaufry of accommodation provides some clue to the national character. It is a country of extremes and contradictions, one that is as entranced as much by the art of bonsai as by Hello Kitty, as entertained by Disneyland as it is by Noh plays, one that can celebrate the marine beauty of Matsushima Bay (officially dubbed one of the "Three Great Sights" of Japan) while allowing a power station to be built right next to it.

Japan, formerly known for an economic vigour that spread its cars, stereos and computers around the world, now faces a variety of problems ranging from deflation to bad-debt burdens. How it tackles these will greatly shape its role both in Asia - where it remains the

most successful industrial economy - and the rest of the world. Japan is made up of some 1,000 islands, strung out in a 3,000-kilometre chain from the icy border with Russia to the tropical climes of Okinawa. The Shinkansen, or Bullet Train, system is one of the miracles of Japan, linking much of the country at speeds of up to 300 kilometres per hour and making punctuality a rule rather than an exception. Quite apart from anything else, the Shinkansen means that visitors can take in an enormous amount of Japan in the matter of a few days. Tokyo remains

one of the most vibrant cities in Asia, contrasting starkly with Kyoto, whose temples, shrines and gardens mark the cultural heart of Japan. Many venture no further than these two centres, but further west the drab town of Himeji is crowned by a five-century-old castle that is one of a handful in

the country to have survived in its original (non-concrete) form. Little remained of Hiroshima after the first atomic bomb was detonated there in 1945, and its Peace Park stands in mute testament to the horrors of war and the folly of militarism.

From the sublime to the ridiculous: theme parks abound in Japan, celebrating all manner of icons from Disney to the more recondite cartoon characters. Away from the cities, there are excellent opportunities for hiking in the mountains, especially in Daisetsuzan National Park on Hokkaido, and the skiing is good even if it is almost as exorbitantly priced the golf. Down south, there are jungle walks, river kayaking and scuba diving on the remote island of Iriomote Jima. Japan's geological make-up has both a good and a bad side - the ever-present danger of earthquake, but also myriad onsen, or hot springs, where you can immerse yourself and rejuvenate after a tiring day.

Hotels in Japan tend to be pricier than in the rest of Asia, in some cases with some reason, but many mid-range hotels are run-

down with shabby service and facilities. But there is an enormous range of choice, from the infamous "capsule" hotels to glittering properties like the Grand and Park Hyatts in Tokyo, which are soon to be joined by other international chains like Ritz-Carlton and Mandarin Oriental. In between there is the charm of ryokan and the rather less traditional minshuku, which are more like bed and breakfasts, while the "hoteru abec" of Love Hotel Hill in Tokyo's Shibuya district are definitely worth a gander, even if you are not in the mood!

Less worldly Japanese sometimes tell visitors at length and with great pride that their country experiences four seasons, and they are indeed quite distinct. Spring (March to May) brings clear skies and cherry blossoms, summer can be sweatily uncomfortable, autumn leaves between September and November turn rural Japan into its most picturesque, while the winter months can be distinctly cold, especially in the northern islands. But 20 degrees south, at the other end of the archipelago, even

December is reasonably balmy.

New Year and Golden Week (April 27 to May 6) are best avoided by visitors as much of Japan is on the move at these times, filling hotels, trains and planes to the max. Other festivals - such as Kyoto's Gion Matsuri parade of exotic floats every July, or the slightly later O Bon when lanterns are floated on water and rivers all over the country - are well worth seeing.

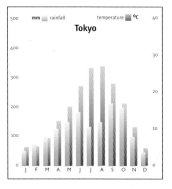

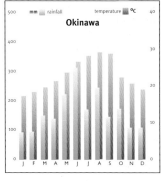

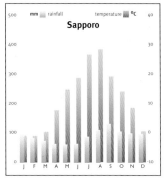

ANA Hotel Tokyo

1-12-33 Akasaka, Minato-ku, Tokyo 107-0052, Japan
T: +81 3 3505 1111 **F**: +81 3 3505 1155
www.HotelClub.com/Hotels/ANA_Hotel_Tokyo

The ANA - which was completely renovated between 2001 and 2004 - is a highly commendable hotel with 873 rooms spread over 37 storeys. All the well-appointed rooms look out onto Tokyo's skyscrapers, the Imperial Palace or Mount Fuji, and are equipped with high-speed Internet, voice mail, satellite TV and some have printers with fax features. Extras like a humidifier, trouser press or VCR are available on loan. The food and beverage side is well covered with a dozen outlets, ranging from traditional meals at Teppanyaki Akasaka to the flavours, textures and aromas of genuine European fare at Italo-Provence.

Recreational facilities are split firmly between His and Hers. The Esthetic Salon lays on fairly heftily priced massages and facials for ladies, while the Sauna (where masseurs are also available) is for men only. However, both sexes are free to use the summer-only outdoor pools, one of which is especially for children.

Rates from: $$$
Star rating: ★ ★ ★ ★ ★
Overall rating: ♕ ♕ ♕ ♕ ♕ ½

Ambience:	8.52	Cleanliness:	9.36
Value:	7.57	Facilities:	8.38
Staff:	9.12	Restaurants:	8.63
Location:	8.95	Families:	8.00

Century Hyatt Tokyo

2-7-2 Nishi-Shinjuku, Shinjuku-ku, Tokyo 160-0023, Japan
T: +81 3 3348 1234 **F**: +81 3 3344 5575
www.HotelClub.com/Hotels/Century_Hyatt_Hotel_Tokyo

Shinjuku is generally reckoned to be one of the most "happening" parts of the Japanese capital, a thriving conglomeration of business, shopping, culture and entertainment that is mirrored in the Century Hyatt, now into its second quarter-century. It is a substantial hotel, packing 744 rooms and suites, a score of banqueting halls, a healthy selection of bars and restaurants, a very stylish top-floor swimming pool and a tea-ceremony room into its two solid, box-like towers. Bland from without, inside the hotel is attractively and warmly decorated. The suites are imaginatively styled with varying themes, whether Japanese-style with futons or situated at a corner with exceptional views over the city. Dining at Chenonceaux may be physically far removed from the celebrated riverside château of the same name, but the flavours are totally authentic. The Rhapsody bar provides marvellous vistas, or you can simply ride the elevator to the 28th floor and take a dip in the glass-roofed Sky Pool with its uninterrupted prospect of the heavens. A five-year renovation plan for the hotel is scheduled to end in 2009.

Rates from: $$
Star rating: ★ ★ ★ ★ ★
Overall rating: ♕ ♕ ♕ ♕

Ambience:	8.42	Cleanliness:	9.13
Value:	8.00	Facilities:	8.18
Staff:	8.87	Restaurants:	8.20
Location:	8.07	Families:	8.22

Four Seasons Hotel Tokyo at Chinzan-so

2-10-8 Sekiguchi, Bunkyo-ku, Tokyo 112-8667, Japan
T: +81 3 3943 2222 **F**: +81 3 3943 2300
www.HotelClub.com/Hotels/Four_Seasons_Chinzanso

One of a pair of Four Seasons properties in Tokyo, Chinzan-so is set in a seven-hectare historic Japanese-style garden that provides a healthy and scenic cordon sanitaire from the surrounding city. The hotel is primarily established as an excellent operations base for the executive traveller, while the sister property at Marunouchi tends toward the more pecunious form of leisure traveller and upmarket marriages. Chinzan-so's 232 rooms and 51 suites are divided into a slightly complex array of 17 different categories - from the spacious 45-square-metre Superior Rooms through Conservatory Rooms all the way up to the 280-square-metre Imperial Suite. While size and facilities will vary with the room rate, all the way through the

hotel guests can expect the customary peerless Four Seasons service. The staff are especially adept at configuring the hotel's 2,000-plus square metres of meeting space, covering 15 function rooms and a 100-seater amphitheatre to guests' conference or other needs - with evening cocktail receptions overlooking the garden a speciality.

Gorgeous though the general surrounds are, the Four Seasons stands head, shoulders and taste buds above the rest when it comes to its restaurants. The luckier sort of trencherman (or indeed trencherwoman) might well

contemplate a four-night stay, dining in a different restaurant each evening, first delving into the casual French Seasons Bistro, then spending several hours overlooking the water garden in Yang Yuan Zhai, where all the dishes are prepared by chefs trained at Beijing's state guesthouse. Day three would be the very Milanese Il Teatro's turn to shine beneath its Venetian glass chandeliers, while Miyuki would provide a classic Japanese finale. In between times weekend breakfasts at Le Jardin are something of a Tokyo tradition, and the Le Marquis bar has a very comfortable and clubby feel to it. Superb for corporate entertaining, these gourmet temples are a delicious personal indulgence too!

Rates from: $$$$$
Star rating: ★★★★★
Overall rating: ♨♨♨♨ ½

Ambience:	9.11	Cleanliness:	9.62
Value:	7.68	Facilities:	8.74
Staff:	9.04	Restaurants:	8.41
Location:	7.79	Families:	8.75

Grand Hyatt Fukuoka

1-2-82 Sumiyoshi Hakata-ku, Fukuoka 812-0018, Japan
T: +81 92 282 1234 **F**: +81 92 282 2817
www.HotelClub.com/Hotels/Grand_Hyatt_Hotel_Fukuoka

Cut across by canals and waterways, Fukuoka is a real delight to explore, as much because - contrary to modern urban layouts in Japan and much of the rest of the world - it does not seem to have taken a dislike to pedestrians, so it's quite easy to get about by Shank's Pony. Added to this is the number of contrasts that a presumably random planning schedule has left on the city centre. The futuristic Canal City is layer upon layer of smart boutiques capped by the enigmatically named outdoor wear and adventure store Vandal. At ground level, a powerful fountain periodically shoots water jets almost as high as the mall's top storey, and a clutch of outdoor cafés and restaurants grants the area a genuine hint of the ambience of a Parisian pavement.

Anchoring the whole complex is the stately Grand Hyatt hotel, beautifully designed with an eye on minimalism that never compromises comfort, and the ideal place to recover over a meal or a drink from a burst of retail therapy, whether in one of its elegant restaurants or in the seclusion of the private roof garden.

There are some 370 rooms, including 14 suites, within the Hyatt. Space comes at a premium anywhere in Japan, but the accommodation here is generous by anyone's standards. A warm, comforting feel is imparted by the wood panelling and soft-tone furnishings, and the bathrooms are indulgent to say the least. There's plenty of room to work and state-of-the-art in-room entertainment on offer includes both movies and music, but make sure you get out at least a couple of times to experience Nadaman, the Japanese restaurant, and the exceptionally popular Bar Fizz.

On related matters, anthropologists may be interested to note that Fukuoka's entertainment district lies only a couple of hundred metres away, however it is pretty much off-limits to monoglot foreigners.

Rates from: $$
Star rating: ★★★★★
Overall rating: 👍👍👍👍

Ambience:	8.61	Cleanliness:	9.00
Value:	7.50	Facilities:	8.76
Staff:	8.56	Restaurants:	8.59
Location:	8.17	Families:	8.36

Grand Hyatt Tokyo

6-10-3 Roppongi, Minato-ku, Tokyo 106-0032, Japan
T: +81 3 4333 1234   **F**: +81 3 4333 8123
www.HotelClub.com/Hotels/Grand_Hyatt_Tokyo

Stand in the rainforest shower of your room in the Grand - and you have to grant that adjective some extra emphasis when you say it - the *Grand* Hyatt, giving yourself a mild rinse down with up-market body scrub, and let your gaze drift outward. Immediately in the foreground stands an adjustable flat-screen TV tuned perhaps to one of myriad satellite channels, right beside the washbasin. Look a little further across the bed (Simmons pocket coil mattress, Frette sheets and pillow cases) and you are presented with a city view out over Roppongi Hills. Obviously,

designer Peter Remedios planned it this way, but the thing is, it just feels so natural.

Indeed, so architecturally faultless is this 389-room property that it is difficult to conceive of a time when the Grand Hyatt was not part of the landscape. It blends seamlessly into a complex that includes designer label retail, one of the funkiest museums in Asia, a technologically superb multi-screen complex, restaurants that scale the uppermost heights of

gourmet-dom, plus - fulfilling the role of "enemy at the gates" and providing a riotous contrast - there's the Roppongi nightlife zone in all its grungy glory just down the road.

It seems invidious to highlight only one aspect of the Grand Hyatt, but it would be folly not to spend some time on the Nagomi Spa, conceived by Takashi Sugimoto of the quintessentially modern Japanese design company Super Potato. Bathing is such an essential part of life in Japan, but Nagomi - with nuances of harmony, well-being, balance and relaxation - has managed to redefine it. The 140-square-metre red granite swimming pool forms the spa's centrepiece, the extravagantly lit jaccuzzi makes for its most daring aspect, and there are also eight private treatment rooms, one with its own granite soaking tub.

Perhaps the Grand Hyatt truly

comes into its own via its ten restaurants and bars, which effortlessly fuse the very best of international and Japanese cuisine. At lunch and dinner times, and indeed at many other times of day, Tokyo's glitterati and gourmets, cognoscenti and CEOs converge here, happy to queue for some minutes as they know the wait will be more than worth it. There are dramatic wood-burning ovens, an original Paul Ching-Bor painting and 3,500 bottles in the cellar at The Oak Door. One room at Maduro is specifically set aside for whisky tasting. Handpicked artisans from around the country contribute ingredients to the sushi menu at Roku Roku. Fiorentina exudes Italian cuisine, aromas and passion. In short, the dining is quite faultless and rarely ceases to amaze.

The Grand Hyatt runs perfectly under the tutelage of hotel veteran Xavier Destribats - born in France, educated in England and Switzerland, and with extensive work experience in Israel and Mexico, he exemplifies the hotel's aura of cosmopolitan sophistication. Few guests come here without finding all their expectations exceeded and eagerly anticipating their next visit.

Footnote: The water distributed in the more exclusive suites in sleek glass cylinders is imported from Norway. Grossly extravagant lily-gilding? More like the hallmark of perfection.

Rates from: $$$$
Star rating: ★ ★ ★ ★ ★
Overall rating: ♦ ♦ ♦ ♦ ½

Ambience:	9.05	Cleanliness:	9.46
Value:	7.91	Facilities:	8.76
Staff:	8.80	Restaurants:	8.59
Location:	8.91	Families:	8.18

Hilton Osaka

1-8-8 Umeda, Kita-ku, Osaka 530-0001, Japan
T: +81 6 6347 7111 **F:** +81 6 6347 7060
www.HotelClub.com/Hotels/Hilton_Osaka

Osaka, as anyone who's ever been there will tell you, means business - the standard greeting here is: "Making much money?" So no surprises then, that the 525-room Hilton, the granddaddy of the city's international hotels and just across the road from the main railway station, means business too.

The 30-square-metre standard rooms - soft blue tones with the windows sporting shoji and fusuma screens - are equipped with everything from speaker phones to bilingual TVs. There is plenty in the way of activities to fill any down-time - a bowling alley for a start - and a pleasant swathe of restaurants and bars that can be earmarked for corporate entertaining. Pop into The Seasons for French haute cuisine, or Genji for the best of Japanese dining. However in both the physical and metaphorical sense the top eatery has to be Windows on the World, the sky lounge, with its celebrated lunch buffet.

Rates from: $$$
Star rating: ★ ★ ★ ★
Overall rating: ⏺⏺⏺⏺ ½

Ambience:	8.80	Cleanliness:	9.47
Value:	7.73	Facilities:	8.49
Staff:	8.90	Restaurants:	8.41
Location:	8.80	Families:	8.39

Hilton Tokyo

6-6-2 Nishi-Shinjuku, Shinjuku-ku, Tokyo 160-0023, Japan
T: +81 3 3344 5111 **F:** +81 3 3342 6094
www.HotelClub.com/Hotels/Hilton_Tokyo

The Hilton has been around in Tokyo for the past four decades, but not always in its present incarnation. This Shinjuku Hilton opened in 1984, with its 38 storeys and 806 rooms enclosed within an unusual S-shaped design. To the outpost of a very American chain are added a number of distinct Japanese touches - so count on digital movies on demand plus shoji screens, voicemail and PC jacks as well as yukata robes and slippers - throughout the hotel. Five floors are dedicated to business travellers, who get a private safe, free high-speed Internet connections and a fax machine as well as their own private - but self-service - lounge.

Above them, a further five executive floors get the additional bonus of a concierge in a rather more luxurious lounge. The amalgam of Asian and international is continued in the Hilton's restaurants, which are uniformly reliable, with Twenty One adding a superior Gallic twist.

Rates from: $$$
Star rating: ★ ★ ★ ★
Overall rating: ⏺⏺⏺⏺

Ambience:	8.30	Cleanliness:	9.21
Value:	7.51	Facilities:	8.37
Staff:	8.99	Restaurants:	8.57
Location:	8.58	Families:	8.44

Imperial Hotel

1-1-1 Uchisaiwai-cho, Chiyoda-ku, Tokyo 100-8558, Japan
T: +81 3 3504 1111 **F:** +81 3 3581 9146
www.HotelClub.com/Hotels/Imperial_Hotel_Tokyo

The story of the Imperial - which over the course of a century has set the benchmark for innovation in concert with deluxe hospitality in Tokyo - mirrors the story of modern-day Japan. The first Imperial was founded in 1890 at the behest of the Emperor. A wooden, Victorian-style hotel was raised next to the royal palace on the same site where the modern Imperial stands today. It was a reassuring pied-à-terre for foreigners, equipped with wood-burning fireplaces, Irish linen and English cutlery, and was the first hotel in the country to serve beef and pork, which Buddhist precepts had traditionally forbidden. In 1923 a spectacular new building designed by Frank Lloyd Wright opened on the very day of one of Tokyo's worst earthquakes. It suffered minimal damage, but was later bombed during the war and by 1967 had to be dismantled. Parts were incorporated into the new building, which threw open its doors in 1970.

Three and a half decades later, the Imperial is embarking on another major make-over, which will see most of the hotel spruced up in the coming years.

Currently divided into a main building and an adjoining tower,

the hotel contains 1,019 rooms, including 64 suites. Firmly aimed at the executive market, all the tastefully decorated rooms embrace complimentary high-speed Internet connections, hands-free phones and a very workable desk. An entire wing is given over to the business centre, which as well as the usual secretarial services and conference rooms also includes a soundproof practice chamber for musicians, a relaxation lounge (for early arrivals and late departures) and even showers.

The 13 restaurants include the

award-winning French cuisine at Les Saisons, and the subtle flavours of Kyoto - season by season - at Isecho, while the ultra-traditional Old Imperial Bar continues to serve up the ambience inspired by Frank Lloyd Wright, as well as some powerful cocktails. The hotel also provides ample opportunity for relaxation at its fully-equipped fitness centre and the heated indoor pool on the 20th floor.

From royal brainchild to high-tech hostelry, the Imperial is as pleasing for its historical antecedents as its current offerings and should continue to go from strength to strength.

Rates from: $$$
Star rating: ★★★★★
Overall rating: ♕♕♕♕ ½

Ambience:	8.99	Cleanliness:	9.41
Value:	7.92	Facilities:	8.42
Staff:	9.23	Restaurants:	8.67
Location:	9.27	Families:	8.44

Keio Plaza Tokyo

2-2-1 Nishi-Shinjuku, Shinjuku-ku, Tokyo 160-8330, Japan
T: +81 3 3344 0111 **F**: +81 3 3345 8269
www.HotelClub.com/Hotels/Keio_Plaza_Hotel_InterContinental_Tokyo

If they ever shoot yet another remake of the classic monster movie *Godzilla*, chances are even it would have a tough job demolishing the Keio Plaza. A true juggernaut of a hotel, it parades a nigh-overwhelming line-up of 1,441 rooms, 29 restaurants and bars and 40 function rooms. What saves it from being a maze is the attention that has been paid to giving it a most welcome and hospitable atmosphere.

All the artwork (exhibits change every two weeks) in the Lobby Gallery is for sale, but guests are welcome just to sit and talk here. Delicate ikebana flower arrangements dot the public areas. And in contrast to the gritty metropolis outside, the rooms - take your pick of executive floor, tatami mats or non-smoking - are all pastel-hued with extra-spacious windows. Perhaps its major draw, though, is its prices - a great value property given its very central Shinjuku location.

Rates from: $$
Star rating: ★★★
Overall rating: ⚜⚜⚜⚜

Ambience:	8.39	Cleanliness:	9.20
Value:	7.70	Facilities:	8.28
Staff:	8.86	Restaurants:	8.33
Location:	9.05	Families:	7.79

Kobe Bay Sheraton Hotel and Towers

2-13 Koyocho-naka, Higashinada-ku, Kobe 658-0032, Japan
T: +81 78 857 7000 **F**: +81 78 857 7001
www.HotelClub.com/Hotels/Kobe_Bay_Sheraton_Hotel_Towers

Pub or the Matsukaze Japanese restaurant. Massage, tennis lessons or simply a laze on the hotel sundeck are a few of the other diversions available. Ten years on from its disastrous earthquake, Kobe is back on its feet again and thriving, as properties like the Sheraton demonstrate very well indeed.

Guests lucky enough to arrive in this part of Kobe by train have only a brief stroll before they gain the Sheraton's doors. Chances are that vacationers will be here to sample Universal Studios, which are only a short shuttle-bus ride away. Having got the location thing down pat, the Sheraton – which is part of an international complex built on reclaimed land - continues with pleasing accommodation and similarly appointed restaurants and bars. The 276 guestrooms enjoy views of Rokko Mountain and out over Osaka Bay, while there's a chance to get stuck in at such diverse outlets as the Arena Sports

Rates from: $$
Star rating: ★★★★
Overall rating: ⚜⚜⚜⚜

Ambience:	8.08	Cleanliness:	9.25
Value:	7.17	Facilities:	8.38
Staff:	8.83	Restaurants:	8.30
Location:	8.92	Families:	8.22

New Otani Tokyo

4-1 Kioi-cho, Chiyoda-ku, Tokyo, 102-8578, Japan
T: +81 3 3265 1111 **F:** +81 3 3221 2619
www.HotelClub.com/Hotels/New_Otani_Hotel_Tokyo

post office, dental and health clinics, an art museum, and a chapel, plus an outdoor pool and a gym with ample space for treading the mill or practising yoga. However, for many the highlight of the New Otani is the wonderful buffet breakfast with a view at Top of the Tower on the 40th floor.

The New Otani is actually over 40 years old, having opened just prior to the Olympic Games in 1964. But the hotel traces its roots back over four centuries, via the exquisitely composed stones, shrubs, ponds, waterfalls and flowers of its celebrated 30,000-square-metre gardens which once belonged to the Samurai warlord Kiyomasa Kato.

Juxtaposed with the adjacent hotel's 1,500 rooms and suites (all with high-speed Internet access) and two dozen restaurants, five bars and 28 banquet and conference rooms, the gardens are a complete contrast. Somewhere in this mini-metropolis there is also a

Rates from: $$$
Star rating: ★ ★ ★ ★
Overall rating: ⚜⚜⚜⚜ ½

Ambience:	8.95	Cleanliness:	9.37
Value:	8.21	Facilities:	8.64
Staff:	8.98	Restaurants:	8.97
Location:	8.98	Families:	8.68

Okura Tokyo

2-10-4 Toranomon, Minato-ku, Tokyo 105-0001, Japan
T: +81 3 3582 0111 **F:** +81 3 3582 3707
www.HotelClub.com/Hotels/Okura_Hotel_Tokyo

South Wing also has a poolside restaurant and a health club. Restaurants and bars are split pretty evenly between eastern and western cuisines in either wing. Focused essentially as a business hotel, the Okura also runs to more than 30 function rooms with the largest able to hold 2,600 people.

Many of the double-winged Okura's 834 guestrooms may be tinged with the 1960s - some greeny-blue upholstery, gilt and white furniture, and the odd item in shocking pink - but in 2005 two floors in the main building were given a total makeover, so the hotel is changing with the times, albeit slowly. Bathrooms are pleasantly marbled

with a deep tub and separate shower, while the views from the upper storeys are especially inspiring at dusk. Choosing which wing you stay in can help cut down on "commuting" times, although the walk along the underpass takes only a few minutes. Both parts of the hotel have shopping arcades, a beauty salon and a pool, but the

Rates from: $$$
Star rating: ★ ★ ★ ★
Overall rating: ⚜⚜⚜⚜ ½

Ambience:	9.03	Cleanliness:	9.46
Value:	8.05	Facilities:	8.37
Staff:	9.21	Restaurants:	8.75
Location:	8.51	Families:	8.62

Park Hyatt Tokyo

3-7-1-2 Nishi-Shinjuku, Shinjuku-ku, Tokyo 163-1055, Japan
T: +81 3 5322 1234 **F:** +81 3 5322 1288
www.HotelClub.com/Hotels/Park_Hyatt_Hotel_Tokyo

If you've seen Sofia Coppola's comedy drama *Lost in Translation*, you will already be enamoured of the Park Hyatt Tokyo. Perched atop the 235-metre 52-storey Shinjuku Park Tower this 14-floor hotel was the first of its brand to open in Asia and remains leader of the pack, besting not only others in the same chain but many kindred properties in the region.

Each of the 178 rooms and suites forms a modernist private residence, tallying hi-tech communications and entertainment options with Egyptian cotton sheets, rare water elm from Hokkaido and original artworks by Yoshitaka Echizenya. Also standard are a luxuriously deep bathtub, separate shower and a walk-in wardrobe. The suites are naturally larger and even better appointed, while the Presidential Suite comes with its own sauna, jacuzzi and formal dining room and library. In fact, dictionaries and encyclopaedia are placed in all the rooms as a matter of course, and they are buttressed by a 2,000-volume library (plus several hundred CDs and laser discs), which is overseen by the concierge.

Similarly impressive is the Hyatt's range of conference and banqueting facilities, which combine sophisticated decor and electronics as both the elegant Ballroom and chandeliered Venetian Room include teleconferencing facilities and video walls.

Four arresting dining outlets at the Hyatt allow guests to put their corporate entertainment allowance to work usefully. However, if there is a single part of the Hyatt that defines its ethos and the particular brand of alchemy conjured up by Japanese architect Kenzo Tange and American interior designer John Morford, it is the Club on the Park, the hotel's two-storey health and fitness sanctuary. Light pours through its 25-metre steel and glass pyramid, 47 floors above the rest of Tokyo, reflecting off the eight-by-20 metre swimming pool. On clear days, a snow-peaked Mount Fuji dominates the horizon like a divinity.

Rates from: $$$$$
Star rating: ★★★★★
Overall rating: 4½

Ambience:	9.19	Cleanliness:	9.51
Value:	7.77	Facilities:	8.77
Staff:	9.09	Restaurants:	8.98
Location:	8.30	Families:	8.11

Prince Akasaka

1-2 Kioi-cho, Chiyoda-ku, Tokyo 102-8585, Japan
T: +81 3 3234 1111   **F**: +81 2 3262 5763
www.HotelClub.com/Hotels/Akasaka_Prince_Hotel_Tokyo

If Japan is a land of contrasts - think kitschy teenage fashion versus the elegance of the kimono - then this particular Prince (not to be confused with others members of this regal hotel family) is a hotel of contrasts.

From a distance you are confronted with a monolith - 761 rooms (including 68 suites) stacked up over 34 floors in a concrete fan designed by the much renowned Kenzo Tange. But step inside and it changes. The outdoor pool is a perfect blue circle, as if it were a resort, not in the middle of a city that inspired Ridley Scott's epic movie *Blade Runner*.

Try Le Trianon, where you dine upon the very reasonable French cuisine beneath glittering chandeliers and powerful Doric columns. So, the Prince is bold without and intimate within, as evidenced by the bedrooms, which have a convenient and homely feel.

Rates from: $$
Star rating: ★ ★ ★
Overall rating: ◊ ◊ ◊ ◊ ½

Ambience:	9.03	Cleanliness:	9.45
Value:	7.67	Facilities:	8.59
Staff:	8.88	Restaurants:	8.50
Location:	8.73	Families:	8.58

Ritz-Carlton Osaka

2-5-25 Umeda, Kita-ku, Osaka 530-0001, Japan
T: +81 6 6343 7000   **F**: +81 6 6343 7001
www.HotelClub.com/Hotels/Ritz_Carlton_Hotel_Osaka

Every year the Ritz-Carlton hosts numerous weddings, with couples in tuxedos and silk gowns plighting their troth in the hotel's chapel or Shinto shrine. They are drawn mainly by the Ritz's intriguing European aura - an anomaly in building-block Osaka - because its 18th-and 19th-century art and antiques, Italian marble, silk wall coverings and large-scale fireplaces are reminiscent of a bygone age of elegance. Fast forward to the 21st century and you have 292 luxuriously fitted rooms, all with marble bathrooms; the suites carry extras like CD players, while there is even a grand piano in the 233-square-metre Ritz-Carlton Suite. Anyone overindulging at the Japanese, Chinese, French or Mediterranean restaurants can take advantage of the free (a rarity in Japanese hotels) gym, with its state-of-the-art workout studio, saunas and indoor and outdoor jacuzzis. Spa services are also available. As the centrepiece of the downtown restaurant, business and shopping zone called Herbis Osaka, the Ritz-Carlton continues to shine.

Rates from: $$$
Star rating: ★ ★ ★ ★ ★
Overall rating: ◊ ◊ ◊ ◊ ½

Ambience:	9.00	Cleanliness:	9.45
Value:	8.03	Facilities:	8.81
Staff:	8.59	Restaurants:	8.57
Location:	8.59	Families:	8.32

Westin Miyako Kyoto

Keage, Sanjo, Higashiyama-ku, Kyoto 605-0052, Japan
T: +81 75 771 7111 **F:** +81 75 751 2490
www.HotelClub.com/Hotels/The_Westin_Miyako_Hotel_Kyoto

Kyoto, with more than 2,000 temples and shrines, a trio of palaces and scores of gardens and museums, is one of the must-sees of Japan - as its 40 million annual visitors might indicate. The more astute of these check into the Westin Miyako, a deluxe 11-storey resort with a history dating back to 1890, on the wooded slopes of Mount Kacho. It commands stunning views over the city and its many treasures.

The Miyako attracted attention right from its early days, as it was the largest hotel in Japan, and soon became known as the place for visitors to stay if they were some sort of bigwig. Apart from the second world war and the years immediately after when it was requisitioned by the Allied Forces, the Miyako welcomed such diverse personages as ballerina Anna Pavlova, explorer Roald Amundsen, the Dalai Lama, Pop Art icon Andy Warhol, Princess Diana, Deng Xiaoping and actress Audrey Hepburn.

The current structure is not exactly boutique, with 502 rooms (including a score of charming rooms in a traditional guesthouse divided into areas named "moon", "snow" and "flower"), nine restaurants - Espoir, the contemporary French restaurant, is especially good, while the Mayfair Tearoom is a particularly charismatic anachronism - and 16 banqueting and conference rooms, but it is extremely comfortable.

Perhaps the Miyako's greatest asset is its circular garden and 800-metre bird-watching trail. A separate "Garden of Philosophy" was designed by the sculptor Bukichi Inoue, with cool clear flowing water from the eastern mountains intended to suggest an aura of stillness. Other recreational opportunities include a sauna, jacuzzi, swimming pools (indoor and out) and tennis courts.

Newcomers to Kyoto will be pleased to take note of the Miyako's downtown office by the station, where they can drop their bags for delivery to their room and so set off sightseeing the moment they arrive.

Rates from: $$$$
Star rating: ★ ★ ★ ★ ★
Overall rating: ♡ ♡ ♡ ♡ ½

Ambience:	8.92	Cleanliness:	9.42
Value:	8.67	Facilities:	8.50
Staff:	9.25	Restaurants:	8.50
Location:	8.33	Families:	8.83

Westin Tokyo

1-4-1 Mita, Meguro, Tokyo 153-8580, Japan
T: +81 3 5423 7000 **F:** +81 3 5423 7600
www.HotelClub.com/Hotels/Westin_Hotel_Tokyo

There are not exactly rolling hectares of greensward at Yebisu Garden Place, but the self-contained community built on an old Sapporo brewery site does offer a respite from the hectic thoroughfares of Tokyo. Capping its museums, cinemas, shopping and dining facilities (plus a 1,700-seat beer hall) is the 22-storey Westin, a deluxe European-style hotel containing 438 rooms and a host of restaurants and other facilities. The rooms are particularly large by Japanese standards - even standard rooms encompass 42 square metres - and the deluxe bathrooms have a separate tub and shower stall. High-speed Internet access is available in all rooms and guests can choose between 1.8-metre-wide king-sized beds, two double beds or three singles. The fitness centre and pool are located in the Club next door, where guests enjoy preferential rates. The combination of location and the excellence of the facilities certainly put this hotel near the top of the shortlist for anyone shopping around for where to stay in Tokyo.

Rates from: $$$$
Star rating: ★ ★ ★ ★ ★
Overall rating: ♭♭♭♭

Ambience:	8.73	Cleanliness:	9.27
Value:	7.65	Facilities:	8.40
Staff:	8.79	Restaurants:	8.28
Location:	8.29	Families:	7.98

Yokohama Grand InterContinental

1-1-1 Minatomirai, Nishi-ku, Yokohama, Kanagawa 220-8522, Japan
T: +81 45 223 2222 **F:** +81 45 221 0650
www.HotelClub.com/Hotels/Grand_Intercontinental_Hotel_Yokohama

Yokohama tends to be overshadowed by its neighbour Tokyo, however here the InterContinental proves it is as good as anything the capital can come up with. Incentive types might want to try a port cruise or a helicopter night flight around the city - both of which can be organised by the hotel's excellent concierge.

Sometimes particular buildings come to symbolise their home city - the Sydney Opera House being a prime example. And so it is with the InterContinental in Yokohama, whose billowing sail-like structure encapsulates all the hope and exuberance of the newly developed Minato Mirai 21 harbourside inner-city area. Impressive from the outside, the hotel continues to notch up points within. Like many Japanese hotels it was built with high revenues in mind - so there are 600 rooms, half a dozen restaurants and two bars, 14 meeting rooms and a 25-strong team of conference professionals.

Rates from: $$
Star rating: ★ ★ ★ ★
Overall rating: ♭♭♭♭

Ambience:	8.75	Cleanliness:	9.25
Value:	7.44	Facilities:	8.22
Staff:	8.56	Restaurants:	8.29
Location:	8.94	Families:	7.91

KOREA (SOUTH)

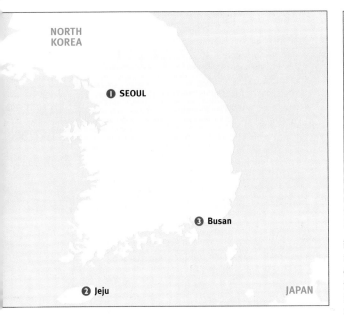

NORTH
KOREA

❶ SEOUL

❸ Busan

❷ Jeju

JAPAN

Looking at the map, the Korean peninsula - divided into two republics with varying ideas about democracy - sticks out like North Asia's sore thumb. Too tempting to ignore, it has endured a long history of invasions and occupations, and it is of little surprise that Korea became introverted and insular, shunning the outside world. A century ago the West referred to Korea as "the Hermit Kingdom", but Koreans have learned that the world just will not have it that way.

In the 20th century, Korean streets echoed to a variety of military boots - including Japanese, Chinese and American. The Korean War tore through the nation after the surrender of the Japanese at the end of World War II, and came to symbolise the world's political struggle of the age. Other nations leapt into the ideological battleground, the devastating war ended in stalemate and the nation broke in two following armistice in 1953. For the past half-century Korea has been split between North and South.

Today the communist North remains very much the international hermit and is jammed in a political time warp. Strident Stalinist statues boldly salute the continuing Cold War. As the world's most heavily fortified and sensitive border, the demilitarised zone (DMZ) separates the two Koreas. Thousands of troops are poised either side of the buffer that is roughly four kilometres wide.

South Korea is a total contrast to its northern neighbour, and has diversified into a modern industrialised powerhouse. South of the demarcation line the peninsula liberally sprouts manufacturing plants and heavy industry, yet untouched countryside remains in many parts. South Korea enjoys a temperate climate with four seasons, the best times to go being the autumn and the spring. In autumn the countryside breaks into vivid reds and golds, and spring is popular for the gentle tree blossoms. Sticky summer sees the country pummelled by typhoons and winter is for the most part extremely cold.

The country is by no means overrun by mass tourism. A high proportion of visitors are on short breaks from Japan and China, although the strong US influence sees quite a few Americans shuttling through on business. There is less to see and do when compared with some other countries in Asia, a legacy perhaps of war, pillage and economic boom. The modern capital Seoul is a sprawling - but not unpleasant - metropolis rather bereft of authentic cultural attractions. It offers some temples and palaces, though mostly reconstructed rather than restored. But one unforgettable highlight is the

surreal tour to the DMZ. Weird but engaging attractions here include exploring invasion tunnels and peering at mysterious North Korea through the observation point's telescopes.

Seoul's shopping is also extensive, with comparatively low prices attracting waves of Japanese shoppers. Restaurants cater mainly for the Asian palate. A visit to Korea is certainly not complete without munching on some kimchi - salted and spiced cabbage. It does not look exciting but one of the first

questions Koreans will ask you is if you have tried it.

In the south, a short way from the port city of Busan lies the unusual ancient site of Gyeongju, a delightful historic area spanning across the plains and hills. Gyeongju is dotted with tombs and cultural artefacts and was luckily spared destruction during all of the invasions of the past millennium. South Korea also has some beautiful natural scenery - wonderful sweeping mountains for hikers, good golf courses, plus

several acceptable ski resorts, and to the south the tourist beaches of Jeju Island.

Visitors tend to find hotels to be big and glitzy but well maintained. Some of the newer ones are as good as any in Asia. Koreans are wonderful hosts, being welcoming and friendly, and the vast majority of hotels convey this, although English can be a problem away from the top ones. Unfortunately, since Seoul is home to a quarter of the population property prices have shot up higher than a North Korean missile and hotels are stiffly priced, and this seems to have set the benchmark for the rest of the country.

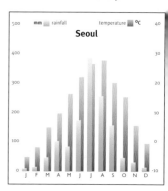

COEX InterContinental Seoul

159 Samseong-dong, Gangnam-gu, Seoul 135-975, Korea
T: +82 2 3452 2500 **F:** +82 2 3430 8000
www.HotelClub.com/Hotels/Coex_InterContinental_Seoul

This is frequently touted as South Korea's leading business hotel, not least for its cheek-by-jowl location next to the exhibition centre. The facilities are excellent with regards to upkeep, ambience, practicality and depth. The open kitchen buffet of the Brasserie on the first floor is popular and diners can drift from section to section nibbling a broad selection of the world's cuisines. Asian Live on the second floor is equally multinational, with fare from Korea, China, Japan, Thailand, India and Indonesia. Other facilities are just as trendy and cosmopolitan - including the aptly named Cosmopolitan Fitness Centre complete with golf room, saunas and massage rooms and a whirlpool spa. Many of the 653 rooms have excellent views. Their design is not quite as adventurous as the rest of the hotel, but they are certainly good enough and are well equipped.

Business facilities are state-of-the-art with 16 meeting rooms with capacities from 15 to 1,500. Eight-language simultaneous translation and teleconferencing are some of the many services available. This is a superb package that should meet the needs of any business traveller.

Rates from: $$$
Star rating: ★ ★ ★ ★ ★
Overall rating: ◗◗◗◗ ½

Ambience:	8.43	Cleanliness:	9.13
Value:	8.00	Facilities:	8.61
Staff:	8.57	Restaurants:	8.38
Location:	8.85	Families:	8.12

Grand Hilton Seoul

210-1, Hongeun-dong, Seodaemun-gu, Seoul 120-710, Korea
T: +82 2 3216 5656 **F:** +82 2 3216 7799
www.HotelClub.com/Hotels/Grand_Hilton_Hotel_Seoul

Having started life as the Swiss Grand, the Hilton now presents a combination of Swiss efficiency and American know-how - not much personality or local colour, but a great place for harried business travellers to hang their hats. The hotel forms part of a bigger complex that includes a 2,500-capacity Convention Centre.

Situated on "Lotus Hill", a 15-minute free shuttle from Itaewon (and one of the closest deluxe properties to the international airport), the Hilton's 396 rooms and suites face either Mount Baekryun or the city, while a terraced garden walkway enjoys views of both. The business centre is efficient, and there is a 25-metre indoor pool, a golf driving range, saunas and massages for de-stressing.

Japanese, Italian, Cantonese and Sichuan head the array of restaurants, although many business executives retreat to the Members' Club for cocktails and cigars.

Rates from: $$$
Star rating: ★ ★ ★ ★ ★
Bellhop rating: ◗◗◗◗ ½

Ambience:	8.63	Cleanliness:	9.24
Value:	8.13	Facilities:	8.58
Staff:	8.87	Restaurants:	8.36
Location:	8.63	Families:	8.57

Grand Hyatt Seoul

747-7 Hannam 2-dong, Yongsan-gu, Seoul 140-738, Korea
T: +82 2 797 1234 **F:** +82 2 798 6958
www.HotelClub.com/Hotels/Grand_Hyatt_Seoul

Certainly among Seoul's better hotels - and arguably one of the best all-rounders - is this outstanding property from the Hyatt Group. Sat on top of a sparsely wooded hill overlooking a quiet neighbourhood around Namsan Park, the big advantage (and disadvantage) of this sizeable hotel is its location. On the map it looks quite central but it is positioned just off a major slip road and has little within walking distance, lending it a suburban feel. Perched comfortably on its fine vantage point, it has plenty of space which it uses well.

The striking granite and marble lobby soothes with the notes of live classical musicians. The subtle lighting, warm woods and greenery all help set a convivial tone. The benefits of the glass exterior then become clear - views from the lobby lounge sweep beyond the greenery and over the capital. The Grand Hyatt's lobby is certainly a triumph. Leading off from it are some very agreeable restaurants indeed, including the Paris Grill brasserie, two Japanese eateries - Akasaka and the more intimate Tenkai - and The Chinese Restaurant, complete with open kitchen. Descending from

the lobby brings you to one of Asia's most creative outdoor swimming pools. Most of the year it is just an attractive, glassy blue swimming pool complete with sundeck and poolside barbeque facilities. But come Korea's chilly winter months the pool mutates into an ice-skating rink. The Hyatt maintains the back-up of an enticing indoor pool and spa all year round, to go with the full complement of other quite excellent business and leisure facilities. Lively JJ Mahoney's, for

instance, is one of Seoul's premier bars.

The 601 rooms are also outstanding - cool, crisp and many offering engaging city views. High-speed "plug-and-play" Internet access is provided throughout, complete with 24-hour technical support. For the privileged, the stylish specialty suites occupy the top three floors, while the five floors of club rooms and supporting facilities are truly world-class and well above other hotels' comparable efforts. The hotel is not particularly well positioned but it is certainly not inconvenient, lying just a few minutes from Itaewon Metro by taxi and five kilometres from the central business district.

Rates from: $$$
Star rating: ★ ★ ★ ★
Overall rating: ♫♫♫♫ ½

Ambience:	8.92	Cleanliness:	8.94
Value:	7.86	Facilities:	8.46
Staff:	8.66	Restaurants:	8.67
Location:	8.39	Families:	8.44

Grand InterContinental Seoul

159-8 Samseong-dong, Gangnam-gu, Seoul 135-732, Korea
T: +82 2 555 5656 **F:** +82 2 559 7990
www.HotelClub.com/Hotels/Grand_InterContinental_Seoul

Now approaching 20 years old, the Grand (by nature as well as name) is the Seoul hotel that wealthy Koreans patronise while their offspring make whoopee in its sister property across the road. The Grand's Fitness Club and Silk Road Club are as full of local members as hotel guests. The overall decor is rich and clubby, the 535 rooms among the city's roomiest, and the cellar at the Tony Chi-designed Table 34 restaurant houses more than 4,000 fine wines. It is very much a property for the mature traveller, business or otherwise. It has a surprisingly Korean personality grafted onto its veneer of sophisticated internationalism (the kimchi-with-everything syndrome).

The outstanding Australian Grill (one of the hotel world's few Aussie fine-dining spots outside of God's Own) is only surpassed by the eclectic Marco Polo, a vertiginous 52 floors up. Marvellous city views are matched by a bewildering array of cuisines from most of the countries the Italian explorer is alleged to have visited. Convenience note: the hotel is right next door to the city airport terminal.

Rates from: $$
Star rating: ★ ★ ★ ★ ★
Overall rating: 🏨🏨🏨🏨 ½

Ambience:	8.92	Cleanliness:	9.13
Value:	7.50	Facilities:	8.67
Staff:	8.68	Restaurants:	8.76
Location:	9.16	Families:	8.20

JW Marriott Hotel Seoul

19-3 Banpo-dong, Seocho-gu, Seoul 137-040, Korea
T: +82 2 6282 6262 **F:** +82 2 6282 6263
www.HotelClub.com/Hotels/JW_Marriott_Hotel_Seoul

This is a splendid hotel in many respects - large, modern, well-situated - but there is no doubting its "killer app": the incredible Marquis Thermal Spa and Fitness Club, hailed as the biggest and most comprehensive in Asia. Not only does it utilise thermal spring water from deep below its foundations, but it includes a rock-climbing wall and a scuba-diving pool among its many physical-workout facilities.

The 34-storey property sits atop a shopping, dining and entertainment complex called Central City, which has a food court, so it's perfect for weary visitors who don't fancy venturing too deep into downtown Seoul. And it's the first stop for the bus from the airport.

Service standards are what you would expect from the Marriott, ditto the food - at the Italian Di Moda, Japanese Mikado, Chinese Man Ho, Marriott Café and JW's Grill. River or mountain views can be had from its 497 large but somewhat uninspiringly furnished rooms, and there are all the appropriate mod cons for business travellers.

Rates from: $$$
Star rating: ★ ★ ★ ★ ★
Overall rating: 🏨🏨🏨🏨 ½

Ambience:	8.83	Cleanliness:	9.19
Value:	7.79	Facilities:	8.71
Staff:	8.90	Restaurants:	8.46
Location:	8.33	Families:	8.73

Lotte Seoul

1 Sogong-dong, Jung-gu, Seoul 100-721, Korea
T: +82 2 771 1000 **F:** +82 2 752 3758
www.HotelClub.com/Hotels/Lotte_Hotel_Seoul

The Lotte claims to be the most prestigious hotel in Seoul, and while this may not be quite true, there is an awful lot going for South Korea's largest hostelry. It is not the smartest, but it must be the most convenient for tourists, especially shoppers, being right in the middle of the prime retail areas. It is a few steps from City Hall Metro and has its own mega-department store attached. Towering at 38 storeys, the Lotte has a staggering 1,486 rooms and just about all the facilities any hotel can possibly have in a city centre, including an indoor golf driving range. There are, for example, 14 restaurants and bars. Standards are good, but maybe not quite internationally five-star. The rooms are flush with tech add-ons including wireless Internet. While the hotel's flamboyant decor is less than subtle, with its location and facilities, the hugely popular Lotte appeals to a wide audience from families to business executives.

Rates from: $$$
Star rating: ★ ★ ★ ★ ★
Overall rating: 🌓🌓🌓🌓 ½

Ambience:	8.87	Cleanliness:	9.15
Value:	7.98	Facilities:	8.63
Staff:	8.51	Restaurants:	8.58
Location:	9.11	Families:	8.68

Marriott Busan

1405-16 Jung-dong, Haeundae-gu, Busan 612-010, Korea
T: +82 51 743 1234 **F:** +82 51 743 1250
www.HotelClub.com/Hotels/Marriott_Hotel_Busan

floors of Executive Level rooms.

Fish features strongly on the hotel restaurants' menus (make sure you visit the nearby market) from Aomi (Japanese), Seascapes (all-day international dining), Ventanas (surf 'n' turf) or the self-explanatory Chopsticks & Pizza. In the evenings, Murphy's Discotheque & Pub romps with true Celtic abandon.

The fact that this gleaming white beacon is stuck out on Haeundae Beach, a fair distance from downtown Busan and even further from the airport, should inspire rather than deter the honeymooners and family groups this hotel appeals to. And business travellers would be silly to pass up a chance to mix work with pleasure in such bracing surroundings.

Most of the 362 rooms have ocean views and all have been recently renovated in a light, airy style. The 19 Corner Suites have separate living and sleeping areas. There are family rooms for guests with kids in tow, as well as two

Rates from: $$
Star rating: ★ ★ ★ ★ ★
Overall rating: 🌓🌓🌓🌓

Ambience:	8.61	Cleanliness:	9.33
Value:	7.56	Facilities:	8.82
Staff:	8.78	Restaurants:	8.88
Location:	8.89	Families:	7.58

Ritz-Carlton Seoul

602 Yeoksam-dong, Gangnam-gu, Seoul 135-080, Korea
T: +82 2 3451 8000 **F**: +82 2 3451 8280
www.HotelClub.com/Hotels/Ritz_Carlton_Hotel_Seoul

The jagged exterior may look half-finished, but the Ritz-Carlton has perhaps the most stylish and classy interior of any hotel in Korea. Right from the six-storey atrium, with its signature waterfall which is illuminated at night, this very chic offering has all the expected facilities, but its refined European feel gives it an edge over other, more modest five-star properties. One of the Ritz's impressive assets is the 600 pieces of modern art collected from around the world that have been thoughtfully placed around the property. The hotel contains a quite stunning indoor pool and spa and the gourmet restaurants are some of the most elegant (and priciest) in Seoul.

These include such gems as the Cesar Grill, which serves US imported beef, lamb, veal and fresh Pacific seafood, and Hanazono, which concentrates on authentic Japanese cuisine. Chee Hong combines Cantonese and Shanghainese fare in a contemporary atmosphere, while Café Fantino features the best food of the Mediterranean from Italy, Spain, France and Morocco using infused oil and specially chosen herbs and spices. Gangnam is not generally noted for its nightlife but the Nyx & Nox pub and disco is as popular for its pizzas as its live entertainment, while suits from all over town converge on The Bar with the express intention of schmoozing while getting mildly sloshed most nights of the week.

In the rest of the hotel, extra little touches are obvious throughout the 410 luxurious but relaxing rooms, such as VCRs and CD players, and mini TVs in the bathrooms. The staff - from the bath butler to the IT assistant - offer very high service standards, and the hotel is fairly well located for business, with Gangnam Metro only 10 minutes' walk away. The Ritz-Carlton is a very good hotel with superior standards to many others in the same price bracket.

Rates from: $$$
Star rating: ★ ★ ★ ★ ★
Overall rating: ♦♦♦♦

Ambience:	8.56	Cleanliness:	8.82
Value:	7.68	Facilities:	8.47
Staff:	8.70	Restaurants:	8.56
Location:	8.32	Families:	7.93

Sheraton Grande Walkerhill

21 Gwangjang-dong, Gwangjin-gu, Seoul 143-708, Korea
T: +82 2 455 5000 F: +82 2 452 6867
www.HotelClub.com/Hotels/Sheraton_Walker_Hill_Seoul

This Sheraton stands apart from Seoul's rather conformist hotels, and has decided to occupy a very different niche. Very leisure-oriented, the hotel is set on the green north-easterly skirts of the capital, 40 minutes from the town centre. Overlooking Mount A-Cha, this huge 623-room hotel has a good spread of sporting facilities, a golf driving range and three pools. Seoul's sole casino is the proud centrepiece, with gambling around the clock and the elaborate Walker Hill Shows - Korean folk dances, bright Latino musicals and raunchy topless extravaganzas - staged in a 720-seat theatre. And with over a dozen restaurants, the hotel-cum-resort caters for virtually anyone.

The rooms are set in two towers and an annex, and range from the slightly ordinary standard rooms (Main Tower) to the detached villas (Annex). At 40 years plus, the hotel is beginning to show its age, but its popularity shows no sign of waning, especially with the Japanese hopping over for weekend gaming breaks.

Rates from: $$$
Star rating: ★ ★ ★ ★ ★
Overall rating: ◊◊◊◊

Ambience:	8.80	Cleanliness:	8.90
Value:	7.67	Facilities:	8.53
Staff:	8.80	Restaurants:	8.67
Location:	7.73	Families:	8.29

Shilla Jeju

3039-3 Saekdal-dong, Seogwipo-shi, Jeju-do, Korea
T: +82 2 738 4466 F: +82 2 735 5415
www.HotelClub.com/Hotels/Cheju_Shilla_Hotel

In Korea's subtropical south lies the volcanic island retreat recently renamed Jeju, a popular escape for Koreans and Japanese. The Shilla Jeju, part of the Chungmun Resort Complex, is the island's top residence. The hotel optimistically suggests that it has been recognised as one of the four best resorts in the world. This it is not, but it is the best in Korea and a fine respite. Launched in 1990, the resort, with its mock-European styling, spreads out over eight hectares of landscaped cliff-top gardens. Hotel facilities are among the most extensive in the country with extras like a casino, a bowling alley and an unusual indoor/outdoor pool. Check into

L'Institute de Guerlain spa for some excessive pampering. Each of the 429 guestrooms is spacious and has a private balcony with views of Mount Halla or the ocean. The complex includes a golf course, a beach and some wonderful areas of natural beauty, so it is no surprise the resort bulges with happy families in the summer.

Rates from: $$$
Star rating: ★ ★ ★ ★ ★
Overall rating: ◊◊◊◊ ½

Ambience:	9.11	Cleanliness:	9.00
Value:	8.14	Facilities:	8.66
Staff:	9.00	Restaurants:	8.93
Location:	8.68	Families:	8.77

Shilla Seoul

202, 2-Ga, Jangchung-dong, Jung-gu, Seoul, Korea
T: +82 2 2233 3131 **F:** +82 2 2233 5073
www.HotelClub.com/Hotels/Shilla_Hotel_Seoul

Standing proud on the pedestal of a green hill, the 23-storey Shilla is a significant monument on Seoul's skyline, not least for its brand new Guerlain Spa which opened at the end of 2004 and has set new standards in the Korean capital.

From a distance the hotel looks dominant and purposeful, almost like a bold, coppery stele. For a relatively central hotel it is huge, somehow managing to have nine hectares of greenery all to itself. It feels much like a university campus in layout when walking up the hill through the gardens and the broad car park. This communal facility feel is maintained inside, the angular lobby with its combination of red brick, grey columns and pine wood making you wonder if you have stepped into an exhibition or performing arts centre.

The award-winning Shilla has a fine reputation but is visually different to typical top international hotel chains inside. Being a very Korean enterprise it tends to be a very well-packaged and smart product, but also slightly lacking in

imagination when it comes to style or flair. That does not mean that it is ugly - it most certainly is not - but expect everything to blend in rather anonymously in unobtrusive comfort. Luxury is not just defined by artistic impression but by standards and services. And for this the Shilla excels - there are few hotels in the city with broader amenities, and due to the generous space they are simply bigger and tend to be more comprehensive. The jogging track, for example, disappears into a four-hectare sculpture park rather than a miserable lap of a hotel wing. The duty-free shopping centre is a packed out plaza. Also expect very Korean service - exemplary. Business facilities are bang up to date technologically (including Bloomberg terminals in the 24-hour business centre), plus there are more than enough large, capable restaurants. And for a real change in scenery, the adjacent Yeong Bin Gwan, Korea's former state guesthouse, has three very Korean-styled banquet halls.

The hotel's 508 light and trim rooms are again generous in size, with traditional Korean fittings and robust and dependable furniture. Internet TV, wireless LAN and multi-

lingual voicemail are just some of the standard facilities. A big plus are the views over the city, which given the hotel's raised position are quite superb. With Dongguk station just a five-minute walk away, the hotel is ideal for those needing a bit of space and fresh air while still being ten minutes from the main financial districts and within half an hour of just about everything else that counts in Seoul.

Rates from: $$$
Star rating: ★ ★ ★ ★ ★
Overall rating: ♔♔♔♔ ½

Ambience:	8.94	Cleanliness:	9.21
Value:	7.94	Facilities:	8.74
Staff:	9.00	Restaurants:	8.77
Location:	7.94	Families:	8.72

Westin Chosun Seoul

87 Sogong-dong, Jung-gu, Seoul 100-070, Korea
T: +82 2 771 0500 F: +82 2 753 6370
www.HotelClub.com/Hotels/Westin_Chosun_Hotel_Seoul

If one had to pick a hotel for its location, at least for tourists, then it would be the Westin Chosun. It is only a few steps from two Metro stations, and over the road from the buzzing shopping maze of Myong-dong. Also within easy walking distance is Toksu Palace, the famed bargains of Namdaemun Market and the stately City Hall, considered by many the centre of Seoul. But the Westin Chosun is also set on the edge of Youido, one of Seoul's main business areas, and so sets itself up primarily as a business hotel.

Seoul's oldest hotel has a distinguished past dating back to 1914, which in this modern city makes it an heirloom. The Westin Chosun is not really old or historic, with no elegant colonial airs about it. It is more stately, grandfatherly, perhaps even a tad stuffy. The dim enclosed interior involves lots of deep dark woods with many underground facilities reminiscent of cellars. Three wings stretch out of a central core, to give three concave faces. Each of the 453 rooms is chic but simple and clearly designed with the executive in mind - first-class Internet connections, four telephone lines, computer, fax, and of course voicemail.

The facilities are in very good shape, bearing in mind the hotel's advanced years. Predictably for Seoul, the facilities are very expensive, especially the restaurants where the prices are well above those outside. The difference is in the menus, since Korean and Japanese restaurants dominate the district. Apart from junk-food joints and the odd pizza bar, the Chosun is one of the only places offering Western food in the area. O'Kim's does not look all that Irish, but the European food is good, as are the offerings from Ninth Gate (continental), Vecchia e Nouvo (Italian) and the Café Royale (international). The hotel's Asian restaurants offer attractive Chinese, Korean and Japanese dishes and an authentic ambience.

The gym is certainly good and the huge business centre is exemplary with the full range of services laid on, while meeting rooms, offices for rent and 24-hour secretarial services make the Westin Chosun one of the preferred business bases north of the river.

Rates from: $$$
Star rating: ★ ★ ★ ★ ★
Overall rating: ◊ ◊ ◊ ◊ ½

Ambience:	8.70	Cleanliness:	9.25
Value:	7.49	Facilities:	8.60
Staff:	8.85	Restaurants:	8.32
Location:	8.91	Families:	7.95

LAOS

Sleepy, landlocked and incredibly beautiful Laos has very few visitors and refreshingly low-key tourism. Unlike other developing Asian countries, you will not be hassled by vendors, nor feel a financial target. With a population of only six million chiefly involved in agriculture, there is little industry and consequently few hotels, which for the most part are basic and rudimentary.

The restful capital Vientiane, with its population of only 130,000, feels like an escape in its own right. This is about as busy as it gets in dormant Laos, a country where the tallest building is only seven storeys. There can be few capitals with cabbage patches lining the busiest districts. Up country lies the magical Luang Prabang, officially designated as the best preserved "city" in Southeast Asia by UNESCO. The streets are mainly dotted with quaint French colonial houses, and the famed temples are ornate and absolutely spectacular. The gentle Mekong winds its way through and the rush hour is an orange tide of monks.

Infrastructure beyond the threads connecting these two is virtually non-existent. The mountains have never really been tamed and their inhabitants remain a law unto themselves. Even if it were safe, such is the state of the roads that it would take several days to navigate through the northern regions. Flying, or boating down the Mekong are the only ways.

Poor old Laos remains one of the most bombed countries in the history of modern warfare. Around the barren and remote cowboy town of Phonsavan the sad legacy of Agent Orange is visible in the useless soils. Farmers try to make the best of it in the bomb-littered fields. Many deal in scrap metal, with shell casings forming props for huts or troughs for pigs. The main reason to come this far out is to scratch your head over the mysterious Plain Of Jars. Hundreds of ancient stone jars are strewn across the hilltops and no-one has quite worked out their purpose. In the Vietnam War these drum-sized oddities were used as bomb shelters and many have been raked with gunfire.

The lazy pace, absence of materialism and strong culture is a breath of fresh air. Higher elevations are cool all year round. Laos undergoes a tropical monsoon and is best visited in the dry season, December to April. It is still quite tough to get around, but the challenge is well rewarded for those who take the time.

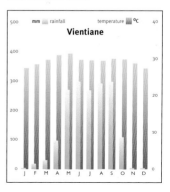

Le Calao Inn

27/3 Ban, Phone Heuang, Khamkong Road, Luang Prabang, Laos
T: +856 71 212 100 **F:** +856 71 212 085
www.HotelClub.com/Hotels/Le_Calao_Inn

Le Calao Inn is one of the loveliest hostelries anywhere in Asia. It cannot quite be classed as a hotel, even though the price on the tariff puts it in the same bracket. The label "boutique hotel" may also be a bit vague. Le Calao is best described as a glorious bed and breakfast, low on facilities but absolutely brimming with character. The name is primarily derived from the origins of the owners (Canada and Laos) but for a rather more romantic explanation turn to your French dictionary. Calao is the French/Malay word for the tropical hornbill found throughout Asia - and incidentally is also the hotel's emblem.

The building is a lovingly restored 1904 French mansion, a true remnant of the romantic Indochine past. The exterior is lusciously Gallic, with archways, shutters and decorative balconies. The interior is a rare glimpse of a forgotten era. The inn is filled with polished dark wood with depth and soul. Floors creak and give a little underfoot, the small cocktail bar surely belongs to another era. Le Calao is rich in colonial history, but less endowed with facilities and luxury. This provides an authentic experience. There are no gyms, TVs or anything else that would have felt out of place in the early 20th century.

The inn's simplicity is absolute, being utterly personal as it has only six rooms. These are spartan and simple, but in a thoroughly enjoyable way. Beds are solid and sturdy, light switches and wiring exposed, and the bathrooms tiled with homely blue and white tiles. The only traces of the modern world are the air-conditioning units and the rather weak electric showers. From the four upper rooms your every footstep is amplified as you slip along the creaky floorboards in your socks to the balcony which overlooks the languid Mekong and provides a perfect spot from which to admire the sunset. The two ground-floor rooms are much larger and spill into quiet terrace gardens.

Hotel amenities are almost non-existent but the tranquillity here is bliss. The location overlooking the Mekong and within a leisurely stroll of the splendour of Luang Prabang's palaces is pretty much unrivalled, the venerable Wat Xieng Thong is less that 150 metres away. The food at Le Calao is simple and unfussy, but the staff are superbly sweet and helpful. A wonderful, wonderful retreat.

Rates from: $
Star rating: ★★
Overall rating: Editor's pick

Ambience:	n/a	Cleanliness:	n/a
Value:	n/a	Facilities:	n/a
Staff:	n/a	Restaurants:	n/a
Location:	n/a	Families:	n/a

La Résidence Phou Vao
Luang Prabang, Laos
T: +856 71 212 194   **F:** +856 71 212 534
www.HotelClub.com/Hotels/La_Residence_Phou_Vao

Whether the fact that Mick Jagger stayed here for a week and was delighted not to be harassed by autograph-hunters says more about La Résidence's exclusivity or Luang Prabang's other-worldliness is a moot point. But by general consensus, it is still the best address in town.

A low-rise property built on the side of "Kite Hill", it commands a captivating view of the surrounding mountains and the town below (whence there is a free shuttle service). La Résidence has 34 Lao-style accommodations, each containing four-poster beds - as well as a day bed - large bathrooms and shaded balconies, ideal for enjoying room service.

The French restaurant, which also serves Lao specialities, is outstanding. The infinity pool is the biggest in town, and the gardens extend to three hectares. If there were a quibble, it would have to be over the English-language skills of its otherwise extremely obliging staff, but this is an endemic problem in this part of the world.

Unlike many mock-colonial piles that have gone overboard on the ethnicity, La Résidence (formerly the Pansea) has kept things clean and simple. Rooms are done in rosewood with cotton linens on the walls. There is ample use of wood and stone throughout and floors are are highly polished but bereft of carpets, as befits the humid climate. Ceiling fans and low-slung Laotian-type seating, plus artfully placed local artefacts, complete the understated exoticism of the ambience.

There is no gym, no nightclub, no sports facilities apart from swimming, in keeping with the country's somewhat austere image. But once the spa opens in 2005, the other side of that image - languid sensuality and an attitude to life so laid-back it is almost horizontal - will be equally represented. All in all, an ideal retreat from which to wind down from the frustrations of exploring this charming but idiosyncratic World Heritage site.

Rates from: **$$**
Star rating: ★ ★ ★ ★ ★
Overall rating: ◗ ◗ ◗ ◗ ½

Ambience:	9.75	Cleanliness:	9.44
Value:	8.81	Facilities:	8.67
Staff:	9.31	Restaurants:	8.60
Location:	8.88	Families:	9.00

Lao Plaza Hotel Vientiane

63 Samsenthai Road, Vientiane, Laos
T: +856 21 218 800 **F**: +856 21 218 808
www.HotelClub.com/Hotels/Lao_Plaza_Hotel_Vientiane

pool, restaurants and a standard fitness offering. The 142 rooms again are a relief - they follow the international mould (including Internet access) without ever trying to be characteristic or clever - exactly what many travellers want in this very undeveloped country. The staff are top-class with a real desire to please.

This is one of Laos' very few "big" hotels. There are not many others in a sleepy land where the capital holds a mere 130,000 residents. In fact, at seven storeys, this is the tallest building in the country and it also has the fullest range of facilities. The formula for a big hotel is applied only at the Lao Plaza. The business facilities, quite frankly, have no real competition so naturally the hotel gets the lion's share of business travellers. A cavernous wood-crafted lobby leads off towards the reassuringly familiar set of amenities including

Rates from: $
Star rating: ★ ★ ★ ★
Overall rating: ◌◌◌◌ ½

Ambience:	8.75	Cleanliness:	9.25
Value:	8.38	Facilities:	8.13
Staff:	9.50	Restaurants:	8.63
Location:	9.25	Families:	8.60

Novotel Vientiane

9 Samsenthai Road, Vientiane, Laos
T: +856 21 213 570 **F**: +856 21 213 573
www.HotelClub.com/Hotels/Novotel_Vientiane

conference venue. The location is reasonably situated halfway between the airport and the town centre and short stroll to the Mekong riverside. Happy-go-lucky staff can sometimes get their wires crossed but overall you certainly get an international product and, thankfully, not an ugly concrete box.

The Novotel Vientiane is the country's sole international hotel chain representative, and is the place to go for those playing it safe. Modest, medium and modern, it squashes in all the facilities that qualify it for four-star status. Some of the facilities are small enough to raise eyebrows but the hotel centrepiece, the lovely pool, is among the very best in Vientiane. The 168 rooms and suites are mass-produced, claiming French influence, with unusually shaped windows - possibly a legacy from the days when this was a hotel training school, indeed some of the staff learnt their trade here. The business facilities are adequate for individuals, but this is no mega

Rates from: $
Star rating: ★ ★ ★ ★
Overall rating: ◌◌◌◌

Ambience:	8.50	Cleanliness:	8.67
Value:	8.50	Facilities:	8.39
Staff:	9.50	Restaurants:	8.17
Location:	8.67	Families:	8.00

Settha Palace Hotel

6 Pang Kham Street, Vientiane, Laos
T: +856 21 217 581 **F:** +856 21 217 583
www.HotelClub.com/Hotels/Settha_Palace_Hotel

A gem of a hotel, the Settha Palace is a beautifully restored piece of French colonial architecture dating from the turn of the 20th century. Of all Vientiane's hotels this is certainly among the most enjoyable – a recollection of a bygone era in Laos, offering just as much historical grace and depth as other Asian grandes dames.

The colonial French first opened the Settha in 1932. It fell into disrepair in the 1970s, and was only reopened after a painstaking renovation in 1999 by the current owner Billy Theodas - who followed in his parents' footsteps.

The authenticity runs deep, with an abundance of stately and solid woods, gently creaking floorboards and delightfully spacious rooms with massive hand-carved four-posters and thick Persian rugs. Authentic shutters, period furniture and landscaped gardens all add to the historic charm. The Settha's 29 spacious rooms and suites are simple but enjoyable with generous marbled bathrooms complete with a separate walk-in shower, and all the modern conveniences demanded these days including IDD, wireless Internet, satellite TV and in-room safe - by no means common amenities in Laos. The same can also be said of the well-equipped business centre, complete with workstations and secretarial services.

The ever-so-slightly stiff Belle Epoque dining room, with its large French windows and a high wooden-studded ceiling, is very elegant to view but a tad pricey; however the cuisine is more than adequate. Al fresco dining by the pool and jacuzzi is much more casual, together with the open-air Sidewalk Café, which offers tasty Asian fare.

As the hotel is just a few minutes' stroll from the town centre it is well-located to take advantage of Vientiane's pleasant little restaurants and cafés, as well as the morning market, Presidential Palace, Wat Sisakhet, Thatluang Temple and broad vistas of the Mekong River; alternatively, board the hotel's London taxi, a charming, anomalous extra to this unique property. Hotels like the Settha are rare indeed.

Rates from: $
Star rating: ★ ★ ★ ★
Overall rating: ♢ ♢ ♢ ♢ ½

Ambience:	9.53	Cleanliness:	9.40
Value:	8.80	Facilities:	8.38
Staff:	9.53	Restaurants:	8.53
Location:	9.00	Families:	8.20

Villa Santi Hotel

Sakarine Road, Luang Prabang, Laos
T: +856 71 252 157 **F:** +856 71 252 158
www.HotelClub.com/Hotels/Villa_Santi_Hotel_Luang_Prabang_The

In many ways, the Villa Santi Hotel sums up the somnambulant land of Laos. It is a lovely little boutique hotel that dovetails perfectly with the quaint northern town of Luang Prabang. Right in the heart of a UNESCO-designated World Heritage site, the Villa Santi was once the residence of a Lao princess and is sprinkled with antiques and ethnic handicrafts. A royal history it may have, but this is no sprawling palace - there are just 25 rooms and suites, all elegantly decorated with rosewood furnishings and silk textiles, yet still with discreet modern conveniences such as air-conditioning.

The overall impression is of modest, comfortably upholstered simplicity with gentle French influences. This is especially notable on the first floor where the open restaurant overlooks the quiet street below. Motorised traffic is virtually non-existent in remote Luang Prabang, and you can sit back and enjoy the surreal non-rush hour over your breakfast, while waves of orange-robed monks drift toward their stunningly ornate monasteries. At dinner, the menu features royal Lao cuisine prepared by a former palace chef, while at any time of day the Elephant Bar is ideal for a snack or a leisurely thirst-quencher.

The Santi never really feels like a hotel - it is more a house party of strangers who have been drawn together by a mutual friend who just happens to be absent. Service is exceptionally graceful but a little slow at times and occasionally handicapped by the language barrier; however, the staff's sincere and heart-warming smiles seem to evaporate any frustration this may

cause. It almost goes without saying that the Villa Santi Hotel (not to be confused with the newer sister Villa Santi Resort just down the road) has enormous personality and charm. This is the place to stay for those looking for a genuinely Lao experience and it is one that will leave a lasting and incredibly favourable impression.

Rates from: $			
Star rating: ★ ★ ★			
Overall rating: ⚘⚘⚘⚘ ½			
Ambience:	9.44	Cleanliness:	9.04
Value:	8.68	Facilities:	7.81
Staff:	9.08	Restaurants:	8.13
Location:	9.44	Families:	8.90

MACAU

In the past couple of years Macau has been catapulted into what the marketing types are calling the "Las Vegas of Asia". Brand new casinos, huge infrastructure projects and the promise of much more to come - certainly nobody is calling the former Portuguese colony a "sleepy enclave" any more.

Macau remains an unlikely mix of two differing cultures - Chinese and Portuguese, although the former predominates nowadays. After the Portuguese dropped anchor in 1557 and blew away the local pirates, China permitted the Europeans to administer just

enough land to park a few galleons. Macau was Europe's first foothold in Asia and the gateway to China until the Opium Wars in the 19th century led to the concession of Hong Kong. China finally resumed sovereignty over Macau in 1999, but 400 years saw plenty of Latin influence and there are many interesting historical remnants. Macau is a surreal hybrid, an intriguing canvas of ornate Portuguese flair and Chinese tradition - together with a massive modern cash injection - and a unique pocket of Asia. Fine examples of centuries-old colonial architecture include the famous ruined facade of St Paul's Cathedral, the symbol of Macau. Other colonial examples include the Guia Lighthouse, and there are historic Chinese highlights such as incense-filled Ah Ma Temple.

Hong Kong lies just an hour away by jetfoil, but nowadays it is mainland China that exerts the greatest influence and basically powers the Macau economy. From a trade base and port, Macau has evolved into a Chinese leisure centre with thousands shuttling over for weekend city breaks. Casinos are the big magnet for Asian visitors with many getting no

further than this glittering world. Around half of Macau's revenue and a quarter of the labour market are tied up in the trade. The newer glitzy Las Vegas razzmatazz showpieces are now competing with the old guard, which are populated by their share of shady characters with grim expressions. Prostitution is also big business here with scores of girls from over the border (and more recently Eastern Europe) strutting around the casinos' outskirts. With all this going on triad gangs are active, although they have kept their heads down since China resumed power.

But it is not all about gambling and groping. Macau has an identity of its own and an undeniable charm and warmth. The pace is a welcome step down from neighbouring cities and there is also the indulgence of Portuguese food and wine. The combination of Portuguese and Chinese food has resulted in Macanese cuisine. And although it is difficult to get excited about a roll, the bread here is some of the best in Asia. Beyond the dining and sightseeing is golf, legitimate bone-cracking massages and the annual Grand Prix - plenty for such a modest pimple of land.

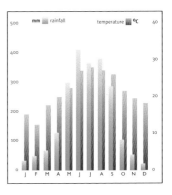

Hyatt Regency Macau

2 Estrada Almirante Marques Esparteiro, Taipa, Macau
T: +853 831 234 **F:** +853 830 195
www.HotelClub.com/Hotels/Hyatt_Regency_Hotel_Macau

The Hyatt sits on Taipa, away from the city lights, although new casinos are giving the island a shot in the arm. The hotel has been here around a dozen years, and it remains a popular choice for business travellers, as the meeting rooms and conference facilities are some of Macau's most comprehensive. But the Hyatt is not restricted purely to collar-and-tie stuff - team-building exercises in the grounds are especially well attended. The hotel has a tangible 1980s hangover with big pillars, beams and angles, but is roomy with nice Portuguese trimmings and 326 well-maintained if fairly average five-star rooms. Scenic Flamingos does a Macanese and Portuguese menu sitting out over leafy carp-filled ponds, or if it rains the Greenhouse is a snug shelter. The broad meandering outdoor pool is attractive and worth lazing around, and there are 1.2 hectares of gardens with plenty of sporting facilities plus a very good children's club, Camp Hyatt. This hotel is neither classy or swanky but works well.

Rates from: $$
Star rating: ★ ★ ★ ★ ★
Overall rating: ♻ ♻ ♻ ♻

Ambience:	8.33	Cleanliness:	8.53
Value:	8.02	Facilities:	8.14
Staff:	8.47	Restaurants:	8.50
Location:	8.00	Families:	8.63

Mandarin Oriental Macau

956-1110 Avenida da Amizade, Macau
T: +853 567 888 **F:** +853 594 589
www.HotelClub.com/Hotels/Mandarin_Oriental_Macau

Handily hugging the Grand Prix track and only a few minutes' taxi ride from Macau's historic centre and the surrounding entertainment areas, this hotel is active seven days a week rather than just at weekends. Having undergone a major renovation in recent years, the Mandarin is Macau's most up-to-date hotel, although it was slightly put in the shadows by the arrival of the Sands casino next door. Not only are the 435 oriental-style rooms smooth and smart, but the hotel facilities are modern yet invitingly decorated with warm Portuguese flair. The addition of the low-rise colonial-style "Resort" to the rear means it now has Macau's most attractive pool (heated), spa facilities (excellent massage treatments) and kids' entertainment, complementing the already fine restaurants, bar and a casino concession. Helpful and friendly staff are another big plus. The Mandarin is a great example of how a previously ageing hotel has very successfully reinvented itself.

Rates from: $$
Star rating: ★ ★ ★ ★ ★
Overall rating: ♻ ♻ ♻ ♻ ½

Ambience:	8.67	Cleanliness:	8.81
Value:	8.42	Facilities:	8.62
Staff:	8.81	Restaurants:	8.79
Location:	8.61	Families:	8.78

Westin Resort Macau

1918 Estrada de Hac Sa, Coloane, Macau
T: +853 871 111 **F:** +853 871 122
www.HotelClub.com/Hotels/Westin_Resort_Macau

The Westin remains by far the most popular retreat in Macau. Set in spacious grounds on the laid-back east coast of the island of Coloane, the hotel backs into a hill and is perhaps the embodiment of the perfect Macanese getaway. The chief reason to come here is for the range of recreational facilities. While they are not the best by Asian standards, they are certainly the broadest for Macau. The adjacent Golf & Country Club makes the resort especially popular. This fine 5,900-metre par-71 championship course is accessed from the ninth floor - just take the lift and stroll across to the starter's box.

The Westin makes a concerted effort to appeal to families, offering a childcare centre, kids' club and a games room. And there is always the choice of enjoyable indoor and outdoor pools plus plenty of sporting facilities such as the eight tennis courts. The Wellness Retreat lists a healthy range of soothing massages and body treatments if you fancy a spot of pampering. There is a lot to do whatever the weather - though the restaurants make no pretensions to fine dining - and the Westin gets lively and boisterous at weekends.

The hotel design is also fully felt in the 208 very large and comfortable rooms. All are sea-facing with spacious private terraces that catch plenty of sunshine. Being on relatively remote Coloane means that transport is essential - there is nothing within walking distance other than the pleasant Hac Sa Beach and the celebrated Fernando's Restaurant. It takes a good 20 minutes for the shuttle to get downtown or to the ferry pier. This remoteness means you finally escape a skyline with a skyscraper on it and find that elusive relaxing holiday mood.

Rates from: $$
Star rating: ★ ★ ★ ★ ★
Overall rating: ◌ ◌ ◌ ◌

Ambience:	8.71	Cleanliness:	8.95
Value:	7.89	Facilities:	8.63
Staff:	8.44	Restaurants:	8.16
Location:	7.99	Families:	8.77

MALAYSIA

THAILAND
❶ Langkawi

Kota Kinabalu ⓮

BRUNEI

❸ Redang
❷ Penang
❹ Kuala Terengganu

❻ Cameron Highlands
❺ Pangkor Laut

⓭ Kuching

INDONESIA

❼ Kuantan

❽ KUALA LUMUR

❾ Port Dickson
⓫ Tioman Island

⓾ Melaka

INDONESIA

⓬ Johor Bahru
SINGAPORE

Malaysia is one of Southeast Asia's most exotic yet most comfortable countries to visit. In many ways this diverse republic of 23 million people is unique, but also seems to be a composite of surrounding influences. Strongly Islamic since the 13th century, Malaysia grew to its present form under the British, who left in 1957. The influx of Chinese and Indians radically altered the ethnic mix, and descendants of these communities now account for almost half of the population.

Malaysia is basically divided into two regions. The busier peninsula dangles from the heel of Thailand, culminating at Johor Bahru next to Singapore. Malaysia's larger but relatively remoter section - made up of the states of Sarawak and Sabah - occupies roughly the top third of the island of Borneo. The two regions differ substantially, and indeed were only united after World War II. You still need your passport when travelling from the peninsula to Borneo, as Sarawak and Sabah still have a high degree of autonomy.

For the tourist, Malaysia is one of the more beautiful and appealing destinations in the region. With rapid economic progress, good infrastructure and English widely spoken, it has also become one of the most safe and accessible places to visit. The modern capital Kuala Lumpur has seen heavy investment and is emerging as a world-class city. Its dining and shopping can now compete alongside the likes of Singapore, Bangkok and Hong Kong. Entertainment is picking up too, although it will probably never match the carefree nightlife of other Asian countries. And "KL", as it is known, has staked a name for itself globally with the completion of the

wonders like the placid orangutans. Sabah's 4,101-metre Mt Kinabalu near the beach resorts of Kota Kinabalu is the highest mountain between the Myanmar and Papua New Guinea, but rises gently and steadily, making it one of the easiest "big" mountains to climb in the world. Offshore and a little to the north is Sipidan, one of many stunning sites for divers.

With hundreds of kilometres of tropical coast, Malaysia has some great beaches that have developed more slowly than their more popular counterparts in Thailand. Laid-back Langkawi island has some fantastic white sandy stretches, far superior to those of Penang. The east coast has good ones too; Tioman, Redang and the backpacking Perhentian islands supply equal beauty, though the monsoon rains affect the winter seasons. Peninsular Malaysia's climate is tropical - sunny, hot and humid year-round with short bursts of torrential rain. The monsoon between October and April hits the east coast harder, while Borneo gets steady rainfall all year. The hill stations of the Cameron Highlands, Fraser Hill and the gambling centre of Genting, with their cool elevated tea plantations, offer a delightful escape from the oppressive heat.

Hotel-wise, Malaysia has the lot - from icons of days gone by such as the E&O in Penang to Langkawi's out-of-this-world Datai, from the highlands' Tudor replicas right down to quaint beachside lean-tos.

Iconic Petronas Towers, at 452 metres two of the world's tallest buildings.

No other Malaysian city is in the same league as the capital, as most are sleepy and quiet. One thing that might strike the visitor is a relative absence of visible historical landmarks. Unlike most of Asia, which is bulging with temples and relics, Malaysia retains an aura of newness. This is largely due to the fact that the Malays have traditionally constructed with wood and earlier buildings have decayed, but even colonial brick-and-mortar contributions are few. A noteworthy exception is in coastal Melaka,

which lies just a few hours south of the capital and huddles together a collection of Portuguese and Dutch architecture. Further north, approaching the Thai border, the island of Penang is the other main area of historical depth.

The really big pull is Malaysia's natural beauty. The country floats just north of the equator and straddles one of the world's great rainforest belts. The biodiversity is spectacular. Despite the logging mania that has ripped through the forests, some amazing flora survives - such as the world's biggest flower, the Rafflesia. Fauna is truly exotic and includes loveable

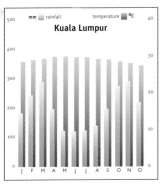

Kuala Lumpur

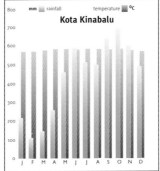

Kota Kinabalu

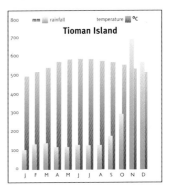

Tioman Island

Andaman Langkawi

Jl Teluk Datai, 07000 Langkawi, Malaysia
T: +60 4 959 1088 **F:** +60 4 959 1168
www.HotelClub.com/Hotels/Andaman_Langkawi_The

Taking its cue from nature, the Andaman incorporates some of the most recent advances in resort design. It is clearly one of Langkawi's leaders. The resort has managed to merge all of the features of five-star luxury with 187 rooms, Malay culture and a rainforest setting. With a couple of four-storey wings clipped either side of an imposing lobby block, the Andaman is big and bold, but structures are built along traditional lines and sit comfortably yards from a 50-million-year-old treeline.

The location on the northwest tip of Langkawi is one of the best for those wanting tropical escapism. Not only is the beach superb (albeit narrow at high tide), it is quiet and peaceful, being shared with only one other hotel. Exploring the surrounding rainforest is a fantastic experience and the Andaman puts on excellent eco-tours. Other facilities are broad with many organised activities, making it a good choice for families, and the spectacular Datai Bay golf course lies nearby.

The impressive lobby sets the tone, lots of wood and firm architecture abounds throughout. The rooms are well done and spacious. Ground-floor rooms open out to their own sun decks (called lanai) and upper ones have superior balconied views over the delightful bay.

The property has been underused to some extent, which means that many of the facilities, although well designed, can feel a little lifeless. Service remains high and the restaurants are excellent,

especially the curries at the Gulai House, a gentle stroll down the beach. The free-form pool is huge but surrounding foliage provides plenty of shade. Perhaps the highlight though is the Jamu Nature spa - have a massage in one of the open pavilions overlooking the bay - which is really quite spectacular.

Rates from: $$$
Star rating: ★ ★ ★ ★ ★
Overall rating: ♦♦♦♦ ½

Ambience:	9.11	Cleanliness:	8.93
Value:	8.07	Facilities:	8.58
Staff:	8.91	Restaurants:	8.53
Location:	8.74	Families:	8.76

Avillion Port Dickson

3rd Mile, Jl Pantai, 71000 Port Dickson, Malaysia
T: +60 6 647 6688 **F**: +60 6 647 6835
www.HotelClub.com/Hotels/Avillion_Village_Resort

Set in lush landscaped beachfront grounds that house three swimming pools (one for kids), the Avillion is more romantic resort than business hotel, and - given its quality - something of a rarity in Port Dickson. Children's diversions include a daily treasure hunt, a "pet farm" with scheduled feeding times and numerous fun activities at a dedicated day centre. There are also daily nature walks, herb and orchid gardens, kayaking, pedal-boating, jet-skiing, fishing and crabbing gear for rent. From a central block, accommodation fans out in seven wings that reach out on stilts into the Straits of Melaka, each tipped with dark timber "water chalets" whose pièce-de-resistance is a breezy veranda. Garden chalets offer similar low-rise structures on solid land. Decoration in all 294 rooms and suites combines old-world and ethnic Malay touches - the legend of Lord Jennings Avery is a constant throughout the resort - day beds and large bathrooms are standard, while the restaurants are uniformly excellent.

Rates from: $$
Star rating: ★ ★ ★ ★
Overall rating: 🌀🌀🌀🌀

Ambience:	8.65	Cleanliness:	8.53
Value:	7.85	Facilities:	8.18
Staff:	8.15	Restaurants:	7.79
Location:	8.08	Families:	8.16

Berjaya Langkawi Beach & Spa Resort

Karong Berkunci 200, Burau Bay, 07000 Langkawi, Malaysia
T: +60 4 959 1888 **F**: +60 4 959 1886
www.HotelClub.com/Hotels/Berjaya_Langkawi_Beach_and_Spa_Resort

The Berjaya Langkawi Beach & Spa Resort is, as the name suggests, especially proud of two things - its beach and its spa. The resort is on the large side with 500 rooms, making it one of the biggest on the island, with facilities to match. The architecture mimics a local village with the large central structures attractively surrounded by smaller satellites - some running throughout the gardens, and others perched directly over the sea. The rooms are contained within chalets, elevated on stilts in traditional Malay style. The bulk of the resort nestles at the foot of a hillside but a tail threads along the rocky section of the beach. This line of chalets stands over the lapping water, making relaxing on the balconies especially appealing. The interiors of all the chalets are comfortable enough, although they are clearly more rustic than luxuriant. Classed as a five-star hotel, while there may be a little fraying at the edges, the rates are very reasonable.

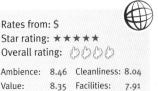

Rates from: $
Star rating: ★ ★ ★ ★ ★
Overall rating: 🌀🌀🌀🌀

Ambience:	8.46	Cleanliness:	8.04
Value:	8.35	Facilities:	7.91
Staff:	8.12	Restaurants:	8.34
Location:	8.39	Families:	8.04

Berjaya Redang Beach Resort

Pulau Redang, 20928 Kuala Terengganu, Malaysia
T: +60 9 697 3988 **F:** +60 9 697 3899
www.HotelClub.com/Hotels/Berjaya_Redang_Beach_Resort_Redang_Island

Once the word got out about Pulau Redang, the rest of the world caught on fast. Happily, the island is not yet overrun, and the few resorts that are here have kept themselves well below the palm trees. The Berjaya's original 152 wooden Malay-style chalets and suites - wedged into a valley that leads down to the breathtaking beach on the north side of the island - were joined by 130 deluxe rooms and suites in early 2005. A pool, tennis courts and jungle treks provide ample diversion. However, the real joy of Redang is still its marine park, which is why both island and resort bespeak an underwater Arcadia for the dive fraternity. Redang lies at the centre of the protected Terengganu Marine Park, whose reefs abound with the largest assortment of coral species the peninsula waters have to offer.

Rates from: $$
Star rating: ★ ★ ★ ★
Overall rating: 🐾🐾🐾🐾 ½

Ambience:	9.11	Cleanliness:	8.57
Value:	8.11	Facilities:	8.28
Staff:	8.25	Restaurants:	8.19
Location:	9.21	Families:	8.39

Berjaya Tioman Beach, Golf & Spa Resort

Pulau Tioman, 86807 Mersing, Johor, Malaysia
T: +60 9 419 1000 **F:** +60 9 419 1718
www.HotelClub.com/Hotels/Berjaya_Tioman_Beach_Resort_Tioman_Island

Back in the 1950s, Hollywood used Tioman as the location for the all-singin' and dancin' movie *South Pacific*. A half-century on, the island remains firmly anchored in the South China Sea and - although tourism has made some inroads - its scenic beaches and bays still provide some stunning multi-coloured backdrops. Tioman is now almost totally geared to tourism, and the Berjaya - on the northwest coast - is a large-scale four-star resort, counting 400 simple Malay-style chalets and rooms sprawling over 80 hectares of beachfront. Perched on the headland, a short buggy ride away, are another 196 more modern one- and two-bedroom suites. The Matahari restaurant is right on the beach, there is a bar by the pool, another restaurant by the 18-hole golf course, plus a snooker bar and a karaoke lounge. Kids get their own playground and a stable of donkeys, plus some wonderful snorkelling.

Rates from: $$
Star rating: ★ ★ ★ ★
Overall rating: 🐾🐾🐾🐾

Ambience:	8.88	Cleanliness:	8.28
Value:	8.05	Facilities:	8.17
Staff:	8.40	Restaurants:	8.16
Location:	8.96	Families:	8.50

Bon Ton Restaurant & Resort Langkawi

Pantai Cenang, 07000 Langkawi, Malaysia
T: +60 4 955 3643 **F**: +60 4 955 4791
www.HotelClub.com/Hotels/Bon_Ton_Restaurant_Resort_Langkawi

Just ten minutes away from the international airport, Bon Ton is one of the island's most interesting boutique-scale resorts. Founder Narelle McMurtie, a highly colourful Australian, set up the Langkawi Animal Shelter and Sanctuary within Bon Ton's grounds in 2000, adding a unique twist to what was already one of the best restaurants on the island and an eclectic collection of rooms.

Accommodation - seven rooms in all - is housed in century-old timber Malay kampong (village) structures with names like Blue Ginger and Yellow Orchid that have been re-erected on a former coconut plantation. Exteriors have

been restored to their original state while air-conditioning, ceiling fans and modern bathrooms have been installed inside, together with antique Malay and Indonesian wooden furniture; bright silk cushions and curtains add splashes of colour.

Bon Ton is all about unwinding from routine life. You won't find a TV in your room, however; satellite viewing is available in a communal lounge, which also has a pool table and dart board. Set among a generous turfed garden studded with mature plantation palms, is a rectangular designer swimming pool and jacuzzi which overlook mangrove-fringed wetlands (rather

than a sandy beach) and nearby Rebak island.

Bon Ton's restaurants and bars are Langkawi destinations in themselves. Chin Chin, slotted within an old Chinese shop house, is the island's only funky lounge bar.

Nam Restaurant - more Balinese than Malay in design - fuses Western cuisine with Asian spice. Its menu has been highly praised in a string of international magazine and newspaper reviews. Tables here offer front-row sunset viewing, which is often accompanied by water buffalo cooling off in the evening breeze and swooping migratory birds at the water's edge. Finally, Buzz Café is a bakery and more casual diner, where tantalising breakfasts are served with the sunrise.

Rates from: $$
Star rating: ★ ★ ★
Overall rating: Editor's Pick

Ambience:	n/a	Cleanliness:	n/a
Value:	n/a	Facilities:	n/a
Staff:	n/a	Restaurants:	n/a
Location:	n/a	Families:	n/a

Casa del Mar

Jl Pantai Cenang, 07000 Langkawi, Malaysia
T: +60 4 955 2388 **F:** +60 4 955 2228
www.HotelClub.com/Hotels/Casa_Del_Mar_Resort_Langkawi

On Pantai Cenang beach on the southwest coast of Langkawi, the Casa del Mar contains just 28 rooms and suites, so this really qualifies as a boutique resort. Ceiling fans spin lazily overhead in the compact terracotta-tiled rooms, each with a small balcony overlooking the sea.

In the far superior Junior Suites, four-poster beds are swathed in mosquito nets. Small-scale and simple just about sums up the aptly named Casa del Mar. The first-class dining room extends past the swimming pool and into the garden, so you can pick exactly where you

want to browse over a thoughtful menu that fuses Japanese cuisine with the Mediterranean, backed up by a cellar that has a strong Californian emphasis. Regrettably, parts of Langkawi have been colonised by larger, brasher establishments. Thankfully, Casa de Mar remains a haven of repose with a very personal feel.

Rates from: $$
Star rating: ★★★★
Overall rating: ♢♢♢♢ ½

Ambience:	8.97	Cleanliness:	9.13
Value:	8.66	Facilities:	8.26
Staff:	9.21	Restaurants:	8.34
Location:	8.95	Families:	8.96

Cheong Fatt Tze Mansion

14 Leith Street, 10200 Penang, Malaysia
T: +60 4 262 0006 **F:** +60 4 262 5289
www.HotelClub.com/Hotels/Cheong_Fatt_Tze_Mansion_Penang

Winner of three conservation awards, this hotel - built around five courtyards and containing just 16 bedrooms - is a Georgetown gem. Two minutes away from the buzz of the city's main thoroughfare Chulia Street - "La Maison Bleue" as it was once nicknamed on account of its indigo façade - is a haven of calm.

A massive restoration in the 1990s resulted in one of the best examples of preserved late 19th-century Chinese architecture in Malaysia. Doors opened to the public in 2001. Cheong Fatt Tse was an entrepreneurial legend, who left China penniless to become "the Rockefeller of the East" with homes

throughout the region; this Penang property was his operational base. Antique furniture and fittings pepper the granite-paved mansion. Common facilities include two historical archive rooms, a small library, a TV lounge and a compact spa and beauty centre. Rates include breakfast, which is taken outdoors in one of the courtyards.

Rates from: $
Star rating: ★★
Overall rating: Editor's Pick

Ambience:	n/a	Cleanliness:	n/a
Value:	n/a	Facilities:	n/a
Staff:	n/a	Restaurants:	n/a
Location:	n/a	Families:	n/a

Concorde Kuala Lumpur

2 Jl Sultan Ismail, 50250 Kuala Lumpur, Malaysia
T: +60 3 2144 2200 **F:** +60 3 2144 1629
www.HotelClub.com/Hotels/Concorde_Hotel_Kuala_Lumpur

This has got to be one of Kuala Lumpur's most practical hotels, and for those seeking no-nonsense comfort it hits the nail on the head. It is centrally placed in the Golden Triangle, close to some of the capital's trendiest nightlife and five minutes' stroll from the Petronas Towers and the city's best shopping, the Suria KLCC. The Hard Rock Café directly adjoins the hotel and the lobby buzzes with activity. As a building it is a bit uninspiring from without, but inside it is rather irregular and spacious with useful facilities, including some popular restaurants and the welcoming option of a good-sized rectangular outdoor pool. The gym is also surprisingly good. Standard rooms are fairly ordinary but the premier rooms are trendy, spacious and represent tremendous value.

Rates from: $
Star rating: ★★★★
Overall rating: ◗◗◗◗ ½

Ambience:	8.42	Cleanliness:	8.82
Value:	8.72	Facilities:	8.53
Staff:	8.59	Restaurants:	8.37
Location:	8.81	Families:	8.28

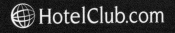

Datai Langkawi

Jl Teluk Datai, 07000 Lankawi, Malaysia
T: +60 4 959 2500 **F:** +60 4 959 2600
www.HotelClub.com/Hotels/Datai_Hotel_Langkawi_The

As timelines go, there is a fair gap between Langkawi's geological genesis 500 million years ago and 1993 AD, when the Datai opened. Bridging these two milestones is resident naturalist, Irshad, whose cheery early-morning treks into the rainforest open guests' eyes to the natural wonders around this wonderfully natural resort. Picking his way along the winding trails, Irshad unravels the complex eco-system, noting a nesting hornbill here, leaf beetles chomping on their favourite foliage there and pointing out medicinal plants that have been used for æons by indigenous tribes.

Indeed, there is an innate feeling at the Datai that it was not so much built next to the rainforest that covers almost two thirds of the island of Langkawi, but grew up as part of it. The 54 rooms in low-rise wings peeking over the canopy, and 58 villas and suites sprinkled throughout the forest floor are linked by open-air corridors and a series of verdant pathways. Cool Langkawi marble and warm red balau wood provide a gentle contrast within generous interiors. The exterior walls and roofs have a hint of Mayan mixed with Japanese. This unpretentious cosmopolitan aura is augmented by a progression of inducements to relaxation - balconies and daybeds in the rooms, Bose sound systems in the regular suites and villas (which also have private sun decks), and personal plungeries in the pool suites and villas. The ultimate of all these treats is the Datai Suite, a two-bedroom hideaway with expansive living and dining areas and surrounded by a sandstone balcony with panoramic ocean views.

Throughout its 10 years in operation, the Datai has been overseen by the genial Canadian Jamie Case, whose love of wine and easy-going charm are reflected both in the resort's cellars and its general character. His staff are uniformly courteous, eager to please without being intrusive or arrogant, and are patently proud of their place of employ. You witness this in the tiniest details - the care with which waiters serve your meals, the

spontaneous affection towards children, the delicate manipulations of the therapists' fingers in the Mandara Spa, an isolated haven out of sight of the rest of the resort yet within earshot of a gently meandering stream.

Spread over 750 hectares on a hillside above a private white-sand beach, the Datai never feels crowded. The peaceful main pool (no children under 16 here) is seemingly suspended within the forest canopy, almost in touching distance of the monkeys and flying foxes that leap from branch to branch. Settle into one of the teak chairs in the Lobby Bar, and you might almost be in a tree house.

Settle down to dinner at the Pavilion, and the authentic Thai dishes might make you think you have stepped across the border. Malaysian and Gallic cuisines mix and match at the Dining Room, while the Beach Club - next to the resort's second pool - is the most relaxed kid-friendly venue.

Just as the waves lap the Datai's beach and the resort merges into the rainforest, so the adjacent 18-hole championship golf course blends into the landscape equally naturally. There

is a similarly elegant synthesis back at the open-sided spa, where the deep petal-strewn tubs and rich wooden textures are totally at one with nature. The signature treatment - two therapists blending Japanese, Shiatsu, Thai, Hawaiian Lomi-Lomi, Swedish and Balinese massage for a spine-tingling 50 minutes - is one very small step away from outright seduction.

It goes without saying that the Datai is incredibly popular with its guests, a testament both to the resort which provides a sense of luxury and sophistication while respecting a remote natural environment, and to the extraordinarily dedicated team who run it so smoothly.

Rates from: $$$
Star rating: ★★★★★
Overall rating: ◊◊◊◊ ½

Ambience:	9.44	Cleanliness:	9.28
Value:	8.13	Facilities:	8.71
Staff:	9.07	Restaurants:	8.64
Location:	8.90	Families:	8.21

Eastern & Oriental Hotel

10 Lebuh Farquhar, 10200 Penang, Malaysia
T: +60 4 222 2000 **F:** +60 4 261 6333
www.HotelClub.com/Hotels/Eastern_Oriental_Hotel

There was no more depressing sight in Penang in the late 1980s than the Eastern & Oriental, a sadly neglected legacy of the pioneering Sarkies brothers. The hotel, fondly referred to as the E&O, first opened in the late 19th century, looked not so much run down as run over and it was not until a RM75 million renovation that it reopened spick and span again, just before the new millennium.

The rejuvenated E&O falls somewhere between the glitz of Raffles in Singapore and the authenticity of the Strand in Yangon. The exterior and many of the original fixtures and furniture have been preserved, but the hotel is not packaged with an unduly commercial slant. And rather than being dwarfed by skyscrapers, it sits securely in the historic part of Georgetown, within walking distance of landmarks like Fort Cornwallis and the Penang State Museum.

The general verdict is that the E&O has emerged looking pretty good, as much a pleasure to stay in

as it is to drop by for afternoon tea or a sundowner. All 101 butler-serviced suites have been thoughtfully appointed to provide a blend of history with modern amenities, and you can elect to stay in one of the Writers' Suites (Kipling, Coward, Hesse et al) or go the whole hog in the E&O Suite which, apart from anything else, has a dining room that can seat 22.

On the subject of food, the hotel has six different wining and dining venues, each especially appropriate to the meal in question. The all-day Sarkies Corner is truly international, as one would expect. A sunrise breakfast outside on the Verandah is a must, and a long colonial-style dinner is almost obligatory at 1885. And after a session at the gym or in the sea-facing pool, stretch out with some fresh juice on the Deck.

Rates from:	$$		
Star rating: ★ ★ ★ ★ ★			
Overall rating: ♦ ♦ ♦ ♦ ½			
Ambience:	9.38	Cleanliness:	9.30
Value:	8.88	Facilities:	8.51
Staff:	9.05	Restaurants:	8.51
Location:	8.80	Families:	8.32

Equatorial Melaka

Bandar Hilir, 75000 Melaka, Malaysia
T: +60 6 282 8333 **F**: +60 6 282 9333
www.HotelClub.com/Hotels/Equatorial_Hotel_Melaka

All in all, the Equatorial is among the best hotels in the historic town of Melaka. It boasts a great location, standing proud over the town centre. Although near a busy roundabout the noise is kept at bay, and it is within easy walking distance of the prime tourist attractions and restaurants of Jalan Merdeka. This thorough four-star hotel is all about straightforward comfort and space. The Equatorial's facilities are inviting, with a selection of six food and beverage outlets and a superb outdoor swimming pool. The 496 rooms are bright, spacious and modern, and represent excellent value. For business, the club floor is well done and the Equatorial has meeting and conference facilities capable of holding up to 1800 people. Staff are generally good, but some find that more demanding guests stretch them beyond their capabilities. For the price, a dependable hotel indeed.

Rates from: $		
Star rating: ★ ★ ★ ★		
Overall rating: 🌐🌐🌐🌐 ½		
Ambience:	8.84	Cleanliness: 8.89
Value:	8.36	Facilities: 8.68
Staff:	8.70	Restaurants: 8.59
Location:	8.86	Families: 8.82

Hilton Kuching

Jl Tunku Abdul Rahman, 93748 Kuching, Malaysia
T: +60 82 248 200 **F**: +60 82 428 984
www.HotelClub.com/Hotels/Hilton_Hotel_Kuching

Facing each other on opposite sides of the Sungai Sarawak River, the Hilton and Fort Margherita make for a sharp contrast; the fort was built in 1879 to repel pirates, the hotel rather more recently to extend a cordial welcome to all comers. And it makes a very successful job of it, with 315 comfortably appointed rooms and suites set back slightly from the city's picturesque waterfront promenade.

Kuching's cosmopolitan population is reflected in the Hilton's eateries, with Chinese, international and local dishes on offer, as well as a sushi and oyster bar. For recreation, there is a flood-lit tennis court, pool (and pool table) and a playground for children.

Business travellers are similarly well catered to here, with Internet connections and fax machines available, and private check-in on the executive floors, whose 12th-floor clubroom and library provide commanding views over the city.

Rates from: $		
Star rating: ★ ★ ★ ★		
Overall rating: 🌐🌐🌐🌐 ½		
Ambience:	8.42	Cleanliness: 8.77
Value:	8.62	Facilities: 8.04
Staff:	8.77	Restaurants: 8.16
Location:	9.15	Families: 8.58

Hilton Petaling Jaya

2 Jl Barat, Petaling Jaya, 46200 Kuala Lumpur, Malaysia
T: +60 3 7955 9122 **F:** +60 3 7955 3909
www.HotelClub.com/Hotels/Hilton_Petaling_Jaya

The Hilton sits in the industrial and commercial satellite city of Petaling Jaya, only half an hour or so from Kuala Lumpur's city centre if the traffic is light, and 45 minutes from the airport. Built in 1984, it might seem to have had its day but it remains efficiently run and hugely popular, especially with businesses in the area. Facilities are predictable, although the practical conference rooms are extensive - no surprise here, given the clientele. Leisure facilities equally are dated but popular - the decent gym barely has a piece of equipment spare during peak hours and the four restaurants buzz with a steady stream of visitors. Uncle Chilli's pub is the best in the area and wonderfully funky with plenty of soul. The 553 rooms are fair, although nothing special, visually at least. But staff are proactive and polite, and despite a little age and road noise, this is one of the best hotels in the up-and-coming city of "PJ".

Rates from: $
Star rating: ★ ★ ★ ★ ★
Overall rating: ♨ ♨ ♨ ♨

Ambience:	8.32	Cleanliness:	8.69
Value:	8.21	Facilities:	8.20
Staff:	8.67	Restaurants:	8.54
Location:	8.31	Families:	8.21

Hyatt Regency Johor Bahru

Jl Sungai Chat, 80720 Johor Bahru, Malaysia
T: +60 722 21 234 **F:** +60 722 32 718
www.HotelClub.com/Hotels/Hyatt_Regency_Johor_Bahru

Of all Johor Bahru's lacking, lustreless hostelries, this is probably the most upmarket, complete with sprawling two-tier resort swimming pool in large grounds that also house two tennis courts, a gym and spa. Sleek-lined rooms are contemporary in flavour and there is a generous four floors of Regency accommodation. The club's exclusive lounge offers complimentary Continental breakfasts, evening cocktails and canapés - with an outdoor seating option, special concierge service and private boardroom. These top floors have sweeping views across the Straits (downtown Singapore is around 30 minutes by road from the hotel). Also visible, and of local cultural interest, is JB's Sultan's palace. Abu Bakar Mosque and the Johor Museum are within easy walking distance. Hotel restaurants include Piccolo, a modern Italian joint near the pool, with an open kitchen, large pizza oven and live music nightly. Aska offers an indoor contemporary Japanese alterative, where sushi and teppanyaki are specialities.

Rates from: $
Star rating: ★ ★ ★ ★
Overall rating: ♨ ♨ ♨ ♨

Ambience:	8.34	Cleanliness:	8.55
Value:	8.09	Facilities:	7.90
Staff:	7.86	Restaurants:	8.23
Location:	7.89	Families:	7.82

Hyatt Regency Kuantan

Telok Chempedak, 25050 Kuantan, Malaysia
T: +60 9 566 1234 **F**: +60 9 567 4677
www.HotelClub.com/Hotels/Hyatt_Regency_Kuantan

The east-coast city of Kuantan does not draw a large number of international visitors despite its great beach, Telok Chempedak, or the primary jungle nearby. Neither the city nor the beach area has a large choice of hotels so the Hyatt Regency Kuantan easily emerges as the area's place to stay. An attractive and airy hotel complex divided into four blocks, it is thoughtfully designed with local Malay architectural lines. Within are 336 bright rooms, all enjoying balconies with garden or sea views. The resort has two beguiling azure pools a stone's throw from the sea. The leisure facilities are happily sufficient, with a well-equipped gym, tennis and squash courts, kids' club, plus beach activities. Three popular restaurants cover Malay, Italian and Sichuan cuisine, and the Hyatt Regency fulfils its obligation as one of the leading hotels in the state capital by laying on a full complement of business amenities and function rooms.

Rates from: $
Star rating: ★ ★ ★ ★
Overall rating: ♦♦♦♦ ½

Ambience:	8.68	Cleanliness:	8.64
Value:	8.19	Facilities:	8.19
Staff:	8.79	Restaurants:	8.37
Location:	8.96	Families:	9.05

Istana Hotel

73 Jl Raja Chulan, 50200 Kuala Lumpur, Malaysia
T: +60 3 2141 9988 **F**: +60 3 2144 0111
www.HotelClub.com/Hotels/Hotel_Istana

Kuala Lumpur is one of the world's most progressive Islamic cities, and there are echoes of the faith in its architecture. This can be said of the Istana, the Malay word for palace, which has incorporated Islamic elements into its design and decor.

The 23-storey exterior seems modestly veiled and within is a characteristic large lobby with tiles, marble, trickling water and thick pillars. The corridors and rooms continue the Middle-Eastern theme, although they are jaded in areas and could do with updating. Nonetheless, the 516 rooms are spacious, comfy and well-equipped, and the hotel facilities are excellent. A good fitness centre lurks unusually next to an underground car park and the neon-clad entertainment centre, Musictheque Club 73, gets loud and lively late on. An otherwise reasonable hotel is elevated by a fine location on the junction of Jalan Sultan Ismail and Jalan Raja Chulan, near the shops and restaurants of Lot 10 and Jalan Bukit Bintang.

Rates from: $
Star rating: ★ ★ ★ ★
Overall rating: ♦♦♦♦

Ambience:	8.38	Cleanliness:	8.57
Value:	8.28	Facilities:	8.16
Staff:	8.22	Restaurants:	8.39
Location:	8.70	Families:	8.33

JW Marriott Hotel Kuala Lumpur

183 Jl Bukit Bintang, 55100 Kuala Lumpur, Malaysia
T: +60 3 2715 9000 **F:** +60 3 2715 7000
www.HotelClub.com/Hotels/JW_Marriott_Hotel_Kuala_Lumpur

Built in 1997, the JW Marriott is still one of Kuala Lumpur's smarter properties and benefits from a modern interior design. The style is somewhat European, even regal, with plenty of pale creamy-beige tones in the polished pillars and marble. The 561 richly elegant rooms embrace a generous floor area, voicemail, call-waiting, desk-level electrical outlets, ergonomic chairs and adjustable desk lighting, and together with the spacious club floor are aimed primarily at the corporate market, and provide the sort of "office-away-from-home" that takes the worry out of road-warrioring. Take your choice of accommodation from a wide selection, starting with the humble king-size room and gravitating via various suites all the way up to the Presidential, which is just short of 2,000 square metres. Conference and banqueting facilities run to 22 broadbanded rooms and a Grand Ballroom.

Given that a number of the guests are en route to one of the two stunning resorts under the same ownership (Pangkor Laut and Tanjong Jara), and the prime location of the hotel, the JW serves the leisure market just as well. And it could hardly be better: right in the middle of the Golden Triangle at the end of the Bintang Walk connecting Lot 10 with the seven-storey Starhill Shopping complex directly adjacent. There is plenty in the way of diversion within the JW, notably the spa, which provides a broad buffet of wet and dry, hot and cold, with a fully-equipped gym, a bevy of treatment rooms and somewhere to put your feet up afterwards.

The hotel restaurants are very much what might be expected of an international chain; the distinctive Satay Club combines the aromas and taste of this idiosyncratic Malay barbecue with smartly designed surrounds. Small wonder all 40 places are often filled with diners concentrating heavily on their food - and that's precisely how it should be.

Rates from: $
Star rating: ★ ★ ★ ★ ★
Overall rating: ◊ ◊ ◊ ◊ ½

Ambience:	8.69	Cleanliness:	8.81
Value:	8.30	Facilities:	8.52
Staff:	8.39	Restaurants:	8.35
Location:	9.08	Families:	8.31

Mandarin Oriental Kuala Lumpur

Kuala Lumpur City Centre, 50088 Kuala Lumpur, Malaysia
T: +60 3 2380 8888 **F:** +60 3 2380 8833
www.HotelClub.com/Hotels/Mandarin_Oriental

300 original artworks - including Malay dancing scenes and symbolic Islamic pieces - decorate the public areas and 643 guestrooms (including 51 serviced apartments), all characterised by warm, invitingly soft furnishings and set against earthy Melakan wood tones.

The executive side of life is catered for by two-line IDD telephones, voicemail and dataports, while thickly upholstered furniture and marbled bathrooms with separate tub and shower induce a definitive air of luxurious relaxation. The top seven storeys of the Mandarin are given over to its club, where breakfast, snacks and cocktails are served in the private lounge that also includes a very civilised billiards room. But the lounge's forte undoubtedly lies beyond its windows, for it is impossible to glance outside and not be stopped short - perhaps for the third or fourth time - by the Brobdingnagian Petronas Towers, whether bathed in glistening sunshine or flashing black and silver at the height of a thunderstorm.

In keeping with the spacious and inviting effect of all its public areas, the Mandarin's restaurants were designed to make the best use of natural light and the views. The all-day dining Biba's Café is divided into three levels that make it informal yet intimate. In contrast, the Pacifica Grill & Bar mixes its design textures and flavours in its Asian open kitchen, so you dine surrounded by a dazzling, contemporary mélange of mosaic tiles, wood, iron, glass, fabric and murals. Lai Po Heen is an entirely different scene again - an

It now seems difficult to believe that what was once the Malaysian capital's racecourse has been transformed into the city's new centre, KLCC. Fusing a 20-hectare park and shopping and performing arts centres, its centerpiece is the totemic Petronas Towers. At the nucleus of this metropolitan hub, the Mandarin has successfully incorporated local aesthetics with an international appeal and a residential feel.

The hotel complements rather than competes with its monolithic, pewter-clad neighbour, even to the extent of camouflaging rooftop fittings to make itself look attractive from above. Custom-made copper lanterns and Malay lattice grills for external louvres add a practical touch of local colour, one that is reinforced inside with custom-carved kris door handles, antique Nonya screens in gold leaf and sword reliefs on the handrails.

Perfectly suited to its environment, the Mandarin also provides a sympathetic, nigh perfect environment for its guests. Some

architectural shell reminiscent of Shanghai's heyday, with a wok-cooking area and private dining areas furnished with Melakan antiques. The Wasabi Bistro is a modern take on intricate, traditional Japanese fare in an elegant and intimate setting.

Despite being in the heart of the city, the Mandarin's extensive recreational facilities ensure it doubles as a resort. From the outdoor infinity pool you can gaze down on the joggers, strollers and tai chi-ers in the park below. You can work off surplus energy at the tennis or squash courts, and surplus frustrations with a bout of kick-boxing in the aerobics studio. Cardiovascular and other state-of-the-art exercise machines throng the gymnasium, while specialists at the Thalgo Marine Spa can personally guide you through a customised, far-ranging menu of beauty and wellness treatments.

For more leisurely exercise, shop until you drop at the adjacent Suria KLCC Shopping Centre, with its extensive range of top retail outlets, where hotel guests enjoy a range of what might be termed pecuniary inducements.

Rates from: $$
Star rating: ★ ★ ★ ★ ★
Overall rating: ⚘ ⚘ ⚘ ⚘ ½

Ambience:	8.79	Cleanliness:	9.06
Value:	8.36	Facilities:	8.66
Staff:	8.56	Restaurants:	8.62
Location:	9.27	Families:	8.41

Mutiara Burau Bay Beach Resort Langkawi

Teluk Burau, 07000 Langkawi, Malaysia
T: +60 4 959 1061 **F**: +60 4 959 1172
www.HotelClub.com/Hotels/Mutiara_Burau_Bay_Beach_Resort_Langkawi

The location and architecture help set this simple resort apart - instead of the usual vertical block, the three-star Mutiara consists of 150 simple cabana chalets. Set among pretty gardens and trees, each is stand-alone with its own private balcony. The cabanas are not luxurious but basic; externally they look somewhat prefabricated, while inside they are compact with low beds and walk-in showers. However, they are great value. Facilities and services are modest, but the resort does manage to offer a fair choice of food, an equestrian centre and a good free-form pool. The big bonus is the splendid remote beachfront - set in front of sprawling gardens complete with sleepy monitor lizards - one of the most pleasant on Langkawi. It is a 20-minute ride from town and therefore more peaceful than some other more expensive alternatives on this peaceful island. A super low-key place for families.

Rates from: $
Star rating: ★ ★ ★
Overall rating: ♢♢♢♢ ½

Ambience:	8.52	Cleanliness:	8.56
Value:	8.52	Facilities:	8.22
Staff:	8.80	Restaurants:	8.16
Location:	8.68	Families:	8.92

Palace of the Golden Horses

Jl Kuda Emas, Mines Resort City, 43300 Kuala Lumpur, Malaysia
T: +60 3 8943 2333 **F**: +60 3 8943 2666
www.HotelClub.com/Hotels/Palace_of_The_Golden_Horses

Part of the mega 400-hectare landscaped Mines Resort City complex and billed, presumably without any intended irony, as "Asia's Most Extraordinary Hotel", the Palace of the Golden Horses was built on top of a disused tin mine. Indeed, "over the top" is the phrase that comes to mind on a tour of the hotel, with its 480 rooms and suites (18 of the latter are categorised "Head of State"), seven restaurants and multiple function rooms, all presented in a blend of Malay and Moorish architecture. On the assumption that you are not one of the many delegates attending the international conference centre, the Palace is within trotting distance of a man-made beach resort and state-of-the-science "health sanctuary", a shopping plaza, an amusement park and an 18-hole golf course, so it is well placed for a one-stop family vacation - and a popular one at that, especially with local residents.

Rates from: $$
Star rating: ★ ★ ★ ★
Overall rating: ♢♢♢♢ ½

Ambience:	8.93	Cleanliness:	8.96
Value:	8.07	Facilities:	8.70
Staff:	8.51	Restaurants:	8.68
Location:	7.86	Families:	8.55

Pan Pacific Hotel KLIA

KL International Airport, Jl CTA 4B, 64000 KLIA, Malaysia
T: +60 3 8787 3333 **F:** +60 3 8787 5555
www.HotelClub.com/Hotels/Pan_Pacific_Kuala_Lumpur

Although there are only two main reasons to stay here - to catch your breath before or after a flight at Kuala Lumpur's isolated international airport, or to catch some action at the nearby Grand Prix circuit - this is an excellent property and it would succeed if placed elsewhere. Unlike other airport hotels that specialise in disappointing a captive market, the Pan Pacific has been well thought out and maintains high standards. The lobby displays flight information and adjoins the airport via an immeasurably convenient walkway. But the hotel is more imaginative than just an airport extension and is well-appointed with cosy rooms, the Pacific Floor being especially good.

Facilities are capable and useful, with late-closing restaurants and a 24-hour spa. There is a small and pleasant tropical pool to soak in, sitting rather memorably in the shadow of the air traffic control tower. The Pan Pacific has some superb staff and is run very smoothly. Definitely one of the best airport hotels in Asia.

Rates from: $
Star rating: ★ ★ ★ ★ ★
Overall rating: 🏨 🏨 🏨 🏨 ½

Ambience:	8.82	Cleanliness:	9.11
Value:	8.58	Facilities:	8.57
Staff:	8.65	Restaurants:	8.57
Location:	8.62	Families:	8.50

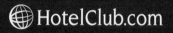

Pangkor Laut Resort

Pangkor Laut, 32200 Lumut, Malaysia
T: +60 5 699 1100 **F:** +60 5 699 1200
www.HotelClub.com/Hotels/Pangkor_Laut_Resort_Pangkor_Island

One of Pangkor Laut's biggest - large pun intended - fans is tenor Luciano Pavarotti, a regular visitor all too happy to sing the resort's praises by rendering the not exactly unpredictable aria: *O Paradiso*. Cue standing ovation from just about everyone who has ever stayed here. Here's why.

The 120-hectare island is covered by a two-million-year-old rainforest, and some seven score villas and suites. Add in top-of-the-range food, drink and recreational diversions and the result is a resort with few peers anywhere in the world.

"Exclusive" and "idyllic" are words easily associated with Pangkor Laut, which opened in 1994 and subsequently added its own spa. No mere massage joint, this is an entire village spread over 1.5 hectares between the sea and the rainforest. Interspersed with open courtyards, lotus ponds, a herb garden and a reflexology path, it also mirrors the country's ethnic make-up, providing Ayurvedic and Chinese herbal treatments in surroundings that are Malaysia at its most ravishing. And forget any idea of hurried, in-out-spa-it-all-about modus operandi. Visits here start with a well-defined ritual that lasts three quarters of an hour: a Chinese footbath and mini massage, a Malay river bath, a Japanese goshi-goshi cloth scrub, an exfoliating Shanghai scrub, a cup of tea and then - and only then - does the real treatment begin.

As might be expected, the 22 new villas built out over the sea next to the spa village are Pangkor Laut's paramount accommodation. But all of the resort's 148 villas are superbly appointed, with spacious interiors and cushioned deckchairs on generous private balconies, so the main question is to decide whether you want to stay overhanging the sea, up the hill overlooking the bay, on the beach or in one of the garden villas. There are CD players in each villa and a wide selection of discs in the library, however anyone looking for a TV is going to have to search long and hard for one of two lounges. The message is clear - never mind Discovery or National Geographic channels, you can find reality TV

right on the doorstep.

This being Pangkor Laut, you do not simply wander off on a jungle trek, but venture forth accompanied by resident naturalist Uncle Yip, who is on first-name terms with the yellow-pied hornbills, monitor lizards and troupes of macaques. Excursions usually end up at Emerald Bay, a stunning crescent-shaped bay often cited as one of the most beautiful beaches in the world. Further afield, you can swim, snorkel and island-hop around the Pulau Seribu, while back at the resort there is a quintet of tennis and squash courts, two swimming pools, a jet pool and a cold dip.

Pangkor Laut's six restaurants round off its almost hypnotic

offerings, for this is somewhere most guests feel they need to hang around and savour everything for far longer than the bounds of a brief holiday. Chef Uncle Lim - one of the resort's characters who has been here from the beginning - runs his eponymous eatery on a rocky outcrop overlooking the sea, serving delicious Nyonya and Hockchew delicacies. The open kitchen at Fisherman's Cove rustles up a mixture of Western, Italian, Chinese and fresh seafood. Or you can hire the resort's teak tongkang junk and spend an evening at sea over a four-course dinner. There are few better ways to end a day in one of Asia's most idyllic resorts.

Rates from: $$
Star rating: ★ ★ ★ ★ ★
Overall rating: ♦ ♦ ♦ ♦ ½

Ambience:	9.28	Cleanliness:	9.01
Value:	8.09	Facilities:	8.55
Staff:	8.88	Restaurants:	8.58
Location:	8.98	Families:	8.41

Pelangi Beach Resort Langkawi

*May '07
with
Charlton
family*

Pantai Cenang, 07000 Langkawi, Malaysia
T: +60 4 952 8888 **F:** +60 4 952 8899
www.HotelClub.com/Hotels/Pelangi_Beach_Resort_Langkawi

It is not often that you stumble across a beach resort with 350 rooms that is almost entirely made of wood. The Pelangi Beach Resort is one of Langkawi's largest but is cleverly spread out - and sensitively designed - to avoid the mass-produced atmosphere often found in hotels this big. Its 12 hectares are plenty on which to liberally sprinkle low-rise buildings among beautifully tended lawns and gardens, quiet lakes and two very large free-form pools.

The impressive timber lobby reveals the principal theme throughout the resort. Everywhere you look there is local kempas and kapor timber. Shunning practical concrete materials and high-rise profiles, the Pelangi's wooden design is inspired by the local Malay kampongs or villages. A total of 51 double-storey chalets or bungalows house the guests below sweeping roofs. Chalets are supported by stilts, with naked beams and broad verandahs very much in evidence. Inside, the rooms are rustic, trim and cosy. The wooden construction has a few drawbacks, though. Windows are small and the deep colours absorb a lot of light, resulting in dark interiors. More problematic are the acoustic properties - footsteps and vibrations carry easily - although the hotel has taken measures to dampen and muffle the noise. Also note that the resort is conveniently close to the airport so the occasional plane passes overhead, but they are few and do little to dent the peace.

Colourful resort facilities are inviting with the fullest range of tours, water sports and activities for all the family. If you are knocking around the tennis or squash courts, the good kids' club can take care of the little ones. The fun pub, Tepian Cenang, includes a 12-metre sampan, and the restaurants are pretty good although they all tend to have an Asian emphasis. Some look out over Langkawi's main beach lining the resort. And if it is the ocean you love then it might be worth opting for the Marina Club rooms - they have the best sea views and the added benefit of free cocktails in the club lounge.

Rates from: $
Star rating: ★ ★ ★ ★ ★
Overall rating: ◗ ◗ ◗ ◗ ½

Ambience:	9.16	Cleanliness:	8.85
Value:	8.46	Facilities:	8.55
Staff:	8.85	Restaurants:	8.51
Location:	8.86	Families:	8.99

Penang Mutiara Beach Resort

1 Jl Teluk Bahang, 11050 Penang, Malaysia
T: +60 4 886 8888 **F:** +60 4 885 2829
www.HotelClub.com/Hotels/Mutiara_Beach_Resort_Penang

Certainly one of the better properties in the tried-and-tested holiday destination of Penang, this is a surprisingly good resort that lives up to each of its five stars. The 16-storey resort sits on seven hectares of palm-studded land, wrapped in hills on one side and lined by a beach on the other. Quiet and secluded, there is little within walking distance, but five minutes' drive away lies the tourist strip of Batu Ferringhi. The facilities of the resort are ideal for a short break, the handsome exterior gardens pointing proudly towards the large swirling pool and an excellent kids' pool. These provide the essential alternative to the shallow beach, which is unfortunately often a minefield of jellyfish. The hotel's 438 rooms (each over 50 square metres) are another highlight - cheerful with rattan furniture and roomy balconies overlooking the sea. Cuisine is good if a tad pricey, with Italian favourite La Farfalla winning numerous local awards.

Rates from: $
Star rating: ★ ★ ★ ★
Overall rating: ◊◊◊◊ ½

Ambience:	8.82	Cleanliness:	8.88
Value:	8.27	Facilities:	8.55
Staff:	8.61	Restaurants:	8.56
Location:	8.36	Families:	8.83

Puri Melaka   *30·11·07 with Mum.*

118 Jl Tun Tan Cheng Lock, 75200 Melaka, Malaysia
T: +60 6 282 5588 **F:** +60 6 281 5588
www.HotelClub.com/Hotels/Puri_Melaka

Walk through the doors of this charismatic two-star boutique hotel in the heart of the old city of Melaka and you seem to have left the 21st century behind. The building was originally the home of Tan Kim Seng (1805-1864), a third-generation Melaka-born Straits Chinese who went on to become one of Singapore's most philanthropic tycoons. The Puri stands in one of the oldest streets in Melaka (once nicknamed Millionaires' Row) and is now surrounded by antique and bric-à-brac shops. The hotel runs back almost 100 metres from the street, and its intricately decorated façade is echoed in details such as antique chairs and bed headboards in its 50 rooms and suites, which all offer basic amenites. The Puri's main restaurant, the Galeri Café, may not be gourmet, but it has atmosphere in spades. Whether you are lolling in the garden or relaxing in the lounge (which has wireless broadband), history fairly gallops about you here.

Rates from: $
Star rating: ★ ★
Overall rating: ◊◊◊◊ ½

Ambience:	9.00	Cleanliness:	8.69
Value:	9.23	Facilities:	7.69
Staff:	8.54	Restaurants:	7.55
Location:	9.46	Families:	8.33

Regent Kuala Lumpur

160 Jl Bukit Bintang, 55100 Kuala Lumpur, Malaysia
T: +60 3 2141 8000 **F**: +60 3 2142 1441
www.HotelClub.com/Hotels/Regent_Hotel_Kuala_Lumpur

As an all-rounder, the Regent excels, putting it well into the first division of KL hotels. This well-established and respected property is parked happily opposite the Starhill Shopping Centre on Jalan Bukit Bintang with its mass of retail outlets. Such is its appeal that the hotel draws people in from the buzzing streets, rather than being anonymous or overlooked - the sweeping lobby is alive with constant activity. All the restaurants, from Lai Ching Yuen (Cantonese) to the Terrace with its high tea at weekends, from the ground floor Brasserie to the ever-so-chic modern Italian menu of Oggi are popular both with guests and shoppers seeking to rest their weary legs. The pleasant service definitely helps. The 468 rooms are perfectly comfortable and surprisingly peaceful given the location. And the recreational and business facilities are complete and well above average. Accessible, both geographically and financially, this is everyone's five-star hotel.

Rates from: $$
Star rating: ★ ★ ★ ★ ★
Overall rating: ۵ ۵ ۵ ۵ ½

Ambience:	8.53	Cleanliness:	8.79
Value:	8.32	Facilities:	8.34
Staff:	8.81	Restaurants:	8.38
Location:	8.92	Families:	8.44

Renaissance Kuala Lumpur Hotel

Corner of Jl Ampang and Jl Sultan Ismail, 50450 Kuala Lumpur, Malaysia
T: +60 3 2162 2233 **F**: +60 3 2163 1122
www.HotelClub.com/Hotels/Renaissance_Hotel_Kuala_Lumpur

One of Kuala Lumpur's giants, with almost 1,000 rooms, the Renaissance offers the works if you want a list of facilities as long as your arm. It is all here in terms of leisure and recreation, with five excellent restaurants offering Chinese, Japanese, Mediterranean and Asian cuisine and a fabulous free-form outdoor pool to relax beside. For business, the hotel certainly rises above others with its impressive Convention Centre and banquet facilities, which are big enough to host major events. The hotel is split into two vast wings, the superior Renaissance wing with its black marble and elegant chandeliers and the rather more simple New World wing. Each has its own entrance, lobby and check-in, which can get quite confusing if you are new to the hotel. The New World rooms are straightforward while the Renaissance rooms follow the more regal decor that the hotel embraces in general. With a good location and many rooms that gaze out over the Petronas Towers, this is a popular and very affordable choice.

Rates from: $
Star rating: ★ ★ ★ ★ ★
Overall rating: ۵ ۵ ۵ ۵ ½

Ambience:	8.66	Cleanliness:	8.91
Value:	8.44	Facilities:	8.56
Staff:	8.71	Restaurants:	8.52
Location:	8.71	Families:	8.39

Ritz-Carlton Kuala Lumpur

168 Jl Imbi, 55100 Kuala Lumpur, Malaysia
T: +60 3 2142 8000 **F:** +60 3 2143 8080
www.HotelClub.com/Hotels/Ritz_Carlton_Hotel_Kuala_Lumpur

Of all the hotels in Kuala Lumpur, some of the most professional, thorough and sincere staff are found at the Ritz-Carlton. Their genuine effort to put the guest first - whether waiting in the lobby, getting into a lift or strolling the corridors - makes your stay here a real pleasure. In keeping with the staff, the hotel itself is intimate and personal. The building is small and snug with a refreshing calm once inside - you could never get lost in a crowd here. The interior design is classic European with Asian touches. Gentle colours are balanced with dark woods and subtle lighting in both the 248 rooms and corridors.

The European-Asian blend permeates the restaurants. From the Mediterranean, Rossini's serves authentic Italian cuisine in elegant surroundings, from the Far East, Li Yen specialises in Cantonese and dim sum. And for a combination of Western and Malaysian food try César's Bistro, a satellite restaurant just away from the hotel on Bintang Walk. A rather civilised bar adjoins the lobby while the club rooms on floors 17 through 20 have the rather plush Club Lounge with its dedicated concierge, 24-hour beverages and five daily food servings.

The soothing and lavishly furnished rooms, at a minimum of 46 square metres, are some of the largest in Kuala Lumpur and refreshingly wide with a T-shaped floor plan. The personal feel is maintained with the attentive services of a 24-hour dedicated butler, and repeat guests enjoy added touches such as having the room laid out to their previous preferences, and their names embroidered on their pillow cases.

Full business facilities, the magnetic pull of the top-end spa, and a handsome outdoor pool (albeit slightly noisy) complete the picture. All are maintained and run with the same style and warmth. The Ritz-Carlton tends to appeal to corporate clients, but there is no reason why its appeal should not be broader, especially as it is located conveniently near the shops of lively Jalan Bukit Bintang, and the service would be appreciated by anyone far away from home.

Rates from: $
Star rating: ★ ★ ★ ★ ★
Overall rating: 🌀🌀🌀🌀 ½

Ambience:	8.96	Cleanliness:	9.32
Value:	8.62	Facilities:	8.72
Staff:	9.23	Restaurants:	8.43
Location:	8.76	Families:	8.93

Shangri-La Hotel Kuala Lumpur

11 Jl Sultan Ismail, 50250 Kuala Lumpur, Malaysia
T: +60 3 2032 2388 **F:** +60 3 2070 1514
www.HotelClub.com/Hotels/ShangriLa_Hotel_Kuala_Lumpur

While maybe not the earthly paradise that its name might suggest, the Shangri-La continues to maintain its position as one of central KL's best. The modern, chic lobby sets the tone for the whole hotel, but is nicely offset by the lush and leafy gardens. Perhaps it is the eight restaurants and bars which stand out most with some excellent and varied choices. The chef's brigade at the Lemon Garden prepares à-la-minute dishes for the "live" buffet in the multi-Asian show kitchen, and the aromas from Cinnamon's oven-fresh pastries are enough to make your tastebuds twinkle. The floor-to-ceiling wine racks, designer lights and central water cascade continue the stylish design at Lafite. Wine and sake is displayed in similar fashion at Zipangu, the contemporary Tokyo-style brasserie. Slightly more traditional is the first-floor English-style pub with pool table, draught beer and live entertainment. The whole package is rounded out with top-class service and 701 well kitted-out rooms. There is a wealth of choice when it comes to picking precisely where you are going to lay your weary head, from the more prosaic executive and deluxe rooms right the way up to the Royal Suite - an aptly named apartment as the Shangri-La has close connections with Malaysia's sultans and royal family. A couple of notches down the scale, the trio of speciality suites provides some of the city's more exceptional accommodation. Italian marble, antique wrought-iron tables, mahogany furniture and European and American fabrics combine to impart a sense of luxury that is as entertaining as it is exclusive, with the whole warmed by plush handmade Australian carpeting. More marble gives the bathroom a superior feel, and Trussardi toiletries from Italy round out the whole package. All in all, the suites epitomise the KL Shangri-La's international standards, which perfectly complement Malaysian hospitality.

Rates from: $$
Star rating: ★ ★ ★ ★ ★
Overall rating: ♦ ♦ ♦ ♦ ½

Ambience:	8.85	Cleanliness:	9.00
Value:	8.35	Facilities:	8.56
Staff:	8.77	Restaurants:	8.71
Location:	8.76	Families:	8.52

October 06

Shangri-La's Golden Sands Resort

Batu Ferringhi, 11100 Penang, Malaysia
T: +60 4 886 1911 **F**: +60 4 881 1880
www.HotelClub.com/Hotels/ShangriLas_Golden_Sands_Resort_Penang

Start the day with a guided two-hour jungle walk through one of the nearby rainforests, ease down a gear with a stretching tai chi lesson at the Pavillion Terrace - now for a hard-earned breakfast at the Garden Café. The boat for Monkey Beach leaves from the Watersports Centre at 10 am, or maybe today just lounge by the beachside pool and have that tension-sapping foot massage. Snack lunch at the Kuda Laut poolside bar before the satay cooking class at 3pm, followed by an archery tournament and evening tennis competition. Sigi's by the Sea for bistro dinner before enjoying the live band over an evening cocktail at the Sunset Lounge. Retire to your seventh-floor Deluxe Room and admire the sea view from the balcony before collapsing into bed - totally exhausted.

To say Golden Sands features a full activity programme would be a gross understatement. Every waking hour, seven days a week, there is something going on, from juggling lessons to table-tennis competitions, from aquarobics to palmistry, from trapeze demonstrations to napkin-folding classes. The focus for the activities is Starfy's, an activity centre-cum-team building village. And the fun is not restricted to adults - children have their own Star Kids' Club broken into the Betty Club (4 to 7 years) and the Kids' Club (8 to 12 years). Circus school, origami, face-painting, trampolining and treasure hunts all ensure the younger ones return at the end of the day equally worn out. And for those difficult in-betweens, the Teen Club is the cool hangout. Oh, and if it rains there is a full menu of indoor to-dos.

The sands and sea of Batu Ferringhi are sub-standard for Asia but the 395-room Golden Sands, with its extensive selection of entertainment and large free-form pools, more than makes up for this. The old adage says that change is as good as a rest - Shangri-La's Golden Sands certainly is a change, whether you return rested is another issue.

Rates from: $
Star rating: ★ ★ ★ ★
Overall rating: 🌙 🌙 🌙 🌙 ½

Ambience:	8.79	Cleanliness:	8.74
Value:	8.62	Facilities:	8.47
Staff:	8.51	Restaurants:	8.44
Location:	8.80	Families:	8.80

Shangri-La's Rasa Ria Resort

Pantai Dalit, 89208 Tuaran, Malaysia
T: +60 88 792 888 **F**: +60 88 792 777
www.HotelClub.com/Hotels/ShangriLas_Rasa_Ria_Resort_Kota_Kinabalu

The defining aspect of the Rasa Ria is its location, some 45 minutes' drive north of Kota Kinabalu. This remoteness lends some of the escape factor that many visitors seek when heading for Borneo, and the resort sits contentedly between a trio of appealing environments - leafy rainforest, a splendid 18-hole championship golf course and a scenic stretch of white-sand beach. It is also well placed for forays into Sabah's country parks, while Mount Kinabalu and the Poring hot springs are within easy day tripping reach.

The 330-room Rasa Ria is similar to its sister property, the Shangri-La Tanjung Aru, in both design and layout. Big and broad wings span out from the spacious open lobby. The ground-floor rooms have private lanais accessible through the verdant, landscaped gardens, while the other accommodation is split-level with private balconies. All rooms are equipped with numerous modern amenities, from air-conditioning to in-house movies.

The resort's recreational facilities are extensive for both adults and kids, with everything from tennis to mountain bikes outside and a professional spa, compact gym and very reasonable games room and kids' club inside.

However, when the sun shines the resort comes into its own - the pool and beach are perfect places to pass your time and there is the immaculate Dalit Bay Golf & Country Club next door.

The most memorable feature of the Rasa Ria is its proximity to nature. The resort's 140 hectares include a dedicated nature reserve complete with walking trails, bird watching and the magic of resident orangutans swinging down from the branches for feeding time. Diners at either the Pool Bar or poolside Tepi Laut, two of the seven restaurants and bars, are in danger of losing their snacks to an enormous, colourful hornbill which sometimes swoops down to scoff French fries. Despite the Rasa Ria's "walk on the wild side" there is no compromise on comfort - this is one of the better resorts in Asia for eco-tourists.

Rates from: $$
Star rating: ★ ★ ★ ★ ★
Overall rating: ۞ ۞ ۞ ۞ ½

Ambience:	9.00	Cleanliness:	8.95
Value:	8.56	Facilities:	8.55
Staff:	8.91	Restaurants:	8.50
Location:	8.77	Families:	8.84

Shangri-La's Tanjung Aru Resort

Locked bag 174, 88995 Kota Kinabalu, Malaysia
T: +60 88 225 800 **F:** +60 88 217 155
www.HotelClub.com/Hotels/ShangriLas_Tanjung_Aru_Resort_Kota_Kinabalu

The Tanjung Aru turns its substantial back on nearby downtown Kota Kinabalu to look out over the South China Sea and, in particular, the five uninhabited islands which lie a short boat-trip offshore. For a morning or even an entire day, you can voyage out here and while away the hours beachcombing, sunbathing and snorkelling, often with no-one else in sight. Talk about a resort with added extras. The basics are not far short of excellent either. The Tanjung Aru's 500 spacious rooms and suites are split between the Kinabalu and Tanjung wings, furnished in local timber, rattan and bamboo to give them an appropriately tropical feel. The blinds are split bamboo, ceiling fans join forces with the sea breezes, the furniture on the verandahs is comfortably cushioned and the views extend out to sea or up to the majestic craggy peaks of the 4,101-metre Mount Kinabalu.

Even if the idea of exploring isolated islands palls, no-one can really complain about getting bored here. Two free-form pools, four tennis courts, and a nine-hole short form golf course complement a full range of water sports and the resort's leisure and health clubs. And if the prospect of jollifications like mah-jong challenges and family egg-tossing competitions lack a certain *je ne sais quoi*, you can always hive off to the spa, poolside or your own room for a massage or reflexology session.

Pre-teen youngsters will be kept fully occupied at the Sunshine Club, with crab-catching, shell-collecting, flower-arranging and a host of other activities. If that is not enough: rock-climbing, horse-riding, jungle-trekking (treetop or earthbound) and a bird sanctuary are all nearby and, of course, Mount Kinabalu is there to be climbed.

On the food front, the six restaurants and bars serve up the best of Malay, Chinese, Indian and Western dishes, with Peppino's - the Italian restaurant - being especially popular, and the Borneo Lounge catering to late-night snackers and drinkers. The Sunset Bar is the place to watch the sun disappear behind those magical islands and plan the next day's fun-filled agenda.

Rates from: $$
Star rating: ★ ★ ★ ★ ★
Overall rating: 🌸🌸🌸🌸 ½

Ambience:	8.97	Cleanliness:	8.93
Value:	8.55	Facilities:	8.75
Staff:	9.03	Restaurants:	8.59
Location:	8.93	Families:	8.89

Sheraton Langkawi Beach Resort

Telok Nibong, Langkawi, Malaysia
T: +60 4 955 1901 **F**: +60 4 955 1913
www.HotelClub.com/Hotels/Sheraton_Langkawi_Beach_Resort

This enjoyable 231-room resort is in many ways typical of Langkawi and of the standards and service one expects from a Malaysian resort. Sitting just metres from the Andaman Sea, the resort is a pleasantly sprawling mass of low-rise kampong-style cabins. Wood dominates both the setting and the decor. The 15 hectares of rainforest are home to a wide variety of wildlife, from the rather cute dusky leaf monkey often spotted in the trees around the lobby to the rather less endearing groups of long-tailed macaque commonly found near the tennis courts. Giant squirrels, flying lemurs and tree shrews can be seen throughout the resort, along with clouded monitor lizards, which grow up to 1.5 metres long.

The rooms (some recently refurbished), at 51 square metres, are very spacious and have a wonderful but rustic charm. Finished in natural hardwoods and local fabrics, each has full-length French-style windows opening on to generous terraces from which to enjoy the forest canopy above or the wonderful sea views. It is a pleasant walk from the rooms through the grounds to the numerous facilities, but a little bus does scoot around every 15 minutes to transport guests between pick-up points.

On the fringes of the shore lies a pretty little beach with a large decked pool and adjacent well-shaded kids' pool. From here a raised wooden walkway, from which it is not uncommon to spot dolphins, winds along the shore to Captain's seafood grill, one of six restaurants and bars. Spice Trader, perched looking over the sea, offers Asian cuisine with an emphasis on Indian, while Karma Jaya is a more international mix. Black Henry, a rather lively nightspot, features some good bands. Given the wonderful natural environment and extensive activities including tennis, fishing, a full spa, eagle-feeding, jungle-trekking and a daily recreational programme for both adults and children, it is no surprise that this resort is adored by families. This is all helped by the staff who are warm, accommodating and attentive and are the resort's chief asset beside its pretty setting.

Rates from: $
Star rating: ★ ★ ★ ★
Overall rating: ♢♢♢♢ ½

Ambience:	9.02	Cleanliness:	8.94
Value:	8.61	Facilities:	8.66
Staff:	8.86	Restaurants:	8.75
Location:	8.86	Families:	8.90

Sheraton Imperial Kuala Lumpur

Jl Sultan Ismail, 50250 Kuala Lumpur, Malaysia
T: +60 3 2717 9900   **F:** +60 3 2717 9999
www.HotelClub.com/Hotels/Sheraton_Imperial_Hotel_Kuala_Lumpur

As an anonymous rectangular tower, the warmth of this hotel's colonial-cum-Art Deco interior is something of pleasant surprise - starting under the four-storey-high ceiling of the wood-panelled reception and lobby. Botanica Brasserie, with its tall palms pushing past a filigree-railed gallery, continues the theme and signature restaurant Villa Danielli has a pleasant outdoor terrace, while its interior recalls elements of a Tuscan villa. The rooms, though dated in interior design, do not want for functionality. Walk-in wardrobe, separate bath and shower units, dual-power sockets, two telephone lines, high-speed broadband connectivity, personal fax and quality audio-visual system are all standard. And the view over the city from this downtown location is impressive - particularly from the upper executive floors. Celestial Court, with its extravagant pagoda-style façade, is reckoned to be one of the city's finest Chinese - mostly Cantonese - restaurants. Imperial Spa by Mandara, sprawling over 1,000 square metres, offers treatments in an elegant environment.

Rates from: $
Star rating: ★★★★★
Overall rating: 🖐🖐🖐🖐

Ambience:	8.78	Cleanliness:	8.93
Value:	8.29	Facilities:	8.45
Staff:	8.43	Restaurants:	8.38
Location:	7.96	Families:	8.25

Sheraton Perdana Resort Langkawi

Jl Pantai Dato Syed Omar, 07000 Langkawi, Malaysia
T: +60 4 966 2020   **F:** +60 4 966 3097
www.HotelClub.com/Hotels/Sheraton_Perdana_Resort_Langkawi

Perched on 42 hectares next to a white-sand stretch of Langkawi Bay and framed by tropical rainforest, this resort is one for those after peaceful solitude. All nine suites and 191 rooms are generously proportioned with king-size or twin beds. There's plenty to do: beach volleyball, two squash courts, four tennis courts, table tennis, a health club, water sports, jungle walks, and boat trips. Or just chill out by the sprawling landscaped pool that offers private nooks and crannies, thanks to thoughtfully incorporated Fred Flintstone boulders. An adjacent restaurant, The Grove, serves international fare. A major refurbishment programme, finishing in 2005, has given the entire resort a fresh new look. For those craving large-scale exclusivity, Jentayu Villa - touted as "a resort within a resort" - contains five bedrooms, extravagantly spacious living areas bordered with reflection pools and landscaped gardens as well as personal valet and chef.

Rates from: $$
Star rating: ★★★★★
Overall rating: 🖐🖐🖐🖐½

Ambience:	8.93	Cleanliness:	8.75
Value:	8.36	Facilities:	8.54
Staff:	8.72	Restaurants:	8.40
Location:	8.55	Families:	8.81

Smokehouse Hotel

By the Golf Course, 39000 Tanah Rata, Cameron Highlands, Malaysia
T: +60 5 491 1215 **F**: +60 5 491 1214
www.HotelClub.com/Hotels/Smokehouse_Hotel_Cameron_Highlands

It used to be called Ye Olde Smokehouse Inn and, in a way, that name best suits this vaguely twee yet prepossessing anachronism. The mock-Tudor beams and latticed windows, creaky corridors and chintzy sofas, lovingly tended lawns and shrubs, unconventional menus and conventional seen-and-not-heard attitude to children all belong to the 1930s in what was then called Malaya. All this makes sense when you know that the Smokehouse opened for Christmas in 1937 and was firmly intended for homesick expatriates, who only got home leave every eight years. The cooler climes of the Cameron Highlands allowed them to pull on woolly jumpers, toast themselves in front of a real fire and turn their backs on the tropics for a weekend or longer.

A succession of Englishmen and a solitary Scot (with a brief interregnum by the Japanese Army) ran the place with varying degrees of success until 1975, when it was taken over by the Lee family, which oversees the hotel to this day.

Recognising that the Smokehouse's attractions lie in being the antithesis of just about every other hotel in the country, they have sensibly altered and enhanced only a little. The 14 (recently refurbished) suites are named after the houses at English boarding schools where the Lee progeny studied, and are variously furnished with four-poster beds and antiques. The kitchen is perfectly at home with staple meals like full English breakfast, steak-and-kidney pudding, and roast beef with Yorkshire pudding, while afternoon tea in the garden (scones, Devon cream, a selection of home-made jams) is practically de rigeur.

The hotel is right next to the golf course, and easily spotted by the traditional red telephone and post boxes outside. Anglophobes, nouvelle cuisine gourmands, modernists and - in all fairness - families with toddlers in tow should seek out diggings more suited to their particular needs. Just about everybody else with any sense of history is going to love it here. Traditionalists should note that a new wing is currently being added to the Smokehouse, though very much in the spirit of the old.

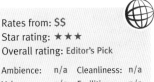

Rates from: **$$**
Star rating: ★ ★ ★
Overall rating: Editor's Pick

Ambience:	n/a	Cleanliness:	n/a
Value:	n/a	Facilities:	n/a
Staff:	n/a	Restaurants:	n/a
Location:	n/a	Families:	n/a

Sutera Harbour Resort

1 Sutera Harbour Boulevard, Sutera Harbour, 88100 Kota Kinabalu, Malaysia
T: +60 88 318 888 **F:** +60 88 317 777
www.HotelClub.com/Hotels/Sutera_Harbour_Resort_Spa_Kota_Kinabalu

The biggest of all of Kota Kinabalu's hotels is set in the sweeping 154-hectare grounds of the ambitious redeveloped area of Sutera Harbour, just minutes from town. This massive resort makes no effort to be subtle; in fact it could be called slightly garish. The colossal lobby is almost like an aircraft hangar and the vast Magellan and Pacific hotel wings house some 956 good-sized rooms. The modern decor is bright and colourful but in keeping with local tastes. Needless to say the facilities are extensive and include a 27-hole golf course, a 41-bay two-storey driving range, 17 bars, restaurants and nightclubs (KK's Sports Bar attracts a regular coterie of party animals, both visiting and local residents), a marina with more than 100 berths, tennis, badminton and squash courts, a 12-lane bowling alley, two kids' clubs, numerous pools, a spa and even a full-sized cinema showing some of the latest releases from around the world. Active, popular and supported by some excellent and attentive staff - it is hardly surprising that families love this place. Of course, the Sutera is also a natural choice when it comes to picking a conference venue, being handy for the airport, well located for jungly expeditions for incentives, and with just short of 12,000 square metres of meeting space under cover (ranking it among the largest in Asia) and extensive grounds for outdoor events. The Sutera's nichest market comes from a rather different group of travellers however, for the hotel is closely associated with the North Borneo Railway, whose Vulcan steam locomotive regularly runs on the century-old railway along the coast, pulling half a dozen beautifully restored Pullman carriages. In short, the Sutera supplies an amazingly diverse package which should suit just about everybody, young and old, from business to leisure travellers. And not forgetting railway nuts.

Rates from: $
Star rating: ★ ★ ★ ★ ★
Overall rating: ♦ ♦ ♦ ♦ ½

Ambience:	8.79	Cleanliness:	8.91
Value:	8.48	Facilities:	8.74
Staff:	8.51	Restaurants:	8.51
Location:	8.85	Families:	8.63

Sunway Lagoon Resort Hotel

Persiaran Lagoon, Bandar Sunway, 46150 Petaling Jaya, Malaysia
T: +60 3 7492 8000 **F:** +60 3 7492 8001
www.HotelClub.com/Hotels/Sunway_Lagoon_Resort_Hotel

The Sunway Lagoon Resort is Malaysian ersatz Disneyland complete with monorail. Think big, think total excess, think fun. The approach to the huge, vivid lobby lets you know what you are in for - giant sculptures of wild animals outside are outdone by what look like mounted flying saucers. Over-the-top decor jumps out throughout. That said, the facilities are absolutely endless. The resort connects with a sprawling theme park and one of the world's largest surf wave pools, an Egyptian "pyramid" shopping and entertainment mall with multiplex cinemas, an ice-skating rink, golf driving range and a 48-lane bowling centre, and more than 10,000 square metres of meeting, convention and exhibition space. The staff are surprisingly welcoming given the huge stream of boisterous visitors and the accommodation (including villas and townhouses) is spacious and well-equipped, though some of the themed suites will raise a smile. The capital and the airport are easily reached in 30 minutes, making this versatile resort useful for business as well as highly appealing to families.

Rates from: $
Star rating: ★ ★ ★ ★ ★
Overall rating: ◗◗◗◗ ½

Ambience:	8.66	Cleanliness:	8.80
Value:	8.17	Facilities:	8.66
Staff:	8.41	Restaurants:	8.59
Location:	8.27	Families:	8.63

Swiss Garden Hotel

117 Jl Pudu, 55100 Kuala Lumpur, Malaysia
T: +60 3 2141 3333 **F:** +60 3 2141 5555
www.HotelClub.com/Hotels/Swiss_Garden_Hotel_Kuala_Lumpur

In south-west downtown KL, almost within touching distance of the city's first skyscraper, Maybank Tower, the Swiss Garden is a very popular leisure hotel a short hop from Lot 10 and several of the city's other major attractions. An opulent marble entrance provides a taste of things to come although decor in the 310 rooms is simpler, if a little dated. On the food front, the Ah Yat Abalone Forum concession specialises in pan-Chinese cuisine with a Cantonese bent - with prized and pricey abalone a house signature. The Garden Terrace serves up a mix of Asian and Western dishes, while for a touch of authentic KL, outdoor hawker stalls dispense traditional Malay street food next to the hotel. At downtime head for the Swiss Garden's most laid-back areas - a small (very) outdoor pool and sun-deck, with a thatched grass-roofed bar, or the basic Samsara Spa, where massage and body and face care treatments all incorporate natural herbal preparations. A simple gym is there for those with energy to burn.

Rates from: $
Star rating: ★ ★ ★ ★
Overall rating: ◗◗◗◗

Ambience:	8.33	Cleanliness:	8.46
Value:	8.47	Facilities:	8.19
Staff:	8.56	Restaurants:	8.24
Location:	8.47	Families:	8.67

Tanjong Jara Resort

Tanjong Jara, Batu 8, Off Jl Dungun, 23000 Dungun, Malaysia
T: +60 9 845 1100 **F:** +60 9 845 1200
www.HotelClub.com/Hotels/Tanjong_Jara_Resort_Kuala_Terengganu

Tanjong Jara - halfway between Kuala Terengganu and Kuantan, an hour from the local airport or a six-hour drive from Kuala Lumpur - is inconveniently situated for the international traveller. This does, however save it from mass tourism and the resort maintains a wonderful aura of a hidden beachside escape. Its traditional architecture, derived from the elegantly crafted wooden palaces of Malay sultans, is set in scenic tropical gardens offering panoramic views over the South China Sea.

First impressions suggest the resort is new, so it comes as a surprise that it is some 25 years old and has had an eventful history.

This part of the east coast was earmarked for tourism and the Tanjong Jara was built to help precipitate it. Opened by the government's Tourist Development Corporation, the resort won widespread praise and scooped up many accolades including the coveted Aga Khan Award for Architecture. But tourism never flourished on this side of the peninsula, and the Tanjong Jara deteriorated before being salvaged by a private company (coincidentally, the owner of the lovely Pangkor Laut Resort) which embarked on a glorious renovation programme. The new design preserved the traditionally constructed buildings

while incorporating an elegant modern theme and maintaining a fundamentally Malay experience.

The accommodation is rich, creative and dominated by a mix of belian wood and teak. Small two-storey buildings contain the Serambi and Bumbung Rooms, both well fitted and catching the tropical mood. The lower Serambis have terraces for sunbathing - the upper Bumbungs are identical but terrace-less, though with better views as compensation. The third category, Anjung, lines the shore - a series of stunningly designed 88-square-metre cottages with sunken baths and canopied terraces.

Comprehensive resort facilities are in the same league - two beautiful pools, a top gym and relaxing spa pavilions. Authentic Malay cuisine is served at Di Atas Sungei overlooking the Marang River, while Nelayan specialises in seafood caught by the resort's own fishermen. The Tanjung Club's gym and spa are well up to standard. Visiting the local prince (second cousin to the reigning Sultan of Terengganu), turtle-watching at a WWF-affiliated sanctuary, jungle trekking along Jara Hill, touring local villages, learning to cook Kari Ayam (chicken curry), and diving off Tenggol Island are just some of the pursuits available at this wonderful backwater.

Rates from: $$	
Star rating: ★ ★ ★ ★ ★	
Overall rating: ◔ ◔ ◔ ◔	
Ambience: 9.16	Cleanliness: 8.84
Value: 7.19	Facilities: 8.09
Staff: 8.63	Restaurants: 8.12
Location: 8.51	Families: 8.53

Tanjung Rhu Resort

Mukim Ayer Hangat, 07000 Langkawi, Malaysia
T: +60 4 959 1033 **F:** +60 4 959 1899
www.HotelClub.com/Hotels/Tanjung_Rhu_Resort_Langkawi

Tanjung Rhu is one of Langkawi's best. But first impressions may have you scratching your head. The approach is not the most flattering angle - the resort resembles an isolated horseshoe-shaped apartment block and the lobby is virtually non-existent. But once you breach the ugly tenement stairwells it indeed transforms into a superb resort, clearly built to be appreciated from within.

The 135 rooms capture the resort essence and abound with that most elusive luxury - space. They are bountifully spacious, among the biggest rooms and best value in Asia. The Damai Rooms are the lowest category but at 50 square metres compare with a typical suite in other establishments. Large bathrooms have shutters that open into the lounge to give that extra feeling of space. Fittings include rosy timber flooring, with full-length windows and balconies overlooking the garden courtyard. The ever-expanding higher-room categories are almost small flats and enjoy beguiling pool or sea views. Each room is equipped like home with TV, CD player and VCR, and an ample selection of videos and discs for all the family is available from the library.

Spread over some 12 hectares with ample lawns and foliage, the Tanjung Rhu faces the Andaman Sea with an impressive 2.5 kilometres of private golden sands. A pleasing 60-metre sunset pool stretches off towards the sundeck and horizon. Alternatively, the lagoon pool is shaded by greenery and wrapped within the ring of the building, broken only to allow access to the sea - and kids just love it. The Jiva Rhu spa is well worth a visit.

No doubt the Tanjung Rhu is remote - a good half-hour by car from town or airport - and with virtually nothing in the surrounding area other than 440 hectares of deserted mangrove-lined coast and forest. The resort benefits from the seclusion and puts on some wonderful nature tours, including spectacular eagle-feeding. The isolation essentially means that popping out for dinner is not an option, and the three resort restaurants meander between the rather average Sands and the truly excellent fine dining of Rhu. That said, there is nothing more relaxing or romantic than a sundowner on the deck of the first-floor reading room with live piano music drifting through the evening air.

Rates from: $$$
Star rating: ★ ★ ★ ★ ★
Overall rating: 🌀🌀🌀🌀🌀

Ambience:	9.23	Cleanliness:	8.77
Value:	8.77	Facilities:	7.10
Staff:	9.14	Restaurants:	8.14
Location:	9.32	Families:	8.93

Westin Kuala Lumpur

199 Jl Bukit Bintang, 55100 Kuala Lumpur, Malaysia
T: +60 3 2731 8333   **F:** +60 3 2731 8000
www.HotelClub.com/Hotels/Westin_Kuala_Lumpur

In the heart of KL's business and glitzy shopping district, with all the best malls just a few minutes away, the 452 guest rooms and suites in this city landmark tower are very easy on the eye. Rooms are minimalist in decor, with a few curves here and there and dark wood accents that prevent starkness. All include the Westin's current big feature, its Heavenly Bed, which it claims meets the average five-star traveller's most sought-after provision from a hotel: a good night's sleep. Panoramas through extra-large windows take in either the KLCC Twin Towers or the historic old city.

High-speed Internet access, separate bath and shower stall and dual-line telephone are all standard.

The Westin's Executive Residences are well-equipped apartments tailored toward longer stays. Featuring a separate entrance from the main lobby, each apartment contains contemporary furnishings, a complete kitchen set-up with appliances, exquisite home entertainment system and a separate study.

As the hotel is relatively new, its Westin Workout area contains some of the most high-tech fitness equipment you are likely to encounter; professionally qualified instructors are well-trained in offering simultaneous hardware and fitness regime advice - all exercise programmes are based on individual assessment. There is also an outdoor pool, and a spa is scheduled for completion in late 2005.

Dining is a real highlight here, with six restaurants to choose from. Prego, a whimsical Italian two-tiered dining room with enormous theatrical copper extractor funnels atop its open kitchen offers Italian fine dining. Qba (pronounced "Cuba") offers a Latin menu and fine cigars in a vibrant relaxed interior. The Living Room is a contemporary take on international cuisine, while Eest (so spelled) sticks to Asian fare. Most casual outlets of all are indoor Treats - a coffee shop - and poolside Splash.

Rounding things off, a Westin Kid's Club allows parents travelling with offspring up to the ages of 12 to do their own thing for a while.

Rates from: $$
Star rating: ★ ★ ★ ★ ★
Overall rating: ♜ ♜ ♜ ♜ ½

Ambience:	8.91	Cleanliness:	9.12
Value:	8.25	Facilities:	8.49
Staff:	8.52	Restaurants:	8.17
Location:	8.87	Families:	8.06

MALDIVES

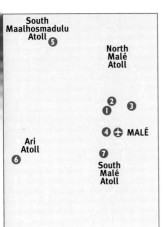

South Maalhosmadulu Atoll ❺

North Malé Atoll

❷ ❶ ❸

❹ ⊕ MALÉ

Ari Atoll ❻

❼

South Malé Atoll

The prototypical tourists to the Maldives would be a pair of newly-wed underwater enthusiasts. Well, make that a flush couple of honeymooning scuba-divers, for this is a potentially pricey destination. But as the old adage runs, you get what you pay for, and the Maldives' 1,190 islands grouped on 26 atolls in the azure waters of the Indian Ocean are without doubt among the most exclusive destinations in the region.

Only around 200 of the islands are inhabited, and some 80 of them are home to resorts fully geared to the whims of "paradise-seekers" and divers. Many of these grace the upper echelons of five-star accommodation, designed with flair and sympathy for their surrounds and dispensing cuisine and service more readily associated with major cities rather than far-flung sandy islets. Expect full-board packages, as there are few dining options off-site, and be aware that your hotel is the only place you will find alcohol; the Maldives is very Muslim in this respect.

The vast majority of visitors fly into the international airport near Malé, the capital city, if that is the right term for a huddle of mosques, markets and a neat maze of streets. In its favour, Malé does offer some inexpensive accommodation, as well as granting a window into local culture.

The Maldives are warm and sunny year round, however the dry season (December - April) is most favoured by visitors. Rain is more likely between May and November. Divers usually agree that the best underwater visibility is during the months of seasonal change in April and November. And it is diving (with the peripheral attraction of other water sports) that acts as the Maldives' chief allure, although El Niño has had a damaging impact in recent years. There are hundreds of easily accessible sites, while more can be reached on diving safari trips. Once below the surface there are veritable academies of fish, magnificent coral gardens, prowling turtles, manta ray, whales and sharks as well as what experts agree is one of the world's most exciting wreck dives, the *Maldive Victory*, off Hulule Airport. Above the waves, parasailing, waterskiing and windsurfing are on offer, and there are some excellent if slightly remote surf breaks. Big-game fishing is also popular, although a strict "tag and release" policy is in force.

As for other recreation, this is a definitely a couples venue rather than singles' vacationland, and there is little in the way of nightlife. However, a blissful tropical island and the seclusion of a four-poster swathed in a mosquito net should be inspiration enough for most couples, whether they have just got married or not.

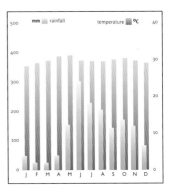

Angsana Maldives Ihuru

North Malé Atoll, Maldives
T: +960 443 502 **F:** +960 445 933
www.HotelClub.com/Hotels/Angsana_Resort_Spa_Maldives_Ihuru

"Ihuru" means "old palm trees" in the Maldivian language. Angsana is a tree found in tropical rainforests and noted for its crown of flowers that burst into a fragrant shower of golden-yellow blooms. So it almost goes without saying that the Angsana Resort and the tiny islet of Ihuru are a flawless marriage of location and concept.

With such inspirational surroundings, it is hardly surprising that many couples elect to hold their nuptials here, surrounded by the natural beauty of the Maldive archipelago. Forget that conventional walk down the aisle - here you can plight your troth on the beach by a crystal-clear lagoon, on a sandbank way out in the ocean, or - assuming you're correctly PADI'd - exchange your vows under water. And come back here for your anniversary and you get a free night's stay.

Even if you are not considering tying the knot, Angsana reeks of romance. Its 45 beachfront villas are set around the island's circumference, thatched with palm, surrounded by a private garden, with outdoor showers and a swing to laze the days away upon. Decorated in fresh, summery colours, all have a queen-size bed and ten come with an open-air jacuzzi.

Assuming you can shake yourself out of a rather pleasing inertia, there is plenty of recreation to fill the hours between buffet breakfasts at the Riveli Restaurant and cocktails at the Velaavani Bar, a vantage point over the reef where turtles and dolphins swim.

The spa's signature therapy is specially designed to relieve tension and aid blood circulation, and there is also a variety of wraps, scrubs and facials. You can also get your circulation going and let off steam canoeing, island-hopping, wakeboarding or windsurfing, all of which can be organised at the resort. And of course the surrounding reefs and dive sites are superb. Just ask anyone who has bubbled "I do".

Rates from: $$$$$
Star rating: ★ ★ ★ ★ ★
Overall rating: ♦ ♦ ♦ ♦ ♦

Ambience:	9.73	Cleanliness:	9.07
Value:	8.07	Facilities:	8.65
Staff:	9.13	Restaurants:	8.67
Location:	9.27	Families:	8.78

Banyan Tree Maldives Vabbinfaru

North Malé Atoll, Maldives
T: +960 443 147 **F**: +960 446 655
www.HotelClub.com/Hotels/Banyan_Tree_Maldives

While many resorts in the Maldives are eco-friendly, the Banyan Tree has gone that extra nautical mile to ensure that its gorgeous undersea surroundings remain exactly that.

The Banyan Tree rests on Vabbinfaru, which means "round island", and is encircled by a coral reef. Arriving here, making an almost regal progress atop the lengthy jetty, there is a tingling sense of excitement as you pass above the aquamarine waters swarming with marine life.

The resort is unarguably lovely, with its 48 rondavel-style villas on the fringes of the white sand beach, their furnishings crafted in polished black granite, and glass doors open to Indian Ocean breezes that will stir the canopy enveloping the four-poster beds. There is a blissful calm here, a palpable sense of indulgence, and an overriding feeling of untrammelled luxury. You can get spa'd in one of the open-air pavilions, fly off sightseeing from a seaplane, or dine à deux at the end of a jetty or on a secluded beach, where you are greeted with chilled champagne and poems hand-written in the sand. More conventionally, there is a smorgasbord of Maldivian, Mediterranean and Asian cuisine at the Ilafaathi restaurant, and barbeques in the Sangu Garden.

All this is as nothing compared to the sub-aqua delights of Vabbinfaru. Quite apart from the reef ringing the island, ten spectacular, top-of-the-world dive sites lie within an hour's boat ride, home to whale sharks, manta rays, moray eels, white-tip sharks and myriad other species. Rather than simply admiring the treasures on display, Banyan Tree guests are encouraged to play a part in preserving the marine ecology. One of the most popular activities is helping to build artificial coral gardens, which enjoy a 70 per cent success rate and are particularly rewarding for guests when they return in years to come.

Alternatively, the Napwatch project logs sightings of the endangered Napoleon wrasse, and divers are urged to photograph any that they come across to add to a database tracking the fish's habits and migration. Naturally, the Banyan Tree's PADI centre is fully equipped and instructors are on hand to advise and teach both qualified divers as well as those making their first tentative strokes underwater.

Rates from: $$$$
Star rating: ★ ★ ★ ★ ★
Overall rating: ♦♦♦♦♦

Ambience:	9.67	Cleanliness:	9.22
Value:	7.96	Facilities:	8.95
Staff:	9.22	Restaurants:	8.58
Location:	9.24	Families:	8.46

Four Seasons Resort Maldives at Kuda Huraa

Kuda Huraa, North Malé Atoll, Maldives
T: +960 444 888 **F:** +960 441 188
www.HotelClub.com/Hotels/Four_Seasons_Resort_Maldives

By launching its 11-stateroom dive catamaran in 2002, the Four Seasons pulled off something no other hotel in the Maldives had quite yet achieved. The 39-metre *Island Explorer* is a mini-resort in itself, ranging the length and breadth of the archipelago in the lap of luxury, to all intents and purposes a floating Four Seasons. Naturally, this is no ordinary cruiser. The 20-strong crew includes a marine biologist to escort divers and snorkellers, and a therapist to massage them once they are back on board. All the staterooms contain a king-size bed and sound and entertainment systems, you can dine inside or on deck, and the Explorer drops anchor at deserted coves and beaches for kayaking or exploring.

Back at Kuda Huraa, the 106 bungalows and villas of the resort proper await. All are beautifully decorated and furnished, but the Water Bungalows each have a

private sun deck and steps leading straight down into the turquoise lagoon, while the villas encompass a larger area and have a private outdoor shower.

On the recreation side, it is difficult to conjecture how anyone could even think about visiting a gym here, but there are treadmills aplenty in the Activity Centre. Rather more sybaritically, the infinity pool has a swim-up bar and is one of the largest in the Maldives. Even less strenuous is the spa, a short trip by wooden dhoni across the lagoon, where Oceanic, Maldivian and Javanese Lulur body elixirs and other treatments are dispensed in thatched pavilions with Arabic, Moroccan and Indian design influences.

Three restaurants more or less complete the picture at Kuda Huraa, with Indian and Maldivian cuisine at Baraabaru, Mediterranean specialties in the Reef Club and all-day dining at Café Huraa. Plus of course it would be sheer folly to miss out on a sunset drink at the Nautilus Lounge when the Indian Ocean goes Technicolor ballistic.

Rates from: $$$$$
Star rating: ★ ★ ★ ★
Overall rating: ♥ ♥ ♥ ♥ ♥

Ambience:	9.64	Cleanliness:	9.39
Value:	7.93	Facilities:	8.77
Staff:	9.38	Restaurants:	8.77
Location:	9.07	Families:	8.41

Hilton Maldives Resort & Spa Rangali Island

South Ari Atoll, Maldives
T: +960 450 629 **F:** +960 450 619
www.HotelClub.com/Hotels/Hilton_Maldives_Resort_and_Spa_Rangali_Island

Let's say, fantasising ever so slightly, that a long and rather lovely - to say nothing of luscious - day at the Hilton is waning, and you are headed on the jet-boat shuttle to your Sunset Water Villa (check Philippe Starke, Bang & Olufsen, Villeroy & Boch) which just happens to be three degrees north of the Equator. Dinner tonight, perhaps à la carte Euro-Asian at Vilu, perhaps seafood in the Grill that's set atop a coral reef out over the turquoise lagoon, is going to be accompanied by one or maybe even two of the inmates of the 10,000 bottle underground wine cellar, chosen with some discreet advice from the resort's resident sommelier. The day, not to put too fine a point on it, has run 99 per cent perfect. A morning dive at Manta Point, ten minutes offshore, was followed by an afternoon in the spa, where, supine in the treatment room you looked down through the glass floor to a gloriously colourful choreographed display by the Maldives' Marine Ensemble. There's just one thing needed to make the day complete - getting back in time to your two-and-a-half-metre wide circular bed which very obligingly rotates to follow the setting sun.

Blending superb attention to detail with the last word in luxury and service the Hilton Maldives is, let's not mince words here, an absolute stunner in an vacation archipelago renowned for doing its fair share of stunning. Spread over two islands, not all the resort's 150 villas get the all-singing-and-rotating bed, but each is set by the beach or over the sea, and even the most simple have their own deck and an open bathroom. Described as "a million miles from nine-to-five ... with a thousand ways of doing nothing" the Hilton Maldives is just about everybody's favourite way of number crunching.

Rates from: $$$
Star rating: ★ ★ ★ ★ ★
Overall rating: ♦♦♦♦ ½

Ambience:	9.67	Cleanliness:	9.15
Value:	7.85	Facilities:	8.70
Staff:	8.79	Restaurants:	9.00
Location:	9.24	Families:	8.39

Soneva Fushi Resort

Kunfunadhoo Island, Maldives
T: +960 230 304 **F:** +960 230 374
www.HotelClub.com/Hotels/Soneva_Fushi_Resort_Spa

If you accept the theory that many of Asia's best hotels are extensions of their owners' personalities, then Soneva Fushi is its prime example. Tycoon Sonu met top Swedish model Eva aboard a yacht in Monaco, and the ensuing Mr and Mrs Shivdasani spent their honeymoon jetting around the world. When they came upon Kunfunadhoo, an abandoned resort on a 40-hectare atoll in the Maldives, they knew at once that this was the place to build their dream. The result, opened in 1995, was Soneva Fushi, an amalgam of their names, vision and inherent taste for good living, together with the Maldivian word for island.

Largely designed by Eva, Soneva Fushi combines simplicity with sophistication, luxury with "back to nature", while emphasising a strong commitment to the environment. The villas are supported by recycled telegraph poles; if guests need wheels to get about they come in the shape of non-polluting sit-up-and-beg bicycles; faxes are distributed in hand-woven reed tubes and if you call for a television it is delivered in a water-hyacinth basket.

With a sturdy, eco-friendly philosophy, the resort - not to put too fine a point on it - is bliss itself.

A seaplane bridges the 60 nautical miles between the international airport at Malé and the island, and on arrival guests are invited to shed their shoes - with the inference of getting rid of cares and inhibitions as well. Kunfunadhoo is just 1,400 metres long and no more than 400 wide, and scattered along the beaches and among the island's unusually rich vegetation are some threescore rooms and villas, including two with their own spa suites. The interiors, whether in one of the two Presidential Villas or a rather more compact Rehendi Room make much of the bathrooms, keep furnishings plain yet attractively simple, and discreetly tuck the CD players away behind rattan screening.

Soneva Fushi is nothing if not seductive, and enthusiastic couples could easily be lured into doing nothing here apart from alternating between bed, beach and bathroom with the occasional stop for sustenance. There are some diversions that, while not compulsory, are pretty unique, such as a private sunrise breakfast on the Sandbank, which lies right out in the ocean 10 minutes away from the resort. The management also throws a weekly cocktail party here - champagne and canapés but otherwise pure Crusoe. Rather than a one-size-fits-all menu, the spa goes for tailor-made, one-on-one treatments, which vault beyond the routine massages, facials and scrubs with some wacky specials like the chocolate and milk bath (which you sit in), accompanied by a glass of iced mocha (which you drink).

The spa should certainly whet your appetite, and the resort's restaurants are fully equipped to assuage it. Two formal dining rooms are backed up by a 500-strong wine list, and there are also informal buffets on the beach, an ice-cream parlour, island picnics and moonlit barbeques. The general feeling is not simply that the food and service should be impeccable, but the setting has to be perfect too. In between meals, there is boules, tennis, badminton, a small gym and a large range of water sports including deep-sea

fishing by dhoni, waterskiing and windsurfing.

Finally, if you do not dive, this is good place to take your first strokes underwater. If you are already qualified - what are you waiting for?

Rates from: $$$$		
Star rating: ★ ★ ★ ★ ★		
Overall rating: 🐚 🐚 🐚 🐚 ½		
Ambience:	9.94	Cleanliness: 9.47
Value:	7.94	Facilities: 8.62
Staff:	8.59	Restaurants: 7.75
Location:	9.06	Families: 8.58

Soneva Gili Resort

Lankanfushi Island, North Malé Atoll, Maldives
T: +960 440 304   **F**: +960 440 305
www.HotelClub.com/Hotels/Soneva_Gili_Resort_Spa

Here is a prime candidate for one of those TV programmes or magazine articles about 50 or 100 things to do before you die. Soneva Gili is another creation from Eva Shivdasani and her husband Sonu, who are also responsible for Soneva Fushi. This resort represents a paradoxical solution to today's done-everything dilemma in terms of luxury hotel accommodation - sheer childlike simplicity served up on a platinum platter.

Your shoes are bagged on arrival, there are no clocks - and what you do is very much up to you. If you hanker after those gilded-by-memory holidays of your youth, but can't live without Dom Perignon and

hand-tied muslin tea-bags, this is the place for you. Needless to say, it is a honeymooners' heaven (especially one of the seven "Crusoe" residences, whose only access is by boat and where room service is rowed out to you).

Consisting of 44 very sophisticated shacks on stilts, connected by wooden jetties to the coral-reef atoll of Lankanfushi (one of the hundreds that constitute the Maldives, from whose language the word "atoll" derives), Soneva Gili is about 15 minutes by speedboat from the capital, Malé. It was the first of the 90-something Maldivan resorts to have all its rooms - the largest in the archipelago - erected

entirely over the water (a trend now, following legal restrictions on the amount of land that can be built upon).

Floodlit portholes in the floorboards afford aquarium-like views of passing shoals of tropical fish, and there is a ladder leading down to a screened bathing area beneath your bathroom. An organic vegetable garden overlaid with Indonesian topsoil grows four types of basil and the fine-dining restaurant (for those fed up with candlelit twosomes) boasts personal curry chefs. Staff far outnumber guests, though they manage to materialise only when you need them.

Rates from: $$$$$
Star rating: ★ ★ ★ ★ ★
Overall rating: 🐚🐚🐚🐚 ½

Ambience:	9.54	Cleanliness:	9.69
Value:	7.46	Facilities:	8.03
Staff:	9.46	Restaurants:	8.31
Location:	9.54	Families:	7.25

Taj Exotica Resort & Spa

South Malé Atoll, Maldives
T: +960 442 200 **F:** +960 442 211
www.HotelClub.com/Hotels/Taj_Exotica_Resort_and_Spa

Seen from the sky, the Taj Exotica - with a shape reminiscent of Neptune's trident - traces an amazing pattern over the silken waters of the Indian Ocean. However most visitors arrive by speedboat from the capital, which is just 15 minutes' ride away.

Luxury-lovers will find much to indulge in here, as the Taj has cloned the impeccable standards gleaned from long years catering for big-city sophisticates and parachuted them down among the lucid waters and flour-soft sand of a purpose-built haven in the South Malé Atoll.

Two-dozen semi-detached and 31 stand-alone Lagoon Villas spearhead out into the sea, complemented by eight Beach Villas, each with their own personal and extremely private plunge-pool, where swimming costumes are definitely optional. And preening itself at the top of the accommodation chain is the Rehendhi Suite with separate living and sleeping quarters, its own exclusive pier and even a mini spa.

Although guests are predominantly European or Japanese rather than Indian, the subcontinent's influence is subtly apparent, and not just in the cuisine at 24 Degrees or the Deep End. An innate conventionality dictates marble rather than sand surfaces. A very superior library is joined by an indoor games room - reminiscent of a hill-station - which resounds to the clack of well-struck pool and snooker balls.

The Spa, where Balinese masseuses reign, is truly divine: try the warm-stone massage. And the infinity pool takes some beating, even by the coral-reefed lagoon it overlooks. Satellite TV and Internet connection provide entertainment for those who cannot survive without access to the wider world.

At the end of the long, lazy day, however, it is the little Taj touches of understated opulence that make the difference: the muted earth tones of the decor, the Mysore sandalwood soap in its own little jute bag, freshly ground coffee beans delivered nightly to your door, and that long, cool "nimbu pani" welcome.

Rates from: $$$$$	
Star rating: ★ ★ ★ ★ ★	
Overall rating: 🖐🖐🖐🖐	
Ambience: 9.67	Cleanliness: 9.00
Value: 8.00	Facilities: 8.38
Staff: 8.78	Restaurants: 8.00
Location: 8.22	Families: 7.50

MYANMAR

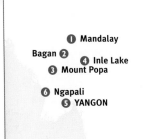

① Mandalay
Bagan ②
③ Mount Popa ④ Inle Lake
⑥ Ngapali
⑤ YANGON

Since independence from Britain after World War II, Myanmar has been torn by ethnic divisions and internal strife, and today finds itself a fractured pariah state run by corrupt generals. It is a great shame because this is one of the most beautiful and interesting countries in Asia. It has a stunningly rich and deep culture, fertile land and wonderful people. As a tourist destination Myanmar has bags of potential but is haunted by the political situation. Many, although not all, democracy activists have implored tourists to keep away.

Myanmar has always had its problems, but since the military junta seized control and stamped out the democracy movement it has been shunned by the international community. There is zero investment and minimal interaction with outsiders. The unintentional result is an unspoiled land that has fallen well behind the progress of the world. Awash with colour and charm, the nation certainly has its problems. Much of this country is shut off to foreigners and is lawless. There are rebel insurgencies, vast poppy fields and a huge smuggling network that the government would rather tourists did not stumble upon.

Infrastructure has not received any major investment for generations. With ground transport erratic and cumbersome, most visitors are realistically limited to four destinations separated by little more than an hour's flight - the capital Yangon (with a possible side excursion to the beach at Ngapali), second city Mandalay, beautiful remote Inle Lake, and Bagan. Dusty Bagan is by far Myanmar's most spectacular site, with thousands of ancient red-brick temples strewn across the arid plains. Trotting around aboard a pony and cart is a great way to soak it up, and the sunsets are quite magnificent.

Yangon is the only place that can be considered international. Hotels are of a high standard with good levels of service but things can disintegrate further out. Most of the country is sleepy and agricultural with simple cottage industries; this lifestyle is reflected in the hotels. Banking is a major problem and credit cards are also almost totally impractical outside the capital.

Myanmar is a difficult country to sum up in terms of weather since it has a varied terrain with tropical beaches, lowland plateaus and the shoulders of the Himalayas. Monsoons sweep up the coast from May to October so a generally better time to visit is during the dry season from November to April. Visiting Myanmar does pose moral questions - those who decide to visit will witness one of the last exotic outposts of a rapidly changing world.

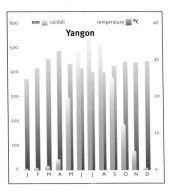

Bagan Hotel River View

Old Bagan, Near Museum and Gaudawpolin Pagoda, Myanmar
T: +95 2 67 145 **F:** +95 2 67 145
www.HotelClub.com/Hotels/Bagan_Hotel_River_View

trips along the Ayeyarwaddy can be timed to admire the luminous sunsets. Or hire a bike or horse and cart (plus driver) to take in some pagodas. The resort's restaurants and bars on wooden decks or on the lawn serve Western and Asian cuisine and provide, to coin a phrase, the icing on the cake of a really excellent small hotel.

There's a temple-like quality and more than a touch of romance at the waterside Bagan Hotel. A wealth of exposed terracotta brickwork, incorporating decorative cut sections, reflects the myriad ancient pagodas nearby, and sweeping views across the resort's trimmed lawns reach up to the hills beyond. Teak floors, stone sculptures, solid bath tubs and satellite TV are standard in the 116 rooms and suites, while the luxurious Bagan Villa is a very superior stand-alone unit. A private butler hovers in all the suites. For recreation, if lounging by the outdoor pool is not enough, boat

Rates from: $
Star rating: ★★★
Overall rating: 🖐🖐🖐🖐 ½

Ambience:	9.23	Cleanliness:	8.77
Value:	8.77	Facilities:	7.10
Staff:	9.14	Restaurants:	8.14
Location:	9.32	Families:	8.93

Grand Plaza Parkroyal Yangon

33 Alan Pya Phaya Road, Dagon Township, Yangon, Myanmar
T: +95 1 250 388 **F:** +95 1 252 478
www.HotelClub.com/Hotels/Grand_Plaza_Parkroyal_Hotel_Yangon

Service throughout is also excellent, and staff show a little more initiative here than at many other hotels in the country. The 312 soothing rooms are well polished in every sense, the teak floors in particular, and some of the upper floors have enviable views of the striking golden Schwedagon pagoda. A highly competitive hotel with no obvious drawbacks.

Centrally located in bustling downtown Yangon, the Grand Plaza Parkroyal (which was once the Sofitel Plaza) is convenience all round. And considering the bargain rates, this makes for an absolutely superb product. This modern property is warm, relaxing and luxurious with contemporary Burmese flashes. Facilities are all top-class and are very popular with the local community. Restaurants brim with yakking, munching diners, especially Yangon's best Japanese outlet, Shiki-Tei. The night spot, the Music Club, is one of Yangon's premier dance venues and the spa deservedly gets rave reviews.

Rates from: $
Star rating: ★★★★★
Overall rating: 🖐🖐🖐🖐

Ambience:	7.56	Cleanliness:	8.61
Value:	8.72	Facilities:	7.20
Staff:	9.11	Restaurants:	7.94
Location:	8.50	Families:	7.76

Governor's Residence

35 Taw Win Road, Dagon Township, Yangon, Myanmar
T: +95 1 229 860 **F:** +95 1 228 260
www.HotelClub.com/Hotels/Governors_Residence_Yangon

The prime appeal of the Governor's Residence lies is its architecture. Formerly a colonial mansion, it has recently been restored to its impressive original self. The structure is almost entirely teak and ornately crafted, and set quite perfectly in a peaceful tropical garden. Lily-padded ponds croak, and satisfying squawks and chirps emanate from the thick surrounding undergrowth. Being set in the quiet diplomatic area, it really does not feel in the slightest like a city hotel. The cocoon of greenery and virtual absence of traffic easily conjure up an imaginary location somewhere much more remote than a mere kilometre or two from downtown Yangon.

The Residence is perfectly proportioned and thoughtfully laid out in graceful European style. Although slightly small it is very personal and does not have a hotel ambience as such, but more that of a glorious bed and breakfast. The facilities are far superior of course, even if not much more extensive. The serene lagoon pool lies languidly beside the garden boardwalk - it is very tempting to just leap in. The Mandalay verandah restaurant is also worth investigating, as its authentic French cuisine draws high praise. A pool table and the Kipling Bar on the breezy open first floor provide a fine place to bide your time. And that is just about all there is to do.

The Residence continues to impress in the rooms - uplifting and beautiful in equal measure and arguably some of the best rooms in all Myanmar. All 48 are teak, the polished floors emitting a contagious rosy warmth, and there's a homely cabin feel and plenty of angles and corners. Bathrooms are also adventurous - each has a splendid big granite bath.

This boutique hotel is a slow and quiet corner of the world, and hits just about every nail on the head. It is wisely hidden away and one of the few places that lives up to its brochure.

Rates from: $$
Star rating: ★ ★ ★ ★
Overall rating: ♙♙♙♙ ½

Ambience:	9.20	Cleanliness:	8.57
Value:	8.31	Facilities:	7.92
Staff:	8.76	Restaurants:	8.19
Location:	8.09	Families:	8.26

Inle Princess Resort

Magyizin Village, Inle Lake, Shan State, Myanmar
T: +95 81 29 055 **F:** +95 81 29 363
www.HotelClub.com/Hotels/Inle_Princess_Resort_Shan_State

The isolated Princess Resort is one of the top properties on the breathtakingly scenic Inle Lake. Partly built on stilts out over the water it is best accessed by boat, lending it true tranquility among the emerald paddies. Some 46 roomy chalets are connected by walkways beside the gently lapping lake. These great little escapes are well constructed, secure and cosy. Big comfy sofas and reliable hot water give the chalets a welcome homely feel. Room facilities are sparse with little technology other than mosquito nets. Hand-cranked telephones link only to reception (shore is reached through the hotel's CB radio). Balconies offer intoxicating views of the lake or the distant mountains. Hotel facilities are refreshingly absent. Forget the typical set-up - the mood can only be helped by the lack of mod cons. In fact there is only is a quiet but finely crafted restaurant-cum-bar, which serves up highly enthusiastic ethnic song and dance shows and very fair Shan food.

Rates from: $$
Star rating: ★ ★
Overall rating: Editor's Pick

Ambience:	n/a	Cleanliness:	n/a
Value:	n/a	Facilities:	n/a
Staff:	n/a	Restaurants:	n/a
Location:	n/a	Families:	n/a

Kandawgyi Palace Hotel

Kan Yeik Tha Road, Yangon, Myanmar
T: +95 1 249 255 **F:** +95 1 256 187
www.HotelClub.com/Hotels/Kandawgyi_Palace_Hotel

Chequered histories look decidedly plain beside the Kandawgyi's tale: former rowing club, maternity hospital, civil servant hob-nobbery, and biological museum (there's still a model dinosaur in the gardens) it achieved its present incarnation in 1996. The hotel's palatial rooftops blend perfectly with the nearby golden tiers of Shwedagon and Maha Wizaya Pagodas and the lakeside location is a reasonable trade-off for being a couple of kilometres from downtown Yangon. Rooms are all elegantly appointed, radiating plenty of warmth from hardwood floors, local carpets, textiles and furniture. The two "Royal Bungalows" enjoy a certain detached opulence. By way of diversion, there's a sprawling resort-style pool and jacuzzi, while a jogging track threads through the lush grounds. Some seven bars and restaurants cater to most Asian and Western preferences. Lakeview Theatre Restaurant and the Naga Pool Terrace are the most relaxed - both with international menus, while Maison Du Lac offers fine French cuisine in a formal dining-room setting.

Rates from: $
Star rating: ★ ★ ★ ★ ★
Overall rating: ◠◠◠◠ ½

Ambience:	9.00	Cleanliness:	8.58
Value:	8.83	Facilities:	7.53
Staff:	8.67	Restaurants:	8.42
Location:	9.17	Families:	8.17

Popa Mountain Resort

Mount Popa, Kyauk Padaung Township, Mandalay Division, Myanmar
T: +95 2 69 168 **F:** +95 2 69 169
www.HotelClub.com/Hotels/Popa_Mountain_Resort_Mandalay

This resort occupies one of the most incredible locations in Asia. An hour's drive from Bagan, the Popa Mountain Resort stands 750 metres above sea-level on the slopes of a forest-clad sacred volcano that last erupted a quarter of a million years ago. That the surrounding plains are semi-arid and Mount Popa is contrastingly lush merely emphasises its significance.

Myriad birds and butterflies flourish in the surrounding greenery, and the hotel enjoys a stunning view of Popa Taungkalat monastery, which is perched atop a crumpled cylinder of rock - a volcanic plug blasted skyward by seismic shifts millennia ago.

The resort contains 50 unobtrusive chalets and cabins on stilts, some with generous balconies looking out towards the monastery.

The entire resort is built from teak and sensitively constructed so as to make the least impact on the environment. Other facilities are limited but fair - the pool is handsome and enjoys those fantastic panoramas. The Sagawa restaurant menu is limited and the service sweet and sincere, but sometimes forgivably erratic.

Rates from: $
Star rating: ★ ★ ★
Overall rating: Editor's Pick

Ambience:	n/a	Cleanliness:	n/a
Value:	n/a	Facilities:	n/a
Staff:	n/a	Restaurants:	n/a
Location:	n/a	Families:	n/a

Sandoway Resort

Mya Pyin Village, Ngapali Beach, Thandwe, Rakhine State, Myanmar
T: +95 43 42 233 **F:** +95 43 42 255
www.HotelClub.com/Hotels/Sandoway_Resort_Thandwe

This stretch of the Bay of Bengal has been compared to parts of (now developed) southern Thailand some 20 years ago. Long turquoise shallows extend to coral outcrops that are ideal for laid-back snorkeling, and Ngapali Bay is one long ribbon of unblemished sand. The Sandoway's understated timber cottages and villas, hidden among coconut palms and set in landscaped tropical gardens a few paces away from the beach, make for a relaxed vacation. An international management and design team has assembled Asian aesthetics for the Western visitor with simple tastes. Though the accommodation is fully air-conditioned, grand flowing mosquito nets and large windows allow for those who prefer a sea breeze. All cottages and villas are two-storey affairs and the latter, at 120 square metres, are particularly spacious. Massage treatments are available in-house, there are boat trips to the best underwater vistas and deep-sea fishing, and hire bikes are great for a peruse of local villages. Pretty much "bliss off the beaten track".

Rates from: $$
Star rating: ★ ★ ★ ★
Overall rating: Editor's Pick

Ambience:	n/a	Cleanliness:	n/a
Value:	n/a	Facilities:	n/a
Staff:	n/a	Restaurants:	n/a
Location:	n/a	Families:	n/a

Sedona Hotel Mandalay

1 Junction of 26th & 66th Street, Chanayetharzan Township, Mandalay, Myanmar
T: +95 2 36 488 **F:** +95 2 36 499
www.HotelClub.com/Hotels/Sedona_Hotel_Mandalay

This is Mandalay's best hotel by a mile. It is the only five-star in fast-developing Mandalay and unquestionably offers the best range of facilities, best rooms and best service. The large, bright and smart lobby sets the tone with its modern and reassuringly familiar upmarket ambience against a subtle backdrop of Burmese decor.

The Sedona successfully competes for the luxury tourist market and is accordingly well positioned directly opposite the moats of Mandalay Fort and facing sacred Mandalay Hill. The 247 rooms are large, but cosy, and equipped as well as the price would suggest. The restaurants are indeed international, and particularly

noteworthy considering the lack of competition. Uno is the city's only luxury restaurant, serving Mediterranean fare. There is a gym, which closes rather inconveniently early, and a pool that offers welcome relief after sightseeing. Hotel standards can slip outside Yangon, but not here.

Rates from: $
Star rating: ★ ★ ★ ★ ★
Overall rating: 🏵🏵🏵🏵

Ambience:	8.20	Cleanliness:	8.40
Value:	8.70	Facilities:	8.17
Staff:	8.45	Restaurants:	8.00
Location:	8.10	Families:	8.88

Sedona Hotel Yangon

1 Kaba Aye Pagoda Road, Yankin Township, Yangon, Myanmar
T: +95 1 666 900 **F:** +95 1 666 911
www.HotelClub.com/Hotels/Sedona_Hotel_Yangon

The Sedona Yangon offers some of the best service in the country and knocks spots off many more expensive hotels across the region. This is noteworthy, as the hotel should by all rights be rather impersonal – it is vast, almost a

cruise liner of a hotel. But the staff are fantastic throughout, genuinely putting the guest first, and a role model for the industry. The 366 homely, spacious rooms are a touch predictable but perfectly decent and the extensive facilities,

including five restaurants and bars, capture a hint of a resort feel, given the slightly inconvenient location three kilometres both from downtown and the airport. Admittedly none of the hotel's facilities is the best of the best, but taken all together and run by exemplary staff, the Sedona is all one could hope for in a big hotel.

Rates from: $
Star rating: ★ ★ ★ ★ ★
Overall rating: 🏵🏵🏵🏵 ½

Ambience:	9.06	Cleanliness:	8.61
Value:	8.94	Facilities:	8.31
Staff:	8.72	Restaurants:	8.28
Location:	7.72	Families:	8.10

The Strand

2 Strand Road, Yangon, Myanmar
: +95 1 243 377 **F:** + 95 1 243 393
www.HotelClub.com/Hotels/Strand_Hotel_Yangon

If you are looking for a slice of colonial Rangoon rather than present-day Yangon, the grand old Strand is where you will find it. This classy throwback is steeped in history, with some exceptionally colourful events stretching back to its opening in 1901. The hotel took a direct hit from a World War II bomb, which landed rather untidily in the GM's office, and the property changed hands in the various struggles that have dotted the country's turbulent history. It also faded into disrepair, even being used as a stable, before being restored to its former glory. The British, the Japanese, the bombs and the decay have all now been swept aside and the Strand remains. Today it captures the sophistication and class of the good old days, with a few modern-day distractions for convenience.

It is in the magnificent chambers of the wood-panelled Strand Bar, or the elegant Strand Grill with its vaulted ceiling and chandeliers, or the oh-so-civilised Strand Café with its huge teak-framed windows staring out on the Strand Road that perhaps you can get rather carried away to a bygone age. The rarefied air has been preserved particularly well, as scruffy riff-raff will indeed find. But if you go along with it, it is a friendly and intimate place. Intimate due to its modest size (and that is all that is modest about the Strand) and the mere 32 enjoyable suites.

Rather than being cocooned in

an exclusive area, the Strand is conveniently set downtown, opposite the river, and not surprisingly it rather sticks out on the cluttered and noisy main road. The view from the quiet, soothing and irregularly shaped River View Suites will not hold your attention for long, but this is far better than the other rather drab views from the Superior Suites, where you may feel the need to pull the curtains. Ignoring the outside world you will enjoy polished wood floors, high ceilings, free-standing baths, enormous beds and the satisfaction that you are staying in a room with personality - something absent from the

mainstream and mass-produced five-star luxury properties.

There are a few minuses, the big one perhaps being the whopping price tag. The rate for one night here is rather perversely equivalent to nearly a year's wages for many locals. Little things that go wrong in other top hotels go wrong here, but more so - this is Myanmar after all, and you are getting ambience for your money rather than the endless list of hotel facilities you would usually get for top dollar in any other city hotel.

Perhaps that is its charm. Still, this is the premier address in Myanmar and an absolute jewel of a hotel.

Rates from: $$$	
Star rating: ★ ★ ★ ★ ★	
Overall rating: ◊ ◊ ◊ ◊	
Ambience: 9.07	Cleanliness: 9.14
Value: 6.50	Facilities: 7.60
Staff: 9.07	Restaurants: 8.69
Location: 8.93	Families: 8.86

Traders Hotel Yangon

223 Sule Pagoda Road, Yangon, Myanmar
T: +95 1 242 828 **F**: +95 1 242 800
www.HotelClub.com/Hotels/Traders_Hotel_Yangon

Beside the bustle of Bogyoke Aung San Market and overlooking the glittering gold façade of Sule Pagoda and the sloping green roofs of the capital's railway station, this is very much Yangon's prime mainstream hotel. The central business district, glitziest shopping malls and a network of narrow streets studded with pastel painted shop-houses are all within a few minutes' stroll. And so is the busy mud-brown Yangon River.

As you would expect from the Shangri-La group, everything about this hotel bears a touch of opulence, especially the marble-floored lobby, with its enormous chandelier and stairway that winds up to the Gallery Bar. The Lobby Lounge with its wicker armchairs is one of the city's most elegant spots for afternoon tea or a cocktail.

The hotel heaves with food and beverage outlets. The best bet for quality Myanmar cuisine is Traders Café, where a selection of local and Asian dishes is available 24 hours a day, albeit in a somewhat dated and uninspired environment. Top-notch Cantonese cuisine and a few other regional Chinese favourites are served at Summer Palace and Tategoto, presided over by a Japanese chef, serves authentic fare.

The 391 guestrooms are spacious and well appointed, and 69 are on the Traders Club floors, which is serviced by a decent river-view executive lounge providing afternoon tea, as well as breakfast and evening cocktails.

A high percentage of guests here are travelling executives, so the business centre is generously proportioned and contains several computers, meeting rooms and secretarial staff. For the long-term business visitor, there are fully-furnished self-contained offices; rental packages include discounts on business centre services, restaurants and bars. On the leisure side, an outdoor pool with whirlpool and a small sundeck and adjacent gym, with sauna and steam and massage rooms, provide a welcome break from what can be a hectic city.

Rates from: $
Star rating: ★ ★ ★ ★
Overall rating: ♦ ♦ ♦ ♦ ½

Ambience:	8.58	Cleanliness:	8.71
Value:	8.82	Facilities:	8.46
Staff:	9.37	Restaurants:	8.65
Location:	9.05	Families:	8.91

NEPAL

CHINA

❶ Pokhara

❷ KATHMANDU

INDIA

This fabled Himalayan kingdom has seen its unfair share of trouble in recent years, from the massacre of many of the leading members of its royal family in June 2001 to wavering governments and continuing problems with Maoist insurgents. Many of the more remote areas of Nepal are now off-limits to foreigners, and visitors should pay special attention to government travel advisories. Yet while the country is no longer automatically synonymous with Shangri-La, its natural beauty, historical wonders and generally hospitable inhabitants are little changed.

While usually viewed as a destination for hearty trekkers, river rafters, and mountain climbers or bikers, Nepal exercises equal appeal for anyone content to shop, visit the myriad of temples and palaces and take in the Himalayas from the comfort of a specially chartered mountain flight. Much of the country is drenched by a monsoon from June to September, so it is best to visit during the rest of the year. While it can be sunny by day during the winter months, it can be bitterly cold at nights, especially at altitude.

Most visitors fly into the capital, Kathmandu, a city that traces its history to medieval times and beyond, although old brick buildings are gradually being replaced with concrete, and pollution from an increasing number of motor vehicles is rearing its ugly head. It would be perfectly possible to spend a fortnight or more exploring the valley, venturing out to the towns of Patan and Bhaktapur, taking in the vast panorama of the Himalayas from the ridgetop at Nagarkot, and wandering the bazaars and back streets of Kathmandu itself. Pokhara is one of the main jumping-off points for trekking, as it sits on the old trade route linking Tibet and India. Further south, Nepal's character changes completely in the Terai, a totally flat area where jungles are still roamed by tiger and rhino. One of the best vacations here combines sightseeing in Kathmandu, trekking around Pokhara and concludes with a wildlife safari.

Accommodation has moved on from the 1960s, when Nepal was besieged by hippies in search of their own personal Nirvana. While there are still plenty of low-budget guesthouses around, international standards of comfort and service are becoming the norm, whether in the old established hotels, newly built ones or the up-and-coming breed of smart trekking lodges.

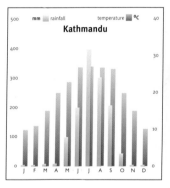

Dwarika's Village Hotel

Battisputali, Kathmandu, Nepal
T: +977 1 447 8378 F: +977 1 447 8378
www.HotelClub.com/Hotels/Dwarikas_Hotel

Dwarika's is so much more than a hotel, and delightfully so. Part museum, part cultural centre, its most remarkable genesis was due to the vision of Dwarika Das Shrestha, who was determined to build a hotel that would preserve Kathmandu's heritage. Mr Shrestha had been salvaging the intricately carved windows, doors and pillars - some dating back centuries - that are characteristic of the Nepalese capital for some time, but he concluded that they needed to be put to their original use. After employing masons and carpenters using traditional building methods, Dwarika's opened in 1978 - a cluster of courtyards and red-brick (handmade) cottages that would act as an architectural showcase as well as generate income for future preservation projects.

Since Mr Shrestha's death in 1992, the hotel has been run by his wife and daughter, and has gone from strength to strength. It now houses some 75 rooms and suites, many with windows that were carved in the 16th century, some with private courtyards, and all furnished with hand-printed fabrics decorated with Buddhist symbols. Dwarika's is infused with a gentle, peaceful ambience; it is somewhere to wander and explore and absorb. The shrine to the elephant-headed god Ganesh is bedecked with offertory flowers; you can browse through the library; cool off from the summer heat by the aquamarine pool, which is fed by gushing stone water spouts; dine on Nepalese specialties at Krishnarpan; or blend with the rhythm of an Ayurvedic massage in your own room.

While the essence of Dwarika's is tradition and history, it has also imported some modern pleasantries - live jazz hums through the Fusion Bar most evenings, and the Internet lurks discreetly in the business centre. As part of its contribution to the community, Dwarika's also runs a workshop where artisans and their young apprentices restore carvings similar to the ones that are already part of the hotel. This may be a property anchored in the past, but it has a firm stake in the future.

Rates from: $
Star rating: ★ ★ ★ ★
Overall rating: ♔ ♔ ♔ ♔

Ambience:	9.17	Cleanliness:	8.67
Value:	8.67	Facilities:	8.25
Staff:	8.50	Restaurants:	8.17
Location:	7.83	Families:	8.00

Fulbari Resort & Spa

Chhinne Danda, Kaski, Pokhara, Nepal
T: +977 61 523 451 F: +977 61 528 482
www.HotelClub.com/Hotels/Fulbari

The phrase "world-class" gets rather over-used nowadays, but it reaches its full worth in Pokhara. To watch passengers disembark at the airport, look up, look further up and then start scrabbling for their cameras is a daily reminder of the stupendous Himalayan panorama that forms the permanent backdrop to this ancient trading crossroads. Add to this a picturesque lake and an entire verdant valley to explore, and you have a destination that is, well - perhaps WC are not quite the right initials.

But for years Pokhara lacked a hotel to complement its surroundings - there was accommodation aplenty, but nothing that really fitted. Enter the Fulbari, to some trumpet fanfare, with a nine-hole golf course and a spa and electricity you could rely on and food that was not simply an approximation. Best of all, as it sits well back at the bottom of the valley, the gently-tinted Fulbari commanded a 200-kilometre view of what folklore throughout the subcontinent holds to be the abode of the gods.

Perhaps the best way to arrive here is by helicopter - 30 minutes' flight from Kathmandu: an adventure in itself over the lush foothills and valleys - touching down at the private helipad. Whether you are here for some conference work, at the start of a trek into the hills, just to kick back for a bit or to indulge in some serious holistic health activities, comfort is the watchword in the hotel's 165 rooms and suites. The outdoor pool might be too much for some, even though it is heated, but activities like horse-riding are suitable year-round whatever the weather. The seven bars and restaurants (fuelled by an organic herb and vegetable garden) face off against the spa and health farm, which offers weight-loss and anti-ageing programmes. A casino is due to open in 2005, though well away from the resort's secluded meditation garden.

Rates from: $$
Star rating: ★★★★★
Overall rating: 4 ½

Ambience:	9.10	Cleanliness:	8.75
Value:	8.30	Facilities:	8.23
Staff:	9.30	Restaurants:	8.10
Location:	7.30	Families:	8.25

Hyatt Regency Kathmandu

Taragaon, Boudha, Kathmandu, Nepal
T: +977 1 449 1234   **F:** +977 1 449 0033
www.HotelClub.com/Hotels/Hyatt_Regency_Kathmandu

The Hyatt Regency is a few score turns of a pilgrim's prayer wheel from the magnificent Boudhanath Stupa, one of the Kathmandu's holiest Buddhist shrines and one of its most recognisable icons. The hotel itself is modelled on a Nepali palace, and sprawls over 15 hectares of landscaped grounds. Rooms are generously proportioned, and clean lines are broken with details such as hand-carved cabinet doors and intricately woven textiles. Large bathrooms all contain tubs and a separate walk-in shower. While the sizeable outdoor pool and jacuzzi is not a huge draw unless visiting in summer, the adjacent café/bar is one of the city's most laid-back watering holes. More lively is the three-storey Rox bar and restaurant, with its intriguing stone wall cladding, a live band most nights and serving attractive Asian and Western food. While the Hyatt is some way from the centre - cycling but not really walking distance - its remoteness does make this one of the quietest hotels in the capital.

Rates from: $	
Star rating: ★ ★ ★ ★ ★	
Overall rating: 🐾🐾🐾🐾	
Ambience: 9.00	Cleanliness: 8.73
Value: 7.73	Facilities: 8.25
Staff: 8.55	Restaurants: 8.27
Location: 7.27	Families: 8.43

Soaltee Crowne Plaza

Tahachal, Kathmandu, Nepal
T: +977 1 427 3999   **F:** +977 1 427 8559
www.HotelClub.com/Hotels/Soaltree_Crowne_Plaza

Spread over 4.5 hectares of landscaped gardens with 283 rooms, this hotel is reasonably close to most city sights and the main shopping areas. A golf course also lies a short drive away. The Crowne's rooms are some of the better ones to be had in Kathmandu, but interior design is not a highpoint. High-speed Internet access, Wi-Fi and a fully equipped business centre are all at hand, along with mobile phone rental and a self-service laundrette. Executive floors offer a handful of larger rooms and suites, and a private lounge that serves breakfast and evening cocktails. Four food and beverage outlets account for most Asian and Western tastes; Bukhara, serving Nepali and northwestern Indian cuisine is a popular Kathmandu destination restaurant. Those visiting in the warmer months of the year can enjoy the large outdoor pool; there is also a tennis court, tended by ball boys who spectate with more than a modicum of enthusiasm.

Rates from: $	
Star rating: ★ ★ ★ ★ ★	
Overall rating: 🐾🐾🐾🐾	
Ambience: 9.00	Cleanliness: 8.75
Value: 7.00	Facilities: 8.50
Staff: 8.25	Restaurants: 9.29
Location: 8.13	Families: 8.83

Tiger Mountain Pokhara Lodge

Pokhara, Nepal
T: +977 1 436 1500 **F:** +977 1 436 1600
www.HotelClub.com/Hotels/Tiger_Mountain_Pokhara_Lodge

Pokhara Lodge is one of the most romantic, sexy even, hotels in the Himalaya. Legend has it that when Prince Siddharta Gautama embarked on his quest for enlightenment, while meditating under a Bodhi tree at Lumbini in Nepal he was tantalised by Mara, lord of the underworld, who one by one offered all his quick and limber daughters to try to tempt the prince away from achieving Buddhahood. Lord Mara failed of course, but temptation is the theme at Pokhara Lodge, suspended seemingly within touching distance of the Himalaya, a spiritual retreat for the senses. Except in summer, it's usually cool at these altitudes, especially come the evening, and the lodge has been built with the emphasis on cosiness. Hewn out of the local stone, the 13 separate bungalows - each with a private verandah - have been sited to take best advantage of the vistas swooping down over the valley 300 metres below and up to the snow peaks of Dhaulagiri, Manaslu, and Annapurna, each of which is over 8,000 metres. Bulky duvets cover the beds, and the rooms - 19 in total - are reassuringly rustic and comforting, decorated with traditional artefacts and local hand-woven fabrics. Life at the lodge, which is set about with indigenous shrubs, bamboo and fruit trees, revolves around the roaring circular open log fire in the bar, where it is all to easy too snuggle up with a hot rum after dinner, reminiscing and chatting with other guests, until the time comes for the brief, brisk walk back to your room and the welcoming frisson of the bedclothes. By day, there is a (mountain-temperature) pool to relax by, excellent opportunities for trekking on the doorstep or, for the airbourne armchair traveller, microlite flights from Pohkara airport, and a unique collection of Himalayan mountaineering literature and photographs belonging to the late Colonel Jimmy Roberts, who pioneered Nepal's modern trekking industry.

Rates from: $$
Star rating: ★ ★ ★ ★
Overall rating: Editor's Pick

Ambience:	n/a	Cleanliness:	n/a
Value:	n/a	Facilities:	n/a
Staff:	n/a	Restaurants:	n/a
Location:	n/a	Families:	n/a

Yak & Yeti Hotel

Durbar Marg, Kathmandu, Nepal
T: +977 1 424 8999 **F:** +977 1 422 7782
www.HotelClub.com/Hotels/Yak_Yeti

The name alone should be enough to sell this intriguing, unique hotel, set back from Durbar Marg and comprising Lal Durbar - a century-old former Rana family palace - as well as a more modern wing. Balancing out the plethora of history - the Chimney restaurant pays tribute to eccentric Russian renaissance man Boris Lissanevitch, who opened the first of Nepal's modern hotels - are the 270 rooms and suites, the more superior of which come with computers and laser printers. Down the years, celebrities have flocked in, from heads of state to princes and princesses and various Hollywoodites including Richard Gere and Goldie Hawn. Kathmandu is starting to host its first international chain hotels, but the Yak & Yeti remains fiercely independent, blending first-class facilities with charm and a great deal of character, not to mention personal service from the staff who tend to welcome guests as if they were personal friends. Tea in the garden (weather permitting) is essential for anyone not actually staying, as quite apart from the surroundings the hotel's bakery produces some of Kathmandu's best cakes and pastries. Indoors, traditional cultural shows are performed at Naachghar, the Nepalese theatre restaurant.

Considerable prominence is now granted to the hotel's art collection, which is fitting considering that the property is a work of art in itself. And on the health side, as yoga hails from the subcontinent, it is only sensible that guru Miss Samjhana Gautam should be conducting daily classes at Club Nirvana, the health and fitness centre. The addition of the Casino Royale may not appeal to everybody, however. It is a slightly rough-and-ready gambling den, not exactly James Bond, and only open to foreign passport holders. The inclusion of a children's crèche on the casino's premises is a touch that could only occur in Nepal.

Rates from: $
Star rating: ★ ★ ★ ★ ★
Overall rating: ♦ ♦ ♦ ♦ ½

Ambience:	8.88	Cleanliness:	8.44
Value:	8.38	Facilities:	7.93
Staff:	9.06	Restaurants:	8.81
Location:	8.81	Families:	8.36

NEW ZEALAND

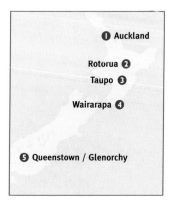

Pristine New Zealand is characterised by its isolation. One look at an atlas will tell you that this boot-shaped double island is one of the most remote countries in the world. A decision to go to New Zealand is therefore entirely deliberate, no-one is just passing through unless they happen to be en route the South Pole.

New Zealand has a population of around four million, nearly all of whom live in and around Auckland and Wellington. These cities suffer little from pollution, and while some of the country's indigenous forests have been chopped down to make room for New Zealand's

countless sheep, it remains one of the greenest and cleanest places in the world. With an acute environmental awareness, New Zealand has a proud reputation for championing the green cause.

Nowhere else can quite match New Zealand for the great outdoors. This is the world centre for adventure sports, and zany activities like bungee jumping were invented here. The sporty Kiwis are into exploring their engaging landscape in the most adrenaline-inducing fashions - tramping, rock climbing, snowboarding, kayaking, and just about any other land, sea or air activity; as a bonus most are easily accessible and safe for novices.

The country is split into North and South Islands which, as they are separated from the major continents, are both filled with unusual wildlife and rare species. The more temperate North Island is the more densely populated and home to the largest city, Auckland. This is the main gateway to the country as well as the centre of

New Zealand's business, and it outstrips the mellow yet urbane capital Wellington for pace and sights. Instead, Wellington is the political and geographical lynchpin of the country, functioning as a balancing transit point between the two islands. North Island's attractions include its native woodlands, barren volcanoes and spouting geysers, and the strong Maori culture. The South Island is sleepier and greener, and many visitors find it more distinctive than the North. Gentle hills roll for kilometres before bursting into the dramatic Southern Alps, with stunning snow-capped peaks and glaciers. Apart from the higher elevations that receive snow all year round, New Zealand's mild weather is comparable to Britain but with the seasons in reverse due to the southerly latitude.

Hotel-wise, New Zealand does not particularly shine, though many of its rural lodges are lovely. It is fair to say that the country has a bed-and-breakfast culture. These small, mainly family-run establishments are generally clean, friendly and good value but are unlikely to win many international awards.

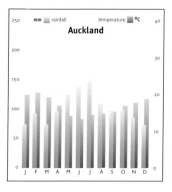

Blanket Bay

Glenorchy, New Zealand
T: +64 3 442 9442 **F:** +64 3 442 9441
www.HotelClub.com/Hotels/Blanket_Bay_Lodge

If you have to spend four years making a movie, being able to relax in a place like this must take some of the strain off. *Lord Of The Rings* star Ian McKellan rates it "the best in the world"; Robin Williams spent Christmas here and Brad Pitt and Jennifer Aniston chose it for their honeymoon.

Only a dozen or so rooms, but what rooms! Nestled on the shores of northern Lake Wakatipu, with snow-capped Mount Earnslaw in the background, this granite-and-timber super-lodge is modelled after Arnold Schwarzenegger's Idaho home. Having bought the land (26,000 hectares of sheep pasture) some 30 years ago, when he finally decided to build on it, Levi Strauss CEO Tom Tusher spared no expense.

A team of Mexican carpenters were flown in to "weather" the wood, and antique furniture was imported from France and the US. The result is that it looks as if it has been here for centuries, the baronial hideaway, perhaps, of an exiled European aristocrat rather than a 20th-century jeans salesman.

Its exclusivity is epitomised by the fact that one of its huge rooms (although admittedly back-facing) is set aside for guests' retinue - personal trainers, pilots, that sort of staff. And unlike at most up-market New Zealand lodges, meals are served at separate tables - in the Private Dining Room with its nine-metre-high beams and lake view, or the ultra-intimate Wine Cave, which seats just six. The Pac Rim cuisine is, needless to say, award-winning, while the Terrace actually has an outdoor log fire.

Deer-antler chandeliers and stuffed ducks, towering picture windows and roaring rock fireplaces, private patios and deep leather couches ... the biggest problem it poses is how to drag yourself away for all that hiking, fishing, boating and horse-riding that the world's newest earthly paradise promises.

Rates from: $$$$$
Star rating: ★ ★ ★ ★ ★
Overall rating: Editor's Pick

Ambience:	n/a	Cleanliness:	n/a
Value:	n/a	Facilities:	n/a
Staff:	n/a	Restaurants:	n/a
Location:	n/a	Families:	n/a

Carlton Hotel Auckland

Corner Mayoral Drive and Vincent Street, Auckland, New Zealand
T: +64 9 366 3000 **F**: +64 9 366 0121
www.HotelClub.com/Hotels/Carlton_Hotel_Auckland

The Carlton's exterior is modern and angular, almost like an office building. On entry the atrium opens 12 floors above you, the glass and marble reinforcing the smart, corporate theme. The decor is professional and suitable, for this bright and efficient property is one of Auckland's top business hotels. It is located centrally, and opposite "The Edge", the city's arts and entertainment complex. A few minutes' walk away is Queen Street, New Zealand's best shopping district. Facilities are tailor-made for the business traveller, with a top business centre and meeting rooms, including one of the city's biggest ballrooms. Restaurants offer broadly Western food, although Katsura serves authentic Japanese cuisine. The heated indoor lap pool, trim gymnasium and steamy sauna give guests the opportunity to unwind. Best of all the Carlton's 455 rooms are large, crisp and good value with great city views through the floor-to-ceiling windows.

Rates from: $$
Star rating: ★ ★ ★ ★ ★
Overall rating: � ♫ ♫ ♫ ½

Ambience:	8.93	Cleanliness:	9.21
Value:	8.64	Facilities:	8.85
Staff:	8.29	Restaurants:	8.80
Location:	9.29	Families:	8.88

Heritage Queenstown

91 Fernhill Road, Queenstown, New Zealand
T: +64 3 442 4988 **F**: +64 3 442 4989
www.HotelClub.com/Hotels/Heritage_Queenstown

If you're expecting to be bang in the middle of Queenstown, bear in mind that this place is a good 20-minute uphill walk away. But the exercise will do you good, the crisp, clean air is a tonic, and there's a free shuttle bus for those who can't quite face the climb.

The views across Lake Wakatipu to the mountain range named, with typical Kiwi understatement, The Remarkables, are surely worth it. The 213-unit (rooms, suites and villas), cedar-and-stone-built Heritage is deceptively large for a lodge-style hotel and the walkways connecting its three wings are uncovered (umbrellas available).

The place is full of blazing log fires, timbered ceilings, wooden chests and stuffed trophies on the walls. The only restaurant, Mackenzies, named after a bygone local family known for its hospitality, dishes up superb Pacific Rim cuisine and has a cosy après-ski ambience. The bathrooms are brilliant, but make sure you book a lake-view room to render that stiff walk worthwhile.

Rates from: $$
Star rating: ★ ★ ★ ★
Overall rating: ♫ ♫ ♫ ♫

Ambience:	8.75	Cleanliness:	9.08
Value:	7.42	Facilities:	8.13
Staff:	7.58	Restaurants:	7.36
Location:	9.00	Families:	8.00

Hilton Auckland

Shed 21 Princes Wharf, Auckland, New Zealand
T: +64 9 978 2000   **F:** +64 9 978 2001
www.HotelClub.com/Hotels/Hilton_Auckland_Hotel

This dramatically designed and situated boutique hotel jutting 300 metres into Waitemata Harbour is probably the most un-Hilton-like Hilton in the world. Built at a cost of NZ$50 million to cater for the America's Cup boom, it has all the verve and contemporaneity you would expect from such an endeavour.

The 166 smallish rooms are simple yet sophisticated, with wonderfully comfy beds and generous bathrooms. And they all have walk-out balconies with jaw-dropping views. Try one of the dozen corner rooms, which feature all-glass walls.

There is not much in the way of facilities, apart from a small pool, but White restaurant is in a class of its own, its award-winning nouvelle Pac Rim cuisine attracting the cream of the city's smart set. And the hip Bellini's cocktail bar serves a mean selection of martinis.

The staff, who seem to have been selected for their looks as much as their accomplishments, compliment the uber-groovy ambience and the place is generally buzzing both inside and out. Its superb Prince's Wharf location - a stone's throw from the Viaduct Basin entertainment district and a catapult-ping from downtown Auckland - ensures you will never be bored, and if you are, just hop on a ferry from the terminal next door.

A word of warning, though: the wharf by the Hilton serves as a berth for cruise liners (and many of the hotel's guests are transiting passengers) and ferries. This means that you may find one of these behemoths parked outside your window, blocking your magnificent harbour view and disturbing your sleep as it re-loads in the early hours of the morning.

They say you can't have everything, and they're right. But the Hilton Auckland makes a damned good stab at it.

Rates from: $$$
Star rating: ★ ★ ★ ★ ★
Overall rating: 🌀🌀🌀🌀 ½

Ambience:	8.95	Cleanliness:	9.38
Value:	7.81	Facilities:	8.63
Staff:	8.67	Restaurants:	8.10
Location:	9.29	Families:	8.67

Huka Lodge

271 Huka Falls Road, Taupo, New Zealand
T: +64 7 378 5791 **F**: +64 7 378 0427
www.HotelClub.com/Hotels/Huka_Lodge

Starting life as a four-hut fishing camp in 1928, Huka Lodge was completely revamped and upgraded in 1985, and is now regarded as the ne plus ultra of New Zealand's luxury rustic retreats. Queen Elizabeth II loves it, Bill Gates and Rupert Murdoch patronise it, as do Diana Ross and Robin Williams. Yet for our money, this is the kind of place Moley and

Ratty would be living if they were real and had become millionaires on the back of *Wind In The Willows* sales.

Situated on the banks of the Waikato River by trout-stuffed

Lake Taupo, just a short walk from the spectacular Huka Falls and a picnic day out from Mount Tarawera volcano, the setting is cosily English rather than dramatically Kiwi. Manicured

awns in landscaped gardens invite gentle strolling rather than the more heart-pumping activities associated with the great NZ outdoors. Petanque, anyone?

Some 20 riverside bungalows offer plush comfort, with large, glass-ceilinged, under-floor-heated bathrooms featuring sunken baths and separate showers, walk-in dressing rooms, pastel decor and private terraces. If there's a party of you, book the Owner's Cottage, which has four double bedrooms, each with its own en-suite bathroom.

The lodge itself is a magnificent affair, exuding a rich, warm ambience by means of log fires, plump armchairs, tartan furnishings, woven wool carpets and panoramic river views. There is a Library adjoining the Lodge Room, which can be used for private dining - as can almost anywhere in the complex, including the Trophy Room, a meeting venue adorned with somewhat inappropriate stuffed African big-game keepsakes.

The Dining Room (it's probably a mark of Kiwi understatement that most luxury-lodge facilities are so unimaginatively named) is a sprawling restaurant with candelabra and Old Would-Be Masters inside and a terrace outside with roaring fire to ward off the chilly evening air. Then there is the Wine Cellar, built under a grassy knoll, with wonderful vaulted ceilings and walls crammed with more than 30,000 bottles of New Zealand's finest vintages.

The lodge's food is so highly regarded that it does a profitable sideline in cookery books based on its own creations. Its hearty, country-style breakfasts are legendary, and gourmets have been known to helicopter in from as far afield as Auckland and Wellington just to sample the superb five-course dinners.

In-room massage is available and there is a small gift shop, as well as a boutique selling warm practical clothing for guests who may have forgotten to pack any along with their evening gowns and diamanté shawls. The staff are as unobtrusive and obliging as you would expect from a favoured haunt of royalty and international statesmen.

Something of a national treasure, then, this superbly civilised hotel masquerades as the country residence of a Kiwi of taste and substance, a source of pride even for those who can never afford to stay here. Motivation, perhaps, for feelings of nationalism of the sort that spur sporting achievements: one can imagine the All Blacks visualising the Huka while they're doing the Haka.

Rates from: $$$$$
Star rating: ★ ★ ★ ★ ★
Overall rating: 🌀🌀🌀🌀🌀

Ambience:	9.29	Cleanliness:	9.14
Value:	8.00	Facilities:	8.56
Staff:	8.86	Restaurants:	9.43
Location:	9.86	Families:	8.50

Langham Hotel Auckland

83 Symonds Street, Auckland, New Zealand
T: +64 9 379 5132 **F:** +64 9 377 9367
www.HotelClub.com/Hotels/Sheraton_Auckland_Hotel_and_Towers

Formerly The Sheraton, the Langham Hotel remains modern and professional with perhaps the most pleasing environment of any city hotel in New Zealand. It is well located - just metres from Queen Street, the backbone of Auckland's best entertainment and shopping.

The city centre and the waterfront can be reached on foot, but it is best to hop on the complimentary shuttle that can get you down there in minutes. The 410 handsome rooms are lively and fully equipped with handy extras like dataports. Glowing facilities are excellent in scope and design, with a choice of outdoor pool and some good upscale restaurants and bars - you can dine at SBF Brassierie 24 hours a day and Paddington's comes highly recommended. Meeting and events facilities are also up to date, with the ballroom catering for up to 900 people. A very capable and complete city hotel.

Rates from: $$
Star rating: ★ ★ ★ ★ ★
Overall rating: ♢♢♢♢

Ambience:	8.75	Cleanliness:	8.67
Value:	8.00	Facilities:	8.39
Staff:	8.08	Restaurants:	8.33
Location:	8.42	Families:	7.88

Skycity Hotel

Corner of Victoria and Federal Streets, Auckland, New Zealand
T: +64 9 363 6000 **F:** +64 9 363 6032
www.HotelClub.com/Hotels/SKYCITY_Auckland

With 1,600 gaming machines and 11 bars and restaurants, guests can drink themselves insensible and/or lose all their money at the hotel attached to Auckland's iconic Skycity casino and entertainment complex. But should they want to smoke they have to use one of seven special outdoor balconies -

or book one of only 92 rooms (the other 252 are all non-smoking but many do have harbour views). The interior designer must have been a Miles Davis fan - all the rooms are kinda blue.

Not that the hotel is just for gamblers: it is sufficiently insulated from the main Skycity action to be well worth using as an Auckland business or sightseeing base.

The beauty of a place like this is that there are many more bars and restaurants than usual - try the stunning views from Orbit and The Observatory in the 328 metre Sky Tower from which you can jump (harness provided).

Rates from: $$
Star rating: ★ ★ ★ ★
Overall rating: ♢♢♢♢ ½

Ambience:	8.64	Cleanliness:	9.29
Value:	7.93	Facilities:	8.68
Staff:	8.36	Restaurants:	8.85
Location:	9.43	Families:	8.55

Treetops Lodge and Estate

351 Kearoa Road, RDI Horohoro, Rotorua, New Zealand
T: +64 7 333 2066 **F**: +64 7 333 2065
www.HotelClub.com/Hotels/Treetops_Lodge_Estate

Natural disasters such as volcanic eruptions can, over a very long period of time, have beneficial effects - witness the lush landscapes of Rotorua that have sprouted from its geothermal terrain. And just 30 minutes' drive from Rotorua city (or a helicopter flight if you're feeling flush), you can stay slap bang in the middle of it all in sybaritic comfort.

The rather unoriginally named Treetops is one of only five such resorts to have earned a place in Qualmark's "Exclusive" category. Nestled in 1,000 hectares of

wooded valley, it is a rural dream come true - a luxurious retreat surrounded by seven of the world's finest trout streams, four lakes, and 70 kilometres of spectacular hiking trails.

The lodge itself has four totally fabulous suites, which open onto a chintzy, oak-beamed lounge with roaring open fireplace and adjoining haute-cuisine kitchen. Then, a short stroll or golf-buggy ride away, there are eight self-contained villas set among the trees (with their own fireplaces and somewhat smaller kitchens - but hey, with five-star room service, who needs to cook?).

Facilities are as simple and unpretentious as the ancient countryside that is this rustic oasis' raison d'être: a well-stocked library,

a games room, a formal restaurant and meeting rooms for conference guests. Structures are made of plain timber and stone, blending seamlessly into their setting. Authentic Maori artwork adorns the walls.

The ideal base for white-water rafting, kayaking, mountain-biking, horse riding, soaking in the area's celebrated mud pools and geysers ... or just soaking up the pristine rurality of it all. And it lies only a three-hour drive from Auckland. No wonder New Zealand is the world's favourite "new" destination, now that it can boast truly world-class accommodations such as this - opened in 2001 - from which to enjoy its æons-old natural attractions.

Rates from: $$$$
Star rating: ★ ★ ★ ★ ★
Overall rating: Editor's Pick

Ambience:	n/a	Cleanliness:	n/a
Value:	n/a	Facilities:	n/a
Staff:	n/a	Restaurants:	n/a
Location:	n/a	Families:	n/a

Wharekauhau Country Estate

Western Lake Road, Palliser Bay, RD3 Featherston, Wairarapa, New Zealand
T: +64 6 307 7581   **F**: +64 6 307 7799
www.HotelClub.com/Hotels/Wharekauhau_Country_Estate

If you want to know what it actually feels like to be vastly outnumbered by sheep, what better way to find out than by staying on a 2,000-hectare working sheep station - that just happens to include one of the country's most luxurious lodges? "Forry-ko-ho" as it is pronounced in Maori (it means "site of knowledge") is set in rolling green pastures, replete with deer forests, trout streams, lakes and vineyards, on the rim of windswept Palliser Bay and its 16 kilometres of black volcanic sandy beaches and stunning coastal scenery, with a backdrop of the cloud-capped Rimutaka Mountains.

The estate is a two-hour drive from Wellington, or a ten-minute helicopter ride ("heli-lunches" are the resort's latest attraction for well-heeled city dwellers). Its cuisine

(mainly French and Italian) and extensive selection of local wines have won almost as many awards as the place itself, which is regularly rated one of the world's top hideaways. Rebuilt in 1998 to resemble an Edwardian country manor-house, the expansive lodge, with its mullioned windows in the Grand Hall and plethora of blazing open fireplaces, manages to exude an air of both period nostalgia and contemporary comfort.

Accommodation in the white-washed cottage "suites" a few minutes' walk away is the very definition of luxury, each boasting a four-poster bed, deep bathtubs with views of the Bay, a sumptuous gold-and-beige colour scheme and under-floor heating (as well as the ubiquitous open fireplaces).

Leisure facilities are in keeping

with the aristocratic theme - apart from the 20-metre indoor pool, gym and astro-turf tennis courts, you can play petanque or croquet in the gardens. And on top of all the usual hunt'n, shoot'n, fish'n and strenuous outdoor activities the area offers in abundance, there are the added lures of a visit to a nearby seal colony and, of course, the chance to participate in some quintessential sheep-shearing or dipping. What about the poor people? Baa-aa-aah, humbug.

Rates from: $$$$$
Star rating: ★★★★★
Overall rating: Editor's Pick

Ambience:	n/a	Cleanliness:	n/a
Value:	n/a	Facilities:	n/a
Staff:	n/a	Restaurants:	n/a
Location:	n/a	Families:	n/a

PHILIPPINES

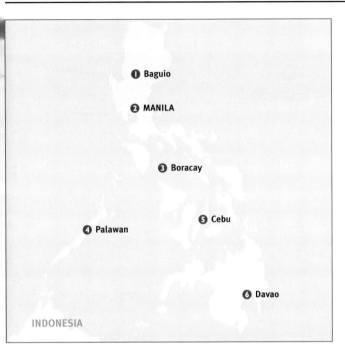

The Philippine archipelago stretches along the fringes of the Pacific Rim from Malaysia's Sabah in the south to Taiwan in the north. The nation cobbles together some 7,000 islands, and it is this geological disintegration that characterises the Philippines.

The infrastructure and development is as broken as the contours of the land, and each province or island has traditionally been somewhat separate from the rule of the capital. Endemic corruption and conflicting religious backgrounds means the country grapples with overwhelming social, economic and political problems. Also, rather unluckily, its location means it suffers a catalogue of natural disasters - typhoons, earthquakes and volcanic eruptions. In fact, the unfortunate Philippines was recently cited as the most disaster-prone country in the world!

So quite why would you come? Could it be the fascinating rice terraces of north Luzon, or Borocay's White Beach, often cited as the best in the world, or the steep limestone cliffs and spectacular diving around the secluded islands of Palawan or the chocolate hills of Bohol, or could it be just that infectious Filipino smile that welcomes all comers to these stunningly beautiful shores?

No doubt for delicate travellers the Philippines might prove intimidating, but for the majority the diversity and sheer beauty make the effort worthwhile.

As the only Asian country to have been colonised by the Spanish, the Philippines is quite distinct. It exudes a Latin flair and pulse and has more in common with South American countries than near neighbours Taiwan, Malaysia, Hong Kong or Japan. The culture is heavily rooted in religion and spirituality, with the vast majority of Filipinos following Catholicism. Most pay more heed to their church leaders than their traditionally weak governments (periodically turfed out by incredible surges of "People Power").

The country can broadly be split into three regions - the northerly fertile island Luzon, the central island band of the Visayas and Palawan, and the large island of Mindanao furthest south. Metro Manila is found on Luzon and is a sprawling and chaotic city. It is not

a pretty metropolis, beset by traffic jams and power cuts, and famed for its "anything-goes" nightlife, which is now being challenged by a sophisticated new breed of restaurants. The commercial centre Makati is orderly and smooth except for the traffic, but the poverty elsewhere is quite obvious and some areas are best avoided.

As soon as you leave the city behind the pace drops. The Visayas and Palawan feel much more remote than they look on the map. Cebu City is a major commercial hub but not far away are the developed beaches of Mactan and countless quieter forgotten ones. The dive sites around this region are absolutely fantastic, with crystal waters and abundant marine life drawing underwater enthusiasts from all over the world.

Distant Mindanao is closer to Malaysia and Indonesia than Manila and culturally separate from the rest of the country. By the time you get down there the capital's influence has all but dissipated. It has a predominantly Muslim population with a strong separatist movement characterised by some guerilla activity. Mindanao has real security issues and it is strongly advisable to seek travel advice before visiting the island.

Filipino hotels are not the best by Asian standards, but this is more down to shaky infrastructure than anything else. Within the mediocrity are some real gems of resorts and some world-class business hotels. The staff are almost always a total delight. Smiles are a constant in the Philippines, no matter what life conjures up, so it is almost impossible not to be drawn to them, and the level of English spoken is remarkably high, among the best in Asia.

Typhoons can bring the Philippines to a standstill so it is best to visit it away from the wet season during the humid and sticky summer months around July to September. Outside this period you can expect beaming sunshine to match the smiles of this happy people.

manpulo

Pamalican Island, Palawan, Philippines
T: +63 2 759 4040 F: +63 2 759 4044
www.HotelClub.com/Hotels/Amanpulo_Resort_Palawan

The Amanpulo experience starts long before you touch down at the airstrip on the remote Philippine island of Pamalican. Cruising south for 80 minutes from Manila over extinct volcanoes, thick jungles and deserted archipelagos in a private 19-seat, twin-engine turboprop, you know you are headed for somewhere distinctly exotic.

It is said that it is better to travel than to arrive, but that well-worn aphorism is utterly disproved here. There is nothing on the island but Amanpulo and its 40 casitas (65-square-metre beachside and hillside bungalows loosely modelled on Philippine village homes) including two villas, all of which come equipped with their own private electric buggy.

Cruise ships will not drop anchor in the bay and vendors cannot come hawking along the silky white sand beaches. As you explore, the realisation steals over you that this five-kilometre-long island (just 500 metres wide) is pretty much all yours, and it is hard to extinguish a spontaneous jiggle of utter pleasure.

Free and easy is the credo here. Nearly half of the casitas' interior is given over to a Cebu marble bathroom, and the romance of the king-sized bed is augmented by details like pebble-washed walls and coconut-shell tables. Outside, the deck and his-and-her divans are hidden behind lush foliage. So let your imagination run wild, and simply wander free around the island and its surrounding seas. Kingfishers, sea eagles and black-napped orioles inhabit the forest, hawksbill turtles, parrotfish and manta ray colour the waters of the reefs. There are canoes, sailing boats and windsurfers, a 30-metre aqua-tiled pool, and of course there are numerous dive sites for water-lovers.

Indeed, the abundant and beautiful reef waters that surround Pamalican and its neighbouring islands could have been specifically devised for water-addicts. The resort lays on a daily complimentary snorkelling and fish-feeding trips and Aquaventure, Amanpulo's dive company, is an exceptionally well-run PADI operation which delivers dive courses ranging from introductory to advanced.

The Sulu Sea also offers fine cruising. Amanpulo keeps a fleet of boats for island hopping, fishing and lazy-day sailing, including the ten-metre *Dolphin 11*. The fibreglass *Gulf Craft* can take up to ten guests on half-day and full-day charters with Manamoc Island, just across the channel, proving a popular cruise and picnic area. Other sea-going options include a sunset cruise or a leisurely voyage around the Sulu Sea by moonlight.

For those preferring dry land there is a library, tennis, massages, nature walks and mountain bikes. The main Clubhouse Restaurant spills out on to a terrace for al fresco dining, although you can also ask for your meal to be set up by the pool, next to a beach bonfire or in a secluded picnic grove. And of course after dinner there is no better entertainment than the Milky Way, brought a little closer by an astronomical refractor telescope.

Amanpulo has become a popular remedy for "too much reality", and its name, by the way, means "peaceful island". As if you needed telling.

Rates from: $$$$$
Star rating: ★ ★ ★ ★ ★
Overall rating: ♙ ♙ ♙ ♙ ½

Ambience:	9.14	Cleanliness:	9.04
Value:	8.24	Facilities:	8.39
Staff:	9.06	Restaurants:	8.35
Location:	8.67	Families:	8.58

Camp John Hay Manor

Loakan Road, Baguio City 2600, Philippines
T: +63 74 446 0231   **F**: +63 74 445 0420
www.HotelClub.com/Hotels/Camp_John_Hay_Manor_Hotel_Baguio

Part of the charm of this four-storey mountain lodge is that, despite being set among 246 hectares of pine forest, its wood panelling is fashioned from Canadian pine. A favourite bolt-hole for frazzled Filipinos (some of whom own chalets here), the resort harks back to Alpine Europe in its sophisticated simplicity, with sing-songs round the roaring open fire in the Piano Bar reminiscent of après-ski in Gstaad, rather than post-hiking in Baguio.

The 176 rooms and suites are basic but comfy. The windows afford stunning views of the Cordillera mountain range, letting in the cool pine-scented air that is the resort's main attraction. There are only two restaurants - the Delicatessen for light snacks, and Le Chef at the Manor, which enjoys a gourmet reputation thanks to the ministrations of the renowned chef Billy King.

The Palm Garden Health Spa will soothe aching muscles after a day spent trekking, strawberry-picking, horse-riding or sifting through Igorot souvenirs. The adjoining par-69 Jack Nicklaus-designed golf course is one of the best in the country.

Rates from: $
Star rating: ★ ★ ★
Overall rating: ♭ ♭ ♭ ♭

Ambience:	8.97	Cleanliness:	8.77
Value:	8.00	Facilities:	8.07
Staff:	8.14	Restaurants:	8.07
Location:	8.48	Families:	8.37

Discovery Suites

25 ADB Avenue, Ortigas Centre, Pasig City 1600, Manila, Philippines
T: +63 2 635 2222 **F**: +63 2 683 8111
www.HotelClub.com/Hotels/Discovery_Suites_Manila

The old cliché "a home away from home" has popped up in many a flowery brochure, but the Discovery Suites is probably one of the few properties here to have truly captured its essence. Why? Because it is not a hotel. The residence presents 225 serviced apartments for the long- and short-stay guest and therefore is designed to act as a true home. Cosy yet spacious one-, two- and three-bedroom suites are decked out in a warm and personal fashion. Each has a great kitchen and all the household appliances one usually tries to escape, while as a back-up there's always Café Berrio on the fifth floor. Crucially, the suites are very habitable - touches include plump pillows, sofas you can snuggle into and fluffy toys in the kids' bedrooms. The communal facilities are accessed via the atrium and have no real sense of luxury, more of comfortable functionality. There is a small gym, lively kids' room, simple lounge and a moderate pool. On a final note, the location near the shopping and office space of the Ortigas Centre is excellent.

Rates from: $
Star rating: ★ ★ ★ ★
Overall rating: ♭ ♭ ♭ ♭ ½

Ambience:	8.48	Cleanliness:	8.52
Value:	8.46	Facilities:	8.48
Staff:	8.50	Restaurants:	8.43
Location:	8.53	Families:	8.51

Edsa Shangri-La Manila

1 Garden Way, Ortigas Centre, Mandaluyong City 1650, Manila, Philippines
T: +63 2 633 8888 **F**: +63 2 631 1067
www.HotelClub.com/Hotels/Edsa_ShangriLa_Hotel_Manila

If big is beautiful, then the Edsa is a corker, with some pretty tempting vital statistics. The hotel is set in mature gardens, giving it a resort feel, which makes it a frequent weekend retreat for locals. It is split into two wings (Garden and Tower) joined at the base, sometimes leading to a bit of confusion in navigation for the uninitiated. The 658 bright and well-appointed rooms follow a typical Shangri-La formula, so there are no surprises here. The clutch of restaurants and bars (Italian Paparazzi is a favourite with locals), lagoon-style pool, first-class gym, banqueting and business amenities are fully rounded, and the service is surprisingly warm and attentive for such a bustling property. The location in the business district near Ortigas, next to several mega malls and within strolling distance of MRT links, makes Edsa a convenient and very popular choice. Renovations to the Garden Café and many of the Garden Wing's rooms should be complete by late 2005.

Rates from: $$
Star rating: ★ ★ ★ ★ ★
Overall rating: ◔◔◔◔ ½

Ambience:	8.61	Cleanliness:	8.71
Value:	8.00	Facilities:	8.42
Staff:	8.47	Restaurants:	8.55
Location:	8.69	Families:	8.54

El Nido Miniloc Island

Miniloc Island, Palawan, Philippines
T: +63 2 759 8482 **F**: +63 2 635 6699
www.HotelClub.com/Hotels/Miniloc_Island_Resort_El_Nido

A 90-minute light-plane ride from Manila followed by an hour's banca ride will get you here. After that it's just you, the 45 nearby islands and the incredible marine life and exotic flora and fauna … and a two-way radio. Most activities and all food are included in the rate, as are the facilities of Lagen, the sister resort across the bay.

Traditional, unassuming, rustic El Nido Miniloc is set in one of the most impressive coves on one of the most beautiful of the 1,780 islands that constitute the provincial archipelago of Palawan, which contains a quarter of the total land area of the Philippines, yet one percent of its population. The owners boast admirable eco-credentials, which include levying a small per-diem conservation fee.

31 cottages - built on water, into the dramatic limestone cliffs or amid cultivated jungle - some with two storeys and a spiral staircase offer typical nipa-and-sawali Filipino lodging, with a communal club-house restaurant serving buffets highlighted by freshly-caught fish.

Rates from: $$$$
Star rating: ★ ★ ★
Overall rating: ◔◔◔◔ ½

Ambience:	9.15	Cleanliness:	8.33
Value:	8.60	Facilities:	8.13
Staff:	9.05	Restaurants:	7.69
Location:	8.96	Families:	9.04

El Nido Lagen Island

Lagen Island, Palawan, Philippines
T: +63 2 894 5644 **F:** +63 2 810 3620
www.HotelClub.com/Hotels/Lagen_Island_Resort_El_Nido

Lagen Island is Palawan personified and personalised - all the natural beauty of one of the Philippines' most gorgeous regions delivered to the doorstep of a five-star resort. A hop, skip and a banca ride from Manila, Lagen is one of the largest islands in the El Nido Protected Area and host to a single resort.

Guarded by sheer cliffs that rise 300 metres out of the sea, its numerous natural coves are perfectly attuned to the needs of snorkellers and other marine-sports lovers, while the forest that covers the island is inhabited by 70 species of birds. Arriving guests are given an eco-checklist to give them an idea of what to watch out for, as Lagen is also home to mammals such as the scaly anteater and the Palawan porcupine, and the surrounding seas host hundreds of different kinds of fish and coral.

The resort itself is horseshoed round a sunset-facing bay; the best of its 51 cottages are built out over the water, others sit on the beach and there are also rooms and suites set in the forest. All the rooms are modern but decorated with indigenous Filipino materials, and have their own video and CD players and a private verandah. Guests are also provided with biodegradable soap, shampoo, conditioner and bath gel to help preserve the environment. As if anyone needed encouraging.

When it comes to food, the best possible dish of the day is a DIY fishing expedition, leaving early in the morning or late in the afternoon. The squid are running between March and May, and back at the resort the kitchen staff are only too happy to prepare your catch to your liking. Otherwise, buffet meals - a blend of Asian and Western with some Filipino specialties - are served in the clubhouse overlooking the beach and bay, although an à la carte menu is available. All meals (and most activities) are included in the price.

A 25-metre swimming pool is situated right in front of the clubhouse, and there are board games and table tennis inside, so it is a natural conclusion that Lagen is a sylvan seaside holiday spot for children.

Rates from: $$$$
Star rating: ★ ★ ★ ★
Overall rating: ♦ ♦ ♦ ♦ ½

Ambience:	9.25	Cleanliness:	8.83
Value:	8.29	Facilities:	8.51
Staff:	8.91	Restaurants:	7.91
Location:	9.10	Families:	9.02

Friday's Boracay Resort

Boracay, Malay, Aklan 5608, Philippines
T: +63 36 288 6200 **F:** +63 36 288 6222
www.HotelClub.com/Hotels/Fridays_Beach_Resort_Boracay

Getting to Boracay is no easy task, which may explain why the island has kept its laid-back lifestyle. The vistas during descent after a 55-minute hop from Manila, followed by a 15-minute banca ride the length of the island, provide a fabulous introduction to White Beach, often rated as one of the best beaches in the world. Wet feet are unavoidable when disembarking but as your toes sink into the soft sand a garland of flowers drops over your head and fresh fruit punch appears to hand, making all the effort of the trip worthwhile.

Friday's is no doubt one of the most visually appealing beach retreats you will find anywhere in Asia. It is certainly not the epitome of luxury, but rustic charm does not come more authentic. The simple construction of weathered wood and wind-raked thatch makes this a perfect place to kick back.

At the far end of White Beach the resort enjoys one of the best stretches of beach in this part of the world. The sand has an almost unbearable, dazzling glare and its talcum powder texture is so fine it squeaks underfoot. Friday's location means that Boracay's gyrating, groovy beach parties are kept at arm's length and the resort maintains an addictive low-key calm. However the "main town" area and its amenable ragbag of restaurants and souvenir galleries is a lazy walk away.

Friday's single restaurant spreads out casually on the sand, with a cool beach bar at its heart. At night the gentle breeze and ambient lighting create an atmosphere as alluring as by day. Food served here, in particular the buffets, is some of the best on the island, although it should be said that Boracay is no culinary Mecca. Behind the restaurant rests a small shaded pool offering cooling respite from the intense beachside sun, that is if the huge thatched sunshades do not suffice.

The 38 rooms, made from local materials, are set in one- and two-storey bungalows that in all honesty are very simple but are more than adequate. Sparse but spacious, the rooms fitted with air-conditioning and mosquito nets are comfy enough but could do with sprucing up. Staff are smart and well drilled, and make a big effort, keeping Friday's well ahead of the competition and a family favourite on this lovely tropical island. The resort's superlative partner Mandala Spa (probably one of the best in the country) is a jeepney ride away.

Rates from: $$
Star rating: ★ ★ ★
Overall rating: ◊◊◊◊ ½

Ambience:	8.79	Cleanliness:	8.36
Value:	8.10	Facilities:	7.95
Staff:	8.89	Restaurants:	8.37
Location:	8.98	Families:	8.82

Makati Shangri-La Manila

Ayala Avenue Corner Makati Avenue, Makati City 1200, Manila, Philippines
T: +63 2 813 8888 **F:** +63 2 813 5499
www.HotelClub.com/Hotels/Shangrila_Hotel_Manila

The Makati Shangri-La is one of the best and most complete hotels in the Philippines. There are no obvious weaknesses in this upmarket property, which maintains its top position through a constant renovation programme, irrespective of the roller-coaster Manila economy. The Makati Shangri-La is superior to competitors in just about every area and its imposing smooth exterior towers over the junction of Ayala and Makati Avenues, making it ideal for business travellers.

The lobby is adorned with a huge chandelier and twin sweeping staircases that say a lot about the hotel in general - smart, spacious, stylish and immaculate. The top feature of the Shangri-La is the standard of the unique rooms - hip, trendy and very high-tech. Irregularly shaped, they include sweeping curves rather than right angles that somehow, although sacrificing space, result in the rooms actually feeling larger. Bright colours and arty flashes here and there are a triumph of interior design, at least as far as hotels go. The ceilings also demonstrate imagination, a domed light source being sunk into a trim circular pit. Bedside lighting is again sleek yet very functional. Extra thought shines through everywhere, such as the dataport located on the desk to avoid having to scramble around at ankle-level to plug in your laptop. These are well-designed, well-equipped and well-maintained rooms.

Rather than the usual long vacant spaces, the corridors too have been remodelled with eye-catching designs and curves, and as ridiculous as it may sound, they are pleasant and warm. Superior hotel business facilities are truly international and include a 24-hour business centre, hence the high proportion of corporate guests who are particularly well catered for at the chic Horizon Club. Leisure facilities are a slight notch down but still very competitive. The outdoor pool, for example, is a tad small but catches every sun ray, and the gym is tidy if not comprehensive. A series of excellent restaurants including the Shang Palace Chinese, the immensely popular Japanese Inagiku, and the fine dining Red complete the picture for this outstanding hotel. If you were being fussy you could say the professional and genuine service can be a little stretched at times, such is the popularity of this top-rate Shangri-La.

Rates from: $$$
Star rating: ★ ★ ★ ★ ★
Overall rating: ◊ ◊ ◊ ◊ ½

Ambience:	8.90	Cleanliness:	8.99
Value:	8.10	Facilities:	8.61
Staff:	8.61	Restaurants:	8.70
Location:	9.06	Families:	8.57

Mandarin Oriental Manila

Makati Avenue Corner Paseo De Roxas, Makati City, Philippines
T: +63 2 750 8888 **F:** +63 2 817 2472
www.HotelClub.com/Hotels/Mandarin_Oriental_Manila

This refined old-timer has finally turned the corner after too many years in the doldrums. Heralding the new dawn is Paseo Uno, a chic and trendy all-day diner that's become one of Manila's most popular eateries. Elsewhere in the hotel, a traditional oriental theme is very prominent - dark combinations of deep woods, black marble, brassy trimmings and Chinese flair in the form of vases and fans, while female staff slink along in elegant cheongsams. The architecture barely allows for any natural light, and on entry your eyes need to adjust. The standard rooms are okay, whereas the upper categories are more than adequate. A popular haunt for the local business community is the buzzing Captain's Bar, leading from the hotel's diminutive lobby, as is the Clipper Lounge on the second floor. Other facilities are well above average and service is consistently courteous and professional. The overall product may slightly disappoint Mandarin fans but the price is very competitive and more renovations are currently underway.

Rates from: $
Star rating: ★ ★ ★ ★ ★
Overall rating: ◖◖◖◖

Ambience:	8.32	Cleanliness:	8.62
Value:	7.98	Facilities:	8.18
Staff:	8.45	Restaurants:	8.48
Location:	8.43	Families:	8.25

Manila Hotel

1 Rizal Park, Manila 1099, Philippines
T: +63 2 527 0011 **F:** +63 2 527 0022
www.HotelClub.com/Hotels/Manila_Hotel

Nostalgia is best cultivated in the mind, rather than in reality. Time was when no visit to the Philippine capital was complete without a visit to the Manila Hotel, with its if-these-walls-could-only-speak history as the hub of Manileño social life and wartime headquarters of General MacArthur. In recent years, however, it has been witness only to a few failed coups and the wholesale movement of both business and nightlife to Makati, a long, frustrating cab ride away.

It still has its devoted fans who swear by the ultra-swish lobby, the hacienda-style decor - all marble and mahogany, narra and capiz - the swim-up bar in the pool, the views over Manila Bay, Rizal Park or Intramuros. And the string quintet in the Champagne Room, the twinkling shells in the Cowrie Grill, the late-night snifters in the Tap Room bar.

But it is a sign of this stubborn old lady's sad refusal to move with the times that the 18-storey tower behind the original Spanish-colonial building, put up in 1970, is still dubbed "the New Wing".

Rates from: $
Star rating: ★ ★ ★ ★
Overall rating: ◖◖◖◖

Ambience:	8.64	Cleanliness:	8.57
Value:	8.00	Facilities:	8.28
Staff:	8.43	Restaurants:	8.45
Location:	8.25	Families:	8.42

Marco Polo Davao

CM Recto Street, Davao City 8000, Philippines
T: +63 82 221 0888 F: +63 82 225 0111
www.HotelClub.com/Hotels/Marco_Polo_Davao_The

Davao is not the swishest of Asian cities, so visiting executives - and the Marco Polo is primarily a business hotel - normally make this convenient retreat their working headquarters. It is efficiently run and only a short hop from the commercial district and airport. While all the hotel's 245 rooms are perfectly acceptable, the two club floors at the top of the 18-storey building make the most sense, with a mini business centre in its lounge, fax machines in every room, clued-up butlers and a roomy boardroom. Food-wise, if the international buffet at Café Marco does not appeal there is the Lotus Court's Cantonese cuisine, or snacks are available from the pool terrace (next to a well-equipped fitness centre) with good views both up to Mount Apo and down to the sea. Potential guests might want to take note of prevailing security issues on Mindanao.

Rates from: $
Star rating: ★★★★★
Overall rating: 👍👍👍👍

Ambience:	8.53	Cleanliness:	8.75
Value:	8.15	Facilities:	8.33
Staff:	8.61	Restaurants:	8.55
Location:	8.52	Families:	8.53

Oakwood Premier Ayala Centre

6/F Glorietta 4, Ayala Centre, Makati City, Manila, Philippines
T: +63 2 729 8888 F: +63 2 728 0000
www.HotelClub.com/Hotels/Oakwood_Premier_Ayala_Centre

The Oakwood is right on top of the Ayala Centre, one of Makati's main shopping malls, and metres from the business district. Successfully cut off from the vibrancy below, it is accessed via a discreet sixth-floor lobby. From a business traveller's perspective, the Oakwood has everything, with smart serviced apartments, extensive meeting facilities and professionally run state-of-the-art (including the latest in videoconferencing) serviced offices all under the same roof. The 306 one-, two- and three-bedroom apartments are spacious and stylish. Elegant furnishings, fully equipped kitchens and even washing machines make it ideal for long-stay guests, although daily stays are welcome. The styling actually does not feature any traditional oak, opting for lighter and crisper tangile. One restaurant, a health club with two tennis courts and a 25-metre pool, a kids' playroom and a few leisure distractions complete a very successful and popular package.

Rates from: $$
Star rating: ★★★★★
Overall rating: 👍👍👍👍 ½

Ambience:	8.62	Cleanliness:	8.95
Value:	8.09	Facilities:	8.68
Staff:	8.39	Restaurants:	8.13
Location:	9.12	Families:	8.69

The Peninsula Manila

Corner of Ayala and Makati Avenues, Makati City 1226, Philippines
T: +63 2 887 2888 **F:** +63 2 815 4825
www.HotelClub.com/Hotels/Peninsula_Manila

There are not many historical remnants in Manila beyond the churches and the old quarter of Intramuros. Certainly no original grandes dames exist in the hotel sector, with the possible exception of the Peninsula, which has been welcoming guests for the last three decades.

It is a graceful hotel that feels like a classic and looks it, at least from the inside. The concrete exterior does nothing to prepare you for one of the most splendid lobbies in Asia. The elegant marble, cavernous ceilings and overall air of extravagance pull in many a movie star, politician and visiting dignitary, with the flashier ones making their grand entrance via the helipad.

Shared between the Ayala and Makati Tower wings, the Peninsula's 497 smooth creamy rooms are slightly irregularly shaped, a welcome touch, and are reassuringly subtler than the extrovert lobby. Bathrooms are thoroughly versatile and the multi-jets of the brass-trimmed surround shower save you from the usual swivelling and rotating that most of us never realised was such a chore.

The Peninsula's food and beverage choices are immaculately presented and the food is rarely short of excellent. The signature restaurant, Old Manila, is decorated with stunning artwork by contemporary Filipino artists and blends Eastern and Western cuisines with a strong French influence. The Lobby is the place to meet for Manila's captains of industry and chattering socialites, with its afternoon tea set and supporting jazz ensemble. Some of the best local soul and blues bands regularly perform at The Conservatory overlooking Ayala Avenue. Mi Piace is rustically Italian, while from Spices you can gaze over the inviting leaf-fringed pool. The kids' pool is one of the few efforts to cater for children as this is very much a hotel for the refined adult. This is nowhere better emphasised than in the spa, a luxurious amalgam of fitness and pampering in cool and crisp surrounds.

Throughout the Peninsula, professional and well-trained staff pride themselves on their service, providing the icing on the cake that makes it far and away one of the most exclusive hotels in the city.

Rates from: $$
Star rating: ★ ★ ★ ★ ★
Overall rating: ♔♔♔♔ ½

Ambience:	8.66	Cleanliness:	8.69
Value:	7.99	Facilities:	8.28
Staff:	8.41	Restaurants:	8.48
Location:	8.84	Families:	8.29

Plantation Bay Resort & Spa

Marigondon, Mactan Island, Cebu 6015, Philippines
T: +63 32 340 5900 **F:** +63 32 340 5988
www.HotelClub.com/Hotels/Plantation_Bay_Mactan

Plantation Bay stretches over seven hectares of tropical grounds, and the emphasis here is on having the space to spread your wings. The most striking feature is the vast inland saltwater lagoon, ringed by the hotel buildings. The man-made lagoon is fine for swimming, being waist-deep for the most part, but deeper in other areas for scuba-diving lessons. And for those who want their waters to be a little more interactive, there is a waterfall, diving rock and two giant slides, and the serene lagoon itself rings the country's largest freshwater pool, equipped with eight whirlpools. Night bathers may (or may not) be pleased to see the pool is beautifully lit. The hotel also opens out on to a short and slightly ordinary stretch of beach, but few swimmers make it this far unless to dive on coral walls and caves just offshore.

Back on land, the location is a mix of convenient and isolated.

Centrally located on Mactan Island and only 20 minutes from the international airport, there is little outside the resort and few taxis pass by, so transport needs to be arranged.

The architecture echoes the theme of a colonial plantation with white wood and deep grey roofs. The 220 rooms are set in lodges and houses around the pools, and feature Waterside Rooms from which you can slip into the lagoon, Club Rooms, which are a combination of bunks and queen beds for up to eight people, and a selection of one- and two-bedroom suites. Within, they are basic but trim and bright, with wood or rattan furnishings.

Facilities lean towards sports and recreation. Extensive water-sport activities take full advantage of the location, with fish-feeding and reel-fishing among the more relaxed choices. Wall-climbing (when open) and a games room are on site, and golf or even pistol-

shooting are available nearby. Children can indulge in various supervised activities from mini-car racing to origami. The Mogambo Springs spa offers a range of massages, body scrubs and facial treatments in its canyon-like setting. Overall the service is usually good but can be erratic. The food at the four restaurants is similar - mostly good, sometimes excellent, but occasionally below par.

Rates from: $$
Star rating: ★ ★ ★ ★ ★
Overall rating: ♙♙♙♙ ½

Ambience:	9.00	Cleanliness:	8.68
Value:	8.07	Facilities:	8.43
Staff:	8.68	Restaurants:	8.10
Location:	8.03	Families:	8.73

Shangri-La's Mactan Island Resort

Punta Engano Road, Lapu-Lapu City 6015, Cebu, Philippines
T: +63 32 231 0288 **F**: +63 32 231 1688
www.HotelClub.com/Hotels/ShangriLas_Mactan_Island_Resort_Cebu

Traditionally the most internationally accessible of the Philippines' holiday spots, Cebu's eastern coast is a quiet and unexpected oasis. The relatively remote northeast tip of Mactan Island points decidedly away from the sprawling metropolis of the country's second city. Little other than resorts dot its blue coastline, and little traffic has a need to come this way. So when staying at the Shangri-La you know that the city is nearby without necessarily feeling it.

It may look functional rather than exotic from a distance, but this resort is very popular indeed and not just with the local residents. It feels like a typical late 1980s resort - large, spread-out (12 hectares), chunky and high-rise (nine-storey) - but with 547 rooms it would be very difficult to be anything else. Close up it is much more appealing - bright, lively and brimming with fun facilities. The airy lobby is big and tropical. Huge floral displays and a flamboyant chandelier encompass the cheerful Filipino exuberance you will find in the staff.

The Shangri-La has a good reputation, mainly for its consistent treatment and high standards since

it opened in 1993. Its second pull is a dazzling length of picture-postcard white beach, whose sand is carefully combed daily. Excellent leisure facilities fully utilise the tropical shoreline and the hotel provides a good programme of things to do. With two huge free-form pools, a complete menu of water sports and other recreation on offer it would be difficult for any member of the family to get bored. Scuba-diving, jet-skiing, fishing, windsurfing, pitch and putt (six holes), parasailing or simple banca rides to outlying islands are all on offer. And if you

need to escape the kids, then toddlers to teenagers have a range of supervised activities.

Seven restaurants and bars are on site, which is just as well, bearing in mind it usually takes 45 minutes to get into town on the free shuttle. Food is generally excellent, especially by Philippine standards. The rooms are well furnished and light but offer few surprises other than perhaps the balconies complete with seating areas. All in all, a fun place for a straightforward holiday escape, and one due to take a step up the five-star firmament with the arrival of its Chi Spa Village in 2005.

Rates from: $$
Star rating: ★ ★ ★ ★ ★
Overall rating: 🌀🌀🌀🌀 ½

Ambience:	8.94	Cleanliness:	8.76
Value:	8.09	Facilities:	8.55
Staff:	8.58	Restaurants:	8.49
Location:	8.45	Families:	8.78

SINGAPORE

MALAYSIA

Orchard / Scotts ❶

Padang / Havelock ❷ ❸ Marina / Suntec City

Chinatown ❹ ❺

Sentosa ❻

A clean, green, hyper-efficient machine, Singapore is the most user-friendly city in Asia. The four-lane freeway from Changi International Airport is bordered with flowering trees and shrubs. The Mass Rapid Transit whisks its way round the island with barely a hint of a rumble or rattle. Taxi drivers help passengers load their luggage into the boot. Glitzy shopping malls rub shoulders with five-star hotels and gourmet restaurants. It is as if the entire republic is wired on broadband to EasyLife.com.

Yet despite the modernity, what makes Singapore so pleasurable is its very traditional Asian identity. Eddies of smoke from smoldering incense sticks waft the streets of Chinatown, the air has a gentle aroma of spices in Little India and the muezzin's call rings out over Arab Street. Conversations

overheard in a lift or a bar might include the sing-song of Mandarin, a lilt of Bahasa, the quickfire jabber of Hindi or the Lion City's own brand of "Singlish", whose quirky expressions often carry the idiosyncratic tag "lah". All in all, the island is like one vast and very cosmopolitan buffet.

When the British colonialist Sir

Stamford Raffles landed in Singapore in 1819, it was little more than a fishing village. But he realised that the island's position - just off the equator in the Straits of Malacca - could be exploited to make it the mercantile crossroads of the Far East. Advocating free trade and laying out a town plan that is still followed today, he only

spent four years on the island, but it was long enough for him to be commemorated as the city state's founder. Following the war and later independence, Singapore - under the helmsmanship of elder statesman Lee Kuan Yew - carved a niche for itself in the financial and service industries. Today it is one of the most prosperous nations in the region, a remarkable achievement considering the lack of natural resources on its 646 square kilometres.

The year-round tropical Singapore attracts two sorts of weather - hot and wet. The temperature rarely falls below 23°C and it rains most between November and January. Storms tend to be heavy and sudden but blow over fairly quickly. The only antidote for the heat and humidity is the city's ubiquitous use of air-conditioning.

As a city attuned to trade, many visitors come here on business, but it also makes for a pleasant family vacation, as well as a jumping-off point to the Malaysian peninsula and Indonesian archipelago. The island of Sentosa has been specifically organised as the city's playground, complete with beaches, attractions and a connecting cable car - although you can get there just as easily by bus. The Singapore Zoo is recognised as one of the best in the world, not simply for its innovative breeding techniques but also for the way in which animals are displayed both by night and in the daytime. Boat Quay and neighbouring Clarke Quay are a mélange of high-rolling bars and restaurants, while Pulau Ubin, one of 58 smaller islands surrounding Singapore, is still a relatively undeveloped kampong.

Shopping is another major Singapore attraction, and while the days of its being a bargain

basement are largely gone, there is certainly a wealth of choice, from the smart boutiques of Orchard Road to the geeks' paradise of computer mazes like the Funan Centre. And beyond mere retail therapy, the city now hosts some of the most significant cultural events in the region.

What Singapore does best, however, is food, largely thanks to its multinational inhabitants who were eating their own brand of fusion cuisine long before anyone thought to put a name to it. The menu ranges from dead cheap and cheerful in the hawker centres, which sell a range of Chinese, Indian and Malay dishes in a no-frills atmosphere, to cutting-edge designer fare in smartly themed restaurants, to absolute gourmet dining with prices to match. Add as garnish African, Middle Eastern, organic and herbal eateries, not to mention Peranakan, a creation derived from early Chinese immigrants and Malay women who married their cuisines.

Singapore's hotels also rank among the finest in Asia. Everyone knows of Raffles, which has been endlessly mythologised, but there are numerous other top-class properties, as well as intriguing boutique hotels brightening up the back streets of Chinatown, providing a dose of the Singapore of yesteryear before it became quite so antiseptically ordered.

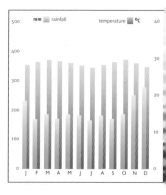

Conrad Centennial Singapore

2 Temasek Boulevard, Singapore 038982
T: +65 6334 8888 **F**: +65 6333 9166
www.HotelClub.com/Hotels/Conrad_International_Centennial_Hotel_Singapore

For many visitors, the Conrad is the surprise card in the pack that clusters in this corner of town. Clumps of bamboo. Swirling sculptured lights. Glistening polished marble. Soft pastel furnishings. It is not just the outstanding food that is fusion at the Conrad, whose 509 deluxe rooms and suites provide a very East-meets-West welcome. Even the smallest rooms cover some 40 square metres, including a bathroom with a separate shower stall, and suites are half as big again.

While being well tailored for the executive (tick off broadband access, audio- and videoconferencing, and a desk that you can happily spread your sheets on) the Conrad should also hold special appeal for leisure travellers. In addition to the pool/spa/restaurant/cocktail bar within the hotel, immediately outside are some 1,300-plus shops and eateries in the adjoining malls, which provide an illuminating undercover walkway to the MRT station and nearby exhibition centre at Suntec City.

Rates from: $$
Star rating: ★ ★ ★ ★ ★
Overall rating: ♪♪♪♪ ½

Ambience:	8.95	Cleanliness:	9.31
Value:	8.35	Facilities:	8.73
Staff:	8.96	Restaurants:	8.63
Location:	8.83	Families:	8.59

Four Seasons Hotel

190 Orchard Boulevard, Singapore 248646
T: +65 6734 1110 **F**: +65 6733 0682
www.HotelClub.com/Hotels/Four_Seasons_Hotel_Singapore

Subtlety is the leitmotif for the Four Seasons, an ultra-discreet retreat just off Orchard Road. High-rise it may be, but the interiors are all rich seclusion. The lobby is more like a drawing room than a public area, and the restaurants - the One-Ninety cafe or the Jiang-Nan Chun - could be the private dining rooms of the sort of club that features a rather long waiting list. Up above, the 254 rooms and suites are sumptuously furnished, with multi-disc CD/LD players as a standard fixture and all requisite electronic business accoutrements to hand. Valets transfer the contents of suitcases into wardrobes. Shoes are burnished to a gleaming shine while you sleep. For larger business gatherings there are two ballrooms and a brace of swish penthouse function rooms. Even the tennis courts are air-conditioned. Overall, the underlying message here would seem to be if you are not a CEO already, you are on the way up.

Rates from: $$
Star rating: ★ ★ ★ ★ ★
Overall rating: ♪♪♪♪ ½

Ambience:	9.13	Cleanliness:	9.29
Value:	8.17	Facilities:	8.71
Staff:	8.99	Restaurants:	8.57
Location:	8.86	Families:	8.54

The Fullerton Singapore

1 Fullerton Square, Singapore 049178
T: +65 6733 8388 **F**: +65 6735 8388
www.HotelClub.com/Hotels/Fullerton_Singapore_The

It would be very hard to miss The Fullerton. Magnificent in both concept and execution, it ranks as one of the most imaginative new hotels to open its doors in Asia in quite some time. The original building was commissioned as part of Singapore's centennial celebrations in 1919, and opened in 1928, when it was the city's largest building. After functioning as the General Post Office for many years, it closed in 1998 prior to its conversion to a luxury, 400-room, five-star hotel. The resulting transformation has been handled with both style and sympathy. The neo-Palladian exterior – marked by towering granite Doric columns that bespeak colonial puissance - is practically unchanged, while within the elegant rooms and public areas are a perfect blend being both hi-tech and highly attractive.

The Fullerton is in the very hub of the city, and within walking distance of Boat and Clarke quays. With its central atrium beaming a cone of light on to the smartly dressed guests nattering over coffee at the Courtyard, and a broad double circular staircase leading down to the ballroom and function rooms, first impressions of the Fullerton are that this is a hotel at the centre of things. Other restaurants include the contemporary Cantonese Jade, and Town, a bistro café and bar serving Mediterranean and Asian fare.

The rooms - all different shapes and sizes - are sensibly laid out, wired and decorated with a distinctive panache. The gym is stacked with a fair range of glistening perspiration-inducers, however the outside swimming pool - with an invigorating infinity view over Marina Bay and up to the skyscrapers which now dwarf the Fullerton - is the hotel's sporting pièce de résistance. Not that it is imperative to exercise here, as you can easily loll in the loungers for an afternoon or more, backed by what imagination could easily prompt to be your very own colonial mansion.

Rates from: $$
Star rating: ★ ★ ★ ★ ★
Overall rating: ◐◐◐◐ ½

Ambience:	9.02	Cleanliness:	9.20
Value:	8.05	Facilities:	8.61
Staff:	8.57	Restaurants:	8.52
Location:	8.85	Families:	8.23

Goodwood Park Hotel

22 Scotts Road, Singapore 228221
T: +65 6737 7411 **F:** +65 6732 8558
www.HotelClub.com/Hotels/Goodwood_Park_Hotel_Singapore

Singapore's second oldest hotel, the Goodwood started life in 1900 as the Teutonia Club, and its two storeys and 235 rooms and suites sit on a hillock overlooking Scotts and Orchard Roads in a measure of refined, semi-colonial splendour. Where the Goodwood notches up points is in its quaint raggle-taggle layout. The best option is to go for one of the rooms opening out onto the second pool - the Mayfair - which is altogether more intimate and charming. Other alternatives include the Parklane Suites, which come with their own kitchenettes and balconies in a separate wing. Top of the range is the Brunei Suite, described by the hotel as "one of the most beautiful rooms east of Suez". Surprisingly for a relatively small hotel, the Goodwood serves up five restaurants and bars within its perimeters, whose chefs can turn their hands to everything from trendy Chinese to trad Yorkshire pud. There is no similar hotel in Singapore, and if it does not quite fit its assumed template of Asian masterpiece, it is still very habitable.

Rates from: $$
Star rating: ★ ★ ★ ★ ★
Overall rating: ♌ ♌ ♌ ♌

Ambience:	8.86	Cleanliness:	8.89
Value:	8.11	Facilities:	8.19
Staff:	8.57	Restaurants:	8.44
Location:	8.84	Families:	8.11

Grand Hyatt Singapore

10 Scotts Road, Singapore 228211
T: +65 6738 1234 **F:** +65 6732 1696
www.HotelClub.com/Hotels/Grand_Hyatt_Singapore

The "Grand" in the Hyatt's name may well refer to its two separate and very smart wings containing 663 rooms and suites, which but for Singapore's firm anti-littering laws could be described as a stone's throw from the retail hubs of Orchard and Scotts roads. "Grand" could equally indicate the chance to indulge not only in deluxe accommodation but also in the hotel's selection of restaurants and bars. The newest arrival is Straits Kitchen, showcasing the best of local cuisine. Pete's Place is an especially atmospheric Italian restaurant, while mezza9's show kitchen serves up Western, Chinese and Japanese alongside a cigar room and a martini bar. Lunch goes down a treat at the al fresco poolside Oasis Bar and Restaurant, and Scotts Lounge overlooking a four-storey waterfall is the place for afternoon tea at weekends. After hours, the basement BRIX offers an immensely popular drinking and dancing double act with the self-explanatory Wine and Whisky Bar and its adjacent Music Bar.

Rates from: $$
Star rating: ★ ★ ★ ★ ★
Overall rating: ♌ ♌ ♌ ♌ ½

Ambience:	8.62	Cleanliness:	8.88
Value:	7.88	Facilities:	8.45
Staff:	8.48	Restaurants:	8.48
Location:	9.27	Families:	8.39

Hotel 1929

50 Keong Saik Road, Singapore 089145
T: +65 6347 1929 **F**: +65 6327 1929
www.HotelClub.com/Hotels/1929_Hotel_Singaopore

The sharpest of the boutiques to have popped up in Chinatown's backstreets, 1929 provides a highly acceptable alternative to yet another chain or the sort of hotel that positively groans under the weight of its heritage.

The brainchild of 30-something former lawyer Loh Lik Peng, who grew up in Dublin, the hotel doubles as a gallery for his collection of classic chairs, with one in each room and more in the public areas. It's a wide and witty range of furniture, whose more eccentric pieces include an Arne Jacobson "Swan" chair, a furry, purple amorphous Kubus sofa that's 90 years old and a less-than-inviting bicycle-saddle seat by Sella.

Otherwise 1929 is all smallish (minute even) rooms balanced with exquisitely hip taste. None of the 32 rooms is exactly alike, but they are all decorated with bold Marimekko fabrics and mosaic tiling, with high-tech add-ons like CD players and flat-screen TVs. Clever wall-mounted hangers take the place of conventional cupboards. The second-floor suites are rather more spacious, with their own roof terraces and outdoor bath tubs, although prudish guests might be alarmed to find these are in sight of the nearby tower blocks.

Catering falls under the ægis of chef Sebastian Ng and his wife Sabrina, who does the marketing for Ember, 1929's signature restaurant that serves zesty modern international dishes. The wine list is relatively short but carefully chosen and balanced delicately between old and new worlds.

Hotel 1929 is probably not the place for young children, though teens might consent that the joint has quite a lot in the way of cool. It's definitely not right if you're built like Yao Ming. The outdoor communal jacuzzi is often filled with the sort of low-key sophisticates naturally attracted to 1929.

The MRT station is in walking distance, as are the more commercial (and artificial) aspects of "Destination Chinatown". The rates, though, are remarkably slim for a quirky fashionable boutique hotel.

Rates from: $
Star rating: ★★
Overall rating: 4 (thumbs)

Ambience:	8.62	Cleanliness:	9.00
Value:	8.54	Facilities:	7.59
Staff:	8.08	Restaurants:	8.00
Location:	8.23	Families:	6.90

InterContinental Singapore

o Middle Road, Singapore 188966

: +65 6338 7600 **F:** +65 6338 7366

www.HotelClub.com/Hotels/Hotel_InterContinental_Singapore

ike all the very best hotels, the InterContinental reveals herself only gradually. Thanks to the dictates of fung shui, the grand entrance is via a set of what could almost be French windows. Marbled floors and an elegant hush distinguish the lobby. Can this really be the way into a 403-room, internationally branded five-star hotel? The reassuring answer is "yes", and this gentle, unassuming theme is continued right the way through the hotel.

The all-day-dining Olive Tree is lit via its skylights, rather as the central areas of Singapore's traditional Peranakan houses were left open to the elements. And the rooftop swimming pool is encompassed by palms and shrubs where you can relax with ease. This

is a garden hotel in a garden city, pleasantly influenced by Singaporean heritage.

While the InterContinental is well suited to the leisure market (especially its signature "shophouse" rooms), executives will fit into its seamless business atmosphere with ease. Designated room desk outlets are wired for laptops, and lie within arm's reach of a state-of-the-art printer/fax/copier/scanner. There is a line each for voice and e-mail, ergonomically designed chairs and enhanced lamps to work by. A cyber-relations desk provides any necessary back-up, and

complements the hotel's ballroom and avant-garde Bugis Vault meeting rooms. And as of 2005, all the hotels rooms will feature a digital video-on-demand service.

For informal corporate entertaining, or indeed a simple drink after the laptop is shut for the day, the Victoria Bar has gained a reputation as the place to wind down, with live international and local bands which usually draw a lively work-hard, play-hard crowd. As a bonus, a side exit from the InterContinental leads straight into the covered streets of the Parco Bugis shopping mall, while an escalator ride downstairs leads to the MRT station.

Rates from: $$

Star rating: ★ ★ ★ ★ ★

Overall rating: ♪ ♪ ♪ ♪ ½

Ambience:	8.79	Cleanliness:	9.12
Value:	8.25	Facilities:	8.50
Staff:	8.65	Restaurants:	8.42
Location:	8.82	Families:	8.37

Keong Saik Hotel

69 Keong Saik Road, Singapore 089165
T: +65 6223 0660 **F:** +65 6225 0660
www.HotelClub.com/Hotels/Keong_Saik_Hotel_Singapore

Small is beautiful, as this pioneering hotel amply demonstrates. Hovering at the upper end of the guesthouse scale, the Keong Saik is not quite a boutique - so perhaps "bootique" would be a more appropriate term. But for ready charm, rates that are more than reasonable, an exotic and authentic location and staff who go out of their way to sort out the most trivial request, this 25-room hotel is a real star. Slap in the heart of Chinatown, right next to an ornate Hindu temple and opposite a Muslim café, this is the sort of Singapore that mainstream hotels can never deliver. The most basic rooms do not even have a window, but are spotless even if they are a

bit of a squeeze. Breakfast (included in the rate) is a matey, DIY affair, and an excellent way to kick off a day of touring the sights.

Rates from: $
Star rating: ★
Overall rating: ♦♦♦♦

Ambience:	7.57	Cleanliness:	8.86
Value:	9.21	Facilities:	7.04
Staff:	8.64	Restaurants:	7.75
Location:	8.43	Families:	8.44

Marriott Singapore

320 Ochard Road, Singapore 238865
T: +65 6735 5800 **F:** +65 6735 9800
www.HotelClub.com/Hotels/Marriott_Hotel_Singapore

a good name, providing a very comfortable urban haven, although the range of treatments on offer is fairly compact. And to cap things off, Bar None at the bottom of the building continues to be the insiders' in place. All in all a stylish and not over-large five-star chain right in the heart of things that delivers on its promises.

Do not allow the Tiger Balm Gardens-type exterior put you off. The 30-storey tower surmounted with green tiles camouflages a property that is Marriott through and through. In fact this selfsame tower gives all 382 rooms an attractive feel, granting each one a window in the shape of an angled L

that sets off the views over the city. Anyone seeking a slightly different venue for a seafood dinner could do a lot worse than make a reservation at the poolside Garden Terrace, the fitness centre never closes and the action continues on Scotts and Orchard roads pretty much 24 hours a day. The Retreat spa capitalises on

Rates from: $$
Star rating: ★ ★ ★ ★ ★
Overall rating: ♦♦♦♦ ½

Ambience:	8.63	Cleanliness:	8.97
Value:	8.02	Facilities:	8.35
Staff:	8.53	Restaurants:	8.40
Location:	9.24	Families:	8.37

Orchard Hotel Singapore

42 Orchard Road, Singapore 238879
T: +65 6734 7766 **F**: +65 6733 5482
www.HotelClub.com/Hotels/Orchard_Hotel_Singapore

An Orchard Road stalwart, this hotel progresses with the well-oiled meticulousness of its lobby's four-faced grandfather clock, very much as it has done for the past 25 years. Changes over the past quarter century have included the addition of the Claymore Wing, where you can't help but remark on the 78-inch wide king-size beds. The Harvesters' Club in the Orchard Wing is in fact the executive wing - and very smart too - rather than any sort of agricultural enclave.

Reliable food and beverage opportunities at Hua Ting and La Terrasse are augmented by the adjacent mall, notably by bars like Muddy Murphy's and Ballymoons. The outdoor pool is generous to say the least; there is no spa but once again the mall slides to the rescue. With gargantuan meeting space and staff who take an obvious pride in their job, the Orchard is an understandably popular hotel for both tourists and executives in downtown Singapore.

Rates from: **$$**
Star rating: ★ ★ ★ ★
Overall rating: ♦♦♦♦ ½

Ambience:	8.58	Cleanliness:	9.04
Value:	8.24	Facilities:	8.40
Staff:	8.61	Restaurants:	8.59
Location:	9.15	Families:	8.65

The Oriental Singapore

5 Raffles Avenue, Marina Square, Singapore 039797
T: +65 6338 0066 **F**: +65 6339 9537
www.HotelClub.com/Hotels/Oriental_Hotel_Singapore_The

Christmas 2004 was celebrated with especial fervour at the Oriental, as the hotel flung open its doors once more after a multi-million dollar renovation. All 527 rooms and suites have been granted a high-tech chic gloss, combining a traditional Oriental feel with Wi-Fi, which also buzzes through all the public areas. On which subject, all the hotels restaurants have a contemporary new feel, from the brasserie-style World Café to the artistic surrounds of the Cherry Garden, which serves haute Chinese cuisine. And of course the Axis Lounge remains the place for an intimate tête-à-tête over afternoon tea or a couple of swift cocktails to bring the working day to a formal conclusion.

All the other great aspects of the Oriental remain unchanged. The building's distinctive fan shape, the ballroom that has dispensed with obstructive pillars, the poolside terrace overlooking the harbour; and of course nowhere is closer to the arts hub of the Esplanade.

Rates from: **$$**
Star rating: ★ ★ ★ ★ ★
Overall rating: ♦♦♦♦ ½

Ambience:	8.71	Cleanliness:	9.03
Value:	8.20	Facilities:	8.54
Staff:	8.72	Restaurants:	8.48
Location:	8.75	Families:	8.36

Nov 1994

Pan Pacific Singapore

7 Raffles Boulevard, Marina Square, Singapore 039595
T: +65 6336 8111 **F**: +65 6339 1861
www.HotelClub.com/Hotels/Pan_Pacific_Singapore

Cue trumpet fanfare! Like Marina Square itself, the Pan Pac got a mega wash-and-brush-up in 2004, and - very definitely among the upper echelons of Singapore's top accommodation - is now pulling the punters back through its doors with a vengeance. The property's most memorable feature, the 35-storey atrium, is still there of course, but now a computer programme lights it according to the time of day, and there are new executive facilities on Level 22.

The hotel's 775 rooms have benefited from little extras like ergonomic chairs and wireless broadband, and the eating (and drinking) is better than ever. The Wine Vault should put many regular cellars to shame, while Keyaki, the Japanese restaurant, has been joined by a dedicated sake bar. Putting the seal on all these multi-million dollar additions is the one-of-a-kind orchid mural in the Atrium, made from square cut-glass tiles specially imported from Italy - an incredible spectacle in itself.

Rates from: $$
Star rating: ★ ★ ★ ★ ★
Overall rating: ♦ ♦ ♦ ♦ ½

Ambience:	8.60	Cleanliness:	8.99
Value:	8.21	Facilities:	8.50
Staff:	8.41	Restaurants:	8.58
Location:	8.84	Families:	8.31

Raffles The Plaza

80 Bras Basah Road, Singapore 189560
T: +65 6339 7777 **F**: +65 6337 1554
www.HotelClub.com/Hotels/Raffles_The_Plaza_Singapore

Not to be confused with Raffles per se, although it is part of the same group, the Plaza sits foursquare in Raffles City, sharing a number of facilities with its sister Swissôtel. The whole property is very much "modern Singapore" - confident, efficient, and with all the essential goods and services delivered with a hint of pizzazz. Even in the smartly decorated Premier Deluxe rooms - the lowest in the 769-strong pecking order - luxury raindrop showers and broadband access are standard; while at the top of the chain the theme suites and penthouses hold their own jacuzzi and sauna. Yoga, Pilates, tai chi and a host of other exercise options at the gym are complemented by the lush, plush Amrita spa. A string of 17 restaurants, two outdoor pools, a hyper-efficient business centre - not to mention the considerable adjacent shopping arcades - round out the picture of this new-millennium Raffles.

Rates from: $$
Star rating: ★ ★ ★ ★ ★
Overall rating: ♦ ♦ ♦ ♦ ½

Ambience:	8.64	Cleanliness:	9.24
Value:	8.24	Facilities:	8.67
Staff:	8.73	Restaurants:	8.54
Location:	9.15	Families:	8.46

Raffles Hotel

1 Beach Road, Singapore 189673
T: +65 6337 1886 **F:** +65 6339 7650
www.HotelClub.com/Hotels/Raffles_Hotel_Singapore

Raffles is a noun, an adjective, a verb - and a much-honoured institution. The hotel itself is the one most readily identified with deluxe Asian accommodation, and being "Raffle'd" has come to mean giving a stately Asian hotel a much-needed makeover.

Opened in 1887 by the pioneering Sarkies brothers, and eulogised over the years by all the usual Asian literary types ("feed at Raffles" is the most-aired Rudyard Kipling quote), there is no question that by the late 1970s the hotel was looking worn at the edges.

After being declared a national monument in 1987, Raffles was given a substantial, spruce revamp and reopened amid much fanfare in 1991. Today guests might feel not so much that they are staying at one of the world's top hotels, but instead invited to take on a part in a long-running costume drama, as the heritage aspect is subject to a fair bit of theatre. The building provides an apposite backdrop, with its stark white columns and colonnades standing out from the lush Singaporean surroundings. Ten of the 103 suites have their own "personality", named and decorated after such long-departed guests as Noël Coward, Joseph Conrad, Charlie Chaplin and the world-famous-in-Chile poet Pablo Neruda.

There are numerous opportunities to feed at Raffles nowadays, from curries in the Tiffin Room to continental at the Grill, and it is de rigueur to knock back a couple of the hotel's signature cocktails, the Singapore Sling, in the two-storey Long Bar. The renovation saw the addition of a number of shops that while not completely authentic, do provide some very upmarket retail opportunities.

Despite its heavily marketed "lifestyle", and top-dollar room rates, Raffles is a welcome change from yet more concrete and glass structures. The suites are especially luxurious, with parlour and dining area leading into bedroom, dressing room and bathroom all beneath 4.3-metre ceilings. The Raffles legend continues unabated, and viewed objectively it is really very enjoyable.

Rates from: $$$$
Star rating: ★ ★ ★ ★ ★
Overall rating: 🏠🏠🏠🏠 ½

Ambience:	9.26	Cleanliness:	9.32
Value:	7.90	Facilities:	8.66
Staff:	8.98	Restaurants:	8.86
Location:	9.01	Families:	8.53

Ritz-Carlton Millenia Singapore

7 Raffles Avenue, Singapore 039799
T: +65 6337 8888 **F:** +65 6338 0001
www.HotelClub.com/Hotels/Ritz_Carlton_Millenia_Singapore

Just about everyone loves this hotel and it takes only the briefest inspection to work out why. A leisurely glance around the 32-storey, 610-room property anchored in three lush hectares on the waterfront sums it all up. It is not simply the design or the facilities. The staff move around their statuesque surroundings with the ease and confidence that comes from knowing that they work in one of Asia's best.

There is no single reason for the Ritz-Carlton's pre-eminence, but there are a lot of contributing factors - and the guestrooms are an obvious help. The mammoth plate-glass windows that let natural light stream into the corridors and lift lobbies are continued in the rooms, where they make up almost the entirety of one wall in both bed and bathroom. A single phone call galvanises the butler into drawing one of the hotel's specialty baths - filled with essences of sandalwood and musk for chaps (accompanied by a Cohiba cigar and a Cognac),

or a creamy Cleopatra mix for ladies, or an encouraging flower and fruit honeymoon mélange for couples, with champagne, strawberries and roses on the side. Sit back, up to your neck with bubbles and bubbly, contemplate the view through the octagonal pane, and it is hard to restrain a triumphant grin. Walk-in showers and closets add to the sense of space - even the standard guestrooms are 51 square metres - and there is nothing in the way of clutter like occasional tables or hat stands. This leaves the main room, with its warm parquet flooring, dominated by a high king-sized bed.

Laptop-carriers can log on via broadband, but Internet access is also possible courtesy of the television and "Guestnet" with a wireless keyboard. Further up the accommodation chain, the 23 suites provide more space. Inhabitants of the upper-storey club floors can make free with an unusually generous five meals and snacks laid out in the course of a day in their private lounge, starting with

breakfast and ending with evening cocktails and snacks.

Most Ritz-Carlton guests commence their day with breakfast in the Greenhouse, a vibrant hub with glass and greenery predominating as the design aspects in a fresh and airy ambience. At other times of the day, dim sum morsels like deep-fried prawn dumplings with diced water chestnuts and yellow chives in homemade XO chili sauce are typical of the outstanding fare in the Summer Pavilion, while Snappers specialises in seafood. And afternoon tea - think freshly baked scones and Devon clotted cream to the accompaniment of a string quartet - is a classic event in the Chihuly Lounge, illuminated by glass artist Dale Chihuly's arresting wall sculpture *Sunrise*.

The elegance and sophistication of the Ritz-Carlton's dining and accommodation options is reflected below ground, with a 1,115-square-metre ballroom and 10 meeting and function rooms. Just outside, the serenity of the swimming pool is

enhanced by threads of water cascading down in a mini cataract at its entrance. On the same level, the fitness centre features a host of free weights, a spa, sauna and massage facilities. Within walking distance of shops, MRT, International Convention and Exhibition Centre (Suntec City) and cultural centres, the Ritz-Carlton is pretty close to faultless and is utterly worthy of the string of

accolades and awards it garners every year.

Rates from: $$
Star rating: ★ ★ ★ ★ ★
Overall rating: ♨ ♨ ♨ ♨ ½

Ambience:	9.09	Cleanliness:	9.36
Value:	8.21	Facilities:	8.86
Staff:	8.98	Restaurants:	8.70
Location:	8.48	Families:	8.47

Sentosa Resort & Spa

2 Bukit Manis Road, Sentosa, Singapore 099891
T: +65 6275 0331 **F:** +65 6275 0228
www.HotelClub.com/Hotels/Sentosa_Resort_Spa_Singapore_The

To an island tailor-made for pleasure comes one of the city's most pleasurable low-key resorts. All the property's 210 rooms and suites (plus its four villas - each with a private pool) are decorated in soft browns and greens, a colour scheme that takes its cue from its surroundings. Every room has high-speed Internet access, flat-screen televisions and swish sound systems too. However, this is primarily a vacation rather than a business spot, so it is fairly certain that most guests will be firmly shutting their room doors and scampering towards the 6,000-square-metre Spa Botanica shortly after check-in. Very much a market leader, this garden spa has 14 indoor rooms and six outdoor pavilions as well as mud pools, floatation tanks, and Turkish-style steam baths, although the latter seems to come with a touch of irony given Singapore's equatorial climate. The overall impression is of a complete escape from the city, and even from the surrounding island with its plethora of regimented amusements.

Capping the Sentosa's tempting offerings is the Cliff, designed by Japanese architect Yasuhiro Koichi, with its glittering open kitchen specialising in contemporary cuisine, water features and a new split-level platform built over lush jungle as well as extended outdoor seating. Alternatively, the Terrace provides a lovely venue for enjoying international fare, whether al fresco overlooking the pool or inside air-conditioned comfort. And the vistas from the Pavilion bar are a ready inducement for a midday aperitif, the first one after the sun is over the yardarm, a nightcap or indeed any excuse you need for a couple of cocktails. This designer-tropical island has always been touted as the groovy getaway on Singapore's doorstep, and indeed there is a beach and two 18-hole golf courses right outside the resort. The Sentosa resort at least grants some licence to the hyperbole.

Rates from: $$
Star rating: ★ ★ ★ ★ ★
Overall rating: ♦ ♦ ♦ ♦ ½

Ambience:	9.07	Cleanliness:	8.97
Value:	8.14	Facilities:	8.52
Staff:	8.51	Restaurants:	8.43
Location:	8.32	Families:	8.52

July 06 ✓

Shangri-La Hotel Singapore

22 Orange Grove Road, Singapore 258350
T: +65 6737 3644 **F:** +65 6737 3257
www.HotelClub.com/Hotels/ShangriLa_Hotel_Singapore

One of the Lion City's largest and best hotels, the 750-room Shangri-La Singapore is divided into three wings - Tower, Garden and Valley - set in a six-hectare botanical garden strewn with more than 133,000 plants, flowers and trees of 110 varieties off the top end of Orchard Road. The extra few yards away from this bustling thoroughfare give the Shangri-La an extra measure of peace, while a dash of exclusivity was added with the March 2005 arrival of The Line, a succulent open-kitchen restaurant in the main lobby designed by Adam Tihany.

The Tower enjoys a contemporary design, and is most suited to business travellers, the bougainvillea-hung Garden has more of a vacation feel to it, while Valley guests can settle back in their own private dining and reception rooms. Needless to say, exceptionally high standards of service and superb facilities combine to ensure you will be exceedingly comfortable wherever you stay here.

Although it markets itself as a business five-star, the Shangri-La's all-pervading jungle ambience could well entice even the most rabidly driven executives to lounge by the free-form pool, scrabble up the electronic rock climbing simulator, play the three-hole pitch-and-putt course and linger over high tea in the Rose Veranda or dabble in the Californian ease and cuisine of BLU. It is in this last restaurant that the true character of the hotel reveals itself. Well tried and tested Shangri-La outlets like Shang Palace and Nadaman have their place here, but it is BLU that sets the real tone. The panoramas over the city have no real rival anywhere else in Singapore, the food could well be summarised as "cool cuisine" and the staff are pleasantly relaxed yet utterly dedicated to their task.

Finally, anyone with a few spare moments should nip into the spa, where a wide range of massages, from reflexology to post-flight therapy, and treatments like herbal baths and body wraps refresh the parts that others fail to reach.

Rates from: $$			
Star rating: ★ ★ ★ ★ ★			
Overall rating: 🦆🦆🦆🦆 ½			
Ambience:	9.12	Cleanliness:	9.31
Value:	8.22	Facilities:	8.78
Staff:	9.02	Restaurants:	8.72
Location:	8.47	Families:	8.71

June 06

Shangri-La's Rasa Sentosa Resort

101 Siloso Road, Sentosa, Singapore 098970
T: +65 6275 0100 **F**: +65 6275 0355
www.HotelClub.com/Hotels/ShangriLas_Rasa_Sentosa_Resort_Singapore

There is still no question in the minds of Singapore's most exacting hotel guest niche market segment about their favourite weekend getaway, and the best place to stay therein. The winner is: "The cabanas at the Shangri-La's Rasa Sentosa Resort". Needless to say, the average age of the members of this select band is about nine and three quarters, for Singapore's only beachfront resort is like a boundless Toys 'R' Us with rooms and restaurants attached.

Sunny, airy, with natural colours and materials predominating, all the Rasa Sentosa's 459 rooms and suites have a balcony or patio. Not that anyone will be spending much time within except to snatch a few hours' sleep. Step out of the room to whizz about on a mountain bike or a set of rollerblades. Dig into the beach, the buffet in the Silver Shell Café or some seafood at Sharkey's down by the water. Surf some video games or splash into the outdoor pool. There is a rock wall to climb, scooters to scoot, petanque and paddle-skiing. Head off on a nature walk or make up a team for volleyball. And this, remember, is before you have even ventured off to the rest of Sentosa.

Singapore's somewhat ersatz playground island is not quite Disneyland but it does encompass a full complement of fun activities all within a short hike of the Shangri-La. The trip by cable car is a thrilling way to arrive, and Sentosa's 500 hectares cover child-friendly aquariums, butterfly parks, mini-golf etc., the only catch being that many attract an admission fee.

With their all-pervading air of good clean wholesome family fun, the Shangri-La and Sentosa have a lot to offer. Adults can tee off on the island's golf courses, then finish off in the resort's spa. And teenagers will be relieved to hear that Siloso Beach also hosts the odd rave. Now for Singapore, that is really cool.

Rates from: $$
Star rating: ★ ★ ★ ★ ★
Overall rating: ♢♢♢♢ ½

Ambience:	9.12	Cleanliness:	9.31
Value:	8.22	Facilities:	8.78
Staff:	9.02	Restaurants:	8.72
Location:	8.47	Families:	8.71

Sheraton Towers Singapore

39 Scotts Road, Singapore 228230
T: +65 6737 6888 **F**: +65 6737 1072
www.HotelClub.com/Hotels/Sheraton_Towers_Singapore

Very much downtown, the Sheraton is a solidly reliable hotel around the corner from Orchard Road with the emphasis on comfort. Bound into any of the beds in the 413 bay-windowed rooms and suites and you find yourself nestling between Egyptian cotton sheets, your head pillowed on goose-down with the whole

atop a Simmons Beautyrest System. And naturally the rooms are fully fitted for the modern executive, while there is also a phalanx of ball, function and conference rooms to cope with meetings and similar events. With the essentials more than adequately covered, a browse round the rest of the hotel embraces a tempting outdoor pool

with attached bar, a gym fairly bristling with chrome, one Cantonese restaurant, one Italian - concentrating on thoroughly authentic dishes from the north - and the fully fledged all-American Dining Room. The Sheraton is a very straightforward business hotel, well-run and well up to the city's high standards.

Rates from: $$
Star rating: ★ ★ ★ ★ ★
Overall rating: ♢♢♢♢ ½

Ambience:	8.69	Cleanliness:	9.04
Value:	8.04	Facilities:	8.45
Staff:	8.91	Restaurants:	8.49
Location:	8.13	Families:	8.42

Swissôtel Merchant Court Singapore

20 Merchant Road, Singapore 058281
T: +65 6337 2288 **F**: +65 6334 0606
www.HotelClub.com/Hotels/Swissotel_Merchant_Court_Hotel_Singapore

If you are going to take a curious squint at the riverside Merchant Court - yet another outpost of the Raffles empire - you might as well do so while seated at Blue Potato, whose name gives a clue both to the sort of cuisine and the location of this poolside restaurant which gives the whole property the sense of an urban resort. Look up and you can see the windows of many of the 476 rooms, smartly decorated and efficiently set up, which lie above the hotel's airy public spaces and very deluxe spa.

Look out and there's both Clarke Quay and River Point, two of the city's main upscale entertainment districts. And if you're blessed with X-ray vision, look down and you'll

see straight into the MRT station. Neatly blending old and new, a reincarnated Sir Stamford would doubtless look upon this place with a fair measure of approval, especially its lobby, which is decorated with some thoughtfully chosen objets d'art.

Rates from: $$
Star rating: ★ ★ ★ ★ ★
Overall rating: ♢♢♢♢ ½

Ambience:	8.62	Cleanliness:	9.04
Value:	8.33	Facilities:	8.48
Staff:	8.63	Restaurants:	8.34
Location:	9.04	Families:	8.41

Swissôtel The Stamford Singapore

2 Stamford Road, Singapore 178882
T: +65 6338 8585 **F:** +65 6338 2862
www.HotelClub.com/Hotels/Swissotel_The_Stamford_Singapore

swimming pools and a cardio theatre.

The gym is open 24 hours a day - a cunning way to combat jet lag if it strikes in the wee hours. If that is not enough, try the stylish collection of restaurants and clubs which make up the Equinox Complex, perched on the 70th to 72nd floors with stunning views over the city.

There are two aspects of the hotel that have to be experienced to be believed. The first is the 360 degree panorama that extends over pretty much the whole city republic, as good a bird's-eye view as anyone will ever get this side of a personal helicopter. And secondly there is the sheer convenience of the Swissôtel, with conference centre and MRT on the threshold and the whole of buzzing get-on-down downtown Singapore immediately outside the imposing entrance.

Some older Asian hands may remember this as the Westin, but the Swissôtel Stamford is the ultra-modern version of a Singaporean institution. Designed by IM Pei, the most successful Chinese architect of the 20th century, the high-rise Swissôtel is a behemoth of a hotel, suspended above an equally outsized shopping and entertainment complex that it shares with its sister Raffles The Plaza. The Raffles that started it all, that Raffles, is just across the road, sitting placidly by like an indulgent grandparent at a family gathering while its more juvenile descendents make whoopee round about. Soaring 72 storeys, counting more than 1,200 tasteful rooms and suites, with a host of restaurants (Kopi Tiam, like an upmarket hawker centre, specialises in Singaporean fare) and more than 8,000 square metres of meeting space, Swissôtel is a multi-functional accommodation umbrella. Just about everything guests might desire is available here, from high-speed Internet access to low-key relaxation in the Amrita Spa, with its 40 private treatment rooms, two free-form

Rates from: $
Star rating: ★ ★ ★ ★ ★
Overall rating: ◊ ◊ ◊ ◊ ½

Ambience:	8.74	Cleanliness:	8.92
Value:	8.30	Facilities:	8.60
Staff:	8.53	Restaurants:	8.60
Location:	9.22	Families:	8.43

SRI LANKA

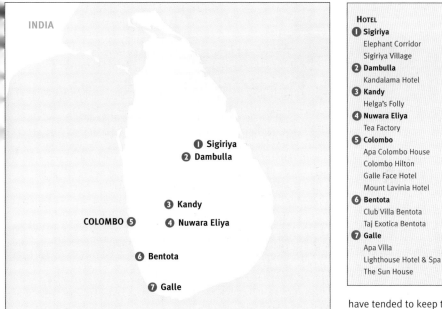

Before the disastrous tsunami in December 2004, Sri Lankan tourism had hit its best-ever numbers. Needless to say, everybody who had anything to do with the trade had their fingers firmly crossed that the country would recover, and many hotels bounced back within a month.

Ravaged by factional violence for the best part of two decades, the island has suffered numerous terrorist attacks and enormous loss of life, but there is a general feeling that it is high time the fighting between Tamil separatists from the north and the Sinhalese majority, who live largely in the south, came to an end over the peace-talks table.

Sri Lanka has had a chequered history. Known to Arab traders as "Serendip", it fell first under Portuguese then later Dutch and British rule. It was the British who imported Tamil labourers from India to work on tea and coffee plantations, and after Sri Lanka achieved independence in 1948, relations between the two main ethnic groups gradually went downhill.

In the past, visitors to Sri Lanka have tended to keep to the south, mainly due to the terrorist problems but also because most of the island's attractions are concentrated there. The chief delight of Sri Lanka is its variety, from the beaches along the coast to the rolling hill country around Kandy, whose main temple is home to a sacred tooth venerated by Buddhists (who make up 70 per

cent of the country's inhabitants) and the focus of a spectacular procession of drummers, dancers and elephants every July. Galle, centred around the beautifully preserved 17th-century Dutch fort, resonates with history, as does Nuwara Eliya, a hill-station highly favoured since British colonial times. Ratnapura forms the heart of the country's gem industry, Arugam Bay on the east coast enjoys a top ranking among the world's surfing community and Kataragama hosts an annual fire-walking ceremony. Wild elephants roam around Uda Walawe and the rainforest is practically untouched in the Sinharaja National Heritage Wilderness Area. Further north, culture vultures can hop between the millennia-old ruins of Polonnaruwa and Anuradhapura and climb the famed rock fortress at Sigiriya.

The ceasefire should see other parts of Sri Lanka opening up again, in particular the untouched beaches of Nilaveli beyond Trincomalee on the northeast coast. The special joy of Sri Lanka is that its relatively small size allows visitors to take in the best of its attractions within a couple of weeks, perhaps starting in the capital, Colombo, venturing into the interior to explore tea country and the historical sights, and then ending with a couple of days kicking back at a beach resort.

Sri Lankan hotels are a mixed bag, starting with the hospitable likes of Mrs Chitrangi de Fonseka's Paying Guesthouse, past some very imaginative boutiques and inspirational villas all the way up to grand colonial dames like the Mount Lavinia and Galle Face hotels, the latter enjoying a new lease of life in the wake of a renovation. International chains are few, and the bulk of the country's accommodation is locally owned and - patience, patience - locally run. Service priorities can see smiles put before speed, and facilities can be a touch makeshift, however rates are generally reasonable, especially in the low season when the monsoon strikes from April to November. Sri Lanka is at its most climatically hospitable between December and March, which is when it sees the majority of visitors, especially Europeans on

packages, escaping the northern winter. Incidentally, every full moon in Sri Lanka is marked by a public holiday (poya), when alcohol is not supposed to be sold in hotels, restaurants or shops, though some establishments have been known to oblige with "special" pots of tea.

Both the island's geography and its multi-ethnic community are reflected in the national cuisine. Spices, in particular cinnamon, initially drew traders from overseas, and they feature strongly in curries, which tend to be rather hotter than their Indian equivalents. "Hoppers", a delicious sort of pancake, make a welcome appearance at breakfast buffets, and a cornucopia of locally grown fruit - mangosteen, rambutan, mango and a host of others - can be turned into juice or eaten at any time of day.

Marco Polo waxed lyrical about Ceylon, as Sri Lanka was then known, and its even more ancient name - Serendip - has come to imply making fortunate discoveries by accident. After a chapter of accidents over the past 20 years, Sri Lanka is in the fortunate position of being at relative peace once more, meaning that the island that Marco Polo described as "the finest in the world" is fully open for business - and even more importantly, pleasure - once again.

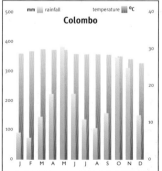

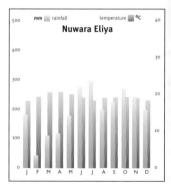

Apa Colombo House

3 Gregorys Road, Colombo 7, Sri Lanka
T: +94 11 268 8017   **F**: +94 11 267 1817
www.HotelClub.com/Hotels/Apa_Colombo_House

Tucked away in the capital's posh Cinnamon Gardens residential district, the century-old Colombo House mixes just three guestrooms with bundles of charm. The two upstairs bedrooms share a private lounge with an open veranda, making them ideal for families. This whole place feels not so much like a hotel, but the well-appointed abode of a friend of a friend who has been kind enough to lend it to you for a few days. Two brilliantly Jeeves-like staff perform the tasks of cook (breakfast is a genuine feast), cleaner and masters of ceremonies while providing a fair dose of local information and generally keeping Colombo House running. Browse

around the library-cum-music room, put your feet up in the garden (home to the house's pet tortoise) in the shade of the frangipani trees, snuggle up on the outsize double bed in your room with a DVD - whatever you do, the pace rarely changes from being utterly relaxed.

Rates from: $$
Star rating: ★ ★
Overall rating: Editor's Pick

Ambience:	n/a	Cleanliness:	n/a
Value:	n/a	Facilities:	n/a
Staff:	n/a	Restaurants:	n/a
Location:	n/a	Families:	n/a

Apa Villa

78 Mile Post, Matara Road, Thalpe, Galle, Sri Lanka
T: +94 91 228 3320   **F**: +94 91 228 3320
www.HotelClub.com/Hotels/Apa_Villa_Thalpe

Each of the villas has its own outside terrace, where meals served beneath swaying palms can easily stretch into repasts lasting several hours. The beach here is not Apa Villa's best asset, but the pool is a delight, and comes with a seaside deck that is perfect for sunbathing or sunset drinks.

There are more than a few places in Sri Lanka where you run into a couple of expats who are, you gradually realise, just a few years ahead of you. They came here on holiday some time back, loved the place, determined to move here and are now running the boutique hotel where you've just arrived. And so it is at Villa Thalpe, where

long-term residents Nikki and Bob Harrison bring their special touch, including a natural gift for both hospitality and interior design.

There are just six Balinese-themed villa-suites, containing four-poster beds swathed in mosquito nets but with no air-conditioning - the gently gusting sea breezes do the trick instead.

Rates from: $$
Star rating: ★ ★ ★
Overall rating: ◐◐◐◐ ½

Ambience:	9.46	Cleanliness:	8.75
Value:	8.18	Facilities:	7.81
Staff:	8.89	Restaurants:	9.15
Location:	8.46	Families:	9.15

Club Villa Bentota

138/15, Galle Road, Bentota, Sri Lanka
T: +94 34 227 5312 **F:** +94 34 428 7129
www.HotelClub.com/Hotels/Club_Villa_Bentota

You don't have to be a railway enthusiast to stay here, but it helps. Perhaps a dozen times a day trains thunder past on the main Colombo line at the bottom of the garden, a momentary intrusion before the villa lapses into tranquillity again. With simply bags of character, this is somewhere that seems to have grown rather than been built. Various extensions were added to the original 1976 structure over the years, with architect Geoffrey Bawa casting an eye over the plans, to arrive at the current 15 bedrooms, which are augmented by colonial furniture, picturesque pool, palm-treed lawns, a beach that is simply fabulous and murals by Lucki Senanayake. There is only one restaurant, but breakfast, lunch, dinner and anything you care for in between times is pretty much faultless. A short way from Bentota, it is true to say there are places to explore around about, but when quartered so idyllically, why not simply let the passing locomotives do that for you?

Rates from: $$
Star rating: ★ ★ ★
Overall rating: ♮♮♮♮

Ambience:	9.42	Cleanliness:	9.08
Value:	7.75	Facilities:	7.75
Staff:	8.42	Restaurants:	7.25
Location:	8.08	Families:	8.75

Colombo Hilton

2 Sir Chittampalam A Gardiner Mawatha, Colombo, Sri Lanka
T: +94 11 249 2492 **F:** +94 11 254 4657
www.HotelClub.com/Hotels/Hilton_Residence_Apartment_Colombo

Smack in the heart of Colombo's business district, next to the World Trade Centre, the high-rise, 384-room Hilton may not have the charm of some of the city's older hotels, but it is certainly the place executives stay. Set on a three-hectare site next to Beira Lake, with views to the Indian Ocean from the upper storeys, it is a highly efficient property yet with a slightly quaint appeal. The Frangipani Floor is specially dedicated to female customers, with women attendants and extra security arrangements, while the Sakura Floor has been adapted to meet the needs of Japanese guests. Whatever their nationality or sex, everyone can enjoy the hotel's nine restaurants and bars (Spoons provides an exciting contemporary kitchen, and the Blue Elephant disco is one of the Colombo's most popular nightspots) plus the rather exclusive pool, gym, tennis and air-conditioned squash courts, which are set slightly apart from the main building.

Rates from: $$
Star rating: ★ ★ ★ ★ ★
Overall rating: ♮♮♮♮

Ambience:	8.30	Cleanliness:	8.60
Value:	7.69	Facilities:	8.23
Staff:	8.47	Restaurants:	8.65
Location:	8.32	Families:	8.70

lephan Corridor

bissa, Sigiriya, Sri Lanka
+94 662 231 950 **F:** +94 662 231 952
ww.HotelClub.com/Hotels/Elephant_Corridor_Hotel

Pic cit" is the mahout's raditional command to his charge o let go. And "letting go" is very nuch the philosophy at Elephant Corridor. Each of the 21 suites has ts own and very discreet plunge pool. You can eat at whatever time of day or night and precisely where you feel like it. Bundle up in a hammock with a view of the ifth-century Sigiriya rock fortress, or spend the day climbing to its summit. Stroll around the property with one of the resident naturalists or go for a bicycle ride. There's even a cricket net. So pic cit. Let go.

Surrounded by 80 hectares of forest, there are no prizes for deducing the rationale behind this superlative resort's name. While the marvellously lofty suites are built too close together for some tastes, they are privacy itself once you close the door. A four-poster, air-conditioning, unusual circular bathrooms, a DVD player - all these and more you can take as standard. But the real treats come with the attention to detail. So break out the easel and paints, reach for the binoculars (there are uninterrupted views of the jungle plains) ease into the pool with the cordless

phone and call some friends for a mild gloat. Pic cit.

Further entertainment abounds. The Ambrosia restaurant more than lives up to its name, and Fables & Tales, the library bar, and Ebony & Ivory, the jungle bar, indulge both thirsts and senses. Make some time to take a trip out to the pool, with its adjacent spa. And of course, with Elephant Corridor more or less at the centre of the Cultural Triangle, guests are ideally placed for jaunts to temples, parks and ancient caves and burial grounds. However the overriding credo here is that you should simply kick back. That is to say, pic cit.

Rates from: $$$
Star rating: ★ ★ ★ ★ ★
Overall rating: Editor's Pick

Ambience:	n/a	Cleanliness:	n/a
Value:	n/a	Facilities:	n/a
Staff:	n/a	Restaurants:	n/a
Location:	n/a	Families:	n/a

Galle Face Hotel

2 Galle Road, Colombo 3, Sri Lanka
T: +94 11 254 1010 **F:** +94 11 254 1072
www.HotelClub.com/Hotels/Galle_Face_Hotel

For decades Asia's grande-dame aficionados have clasped the Galle Face to their collective bosom, boasting of its antiquity - both the building and the redoubtable staff who totter around its interior - and revelling in the management's insouciant attitude to modern trends. Then - some 140 years after first opening - the hotel suddenly had a renovation fit. The 82-room Regency Wing was unveiled, likewise a 1,800-square-metre spa, new restaurants and an all-encompassing air of renaissance. Traditionalists will be glad to hear that the original 65 rooms, the statuesque lobby and that marvellous spume-flecked verandah are little changed. Tip-top up-to-date or securely anchored in the past, the hotel is still all things to all guests. Speaking of which, the Aga Khan's statement that "happiness is the Galle Face Hotel" rings as true as ever. And they're just as proud of other prior guests like Richard Nixon and Yuri Gagarin. Plus ça change, plus c'est le meme Galle Face.

Rates from: $
Star rating: ★ ★ ★ ★
Overall rating: 🖐🖐🖐🖐

Ambience:	9.13	Cleanliness:	8.13
Value:	8.65	Facilities:	7.01
Staff:	8.46	Restaurants:	7.55
Location:	9.08	Families:	7.75

Helga's Folly

70 Rajadhilla Mawatha, Off Mahamaya Mawatha, Kandy, Sri Lanka
T: +94 81 447 4314 **F:** +94 81 447 9370
www.HotelClub.com/Hotels/Helgas_Folly_Hotel_Kandy

When bound for Helga's Folly, it is essential to leave behind your preconceptions. Mrs de Silva - possibly Kandy's most eccentric inhabitant - prefers it when some of her inventory of uniquely styled rooms (pink, lime green, or even dashing yellow) remain empty, and describes her property as an "anti-hotel." Package groups are banned and forget mini bars and televisions - who would want them when the whimsical decoration encompasses 1960s furniture, Buddhist temple paintings and antique Dutch chests? Anyway, who needs a mini bar when the staff will happily bring a whisky soda or whatever you want to drink to the drawing-room or library. The kitchen will not countenance buffets, while both the pool and simple massage treatments will assist in offsetting any overindulgence. With modern life beset by globalisation and bland uniformity, this is a rejuvenating oasis that is at once charming and mildly shocking. Bizarre barely begins to describe Helga and her Folly - which in truth is anything but. Remember, though, to bring sunglasses and a sense of humour.

Rates from: $
Star rating: ★ ★
Overall rating: Editor's Pick

Ambience:	n/a	Cleanliness:	n/a
Value:	n/a	Facilities:	n/a
Staff:	n/a	Restaurants:	n/a
Location:	n/a	Families:	n/a

~~K~~andalama Hotel

~~K~~ndalama, Dambulla, Sri Lanka
+94 662 284 100 **F:** +94 662 284 109
~~www~~.HotelClub.com/Hotels/Kandalama_Hotel

The Kandalama is one of the most amazing hotels in Asia, let alone Sri Lanka, a masterful blend of hospitality and eco-engineering that looks wonderful and feels even better. Much more than just rooms, restaurants and rest and recuperation, it combines history with an unparalleled natural location in the heart of the island.

For a start, as the hotel is built into a cliff and festooned with greenery, it is barely visible from a distance and up close practically merges into its surroundings. Set near the foot of two mountains - Ereulagala and Dikkandahena - on the border of Sri Lanka's intermediate and dry zones, the Kandalama's environs enjoy an especially rich bio-diversity. The hotel looks down on the Dambulla tank, a two-millennia-old reservoir that still supplies water to farms in the area, and is right in the middle of a 22-hectare forest that encompasses trees, medicinal plants and 165 species of arboreal, terrestrial and aquatic birds including the dusky blue flycatcher, yellow-fronted barbett and grey hornbill.

Containing 158 rooms and four suites, the Kandalama was designed on strict eco-friendly lines, unobtrusively strung out along the hillside for a full kilometre. Through its architecture, the hotel ingeniously grants nature centre stage: rocks, caves and cascades of rainwater add drama and charm to the corridors. Forest trees brush against galleries and the windows of public rooms, while flowering woodland creepers

curtain balconies and the roofs are terraces of wild grass. The rooms are sparingly yet comfortably decorated, providing 21st-century amenities like satellite TV and IDD phones while still retaining something of the placid aura of a cliffside monkish cell.

The slightly confusingly named trio of restaurants - Kashyapa, Kanchana and Kaludiya - and brace of bars - Kachchan and Kachana - belong more to the surrounding land than the hotel itself, with vistas stretching out to the tank, mountains and jungles. Using fresh farm produce and locally grown fruit whenever possible, the kitchens serve up a variety of delicious local and international cuisines.

One of the Kandalama's top draws is its Eco Park, where guests can see at first hand sewage being dried by the sun and composted, water being recycled for the rooftop gardens and garbage being sorted and dispatched for appropriate disposal. It is not by any means the sort of excursion that normally confronts five-star habitués, but one that expresses the entire ethos of the hotel. Guests can also tour the plant nursery and beehives, and delve into the extensive eco-library.

More conventional entertainments include tennis, ping-pong, a fully equipped gym, billiards and the board game Carrom. And beyond the Kandalama - whose site was chosen only after an extensive search by helicopter - sits the heartland of the Cultural Triangle. The rock fortress of Sigirya is in sight of the hotel's infinity swimming pool (one of three pools), and the ancient cities of Anuradhapura and Polonnaruwa are both within driving distance. You can venture to the surrounding areas by horse, elephant and bicycle, or board a dugout canoe for a safari on nearby irrigation tanks like the Sea of Parakrama. On foot, an hour's hike leads to the pond named Kaludiya Pokuna, an ancient archaeological site where the ebo trees reach more than five metres circumference. Returning mentally invigorated but possibly physically lacking, there is a whole range of treatment at the Ayurvedic health centre - the most natural form of therapeutics in a hotel inspired by and devoted to, nature.

Rates from: $$
Star rating: ★ ★ ★ ★
Overall rating: ♘ ♘ ♘ ♘ ½

Ambience:	9.39	Cleanliness:	8.64
Value:	8.82	Facilities:	8.32
Staff:	8.75	Restaurants:	8.68
Location:	8.86	Families:	8.80

Lighthouse Hotel & Spa

Dadella, Galle, Sri Lanka
T: +94 91 222 4017 F: +94 91 222 4021
www.HotelClub.com/Hotels/Lighthouse_Hotel_And_Spa

With a style that might be called "Robinson Le Corbusier", the Lighthouse is a constant surprise, dominating a headland near the historic city of Galle. Designed by Sri Lankan architect Geoffrey Bawa, who was inspired by the nearby three-century-old Dutch fort, the hotel is a delirious expanse of cinnamon-coloured buildings topped with red tiled roofs, linked by airy open corridors looking down on to the ocean and a beach that stretches away to the horizon.

Opened in 1997, the Lighthouse comprises just 60 rooms and three suites. The rooms are floored with teak, with large en-suite granite and wood bathrooms and a separate shower, and give out on to a private balcony or terrace. Each of the suites, which come with a jacuzzi, pantry and separate sitting room, enjoys a playful individual theme that draws on Galle's long-time global trading associations. The Ibn Batuta echoes a Moroccan souk, Fa Hsien provides a taste of China, while the Spielbergen is solidly Dutch.

Dining at the Lighthouse is similarly inspired and likewise international. The Cardamom Café is open round the clock, while the Cinnamon Room - noted for its fondues - opens only at dinner. The Anchor Bar occupies a convenient spot near both the main and children's pools, while the Coat of Arms Bar must have a deal going with whoever organises the dazzling sunsets that manifest themselves almost without fail each evening. Al fresco fans can also request an evening barbecue down on the beach, with fresh seafood cooked over crackling open fires and the waves crashing on the rocks as a symphonic backdrop.

By day, there is an enormous amount to occupy guests - billiards, squash, ping-pong and tennis for anyone who likes knocking balls about, and of course a fully-equipped gym. An array of excursions are available or just stay on the beach which is ideal for fishing - and pretty good for toasting in a few UVs as well.

Rates from: $$
Star rating: ★ ★ ★ ★ ★
Overall rating: 👍 👍 👍 👍

Ambience:	8.95	Cleanliness:	8.75
Value:	8.05	Facilities:	8.04
Staff:	8.45	Restaurants:	8.00
Location:	8.85	Families:	7.62

Mount Lavinia Hotel

100 Hotel Road, Mount Lavinia, Sri Lanka
T: +94 11 271 5221 **F:** +94 11 273 0726
www.HotelClub.com/Hotels/Mount_Lavinia_Hotel_Colombo

From a British governor's secret love nest, to a holiday home, to a wartime hospital, Mount Lavinia has gradually metamorphosed from its genesis in the 19th century to its incarnation as a luxury hotel. The hotel's present form neatly reflects its antecedents, as this 210-room (private) beachside property is as well placed for honeymooners as it is for guests who simply need to relax and recuperate.

The Mount Lavinia's nucleus is the marbled Governor's Wing, one-time residence of Sir Thomas Maitland, who built the house so he could rendezvous with a dancing girl - one Lovina Aponsuwa - who had unduly excited his passions. It now contains 40 rooms - with wooden floors and windows that open wide to the sea breezes, accentuating its colonial charm - as well as the duplex Governor's Suite. Other accommodation is split between the Bay Wing and Sea & Garden Wing, more recently built but all with the requisite sea view, as well as more current amenities like satellite TV and IDD phones.

The Lavinia's main dining room also takes its name from the Governor, with bay windows and lofty pillars and palms providing the backdrop to the Western and oriental menu. Lobster and outsize prawns are the prime fare at Seafood Cove and sunset cocktails slip down easily at the thatched Tropical Bar on the beach. Dancing at the hotel nightclub - Little Hut - encouraged by the live band, usually lasts until the wee hours.

Above all, Mount Lavinia is an especially stylish hotel, with a talent for organising unusual events. This might be a wedding, complete with Kandyan drummers and dancers, elephants and a chorus of local girls, or simply the regular Saturday film night, when classic movies are shown on the terrace with nothing to cover the audience but the stars and moon above.

Rates from: $
Star rating: ★ ★ ★ ★
Overall rating: 🌐🌐🌐🌐 ½

Ambience:	8.92	Cleanliness:	8.92
Value:	9.08	Facilities:	8.17
Staff:	8.83	Restaurants:	8.50
Location:	8.92	Families:	8.58

Sigiriya Village

Sigiriya, Sri Lanka
T: +94 662 231 803   **F**: +94 662 231 805
www.HotelClub.com/Hotels/Sigiriya_Village

There's a specific, almost magnetic energy at the sprawling Sigiriya Village - a legacy perhaps of the magnificent 200-metre-high monolith that seems close enough to touch. One-time fortress, for some years a monastery, it is one of the ultimate symbols of the Cultural Triangle and basing yourself in the village at its foot makes a lot of sense. The resort is spread out over 12 hectares, with the 120 chalets gathered together in clusters of a score or so with names like Kingfisher and Temple. On the accommodation side, facilities are not exactly stellar, however the rooms are adequate for a short stay. Previous guests recommend trading up to the more pricey options. Food and beverage score rather higher - the resort's buffets are popular and much of the food comes from the home farm, which is open to visitors. A small pool offers respite from the heat when you are not culture vulturing and is a fine spot to view Sigiriya Rock with a locally brewed Three Coins lager in hand.

Rates from: $
Star rating: ★ ★
Overall rating: 🌸🌸🌸🌸

Ambience:	8.75	Cleanliness:	7.95
Value:	7.95	Facilities:	7.68
Staff:	8.75	Restaurants:	8.75
Location:	7.95	Families:	8.55

The Sun House

18 Upper Dickson Road, Galle, Sri Lanka
T: +94 91 438 0275   **F**: +94 91 222 2624
www.HotelClub.com/Hotels/Sun_House_Galle

One of the forerunners of the new breed of Lankan boutique hotels, the Sun House sits next to its sister property the Dutch House on the hill above Galle. Home to a Scottish spice merchant in Victorian times, the Sun House assumes its current mantle of deluxe retreat with consummate ease. A trio of truly lovely double bedrooms opens out onto the mango tree garden, while there is fierce competition for the three larger but equally alluring suites, especially Dumas with its own balcony and Hibiscus. As in many very good small hotels, life here focuses on the convivial main living room. Dinner times are eagerly anticipated, with guests first lolling on sofas, browsing through the very catholic library and the equally adventurous cocktail menu. Chef Ranavira is well known for returning from the market laden with the freshest ingredients which are then transformed into amazing fusion creations, and it is a rare occasion when these fall short of expectation.

Rates from: $$
Star rating: ★ ★ ★ ★
Overall rating: Editor's Pick

Ambience:	n/a	Cleanliness:	n/a
Value:	n/a	Facilities:	n/a
Staff:	n/a	Restaurants:	n/a
Location:	n/a	Families:	n/a

Taj Exotica Bentota

Bentota, Sri Lanka
T: +94 34 227 5650 **F:** +94 34 227 5160
www.HotelClub.com/Hotels/Taj_Exotica_Bentota

which while it may pale when compared with its international brethren has few rivals locally. Bentota is one of the more exclusive resort areas on the coast, on the beaten track but by no means beaten to death, and the Taj is by far the most exclusive resort here. Stepping off the train and into the hotel is a real thrill,

When the cold-climate wage-slaves of the world dream of a Sri Lankan beach resort, the Taj Exotica - a maze of marble with just 162 rooms set about with hanging gardens - is pretty much what comes to mind. A sunny conglomeration of beach and sea and pool and bars, swaying palms and azure skies, this is the sort of place where you might start the day off with a yoga session and end it deep-sea fishing for your supper, having gone for an elephant ride some time in between, made free with the lunch menu, bagged a bit of sun and fitted in a languorous siesta. Other diversions include the Mkop disco,

Rates from: $$
Star rating: ★ ★ ★ ★ ★
Overall rating: 🏵 🏵 🏵 🏵 ½

Ambience:	8.64	Cleanliness:	8.75
Value:	7.97	Facilities:	8.35
Staff:	9.08	Restaurants:	8.64
Location:	9.31	Families:	8.86

Tea Factory

Kandadola, Nuwara Eliya, Sri Lanka
T: +94 52 222 9600 **F:** +94 52 222 9603
www.HotelClub.com/Hotels/Tea_Factory_Hotel

If you like your hotels with a capital H for Heritage, make haste for the Tea Factory. The old withering lofts now contain the 57 guest rooms, the former Rolling Room is now the Goatfell Bar and the whole place - a euphoric eyrie perched on a hilltop - is a real triumph for sustainable tourism. Ten years on from its opening, the Factory is more popular than ever, despite its remoteness, with guests queuing up to dine in its one-of-a-kind railway carriage, indulge in the spa or simply to breathe deeply of the fresh mountain air. The hotel management's obvious pride and relish for its history is rather touching - even the laminated wooden fans that were used to dry the tea have been preserved, and links have been established with Hethersett in England, whence the original owner came. Plucking your own tea from the surrounding estate and curing it in the hotel's miniature processor makes for the country's most unique souvenir.

Rates from: $$
Star rating: ★ ★ ★ ★
Overall rating: 🏵 🏵 🏵 🏵

Ambience:	8.25	Cleanliness:	7.75
Value:	8.25	Facilities:	6.35
Staff:	8.75	Restaurants:	7.50
Location:	8.75	Families:	7.42

TAIWAN

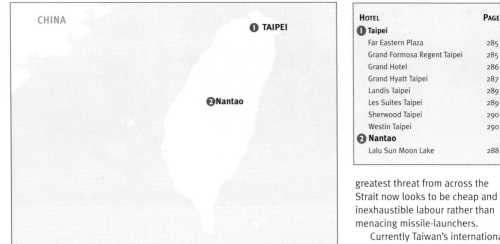

The emerald island lying just 160 kilometres off the Chinese mainland is a feisty character. It lives an uneasy existence, precariously overshadowed by its vast and uncompromising neighbour. Taiwan is a land at peace, but embroiled in one of the thorniest dilemmas of the East.

Originally populated by seafaring peoples from the Pacific islands and groups from the archipelago that today forms the Philippines, Malaysia and Indonesia, Taiwan remained a backwater for millennia. By the time the Portuguese dropped anchor in 1517 and christened it Ilha Formosa - Beautiful Island - it was being steadily settled by Fujianese from across the Strait, and displaying a predominantly Chinese population. In subsequent centuries, the Chinese, Spanish and Japanese were to play a game of musical chairs with the island until after World War II, when the newly formed United Nations decreed that Taiwan would be returned to China. But before that could happen, the communists won the bloody civil war on the mainland, the nationalists fled to the province of Taiwan and each side settled down to plot the other's downfall.

The dispute simmered for decades and the two governments were to diverge along very separate paths. Both sides have evolved into different entities, and much to China's indignation Taiwan did very well for itself. The economy boomed, leaving the then-sluggish mainland in its wake. Since taking control of its own affairs in the 1950s, Taiwan has enjoyed an average GDP growth of nine per cent a year, ensuring it emerged as one of the four "tiger economies" alongside Hong Kong, Singapore and South Korea. Despite wobbles in the Asian financial arena in the late 1990s, Taiwan remains financially robust and a major manufacturing base. Finally China is blossoming economically and, ironically, the greatest threat from across the Strait now looks to be cheap and inexhaustible labour rather than menacing missile-launchers.

Currently Taiwan's international status is a grey area, so its awkward position means it falls into a category all of its own. It exists in diplomatic no-man's-land. For the apolitical it is best described as an unofficial country. Taiwan never declared independence, and Beijing's non-negotiable stance is that Taiwan is a renegade province - and that

reunification is inevitable. Chinese foreign policy is almost defined by the issue and takes a very dim view of anyone in the international community daring to treat Taiwan as a country. No country may maintain official diplomatic relations with both Taipei and Beijing, and for the Taiwanese it has been a long diplomatic march into oblivion. Faced with the choice, only a handful of nations now recognise Taiwan, most of which are Third World recipients of economic aid. Taiwan, incidentally, held the Chinese seat at the United Nations until 1971, when it was replaced by the PRC.

Despite the diplomatic slide, Taiwan booms and the capital Taipei encapsulates a boundless entrepreneurial energy. A sprawling, gritty metropolis, it is home to three million and known for its tide of zipping mopeds and - to be brutally honest - ugly architecture. Most visitors are here for business, but you do not need to look too hard to find pockets of tradition, impressive monuments, good food and uncommonly friendly inhabitants. Taipei also

hosts the National Palace Museum, one of the best collections of Chinese artefacts in the world. Away from the big city are traditional temples and some prime hiking country. Majestic scenery exists along the east coast, across the dramatic mountainous interior and within national parks such as Taroko Gorge and Hsiukuluan River. Across the Strait are more islands dotted like stepping stones to China. From one, Kinmen, you can actually see the mainland.

Taiwan's hotels mirror its persona - functional business hotels with below-average architecture. First-class friendly service is a major plus even if English is not widespread. The best hotels are in the capital and the standards deteriorate pretty quickly outside, although there are some pockets of excellence.

Being comparatively small, Taiwan shares a fairly uniform climate, with slight variations due to latitude and altitude. Generally speaking, the north and the mountainous regions are colder and wetter than the south. Despite

its northerly latitude, the island experiences a tropical monsoon climate, seemingly drawing the leftovers of the various typhoons that have battered Southeast Asia. Most are dissipating by the time they get there but occasionally it is buffeted by vicious storms. Intermittent typhoons and torrential rains wash over Taiwan during the otherwise humid summer - roughly June to September - while the winter is mostly cold, blustery and cloudy. Taipei can be visited all year round, but, like the rest of the country, is at its best around spring or autumn.

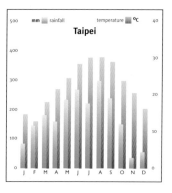

Far Eastern Plaza

201 Tun Hwa South Road, Section 2, Taipei 106, Taiwan
T: +886 2 2378 8888 **F**: +886 2 2377 7777
www.HotelClub.com/Hotels/ShangriLa_Far_Eastern_Plaza_Hotel

Well-established and reliable, this shiny 420-room tower (part of the Shangri-La group) is well up to international five-star service and standards, even if the somewhat dark interior is now starting to show its age. Considerate staff do a splendid job and the Far Eastern is well located in the busy eastern sector of the city, with an array of shops, restaurants and bars close by. The competitive facilities ensure this hotel's appeal is broader than just business, even though this is where it principally excels. It has fine views from the small heated rooftop pool (one of two) and since there is only a small number of rooms on each of its 43 floors, there is a pleasant impression of privacy. Add to this eight restaurants, the 40th-floor spa and well-equipped health club and it is not difficult to see why the Far Eastern Plaza consistently ranks as one of Taipei's, and therefore Taiwan's, most popular hotels.

Rates from: $$$
Star rating: ★ ★ ★ ★ ★
Overall rating: ♦♦♦♦ ½

Ambience:	8.99	Cleanliness:	9.20
Value:	8.20	Facilities:	8.71
Staff:	8.62	Restaurants:	8.76
Location:	8.61	Families:	8.41

Grand Formosa Regent Taipei

41 Chung Shan North Road, Section 2, Taipei, Taiwan
T: +886 2 2523 8000 **F**: +886 2 2523 2828
www.HotelClub.com/Hotels/Gand_Formosa_Regent_Taipei

Sitting on Taipei's main boulevard, the Grand Formosa Regent is well placed, appealing especially to business guests but also to tourists. Its 21 storeys firmly encompass 538 traditionally styled, spacious rooms and suites, all with floor-to-ceiling bay windows and separate bath and shower. Even the lowest category Deluxe Rooms measure a generous 45 square metres. Regular visitors to Taiwan will appreciate the relative novelty of the non-smoking and women's floors, so single female guests can rest assured of extra security.

The hotel interior opens up with a bright atrium and is smart and professional, while its dedicated Tai Pan Club floors and conference facilities are well run. The pool is small but good restaurants offer diverse cuisine choices for the varied guests - Chinese, European and Japanese. The Formosa may not be the cheapest option, but it is complete and very practical.

Rates from: $$$
Star rating: ★ ★ ★ ★ ★
Overall rating: ♦♦♦♦ ½

Ambience:	8.86	Cleanliness:	9.14
Value:	8.10	Facilities:	8.79
Staff:	8.84	Restaurants:	8.90
Location:	8.73	Families:	8.49

Grand Hotel

1 Chung Shang North Road, Section 4, Taipei, Taiwan
T: +886 2 2886 8888 **F**: +886 2 2885 2885
www.HotelClub.com/Hotels/Grand_Hotel_Taipei

As Greater China speeds up its relentless Long March towards total modernisation, this is probably one of the last refuges of the old culture, albeit erstaz ones such as a Forbidden City of a hotel, conceived by Madame Chiang Kai-shek as a tourist lure back in the early 1950s. It was the first five-star property in Taiwan and is now almost a national heritage site in its own right.

Built atop a small hill in an off-centre suburb, the Grand is a veritable riot of Chinoiserie, from its traditional tiled roof to its bright red columns and gold-painted lotus flowers, its four-metre-high entranceway to its calligraphy-covered interiors, its stone lions and golden dragons. In keeping with its imperial pretensions, two secret underground tunnels are said to lead to the late Generalissimo's private residence. Oh, and all its floors are named after dynasties.

But for all the ostensible pomp and circumstance, service is unintimidatingly friendly and solicitous. Owned by the non-profit Duen Mou Foundation, its mission is still to impress visitors to the beleagured isle with the warmth of Taiwan's welcome. Rooms are large and spotlessly clean, with big bathrooms and private balconies from which to survey the city of Taipei spread out below.

The food is among the most authentic Chinese cuisine anywhere, ranging from the huge buffet breakfast spread to Sichuan and Yangtze specialities, Cantonese and northern dim sum. The Western fare is of a satisfactory standard, too, even running to classic afternoon English tea in the Edwardian-style lounge and live jazz with the snacks in the '60s Bar.

An eight-lane bowling alley and an Olympic-size outdoor swimming pool complete with lifeguards are among the leisure facilities, and the comprehensive conference resources include a 400-seat theatre. Rather than trying to make it to downtown Taipei under your own steam - which entails crossing a murderous expressway - hop on the free hotel shuttle bus. Although far from perfect the sheer experience of staying here is well worth the slight logistical inconvenience.

Rates from: $
Star rating: ★ ★ ★ ★ ★
Overall rating: ♔ ♔ ♔ ♔ ½

Ambience:	9.00	Cleanliness:	9.02
Value:	8.34	Facilities:	8.37
Staff:	8.69	Restaurants:	8.55
Location:	8.47	Families:	8.37

Grand Hyatt Taipei

2 Song Shou Road, Taipei, Taiwan
T: +886 2 2720 1234 **F**: +886 2 2720 1111
www.HotelClub.com/Hotels/Grand_Hyatt_Taipei

The Grand Hyatt is Taipei's spiffiest five-star hotel with absolutely everything, plus a familiar name for those who do not wish to stray outside their comfort zones. Its 856 rooms make it one of the biggest in Taiwan. The prime advantage of staying here is the Hyatt's spectrum of facilities, but of equal importance is its strategic location. The hotel lies right next to the landmark World Trade Centre with direct access to the Exhibition Hall and Convention Centre, in Taipei's emerging business and entertainment district. Despite opening in 1990, this is one of Taipei's newer breed of hotels and is broadly considered still one of the best.

The interior design is especially smart and stylish. Contemporary fittings, deep colours and subdued lighting makes for a refined yet relaxed appearance throughout. The lobby enjoys a classical mood and feels a little like a giant conservatory, with grand pillars and arcing balconies sealed beneath a modern glass-paned roof that allows natural light to flood in. Eight excellent restaurants cater for cosmopolitan palettes; Ziga Zaga mutates at 9.30pm from an Italian dining outlet into a chic dance hang-out with live music; Shanghai Court captures the 1930s with its haute cuisine; the Irodori features modern Japanese buffet style; and the show kitchens of Café serve up fresh Western and Asian fare. The Oasis Fitness Centre includes an excellent temperature-controlled outdoor pool (complete with underwater stereo sound system), a sharp, spacious gym and full spa treatments. Appealing guestrooms - pick of the bunch being the newly-opened Tony Chi-designed suites on the top floor - are smooth and trim, generously fitted including three phone lines and broadband Internet access.

The business centre runs conveniently from dawn untill late evening and the club floors have several plush conference rooms. Such is the overall appeal of the Grand Hyatt that it can occasionally fall victim to its own success. The lobby is busy to the point of noisiness and if the adjacent World Trade Centre is hosting an exhibition then the hotel seems to function as an overflow and is swamped by hundreds of visitors. The hotel is hugely popular, and rightfully so, but be prepared for the crowds.

Rates from: $$
Star rating: ★ ★ ★ ★ ★
Overall rating: ⟆⟆⟆⟆ ½

Ambience:	8.66	Cleanliness:	9.00
Value:	7.92	Facilities:	8.48
Staff:	8.67	Restaurants:	8.46
Location:	8.68	Families:	8.16

Lalu Sun Moon Lake

142 Jungshing Road, Yuchr Shiang, Nantao, Taiwan
T: +886 49 285 5311 **F:** +886 49 285 5312
www.HotelClub.com/Hotels/Lalu_Sun_Moon_Lake

The best guide to a country's most desireable hideaways, if they happen to have undergone a period of one-man rule, is to search out the fallen dictator's favourite retreats. The Lalu was built as a holiday home for Chiang Kai-shek and if today's luxury resort is anything to judge by, Taiwan's departed strongman certainly knew how to pick 'em.

Built on the shore of the island's largest freshwater lake, Sun Moon - so named because one end of it is disc-shaped, the other contoured like a crescent - it is in an idyllic spot: shimmering blue waters heaving with fish and shrimp reflect the jade-green mountains that surround it, and the whole area is a time-travel experience, dotted with temples and pagodas and much earlier manifestations of the Thao people's aboriginal lifestyle.

Consisting of 98 rooms, suites and a number of villas built around a courtyard with its own 12-metre pool and al fresco dining pavilion, all accommodation has lake views and is the last word in contemporary comfort, with platform beds and chic furnishings, Internet access, Bose stereo systems, IDD phones, satellite TV and individual airconditioning.

A state-of-the-art spa offers such exotica as volcanic mud wraps and green-tea baths, and there is a 60-metre heated pool as well as a masochistically equipped fitness centre. Organic health-food is available in addition to more fattening Western fare, and Hong Kong, Shanghainese and Japanese cuisine are also featured. Honey-sun-mooners are catered for with special "romantic" dinners.

Stand in the Lobby Bar at dusk, warmed by a blazing fire and a scotch-and-soda, and watch the flocks of birds rise in huge clouds above the lake and listen to the fish rustling through the reeds. And reflect on the fact that sooner or later, even the most exclusive of pleasures will be attainable, if not by the "ordinary" citizens, then at least by a well-heeled minority.

Rates from: $$$$$
Star rating: ★ ★ ★ ★ ★
Overall rating: ♦ ♦ ♦ ♦ ½

Ambience:	9.43	Cleanliness:	9.14
Value:	7.57	Facilities:	9.00
Staff:	9.00	Restaurants:	8.43
Location:	9.29	Families:	7.43

Landis Taipei

41 Min Chuan East Road, Section 2, Taipei, Taiwan
T: +886 2 2597 1234 **F**: +886 2 2596 9223
www.HotelClub.com/Hotels/Landis_Hotel_Taipei

The Landis sits conveniently downtown, a five-minute taxi ride from just about all the major landmarks and communications hubs. The hotel is not far from the main business districts, whence it lays on free shuttle services. This is a warm and enjoyable boutique hotel - small, cosy, yet complete.

There's an appealing and intimate interior decor, and a blend of arty modernism with a hint of pre-war years. The 200 rooms are bright and smart, even perhaps a tad groovy despite their age. However it is the staff who are the prize asset. Helpful, cheerful and courteous, the personal Landis is

one hotel where everyone makes an effort to remember your name. The facilities are compact and sensibly limited, the restaurants reasonable and Paris 1930 in particular gets regular thumbs up for food and ambience. A health centre with sauna, rooftop jacuzzi, sundeck and massage services rounds things out nicely.

Rates from: $$
Star rating: ★ ★ ★ ★ ★
Overall rating: ◖◖◖◖ ½

Ambience:	9.18	Cleanliness:	9.23
Value:	8.68	Facilities:	8.72
Staff:	9.18	Restaurants:	8.85
Location:	8.35	Families:	8.23

Les Suites Taipei

135 Da-an Road, Section 1, Taipei 106, Taiwan
T: +886 2 8773 3799 **F**: +886 2 8773 3788
www.HotelClub.com/Hotels/Les_Suites_Taipei_Daan

Browned off with the bland uniformity of the big chains? Epoque's two Les Suites properties in Taipei offer an interesting boutique alternative. The better-known of the pair, the 90-room Ching-Cheng is tucked away behind Nanking East MRT station in the heart of the financial district, while the 59-room Da-an is likewise

discreetly located downtown.

Neither has a restaurant (though they both boast a small gym and business centre), but the residents-only lounge does breakfasts, all-day drinks and snacks and complimentary cocktails. It also acts as a sort of upmarket cyber-café, with an array of free Wi-Fi computers.

Rooms are tastefully furnished with mood lighting and muted colour schemes, and extremely high-tech, with touch-button curtain control and world-time clocks, as well as the amazing Toto toilets - three wash cycles and a warm-air dry! If you can get your head, or rather the opposite end of your anatomy, round that, you

definitely qualify as a child of the technological age.

Service is impeccable - some of the staff at the Da-an even speak Spanish, as well as Mandarin, Japanese and English. But be warned: occupancy of both hotels is high as savvy Asian business travellers have long been in on this "secret".

Rates from: $$
Star rating: ★ ★ ★ ★
Overall rating: ◖◖◖◖

Ambience:	9.00	Cleanliness:	9.17
Value:	8.00	Facilities:	8.42
Staff:	8.83	Restaurants:	7.50
Location:	8.83	Families:	7.93

Sherwood Taipei

111 Min Sheng East Road, Section 3, Taipei, Taiwan
T: +886 2 2718 1188 **F**: +886 2 2713 0707
www.HotelClub.com/Hotels/Sherwood_Hotel_Taipei

That classic Asian combination, art and money, are the dominant themes here: a fascinating if eclectic collection of Eastern and

Western art adorns the walls, while there are more than 30 international banks within a 10-minute walk of this elegant business hotel.

Its 350 rooms and suites on 20 floors are discreetly decorated in subtle colours and have sound-proofing and filtered-air systems. For added security, they are served by guest-only lifts. There are indoor and outdoor pools and fully equipped business and fitness centres.

The Toscana is many residents' choice of Italian eaterie in Taipei, George Bush Snr and Margaret Thatcher have enjoyed the fusion food at Yi Yuan, while Henry's Bar is a popular power-drinking spot.

The highlight of a stay at the Sherwood is its museum-quality original art: 18th- and 19th-century European is mingled tastefully with Chinese, classic and contemporary, and apart from the paintings there are tapestries, wall clocks, collages, woodblocks and lithographs to admire. The best-known work on show is probably Deschamps' *Le Petit Patissier*.

Rates from: $$
Star rating: ★ ★ ★ ★ ★
Overall rating: 🐾🐾🐾🐾 ½

Ambience:	8.75	Cleanliness:	9.09
Value:	8.09	Facilities:	8.49
Staff:	8.77	Restaurants:	8.53
Location:	8.48	Families:	8.09

Westin Taipei

133 Nanking East Road, Section 3, Taipei 104, Taiwan
T: +886 2 8770 6565 **F**: +886 2 8770 6555
www.HotelClub.com/Hotels/Westin_Hotel_Taipei

Looking good six years after opening, the Westin Taipei is spotlessly clean, shiny and fresh. Do not let the rather sober hospital-like exterior put you off - a step inside reveals much more imagination. This is a warm and homely hotel with a chic European ambience. The Westin is especially well put together for business travellers, with sharp and well-appointed facilities including Internet and fax hook-up in the 288 rooms, and a 184-seat auditorium. The excellent restaurants (Chinese, Japanese, Italian and international) have creative menus. Other welcome add-ons include gym, spa, sauna, and a sleek indoor swimming pool. The central

location on Nanking East Road is great for Taipei's business and financial districts and near to the metro station. The Westin is well staffed by competent and friendly professionals who run things very smoothly. Let's finish with a thunderous round of applause for the in-house cinema and its 15 snuggly sofas.

Rates from: $$$
Star rating: ★ ★ ★ ★
Overall rating: 🐾🐾🐾🐾

Ambience:	8.62	Cleanliness:	8.94
Value:	7.85	Facilities:	8.30
Staff:	8.46	Restaurants:	8.39
Location:	8.27	Families:	8.27

THAILAND

Swiftly back on its feet after the tsunami that struck prime coastal resorts like Phuket, Khao Lak and Phi Phi in 2004, Thailand is regaining its reputation as a vast holiday buffet, where visitors can gorge to their hearts' content on culture, shopping, sun, sand and several other sybaritic recreations. Better still, the kingdom is refreshingly affordable by any standards, making it a favourite for everyone from parents with children in tow to honeymooning couples to greenhorn backpackers.

Travelling executives will usually find themselves in Bangkok, where the great majority of hotels blend the Thai tradition of gracious hospitality (served up with the - usually genuine - smile that is the national marketing tool) with ultra-modern facilities. Indeed, with properties like the Amanpuri, the

Four Seasons and the 2004-opened Mandarin Oriental Chiang Mai that complements the one-and-a-quarter-century-old Oriental in Bangkok, Thailand can lay claim to hosting some of the world's most stunning hotels. In contrast, there are also many very pleasant but rather more modest and modestly priced properties, especially in the main beach resorts.

Shaped roughly like an elephant's head and trunk, the country's diverse offerings begin in the north with opportunities to trek in the jungles around Chiang Mai

and Chiang Rai and take a first-hand look at the ethnic tribes who live in the region. Bangkok, known locally as Krung Thep, has been greatly liberated by the introduction of the SkyTrain, which when combined with the ferry system is a superb way to get around the awesome temples, palaces, retail areas and restaurants - to say nothing of the nightlife. Pattaya, the resort area closest to the capital, remains more attuned to the single male than anyone else. To the south, laid-back Hua Hin has a wealth of golf courses, while the

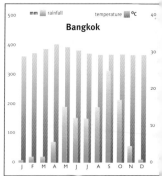

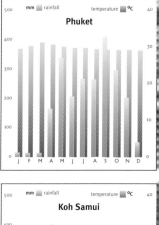

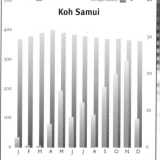

more remote Krabi entices both those who want to scale its picturesque limestone karsts or simply admire them while basking on sugar-sand beaches. The less-developed islands of Koh Samui and Koh Phangan draw the younger crowd, Phuket exercises a universal appeal with beaches, nightlife, sports and shopping, while sleepy places like Koh Lanta are attracting visitors seeking to live out the get-away-from-it-all cliché. Southern Thailand was the scene of some terrorist-related violence in 2004, however the area soon settled down. Families will welcome the news that children are always accorded special treatment by Thais, who happily drop whatever they are doing to coo over babies and natter to youngsters.

Wherever visitors end up, there will be no shortage of recreations and diversions on offer. The worldwide popularity of Thai cuisine has led many hotels to open their kitchens as cooking schools, taking guests into the markets in the morning, showing them how to prepare the food, and finishing off with a gourmet lunch or dinner. Water sports are a given at beach resorts, and mountain-biking and horse-riding provide a new way of exploring the countryside. Massage is an ancient Thai art and most major hotels now sport a spa offering a variety of body scrubs, facials and other similarly rejuvenating treatments. It needs to be said that some independent establishments use

"massage" as a cover for more adult-oriented activities and, while highly publicised official efforts have been made to curb the more outrageous side of red-light areas in Bangkok, Pattaya, Phuket and elsewhere, the sex industry continues to function. Personal indulgence remains a matter of choice, but AIDS is an acronym no one can afford to ignore.

Thailand's variable geography is mirrored by its three-season climate. The rainy season (June - October) hits Phuket and Krabi especially hard, but not Koh Samui, which faces its own monsoon between October and January. The cool season (November - February) is one of the best times to visit. And between March and May expect the temperature to rise to around 40°C. Peak visitor periods (with corresponding accommodation prices) are Christmas and Lunar New Year.

The chance to take in one of Thailand's major festivals is a real bonus; a free-for-all public water fight celebrates Songkran or Thai New Year in mid-April, an event that attracts particular fervour in Chiang Mai. December 31st is also a signal for a wild party, and Loy Kratong in November is especially picturesque as couples and children launch candle-lit floats into waterways at night.

Two Thai words - "sanuk" and "sabai" - sum up the main reasons why so many foreigners return to Thailand time and again. Sanuk

means having a good time and, whether on a beach holiday or trekking through malls or mountains, it is difficult not to have fun here. Similarly, Thailand emanates a very happy-go-lucky atmosphere. Whether you are lying prone beneath a masseur's fingertips, downing a beer in a plush bar or just watching the sun go down on a deserted beach "sabai", or taking it easy, is the watchword.

Allamanda Laguna Phuket

29 Moo 4, Srisoonthorn Road, Cherngtalay, Talang, Phuket 83110, Thailand
T: +66 76 324 359 **F**: +66 76 270 969
www.HotelClub.com/Hotels/Allamanda_Laguna_Phuket

Family friendly? The Allamanda practically invented the term, so jump into its 235 suites, which come in various different flavours. Top of the range are the triplex Allamanda Suites, each containing a double and twin bedroom with ensuite bathrooms, and capped with a rooftop deck that is tailor-made for sunbathing or evening drinks. The duplex two-bedroom suites are not quite so accessoried, but are still eminently comfortable, while the one-bedroom suites are ideal for couples and the Junior Suites just lack a dining area. Each suite contains a kitchenette and separate living area together with tidy little balconies with views of the golf course fairways, the lagoon or one of the three pools, So far, so predictable. But this resort really comes into its own with the two exclusive Kids' Suites - each adjoining an adult bedroom and specially equipped with bunk beds, games, videos and even Gameboys. Even the bathroom is brightly decorated, right down to a duck suspended from the shower head.

Suite deals apart, the Allamanda is a full-on, hands-on, on-and-on activity centre for anyone who cares to dabble in canoe tours round the lagoons (which camouflage old mine shafts beneath the entire Laguna complex), sailing lessons, Thai language lessons, aquaball and basketball, darts tournaments, water polo, croquet competitions, garland-making, paddle-boat races, frisbee tourneys, fruit-carving, coconut-bowling, bike, elephant- and horse-riding, egg-tossing, snorkelling lessons and a whole load more. Phew. Most of these are free or attract only a minimal charge, and there is also a fully functioning Camp Laguna Kids' Club to get the little tykes off your hands for a few hours.

Food gets served up here in a similarly fun, outdoorsy fashion - guests can choose from the Lagoon Grill or the Courtyard Café, or hop on a shuttle to any of the other restaurants in Laguna's four other hotels. The Allamanda is ultra-ideal for families with children in tow, and remains the most inexpensive deal in the whole of the Laguna complex.

Rates from: $
Star rating: ★ ★ ★ ★
Overall rating: ◊ ◊ ◊ ◊ ½

Ambience:	8.38	Cleanliness:	8.40
Value:	8.60	Facilities:	8.27
Staff:	8.40	Restaurants:	7.84
Location:	8.60	Families:	8.90

Amanpuri

Pansea Beach, Phuket 83000, Thailand
T: +66 76 324 333 **F**: +66 76 324 100
www.HotelClub.com/Hotels/Amanpuri_Resort_Phuket

dozen treatment salas spread across the hillside and room for everything from massage to meditation to tai chi. Spa treatments can be as simple as hand and foot massages - using reflexology to cleanse, exfoliate and invigorate. Or it might be something a little more intricate, like a lymphatic draining massage, which is recommended for stimulating the circulation. And after a long day out in the sun, a full-body treatment using yoghurt and aloe vera is the perfect skin conditioner before heading for the hushed bliss of your sea-facing villa.

Since Amanpuri started the upmarket stampede to Phuket, many other hotels have opened their doors on the island, but very few have matched its sophistication that is delivered without effort or very much in the way of pomp. Definitely a world-class classic.

This is the place that launched a thousand trips - the first of the deservedly legendary Amanresorts that is now well into its second decade. However, it's fair to say that Amanpuri's distinctive unassuming style has only improved with age. Some 40 private pavilions (go for numbers 103 or 105 for the almost hypnotic sea views) are complemented by an additional 30 villas set a little apart from the main hotel. Amanpuri means "place of peace", and as far as names go, this could hardly be more apt. Set on its own headland, looking down on

what is practically a private beach, this is a place to utterly relax, totally detox and completely wind down. Naturally, the food and beverage arrangements are everything that you would expect of an Aman - likewise the rates - but here nearly everything is perfect, from the folded towel laid just so on your lounger by the pool to the librarian's omniscient acquaintance with the 1,000-plus books and CDs under her care.

The Amanpuri idyll reached its apogee with the addition of a purpose-built spa - with a half-

Rates from: $$$$$
Star rating: ★ ★ ★ ★ ★
Overall rating: ♦♦♦♦♦

Ambience:	9.62	Cleanliness:	9.49
Value:	8.26	Facilities:	8.87
Staff:	9.35	Restaurants:	8.93
Location:	8.94	Families:	8.47

Amari Palm Reef Resort

14/3 Moo 2, Tambol Bopud, Chaweng Beach, Koh Samui, Surat Thani 84320, Thailand
T: +66 77 422 015 **F**: +66 77 422 394
www.HotelClub.com/Hotels/Amari_Palm_Reef_Resort_Samui

Sooner or later on Koh Samui everyone gravitates to Chaweng Beach. The Thai-style Amari stands at its heart. This is a resort tailor-made for parents with kids in tow, not over-large with 187 rooms and suites, but with just about everything the nuclear family might write on its vacation wish list.

The ideal accommodation lies within the 22 deluxe family duplexes, although the regular rooms all have a balcony or terrace and wide windows that seem to allow a touch of Samui inside.

Once unpacked, there is the entire resort to romp around, with two free-form pools for swimmers and two splash pools for kids, a jacuzzi and an air-conditioned squash court. The beach swarms with water sports merchants, from jet-skis to windsurfers to banana boats, and there is also a fleet of mountain bikes for hire for a little two-wheeled exploration along the Chaweng strip. The addition of the Sivara Spa rounds out the Amari nicely.

Rates from: $
Star rating: ★ ★ ★ ★
Overall rating: 🏨🏨🏨🏨 ½

Ambience:	9.22	Cleanliness:	8.78
Value:	8.26	Facilities:	8.50
Staff:	9.00	Restaurants:	8.42
Location:	8.67	Families:	8.86

Amari Watergate Hotel

847 Petchburi Road, Pratunam, Rajthevi, Bangkok 10400, Thailand
T: +66 2 653 9000 **F**: +66 2 653 9045
www.HotelClub.com/Hotels/Amari_Watergate_Hotel

Fulfilling the old dictum about "location, location, location" to the letter, the Amari Watergate's 569 rooms and suites are slap bang next to the World Trade Centre in one of Bangkok's mainstream commercial and retail areas, and within walking distance of the SkyTrain. This is a thoroughly business-friendly hotel,

the three uppermost floors are specifically dedicated to executives, and in addition to the standard 40 square metres, rooms come with 24-hour butler service and their own cocktail lounge. Conferences and meetings can be accommodated in a variety of rooms, while one Clark Hatch has

consented to add his name to the de-stress fitness centre. The pool and sun deck are similarly relaxed. Returning to the corporate theme, both Grappino, the Italian restaurant, and Heichinrou, serving Chinese fare, are well set up for business dinners or lunches, while the Henry J. Bean's offers a more relaxed atmosphere.

Rates from: $$
Star rating: ★ ★ ★ ★ ★
Overall rating: 🏨🏨🏨🏨 ½

Ambience:	8.60	Cleanliness:	8.86
Value:	8.40	Facilities:	8.42
Staff:	8.70	Restaurants:	8.57
Location:	8.73	Families:	8.46

Anantara Resort & Spa Golden Triangle

229 Moo 1, T. Wiang, Chiang Saen, Chiang Rai 57150, Thailand
T: +66 5 378 4084   **F:** +66 5 378 4090
www.HotelClub.com/Hotels/Baan_Boran_Resort_Golden_Triangle_Chiang_Rai

As just about everybody seems to know, this is where you come to learn to be a mahout, fetching your own personal pachyderm from the forest in the morning, bathing it and feeding it and learning to drive it in a fashion that would make Tarzan jungle green with envy. Eco-friendly, feel-good vacations don't come much better. There is a lot more to do here than playing jumbo jockey of course, with 90 rooms and suites hovering over what could be the acupuncture point for the Golden Triangle and views rolling out to Laos and Myanmar. Terraces leading off from the spa's treatment rooms contain flower-filled baths where you can loll to your heart's content. There's a choice of northern Thai or Italian cuisine in the restaurants, but only alcohol as an aid to recreation in the Opium Terrace Bar. Best of all is the host of cultural diversions - from gem markets to Mekong boat trips - just outside the front gate.

Rates from: $$
Star rating: ★ ★ ★ ★ ★
Overall rating: ◌ ◌ ◌ ◌ ◌

Ambience:	9.29	Cleanliness:	9.47
Value:	8.59	Facilities:	8.74
Staff:	9.12	Restaurants:	8.59
Location:	9.18	Families:	8.65

Anantara Resort & Spa Hua Hin

43/1 Phetkasem Beach Road, Hau Hin 77100, Thailand
T: +66 32 520 250   **F:** +66 32 520 259
www.HotelClub.com/Hotels/Anantara_Resort_Spa_Hua_Hin

Once a year Hua Hin goes wild for a bizarre event that rolls the Olympics, football World Cup and Barnum and Bailey's circus into one. Sports fanatics, playboys, playgirls and even a team of ladyboys jet in from around the globe for the King's Cup Elephant Polo Tournament, which ebbs and flows around the Anantara. It's fitting that such an exclusive event should be held at a very exclusive beachside hotel, which for the rest of the year provides rather more mainstream diversions for guests occupying its 187 rooms and suites.

Naturally the spa is splendid, but if you fancy something a bit more active than a facial and a massage, there is a small fleet of sailing dinghies, mountain bikes and even kickboxing classes. And there's Thai, Italian or international cuisine to restore you in time for another day at one of the region's more unusual resorts - the elephas maximus equivalent of Twickenham or Shea Stadium.

Rates from: $
Star rating: ★ ★ ★ ★ ★
Overall rating: ◌ ◌ ◌ ◌ ½

Ambience:	9.31	Cleanliness:	9.42
Value:	8.55	Facilities:	8.77
Staff:	9.14	Restaurants:	8.78
Location:	8.58	Families:	8.71

Bangkok Marriott Resort & Spa

257 Charoennakorn Road, Thonburi, Bangkok 10600, Thailand
T: +66 2 476 0022 **F:** +66 2 476 1120
www.HotelClub.com/Hotels/Marriott_Resort_and_Spa_Bangkok

Twice a week a 100-year-old teak rice barge fitted out with cabins and galley sets off from the Marriott, taking guests on a cruise for cocktails, dinner or even an overnight onboard stay at the old Thai capital Ayutthaya.

The Bangkok Marriott Resort & Spa was one of the first of the city's riverside hotels to come up with the idea of getting hold of a restored barge, and suffice to say the *Manohra Song* is a glorious way to take in the sights and sounds of Bangkok, almost as if a part of the hotel itself had been floated away on the water. And the innovation and style behind the idea are characteristic of its parent resort and spa.

Made up of some 413 rooms and suites on a five-hectare site beside the Krung Thep bridge, its only disadvantage (though some might view it as a positive - especially as there is a shuttle to the SkyTrain) is the slightly remote location, 15 minutes (depending on the traffic) from the heart of Bangkok. Rather than yet another tower block, this particular Marriott is a low-rise, quasi-colonial-style pile, spread between three buildings with the outdoor swimming pool as its centrepiece. Every room gives way to a balcony - a rarity to be treasured here in Bangkok. Within, guests may count on a gentle Thai-themed decor and all the mod cons that make life so much easier.

No-one is going to starve here either. The Marriott's healthy complement of nine restaurants and bars embraces a fair amount of theatre; there is a Thai cultural show to spice up meals at the Riverside Terrace, while the acrobatic Japanese chefs at Benihana dispense teppanyaki with a showmanship that goes hand in hand with their culinary skills, making a real feast for the eyes.

Topping off the Marriott menu is the Mandara Spa - purpose-built as a mini city escape with half a dozen treatment suites overlooking the hotel gardens dispensing therapeutic pampering by the hour, or even longer.

Rates from: $$
Star rating: ★ ★ ★ ★ ★
Overall rating: 🐾🐾🐾🐾 ½

Ambience:	9.07	Cleanliness:	9.15
Value:	8.61	Facilities:	8.71
Staff:	8.90	Restaurants:	8.87
Location:	8.36	Families:	8.72

Banyan Tree Bangkok

21/100 South Sathon Road, Bangkok 10120, Thailand
T: +66 2 679 1200 **F:** +66 2 679 1199
www.HotelClub.com/Hotels/Banyan_Tree_Hotel_Bangkok

This city hotel is very different from a Banyan Tree resort. While it doesn't really approach being a tropical paradise grafted into the middle of a sprawling capital, it is at least a drop in gear. The exterior of the tall, slim building is a little out of the ordinary, and thankfully it is set back away from the main road, drastically cutting down the noise. The interior is surprisingly dark for a building with so many windows, but the trickling waters and leafiness create that spa-like ambience for which the chain is so famed, and throughout the property are those little Banyan Tree touches such as scented incense sticks. The quiet rooms echo nature's colour scheme with brown tweed-like wallpaper, and the bathrooms are stocked with the superior accessories one comes to expect from this upmarket group.

The Banyan Tree Bangkok excels in the spa area, and boasts one of the capital's largest spa gardens. The white pebbled walls in the 23 spa rooms have soothing water cascades and wall-to-ceiling windows with some fine views over the city. Gilding the lily ever so slightly, there are also three exclusive residential spa suites - named Lavender, Champaka and Sandalwood - each with a dedicated en suite treatment room. In addition to the numerous massage and body scrubs, meditation, aerobics or aqua-aerobics classes are also on offer. To complete the picture the multi-floored spa has a jacuzzi, sauna, steam bath, dip and current pools.

The hotel has some additional bonuses like the architecturally stunning Bai Yun restaurant and the open air panoramic 61st-floor champagne and grill bar, aptly named Vertigo. For those wanting action, the hotel is just ten minutes' walk from the Silom Road shopping district and the SkyTrain. The Banyan Tree Bangkok is no doubt a small oasis of calm amid the crazy pace of the capital, and provides an unusual opportunity to be totally pampered and rejuvenated right in the centre of town.

Rates from: $$
Star rating: ★ ★ ★ ★ ★
Overall rating: ◔ ◔ ◔ ◔ ½

Ambience:	8.91	Cleanliness:	9.28
Value:	8.25	Facilities:	8.73
Staff:	8.98	Restaurants:	8.60
Location:	7.85	Families:	8.23

Banyan Tree Phuket

33 Moo 4, Srisoonthorn Road, Cherngtalay, Amphur Talang, Phuket 83110, Thailand
T: +66 76 324 374 **F**: +66 76 324 375
www.HotelClub.com/Hotels/Banyan_Tree_Resort_Phuket

Loved-up? Stressed-out? A combination of both?

Whether your stay is spread over a fortnight or a couple of nights, there is no contradicting the overwhelming sexiness of this dazzling resort's 121 villas. Kick off the duvet and throw open the bedroom doors to the pool, which is concealed from without by a high wall and extensive foliage. Plunge in together, then turn your gaze upwards. Whether the sky is a vast palette of cobalt and azure or lit by a galaxy of silver asterisks, that delirious, aqueous sensation of luxury and privacy is all utterly Banyan Tree Phuket.

Although it is part of the Laguna complex, you cannot really call this a hotel, nor a resort.

Banyan Tree was designed to reflect the most harmonious elements of an Asian village. The buildings are set in clusters, while the bathrooms are open to the elements, granting a luscious back

to nature effect. The deeply pitched roofs and open-air pavilions - salas - here characterise traditional Thai architecture, which evolved in response to the country's climate.

The overall effect is one of total tranquility, while the interiors' warm colours, rich textures, smooth surfaces and subtle fragrances create sensuous aesthetics that are simultaneously restrained yet exuberant.

Tempting though it may be to linger endlessly chez villa, with its dictator-sized bed and au naturel bathroom, there are other temptations outside. The first tee of the 18-hole, par-71 Max Wexler-designed championship golf course is more or less opposite the hotel lobby. Its undulating fairways are dotted with coconut groves and scenic lagoons while the signature hole - the 16th - enjoys glorious views of the Andaman Sea: assuming you can tear your eyes away from the 12 surrounding bunkers.

Guests who find golf a bit active can while away the days by the 40-metre pool or take classes in tai chi, batik painting or yoga. But the quintessence of the Banyan Tree Phuket lies in its spa, which is the perfect mirror for its philosophy. It is an experience that can only be described as wholly holistic. Guests are bidden to recline on massage beds draped in green and gold silk brocade. The loudest noise comes from the therapists' fingers, unknotting muscles and smoothing sinews as if they were deftly unwrapping a birthday present. At the end of their spa session, guests are gently directed to a wooden sofa (or "dang") where they are given a refreshing herbal drink and - much more importantly - time to reflect on all that they see and feel. The spa menu is nothing if not comprehensive; to a full range of massages add body treatments - perhaps a mud or a seaweed wrap - as well as a panoply of facials, waxing and hair care. Not signing up for a seven-hour programme, which includes lunch at the Tamarind Spa Restaurant, takes a lot of will power.

The Tamarind's cuisine places due emphasis on healthy eating and carefully balanced dishes, but if you need to offset somewhat the effects of being cleansed inside and out at the spa, there are seven other restaurants and bars featuring international and Thai food as well as numerous other options at the other four Laguna sister resorts. Best option of all is to order up a fully fledged barbecue - or even a simple sandwich - back in that haven, your villa.

Rates from: $$$$	
Star rating: ★ ★ ★ ★ ★	
Overall rating: ♻ ♻ ♻ ♻ ½	
Ambience: 9.23	Cleanliness: 9.20
Value: 7.86	Facilities: 8.86
Staff: 9.09	Restaurants: 8.45
Location: 8.46	Families: 8.62

Central Samui Beach Resort

38/2 Moo 3, Borpud Chewang Beach, Koh Samui, Surat Thani 84320, Thailand
T: +66 77 230 500 **F**: +66 77 422 385
www.HotelClub.com/Hotels/Central_Samui_Beach_Resort

Wander along the beach past the Central Samui Beach Resort, you could easily be led astray by the exterior - an unusual mélange of lofty, stark white columns and glass capped by brick-red roof tiles. A coconut expo centre? A museum dedicated to hedonism? Well, both are partly right. Central is not unacquainted with the pursuit of pleasure, and the island's signature fruit crops up regularly in both the resort's cocktails and cuisine - and of course there are a fair few palm trees dotted around the grounds.

Central is big and bursting with energy. Its four storeys contain 208 rooms and suites, all facing the ocean and all tastefully and freshly decorated in a style that is both island and international. The pool

forms the resort's focus - a huge stretch of water that is big enough for an Olympic-style water-polo match yet with semi-concealed channels and jacuzzis where couples can snuggle up together. It also features the Dip & Sip, a swim-up bar where guests can stop for a drink and a snack with their feet still dangling in the water.

Elsewhere, there are playrooms and special pools for children, two tennis courts and a deluxe spa with treatments tailored specifically for men, women and couples.

Despite the sporting and recreational facilities on offer, and the chance to swim in or walk by the ocean, anyone arriving at Central and planning to lose a bit of weight by the end of the holiday should think again. Of the resort's

nine restaurants and bars, Hagi's Japanese is utterly authentic and equally delicious, Spice Island serves up traditional and sometimes fiery Thai, the Seabreeze terrace offers great beach views and Surfers provides a heady mix of drinks, Internet access and a wide-screen TV for international sporting events. Central may be pretty mainstream, but it's pretty good fun too.

Rates from: $$
Star rating: ★ ★ ★ ★ ★
Overall rating: 🐚🐚🐚🐚½

Ambience:	9.03	Cleanliness:	8.87
Value:	8.55	Facilities:	8.36
Staff:	8.68	Restaurants:	8.47
Location:	9.02	Families:	8.90

The Chedi Phuket

118 Moo 3, Pansea Beach, Cherngtalay, Amphur Thalang, Phuket 83110, Thailand
T: +66 76 324 017 **F:** +66 76 324 252
www.HotelClub.com/Hotels/Chedi_Hotel_Phuket

No need to feel that your tropical beach cred is lacking because you're staying here rather than at the Amanpuri up the road. The Chedi enjoys similar if not quite such highfalutin' facilities, and is unlikely to cause you to take a deep breath when you come to pay your bill at the end of your stay. It is also a touch more down to earth, with a less rarefied atmosphere. Rather than design-diva villas, the Chedi puts its guests up in thatched cottages, the sort of place you might hope to borrow from a well-placed friend or distant relation. The accommodation is carefully spaced up the steep hillside that

rises from Pansea Beach - the 89 one-bedroom cottages are fine for a couple even with a child in tow, and there are 19 with two bedrooms which can happily take in your average mum, dad and 2.4 children. Each cottage has its own sundeck, and the interior design - panels of woven palm fronds and earthen-coloured fabrics - brings the outdoors inside. All in all, this is a resort that is at one with nature.

With a swimming pool dramatically tiled in black, a brace of tennis courts and a full fleet of water sports facilities, the Chedi's corporate side is easy to overlook. The floor-to-ceiling windows of the

50-square-metre conference room provide a sensational backdrop and there is a phalanx of audio-visual equipment on hand as well. That five international-standard golf courses - where, after all, most deals are clinched anyway - lie within 30 minutes' drive of the Chedi's front door can only be an additional incentive.

A word of warning - not many guests leave the Chedi weighing less than when they arrived. This is largely due to the Thai and Asian specialities served beneath the soaring rafters of the Lomtalay restaurant, which overlooks the Andaman Sea and remains one of the best locations to dine on the island.

Rates from: $$
Star rating: ★ ★ ★ ★
Overall rating: ◊ ◊ ◊ ◊ ½

Ambience:	9.00	Cleanliness:	9.05
Value:	8.51	Facilities:	8.38
Staff:	9.25	Restaurants:	8.22
Location:	8.89	Families:	8.51

Chiva-Som International Health Resort

73/4 Petchkasem Road, Hua Hin, Prachuabkhirikhan 77110, Thailand
T: +66 32 536 536 **F**: +66 32 511 154
www.HotelClub.com/Hotels/Chom_View_Hotel_Hua_Hin

The Alpha Male (and Female) of Thai signature spas, Chiva-Som continues to go from strength to strength. Primarily a spa rather than a hotel - as opposed to vice versa - its plethora of treatment rooms remain its centrepiece and core competency with 57 pavilions - a refreshing blend of Thai-tinged elegance and simplicity - clustered around about.

As the first purpose-built health resort in Asia, it has enjoyed a distinct measure of success (even the Beckhams have stayed). Many of Chiva-Som's treatments and facilities are unrivalled anywhere else in the region, so guests are free to therapy themselves as healthily as imaginable, but they can also simply sit back and enjoy being surrounded by three hectares of lush gardens right on the beach at Hua Hin. It is not by any means a "fat farm" - the dishes at the buffet (steak - yes, chips - no) are discreetly labelled for calorie content and avoid oily cooking fats, but no one is weighing up how many times you go back and forth. There are some house rules, though - children under 16 and mobile phones are forbidden, as is smoking, except in designated areas, coffee is frowned upon and a limited alcohol selection is available in the evenings.

Visits to Chiva-Som start with an informal check-up, a mild holistic assessment of your fitness chiefly to advise on the best treatments to go for, whether deep tissue massage or an eyelash tint. As in the restaurant, no one is brandishing a list of rules and regulations, and you are free to pick and choose whether your stay is ultra active or downright idle. With 80-plus treatments and activities from lifestyle coaching to traditional Chinese acupuncture, the choice is extensive. Lying suspended in salt water in the flotation suite, it is very difficult to avoid drifting off to sleep - surely one of the most relaxing therapies available anywhere. Slightly higher on the vigor-ometer, you can indulge in tai chi, yoga lessons, Pilates sessions, a bit of sea kayaking or take out all your pent-up frustrations with a bout of Thai boxing. Programmes are typically one-on-one and tailored to the individual, although some sessions offer group therapy - or maybe peer pressure.

Rates from: $$$$
Star rating: ★ ★ ★ ★ ★
Overall rating: 🌸🌸🌸🌸 ½

Ambience:	9.16	Cleanliness:	9.08
Value:	8.72	Facilities:	8.23
Staff:	9.40	Restaurants:	8.48
Location:	7.96	Families:	7.59

Conrad Bangkok Hotel

87 Wireless Road, Pathumwan, Lumpini, Bangkok 10330, Thailand
T: +66 2 690 9999   **F**: +66 2 690 9000
www.HotelClub.com/Hotels/Conrad_Hotel_Bangkok

Chinese or the Photoshop splendours of 87, which describes itself as a "Cuisine Lounge Studio Club". There's loads of fun to be had with the fitness facilities too, from the rooftop jogging track to the spa's dozen treatment salons. The hotel describes itself as funky and unconventionally stylish - no arguments with that.

Every so often in Bangkok a new hotel opens that is just so good even its competitors have to purse their lips and nod in admiration. So it was with the Conrad in March 2003. Perhaps the best way to sum it up is "Wow Factor". Just about everywhere you wander in this arresting 392-room property there's an occasion to perform a double-take. Thai silks and wood predominate in the sleeping quarters - the deluxe corner rooms are especially well fitted-out. Each of the restaurants and bars has a bold, individual style, be it the Japanese Drinking Tea Eating Rice, the culinary high-jinks of Liu's

Rates from: $$$
Star rating: ★ ★ ★ ★ ★
Overall rating: ♨ ♨ ♨ ♨ ½

Ambience:	8.91	Cleanliness:	9.38
Value:	8.41	Facilities:	8.82
Staff:	8.87	Restaurants:	8.74
Location:	8.37	Families:	8.46

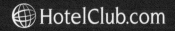

Dusit Laguna Resort Hotel

390 Srisoontorn Road, Cherngtalay, Amphur Talang, Phuket 83110, Thailand
T: +66 76 324 324 **F**: +66 76 324 174
www.HotelClub.com/Hotels/Dusit_Laguna_Phuket

The Dusit was the first of the hotels to rise like a phoenix from the ashes of the abandoned tin mines on Bang Tao Bay. And one eco-triumphant, multi-million dollar restoration project later, it remains one of the leading resorts among the lagoons of Laguna, or indeed the whole island.

Despite having opened its doors in 1987, the resort is far from showing its age. Its 226 balconied rooms and suites have a fresh, clean feel to them, and the Dusit is so laid out that it is only a short walk to the half-dozen restaurants, the multi-taskable recreation centre

including the Busy Bee Kids' Klub or the glories of the isolated Bang Tao Beach, which runs for kilometres in either direction. Plus there is the added merit of being able to hop aboard the shuttle boat which putters around the rest of 400-hectare Laguna site.

Set right next to the sea, the Dusit is unique among the Laguna properties in having a wide and shady lawn between its pool and the beach. With a calm, restful air, this is somewhere to chill, submit to an outdoor massage, drink fresh coconut juice straight from the husk, or laze for a while out of

range of the ultraviolets. It may seem bizarre to think of anything but rest and recreation here. However, the Dusit also holds three large meeting halls and a slightly smaller function room, all adaptable to various business needs and is popular with conventioneers and incentivees.

Whether here on business or pleasure, guests can be sure of eating exceptionally well. There is a choice of royal Thai cuisine - once the exclusive preserve of the upper crust but now available to all and sundry - at Ruenthai, or traditional Italian at La Trattoria. But quite the most "Dusit" of the resort's eateries is the Casuarina Hut, a lovely al fresco location dishing up the freshest seafood and barbecues.

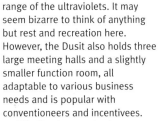

Rates from: $
Star rating: ★ ★ ★ ★ ★
Overall rating: ♌ ♌ ♌ ♌ ♌

Ambience:	9.32	Cleanliness:	9.13
Value:	8.62	Facilities:	8.54
Staff:	9.16	Restaurants:	8.52
Location:	8.94	Families:	9.21

Dusit Resort Hua Hin

1349 Petchkasem Road, Cha-am, Petchburi 76120, Thailand
T: +66 32 442 100 **F**: +66 32 520 296
www.HotelClub.com/Hotels/Dusit_Resort_and_Polo_Club_ChaAm

Although the resort's full name is the Dusit Resort & Polo Club, it is not even an open secret that there is actually no such thing as a polo club, so put aside any thought of getting in a few chukkas on the coast. The resort does have its own stables, though, but the old polo pitch is sadly set aside for more sedate cricket matches. There are few more exhilarating ways to greet a new day than to saddle up and go for a leisurely canter along the beach, with the sounds of rolling surf and the measured thud of hooves mixing with the fresh dawn breeze. You do not have to be an accomplished equestrian either -

both the Dusit's grooms and the horses they care for are used to novice riders, and will set the pace accordingly.

And you can set your own pace in the rest of this very well tended resort nestling outside Cha-am, some 15 minutes from Hua Hin town. The equine theme runs throughout the hotel, with polo sticks for door handles, bellboys in jodhpurs and the horsebox-style corridors. Doubtless you could bed down on straw if you asked, but in fact the 300 rooms and suites are supremely comfortable, and all equipped with their own balcony. Grab a sea-facer if you can, as the

views down over the pools - each with a palm-tree'd mini-island in the centre - and out to sea is worth a 24-channel TV any day.

No real surprises that the resort's main drinking hole is called the Polo Bar, but there is a live band here playing "the sound of surprise" with a good mixture of blues every night. On the food side, the royal Thai cuisine at Ban Benjarong by the lagoon is indeed fit for a King while San Marco serves up pizza and pasta in a casual terrace setting, and international fare is served at the Palm Court. Finally, the long-anticipated Devarana Spa is now up and running, if that's an appropriate phrase for somewhere you spend most of your time supine.

Rates from: $$
Star rating: ★ ★ ★ ★
Overall rating: 🌙🌙🌙🌙 ½

Ambience:	9.13	Cleanliness:	9.28
Value:	8.55	Facilities:	8.82
Staff:	9.06	Restaurants:	8.89
Location:	8.62	Families:	9.14

Dusit Resort Pattaya

40/2 Pattaya Beach Road, Pattaya City, Chonburi 20150, Thailand
: +66 38 425 611 **F**: +66 38 428 239
www.HotelClub.com/Hotels/Dusit_Resort_Pattaya

one Chinese restaurant and two serving international fare make the whole resort very user-friendly. The entertainment side is cranked up a final notch by the Devarana ("garden in heaven") Spa. The hotel is of modern design, so expect concrete and glass rather than anything too traditionally Thai.

The initial raison d'être of "Pattaya Resort Inc" was to provide sun-n-fun R&R for American troops on leave from the Vietnam War, and it is similar diversions that keep hotels like the Dusit doing a thriving trade, though its extensive convention facilities do more than their fair share to attract the corporate crowd. What you get for your baht is a smart, 462-roomer, set at the northern end of the beach away from the whirligig entertainments of the city centre. Two swimming pools - a lap and a lagoon - a sports club, a fitness centre containing gym, sauna and steam rooms, tennis courts, and

Rates from: $$
Star rating: ★ ★ ★ ★ ★
Overall rating: ◐◐◐◐ ½

Ambience:	9.21	Cleanliness:	9.02
Value:	8.51	Facilities:	8.75
Staff:	8.72	Restaurants:	8.83
Location:	8.77	Families:	8.78

Dusit Thani Hotel

946 Rama IV Road, Silom, Bangkok 10500, Thailand
T: +66 2 200 9000 **F**: +66 2 236 6400
www.HotelClub.com/Hotels/Dusit_Thani_Hotel_Bangkok

butler service. Adjacent to the lobby, the cocktail lounge, MyBar, with its live jazz and silky blues is one of the trendy venues in Bangkok. And the hexagonal outdoor swimming pool provides a sunny counterpoint to the fitness club. In short, this is a hotel that is hard to fault for its age.

If you want a classic Thai city five-star, 35 years old and stronger than ever, then shoulder your way into the Dusit Thani Bangkok. Sandwiched between Rama IV, Silom and Sathorn Roads, its 517 sumptuous rooms and suites - decorated with silks and teak - dozen bars and restaurants, heavenly garden spa, and golf driving school and range (plus resident professional) make it an ideal pied-à-terre. Executives will approve the ballroom and attendant meeting rooms' audio visual and similar add-ons. Other facets that deserve to be singled out include the 59-square-metre Dusit Grand rooms - rarely do they come larger - and the 24-hour

Rates from: $$
Star rating: ★ ★ ★ ★ ★
Overall rating: ◐◐◐◐ ½

Ambience:	8.96	Cleanliness:	9.12
Value:	8.63	Facilities:	8.72
Staff:	9.09	Restaurants:	8.89
Location:	8.97	Families:	8.74

Evason Hua Hin Resort & Spa

9 Moo 3, Paknampran, Pranburi, Prachaupkhirikhan 77220, Thailand
T: +66 32 632 111 **F:** +66 32 632 112
www.HotelClub.com/Hotels/Evason_Hua_Hin_Resort_Spa_Hua_Hin

Twenty minutes' drive south of Hua Hin, guests might be content never venturing out of this self-contained resort. Fronted by a beach with shingle-like sand, the infinity-edged pool - or private plunge pools, if you check into one of the 40 or so luxury villas - is all the more appealing. Or you can sprawl on floor cushions on the breezy upper level of the The Bar - overlooking both main pool and sea; a prime spot for sundowners. Poolside, ivory silk-clad staff blend with the minimalist facade of the adjacent Other Restaurant - where mostly Mediterranean and Thai fare looks and tastes great. Otherwise on the culinary side The Restaurant and The Beach Restaurant are the definitive articles. Eight courts should keep tennis fans content. And a Six Senses spa, with open-air treatment pavilions, offers a long list of pampering options. Rooms and villas are simply decorated, incorporating bamboo and red roof tiling; quirky details such as outdoor umbrella stands are a signature of the group's designer, Eva Shivdasani.

Rates from: $
Star rating: ★ ★ ★ ★ ★
Overall rating: ○○○○ ½

Ambience:	9.19	Cleanliness:	9.19
Value:	8.47	Facilities:	8.53
Staff:	8.77	Restaurants:	8.42
Location:	7.74	Families:	8.77

Evason Phuket Resort & Spa

100 Vised Road, Muang, Phuket 83100, Thailand
T: +66 76 381 010 **F:** +66 76 381 018
www.HotelClub.com/Hotels/Evason_Phuket_Resort_and_Spa_Phuket

What happens when a clunky old three-star gets a TV-style makeover? Look no further than the Evason, well away from anywhere else in Phuket and sporting its own private island - Ko Bon - whose lovely beach is topped by a singular honeymoon villa. It's amazing what can be done with a bit of imagination and taste. This is best exemplified in the spa area - previously home to a pile of tired mattresses and ditto masseuses - and now a glorious set of treatment rooms dedicated to the art of pampering. There are quite a lot of steps at this hillside property, but the grounds are a delight and there's always space at one of the three pools or on the beach on Ko Bon. Non-newlyweds can hole up in one of the 260 spacious and cleverly decorated rooms or ultra-private pool villas; the picture's filled out with Thai, international and fusion restaurants. This sort of healing recipe could be applied to so many other hotels in the region.

Rates from: $$
Star rating: ★ ★ ★ ★ ★
Overall rating: ○○○○ ½

Ambience:	9.13	Cleanliness:	8.93
Value:	8.64	Facilities:	8.55
Staff:	8.54	Restaurants:	8.22
Location:	7.90	Families:	8.55

Four Seasons Bangkok

55 Rajadamri Road, Bangkok 10330, Thailand
: +66 2 250 1000 **F:** +66 2 253 9195
www.HotelClub.com/Hotels/Four_Seasons_Hotel_Bangkok

A rose by any other name and all that jazz ... this used to be called the Regent. Now it goes under the Four Seasons moniker. Look for any other changes at this marvellous 21st-century version of a caravanserai and you would be hard pressed to find a single one. Few hotels combine the aura of luxury with the business of efficiency and the art of relaxation so seamlessly.

Kick back over a drink at Aqua, the semi-outdoor bar in the hotel's spruce shopping arcade, and before long a brace of Mandarin ducks will be wandering along from the nearby pond to cadge a few peanuts. Stroll over to the concierge and pick his brains for a tailor-made shopping itinerary. Or smack your lips over the celadon pots of sauces from the Spice Market restaurant. Natural, original, inspirational, this hotel has a wealth of unusual ideas that it never hesitates to share with its guests. Next to the SkyTrain and opposite a nine-hole golf course, the Four Seasons' 340 rooms (including 33 suites and eight rather unusual garden cabanas) each feature hand-painted silk murals and digital telephones, blending the best of Thai art with modern technology.

Of course this is a natural bolt-hole for executives, but a special mention needs to be directed towards the leisure facilities which embrace a 25-metre outdoor jungly pool and sundeck, whistles-and-bells gym and very superior spa. Youngsters will rather enjoy checking in here, as they get a gift on arrival, special kids' toiletries and bathrobes and milk and cookies at turndown. As any marketing executive will tell you, there is nothing like building brand loyalty at an early age.

A final word of praise for the pastry chef's brigade whose truly amazing creations - it is pretty much universally agreed - refresh the parts others cannot reach.

Rates from: $$
Star rating: ★ ★ ★ ★ ★
Overall rating: ◊ ◊ ◊ ◊ ½

Ambience:	8.97	Cleanliness:	9.24
Value:	8.36	Facilities:	8.61
Staff:	9.13	Restaurants:	8.91
Location:	8.93	Families:	8.51

Four Seasons Resort Chiang Mai

502 Maerim-Samoeng (Old) Road, T. Rimtai A. Maerim, Chiang Mai 50180, Thailand
T: +66 53 298 181   **F:** +66 53 298 190
www.HotelClub.com/Hotels/Four_Seasons_Resort_Chiang_Mai

Think northern Thailand and the images that spring to mind are of hill tribes in ethnic dress, elephant treks through dense jungle, antiques, art and culture. All of these come together in an ethos brilliantly celebrated by the Four Seasons, where 80 Lanna-style pavilions merge into the paddy fields and groves of trees in a picturesque river valley outside the kingdom's second city.

The pavilions are more like mini palaces than anything else. The regular suites are some 70 square metres, filled with locally made furniture and textiles, and with a luxurious bathroom and private verandah-style sala that simply invite languorous lazing. The largest of the Residence Suites covers nearly 530 square metres, encompassing three bedrooms,

lounge, dining room, kitchen and a live-in mae baan, or housekeeper, who is on 24-hour call. The air is soft and fresh here, and there is little noise to disturb the idyllic panoramas that lie outside every pavilion.

The main restaurant, Sala Mae Rim, provides similar vistas. With its high gabled ceiling and exposed beams, rich tapestries, crafted teak tables and cane-backed colonial dining chairs, the room exudes a sophisticated but rustic atmosphere. This then is the place to dine on northern Thai cuisine, and signature dishes such as Yum Hua Plee (banana blossom salad), Kaow Soi Kai - Chiang Mai's own version of curry noodle soup with chicken - or Thom Som, a robustly flavoured sea bass cooked in young tamarind leaves and coriander root.

For a more casual snack, afternoon tea or a couple of drinks in the evening, the open pavilion-style Elephant Bar is the perfect place to relax after an active day of sightseeing and elephant-trekking.

Rest and recuperation being the predominant theme here, guests can pick up a few tips from the resident tennis professional, work out on the strength and cardiovascular equipment in the fitness centre, shoot a few holes in one of three world-class golf courses nearby, go horse-riding or ballooning (October to March) or

drop in on the resort's cooking or language schools - both very informal and fun. And if all that seems overly active, the Lanna Spa provides everything from couples' tropical rain-shower massage tables to its own beauty salon. Rather than treating it as a mere adjunct to other leisure facilities, the resort has really gone to town on making the spa a major attraction. Housed in a magnificent three-storey building, it covers some 900 square metres and is practically camouflaged by the surrounding lush tropical vegetation. The treatment suites are elegant and exceedingly spacious, offering total privacy for individuals or couples. You can shower outdoors in a secluded garden, or gently poach yourself with a variety of herbs inside a steam room, while there are also romantic tubs quite big enough for two where you can soak al fresco. The individual changing areas, showers and bathroom facilities in all the treatment suites grant extra privacy.

The Spa offers an eclectic range of treatments that make extensive

use of Thai herbs and aromatic oils, sourced from their traditional rural origins. Most indulgent of all are the "Spa Rituals", lasting three or four hours, which combine herbal steam with massage, body scrubs, wraps, facial treatments, and hair care - total pampering packages for the body, mind and spirit.

And as a souvenir both of your time in the spa and at the Regent you can always purchase any of the range of aromatic oils,

essential oils, soaps, candles, incense - or even the spa robes and slippers.

Rates from: $$$$
Star rating: ★ ★ ★ ★ ★
Overall rating: 🐾🐾🐾🐾🐾

Ambience:	9.57	Cleanliness:	9.59
Value:	8.06	Facilities:	8.71
Staff:	9.31	Restaurants:	8.57
Location:	8.55	Families:	8.43

Grand Hyatt Erawan Bangkok

494 Rajdamri Road, Bangkok 10330, Thailand
T: +66 2 254 234 **F:** +66 2 254 6308
www.HotelClub.com/Hotels/Grand_Hyatt_Erawan_Hotel_Bangkok

One of Bangkok's more venerable hotels, the Grand Hyatt takes its cue from the shrine on the street at its northwestern corner, which was installed to ward off ill fortune during the original Erawan Hotel's construction half a century ago. Every day, thousands of supplicants pray that the deity Than Tao Mahaprom will grant their wishes, draping his golden image in garlands of marigolds and jasmine or paying the resident troupe of classical dancers to perform as a mark of gratitude. Right next to one of the city's most

hectic intersections, the shrine is a picturesque haven of serenity. The same might also be said of the Grand Hyatt, which has adopted the Brahma god's personal vehicle, the three-headed Erawan elephant, as its logo.

It's fair to say that the Hyatt's 380 rooms go the extra mile that executives on a marathon trip should appreciate. The glass-topped desk is right next to the window, and backed by a full-length mirror that not only makes the room look bigger but also reflects natural light. The decor is

subtle, subdued and thoroughly functional with a convenient bedside control panel set against the lacquered coconut-shell headboard.

Essentially spiritual, decidedly comfortable, eminently practical, the Grand Hyatt also offers up a rooftop heliport for high-flyers, three club floors, a smart fitness spa plus outdoor swimming pool and walkways to adjacent shopping centres and the mass transit system. Of the eight restaurants and bars, You & Mee is a refreshingly unusual concept, serving noodles and congee as an alternative to a full meal. But pride of place must go to Spasso, which masquerades as an Italian restaurant by day but come late evening transmogrifies into a high-decibel live music joint with more than a little boy-meets-girl thrown into the mix.

Rates from: $$
Star rating: ★ ★ ★ ★ ★
Overall rating: ◖◖◖◖ ½

Ambience:	8.93	Cleanliness:	9.07
Value:	8.15	Facilities:	8.62
Staff:	8.93	Restaurants:	8.83
Location:	9.14	Families:	8.49

Hard Rock Hotel Pattaya

429 Moo 9, Pattaya Beach Road, Chonburi 20260, Thailand
T: +66 38 428 755   **F:** +66 38 421 763
www.HotelClub.com/Hotels/Hard_Rock_Hotel_Pattaya

This brash and totally unabashed pile segues perfectly into sun-'n'-fun Pattaya, with its much-touted promise of non-stop rollicking entertainment. More a club plus beds than regular hotel, the Hard Rock's 320 rooms certainly raise a smile - with relentless musical references and nothing left un-logo'd. While it might not be first choice for some starchier corporate get-togethers, the hotel's meeting rooms (how best to put this?) rock. Perhaps it's easier to brainstorm in the Stones or Zeppelin rooms, and who needs a boring old ballroom when you've got a 400-square-metre Hall of Fame? Naturally after-hours dance parties with churning suds two metres deep are all part of the deal. The food is always going to be burger-style predictable or snacks in the eBar Internet café. Those seeking a touch of solitude will be glad to find that the beat goes off in the spa, which is far superior to many similar establishments in town.

Rates from: $
Star rating: ★ ★ ★ ★
Overall rating: 🐾🐾🐾🐾

Ambience:	8.43	Cleanliness:	8.65
Value:	8.16	Facilities:	8.43
Staff:	8.59	Restaurants:	8.35
Location:	8.27	Families:	8.84

Hilton Hua Hin Resort & Spa

33 Naresdamri Road, Hua Hin, Prachuabkhririkhan 77110, Thailand
T: +66 32 512 888   **F:** +66 32 511 135
www.HotelClub.com/Hotels/Hilton_Resort_Spa_Hua_Hin

Long a major landmark on the Hua Hin waterfront, this towering 296-room hotel has blossomed under the Hilton brand and also with the benefit of a major renovation.

The rooms are large, and by no means conventionally decorated as there is no writing desk - who needs to write when they're on holiday? The spa - inevitably touting its "royal" massage - is well-proportioned and thoroughly up to date. And on the real recreation side, the only brew house in town serves up the likes of Sabai Sabai Wheat Ale, Dancing Monkey Lager and Elephant Tusk Ale.

Right on the beach (probably the best one in the area), the Hilton is also in the very centre of town, and a few steps outside the front gate lead to a maze of lanes filled with characterful bars and eateries. Thanks to Hua Hin's royal connections, the "adult" nightlife is kept to a minimum, making this an excellent family hotel.

Rates from: $
Star rating: ★ ★ ★ ★ ★
Overall rating: 🐾🐾🐾🐾 ½

Ambience:	8.98	Cleanliness:	9.12
Value:	8.77	Facilities:	8.72
Staff:	8.88	Restaurants:	8.76
Location:	9.00	Families:	9.16

Holiday Inn Resort Phuket

52 Thaweewong Road, Patong Beach, Phuket 83150, Thailand
T: +66 76 340 608 **F:** +66 76 340 435
www.HotelClub.com/Hotels/Holiday_Inn_Resort_Phuket

Mainstream Americana hotel makes it to Asia's Best 400: huh? The Holiday Inn may seem an unusual choice, but this Patong property is one of those rare beings - a resort that is first and foremost highly adaptable. To start with, it is not really one hotel but three. To the main building's 265 rooms add the Busakorn Wing, with 104 studios, and then pile on 36 villa-style suites. Given that the Holiday Inn is at the southern end of Patong Beach (somewhere you "get into" rather than "get away from" it all), the resort's semi-oasis status is a cause for celebration.

Executives might be tempted by the Holiday Inn's modest yet adequate business facilities - two conference rooms and a fully equipped business centre. Libertines will be happy to know it is only a short stagger to the adult playground called Soi Bangla. But this is primarily a resort that families can fit into seamlessly. So popular are the specially designed Kids' Suites (room within a room featuring bunkbeds, TV and PlayStation) and Family Suites (connecting themed rooms) that they are difficult to book. The Busakorn Wing, with its own swimming pool, is preserved for those wishing to escape the din of children, while the villa rooms have their own private swimming facilities, making an ideal retreat for couples. Guests can enjoy the two free-form pools with swim-up bars and shallow pools for kids. Even the most furiously sulky teenagers might deign to admit that Club 12+ - with Internet, movie lounge, MTV, games and books - is "alright", while their younger siblings can be safely occupied in the Kids' Club. Which leaves parents as carefree as in pre-progeny days to kick back, partake of Sam's Steakhouse or the pizzeria, dip into the 13-room (six specially for couples) Aspara Spa, or even make the trek to the beach just a few steps away.

Rates from: $
Star rating: ★ ★ ★ ★
Overall rating: ◗◗◗◗ ½

Ambience:	8.78	Cleanliness:	8.97
Value:	8.69	Facilities:	8.55
Staff:	9.02	Restaurants:	8.54
Location:	9.06	Families:	9.02

Hyatt Regency Hua Hin

91 Hua Hin-Khao Takiap Road, Hua Hin, Prachuapkhirikhan 77110 Thailand
T: +66 32 521 234   **F**: +66 32 521 223
www.HotelClub.com/Hotels/Hyatt_Regency_Hua_Hin

A relatively new arrival, this 204-room property very soon became recognised as one of the most hospitable hostelries along Hua Hin's welcoming strand. The ground floor rooms feature an extended living area, while those on the upper storeys get their own balcony. Central to the hotel, and also to enjoying yourself here are the pools, which include a fast flowing "river" system, a waterfall and a slide seven metres high and 22 long - guaranteed to bring out the nine-year-old in everyone.

Food stresses fun rather more than gourmet dining, with a choice of Mediterranean, home-style Thai and the ultra-casual You & Mee Noodle Shop.

Adding a spa to the hotel's luxuriant five hectares - offering everything from Thai massage to wholly holistic treatments - rounded out the resort into a true haven of rest and relaxation. Anyone new to Hua Hin or Hyatt is in for a splendid treat.

Rates from: $
Star rating: ★ ★ ★ ★ ★
Overall rating: ◔◔◔◔ ½

Ambience:	9.21	Cleanliness:	9.05
Value:	8.64	Facilities:	8.69
Staff:	9.02	Restaurants:	8.46
Location:	8.48	Families:	9.28

JW Marriott Hotel Bangkok

4 Sukhumvit Road, Soi 2, Bangkok 10110, Thailand
T: +66 2 656 7700 **F**: +66 2 656 7711
www.HotelClub.com/Hotels/JW_Marriott_Hotel_Bangkok

This particular Marriott has garnered a select bunch of fans over the years. Some guests rave about its 441 "exec-slick" rooms, specially designed for business travellers living out of a suitcase and off their laptops. Others refer to it as "Sukhumvit Central" in praise of its convenient location. Still others wax lyrical about its outdoor pool and sixth-floor indoor spa. But a lot make little comment at all, the reason being they are fully occupied with the hotel's food and beverage operations, which they cite as the prime reason for staying here.

Speaking of prime, the New York Steakhouse delivers quite outstanding cuts of beef, while the White Elephant is something of a misnomer, serving Thai food that is as delicious as it is authentic. And for an all-round, all-day, all-you-can-eat breakfast, lunch or dinner, call in at the Marriott Café buffet, winner of many local dining awards.

Rates from: $$
Star rating: ★ ★ ★ ★ ★
Overall rating: ◔◔◔◔ ½

Ambience:	8.88	Cleanliness:	9.17
Value:	8.40	Facilities:	8.62
Staff:	8.98	Restaurants:	8.81
Location:	8.80	Families:	8.61

JW Marriott Phuket Resort & Spa

231 Moo 3, Mai Khao, Talang, Phuket 83110, Thailand
T: +66 76 338 000   **F:** +66 76 348 348
www.HotelClub.com/Hotels/JW_Marriott_Phuket_Resort_and_Spa

You might be fresh off the plane on your first-ever visit to Phuket. Or you might have been here so often you know the island as well as you do your own home town. Check in at the breezy lobby and your eye keeps getting drawn away from the forms you are supposed to be filling in to the Reflecting Pond that is flanked by graceful colonnades and stretches away toward the horizon with a vista that bids a glorious welcome to what - quite without hyperbole - could be described an Andaman Arcadia.

Nothing could set the tone better at this 265-room resort, which lies north of the airport, well away from the more popular areas on Phuket, on Mai Khao beach, which is still used by turtles as a hatchery.

Wander about the JW, and there's an endless train of fun features to discover. A sala covers the waterslide into the children's pool, which is ringed by turtle statues. The resort's chefs fill the Siam Deli with a host of goodies that beg to be taken on a picnic or home as a souvenir. The Mandara

spa, one of a chain that shows no drop in standards for all its stretching around the world, gives new meaning to the terms oasis and haven. The Royal Suite is as regally appointed as you would expect, however even the bottom-of-the-range deluxe room includes a cushioned platform (as opposed to a dreary old sofa) where you can loll for ages. And if you want to wander off into the 11 hectares of lush tropical gardens which surround this elegant low-rise hotel, they are set about with peaceful salas where you can conduct your own private retreat.

No commentary on this resort would be complete without a measure of praise for the food and beverage operation; whether dining on Japanese, Italian or Thai in the speciality restaurants you simply can't go wrong.

Rates from: $$
Star rating: ★ ★ ★ ★ ★
Overall rating: ♗ ♗ ♗ ♗ ♗ ½

Ambience:	9.27	Cleanliness:	9.31
Value:	8.47	Facilities:	8.85
Staff:	9.00	Restaurants:	8.70
Location:	7.92	Families:	9.04

August 06

Laguna Beach Resort ✓

Bangtao Bay, Phuket 83110, Thailand
T: +66 76 324 352 **F**: +66 76 324 353
www.HotelClub.com/Hotels/Laguna_Beach_Resort_Phuket

Cue mammoth burst of applause for this cheerful resort and its 254 generous balconied rooms and suites. Laguna Beach's seven-year-old pet elephant Nong Puggy, the colourfully designed children's playground, the breezy informality of the Andaman Pool Bistro (one of five bars and restaurants), the proximity of the Angsana Spa with its 28 exclusive treatments - all contribute to one of the most relaxed and fun of the five Laguna properties. There is a wealth of different recreational activities, including a 1.5-hectare water park feature incorporating a 50-metre waterslide, three outdoor and one indoor tennis courts, golf driving range, squash, sailing, windsurfing or snorkelling lessons, and even a scuba session in the dive pool - all at no extra cost. Even the kids (four to 12 year olds) have a full daily programme of outings and activities, and there's a special camp for older children. Small wonder everyone has huge and permanent grins etched across their faces here.

Rates from: $$
Star rating: ★★★★★
Overall rating: ½

Ambience:	9.03	Cleanliness:	8.94
Value:	8.38	Facilities:	8.74
Staff:	9.04	Restaurants:	8.34
Location:	8.78	Families:	9.23

Landmark Bangkok

138 Sukhumvit Road, Klong Toey, Bangkok 10110, Thailand
T: +66 2 254 0404 **F**: +66 2 253 4259
www.HotelClub.com/Hotels/Landmark_Hotel_Bangkok

The Landmark took a very definite step upmarket in 2004 with the addition of 44 rooms on its "Lifestyle Floors" - contemporary accommodation designed for maximum comfort and space whose subtle hues are complemented by stainless steel and sand-blasted glass and augmented by DVD players and broadband Internet access.

Choice characterises the rest of this super-size property, with a total 414 rooms, a wealth of meeting and conference facilities and restaurants running from Nipa (traditional Thai with cooking classes) via the Kiku No Hana Japanese to an English pub called The Huntsman.

At 2,500 square metres, the fitness centre is one of the largest in town. And while it is the current fashion to question the need for business centres any more, it is still reassuring to know that you can call into the Landmark's at any hour of the day or night and still be met with an efficient smile.

Rates from: $$
Star rating: ★★★★★
Overall rating: ½

Ambience:	8.46	Cleanliness:	9.03
Value:	8.48	Facilities:	8.56
Staff:	8.86	Restaurants:	8.71
Location:	9.28	Families:	8.74

Le Méridien Phuket Beach Resort

8/5 Moo 1, Karon, Muang, Phuket 83100, Thailand
T: +66 76 340 480 **F:** +66 76 340 479
www.HotelClub.com/Hotels/Le_Meridien_Phuket_Bech_Resort

With a whole private cove - Relax Bay - to itself, midway along but well below the road running between Karon and Patong, the Méridien is almost totally secluded. This cosmopolitan resort's 470 rooms are popular with European families, and the comparison that most readily suggests itself is a Mediterranean cruise liner beached on a tropical shore.

While all beaches in Thailand are open to the public, the strand here is not really accessible except via the hotel. So you can hunker down on your lounger knowing that you will not be bothered by hawkers or similar types constantly badgering you to take out a jet-ski. Steeply wooded hills flank the beach so there are no ramshackle cafés, and you are left to enjoy sun and sea in peace.

The beach is backed by an extensive swimming pool that stretches practically across the width of the entire hotel. There is also a host of other sporting and recreational facilities on daily offer. Sporting types can indulge themselves on two hard and two artificial grass tennis courts, two squash courts, a rock-climbing wall, a golf practice range or the putting green, and archery is a further option. Instructors are available for anyone who wants to improve. No question about it, this is primarily a resort for vacationers who want to join in the fun rather than take a quiet break. Under-12s, incidentally, can waddle off to their own "Penguin Club".

Of course, it is not all 100 per cent non-stop action here. The Massage Centre provides a range of facials and body treatments as well as Pilates, and you can also indulge at the hotel's 11 restaurants and bars. The Seafood Restaurant offers Mediterranean dishes and the freshest catch from the Andaman Sea, while Ariake, a casual Japanese restaurant, features a sushi bar and teppanyaki table. Portofino, the Italian restaurant, offers traditional cuisine with home-made pizza, fresh pasta and ice cream. Le Café Fleuri - with its hand-painted murals in soft pastel shades, exotic cane chairs and views of the hotel lagoon - serves a large selection of Asian and European dishes.

Rates from: $
Star rating: ★ ★ ★ ★ ★
Overall rating: ♦♦♦♦ ½

Ambience:	9.03	Cleanliness:	9.01
Value:	8.50	Facilities:	8.71
Staff:	8.96	Restaurants:	8.81
Location:	8.91	Families:	9.01

Le Royal Méridien Baan Taling Ngam

295 Moo 3, Taling Ngam Beach, Koh Samui, Suratthani 84140, Thailand
T: +66 77 429 100 **F**: +66 77 423 220
www.HotelClub.com/Hotels/Le_Royal_Meridien_Baan_Taling_Ngam_Samui

It takes only the merest soupçon of fantasy to picture Baan Taling Ngam as suspended in mid-air rather than built on a hillside overlooking the Gulf of Thailand and on out toward the aquatic splendours of Ang Thong Marine Park. And gravity disappears altogether in the infinity pool, its lip gazing down on to the coconut groves and beach below. Very much removed from the frenetic party atmosphere on the east of Koh Samui, Baan Taling Ngam is surely one of the most lovely resorts on the the island. Electric buggies swoop and wheel around the resort's vertiginous slopes like circling kites, from the uppermost of its 70 rooms, suites and villas - elegant yet simple with exotic Thai tinges - down past the main building to the secluded sandy shore, seaside restaurant and beach villas.

The happy result of the extreme topography is to divide the resort into secluded sections. The one-, two- and three-bedded villas - with outsize sliding glass doors and magnificent balconies - are clustered together around their own plunge pool, perfect for a private early-morning or late-night dip. The beach is shaded by the arching trunks of postcard-perfect coconut palms, where you can launch into football or volleyball games, venture out to the coral reef for a bit of snorkelling and diving, or simply put in some serious work on a tan. The spa is excellent, and the ideal chill-out hang-out has to be the cushioned, open-sided sala that stands slightly away from the pool.

Come evening, guests tend to congregate in the Verandah Bar, just by the lobby where a Thai lady may well be sitting cross-legged patiently carving soap or tropical fruit into intricate, beautiful shapes. Transforming the mundane is something of an art form here, and it only takes a short time before you begin to appreciate that.

Rates from: $$
Star rating: ★ ★ ★ ★ ★
Overall rating: 🦢🦢🦢🦢 ½

Ambience:	9.30	Cleanliness:	9.23
Value:	7.73	Facilities:	8.61
Staff:	9.03	Restaurants:	8.27
Location:	8.47	Families:	8.57

Le Royal Méridien Phuket Yacht Club

23/3 Moo 1, Vises Road, Rawai, Muang, Phuket 83100, Thailand
T: +66 76 380 200 **F**: +66 76 380 280
www.HotelClub.com/Hotels/Le_Meridien_Beach_Resort_Phuket

You're more likely to see a fishing boat than a yacht - royal or otherwise - here, but there is no question that this top-class hotel overlooks what is arguably the best beach in Phuket. The surfers head for the far end, a monastery sited in the middle has precluded any other development, and the Méridien's guests only have to step a short way past the pool to reach their own designated patch of Nai Harn beach. Possibly the best feature of the misleadingly named Yacht Club is that all 110 rooms and suites have a generous private terrace overlooking the bay. The hillside site means that there is not an enormous amount of space to play with here - spa and fitness facilities are on the small side. Three restaurants take best advantage of the view; you might find better food elsewhere on the island, though not in the immediate vicinity.

Rates from: $$			
Star rating: ★ ★ ★ ★ ★			
Overall rating: ♨♨♨♨ ½			
Ambience:	9.00	Cleanliness:	9.13
Value:	8.21	Facilities:	8.57
Staff:	9.15	Restaurants:	8.60
Location:	9.10	Families:	8.57

Marriott Hua Hin Resort & Spa

107/1 Phetkasem Road, Hua Hin 77110, Thailand
T: +66 32 511 881 **F**: +66 32 512 422
www.HotelClub.com/Hotels/Marriott_Resort_Spa_Hua_Hin

Some of the very best aspects of Thailand are packed into the Hua Hin Marriott. Backing up the 216 rooms and suites are a perfectly gorgeous swimming pool, with its low-hanging thatched-roof bar, a luxurious spa and the chance to pick up some Thai cooking tips on the hotel's specially run courses. Invigorating both spiritually and physically, the Marriott also lays out some gourmet surprises at its half-dozen restaurants and bars, including the Chicago Grill, serving grain-fed cuts from the United States and Australia.

All the Marriott's rooms are well-appointed, with views of the gardens, pool or ocean, however the jacuzzi and roof garden of the Penthouse Suite - making all the usual assumptions about "money" and "no object" - should provide a really memorable stay.

This beachside haven also benefits from an excellent location; apart from the white and sandy, albeit narrow, beach, six championship golf courses are within driving range, including the Royal Hua Hin - Thailand's oldest golf course, which teed off in 1924.

Rates from: $			
Star rating: ★ ★ ★ ★ ★			
Overall rating: ♨♨♨♨ ½			
Ambience:	9.11	Cleanliness:	9.02
Value:	8.23	Facilities:	8.44
Staff:	8.81	Restaurants:	8.71
Location:	8.72	Families:	9.00

Novotel Bangkok On Siam Square

Siam Square, Soi 6, Pathumwan, Bangkok 10330, Thailand
T: +66 2 255 6888 **F:** +66 2 255 1824
www.HotelClub.com/Hotels/Novotel_Bangkok_On_Siam_Square

Very much back on form after a long renovation that has seen the hotel spruced up pretty much from top to bottom, the Novotel and its 429 rooms are back in business with a vengeance. The hotel - into its second decade of operation - certainly needed it. However, even though the property is now spick and span, the Novotel's trump card has always - as its name might indicate - been the fact that it is surrounded by some of the most amazing shopping, dining and entertainment in Asia, and of course the SkyTrain station is handy too. Once you've dumped your purchases in your room there's plenty in the way of restoratives. Check off pool, spa, gym, restaurants, bar and nightclub. This is not the lap of luxury but a very affordable hotel. And did anyone mention the location?

Rates from: $
Star rating: ★ ★ ★ ★
Overall rating: ♦ ♦ ♦ ♦

Ambience:	8.12	Cleanliness:	8.52
Value:	8.31	Facilities:	7.98
Staff:	8.46	Restaurants:	8.12
Location:	9.02	Families:	8.09

Novotel Coralia Resort Phuket

282 Prabaramee Road, Patong, Kathu, Phuket 83150, Thailand
T: +66 76 342 777 **F:** +66 76 342 168
www.HotelClub.com/Hotels/Novotel_Phuket_Coralia_Resort_Phuket

Outside Patong, but close enough to wade in if the fancy takes you, the Novotel stands apart from Phuket's most high-density, high-activity tourist centre. Set on a hill at the very northern end of the beach, it presents guests with a unique twin opportunity. Plunge down the hill for shopping, R&R or to join the ranks of cerise, bikini'd sardines that carpet the sands from dawn till dusk; or simply gaze down on the town from the sanctuary of the Novotel's triple-decker swimming pool, the social hub of this thoroughly amenable and smart property. Designed in the Thai style and sensitively landscaped, the Novotel hosts 215 guestrooms, each with its own balcony - a mini private retreat within a retreat. Of the five restaurants and bars to graze, cognoscenti pick Le Mirage poolside bar for an aptly named sundowner looking out over the Andaman Sea.

Rates from: $
Star rating: ★ ★ ★ ★
Overall rating: ♦ ♦ ♦ ♦

Ambience:	8.54	Cleanliness:	8.51
Value:	8.37	Facilities:	8.32
Staff:	8.56	Restaurants:	8.50
Location:	8.34	Families:	8.70

The Oriental Bangkok

48 Oriental Avenue, Bangkok 10500, Thailand
T: +66 2 659 9000 **F:** +66 2 659 0000
www.HotelClub.com/Hotels/Oriental_Hotel_Bangkok

To the question of whether the Oriental is a world-class hotel or a very well appointed museum with rooms attached, there is really only one answer. More than a century and a quarter old, presided over by the legendary Kurt Wachtveitl for the past four decades, it is the Far Eastern must-stay for numerous *Who's Who* entries, venerated for its double-plus plush spa and riverine purlieus. Cock your ear in the lobby near the sign proscribing backpackers (it might as well say riff-raff) and you can practically hear the sacred cows mooing. Let it be said that there are other, newer, less snooty places along the River of Kings where you can sleep and eat just as well as at the Oriental. But this one-time seamen's hostel turned jewel in the crown of accommodation has charisma in spades.

The bulk of the hotel's 393 rooms and suites are in the River Wing; the Garden Wing's split-level suites are rather more attractive, however cream of the crop is the Authors' Wing, with four rooms named for former guests Conrad, Maugham, Michener and Coward. Afternoon tea in the ground-floor Authors' Lounge, which is open to the public, is something of an event.

Indeed, there is no such thing as mundane eating and/or drinking anywhere in the Oriental. Weather permitting - and it usually is - breakfast should be taken at the Riverside Terrace, with a characteristic cavalcade of traffic steaming back and forth along the Chao Praya. Alternatively, the Verandah has both indoor and outdoor seating and a slightly more secluded feel. Just outside the hotel, but still a part of it, the China House is a beautifully restored and decorated colonial-style residence offering classic Cantonese cuisine and other regional food from China prepared by leading Chinese chefs, with the highlight being the dim sum lunches. As well as the main restaurant, there are also six private dining rooms here for a more intimate meal. Or you can spend a long lunch picking your way around

the magnificent seafood buffet in the recently renovated Lord Jim's.

Come cocktail hour, the sound of surprise emanates from the Bamboo Bar when the jazz band strikes up - an excellent precursor to dinner. Very much top of the bill is Le Normandie, with splendid French cuisine, impeccable service and superb wines from an exceptional cellar.

Rather less formal, Ciao's pizzas and other Italian dishes go down well on the marble terrace beside the lush tropical gardens. Or you can sail away on a veritable slice of

hotel's sporting facilities. Its splendid antique style, with 14 private treatment suites, contrasts gently with ultra-modern treatments like hydrotherapy, yet also blends with the traditional curative Thai massage. Catch the shuttle boat across and submit to the tender ministrations of the therapists for an hour, or rather longer, and you return to the hotel almost as if you had been reborn.

The Oriental itself has undergone a number of reincarnations, consistently winning awards and high praise. If nothing else, it deserves a visit from everyone at least once - but no riff-raff please.

the Oriental, dining on northern Thai-style food aboard the hotel's own golden teak rice barge *Maeyanang* - an evening that is as memorable for the night-time river sights as it is for dinner.

But without doubt the Oriental's ace in the hole is its spa - which got a US$1.2 million renovation in 2004 - situated across the river next to the Sala Rim Naam Thai restaurant and the

Rates from: $$$
Star rating: ★ ★ ★ ★ ★
Overall rating: ♦ ♦ ♦ ♦ ♦

Ambience:	9.27	Cleanliness:	9.46
Value:	8.30	Facilities:	8.89
Staff:	9.36	Restaurants:	9.14
Location:	8.71	Families:	8.85

April 08

Pathumwan Princess

444 Phayathai Road, Wangmai, Pathumwan, Bangkok 10330, Thailand
T: +66 2 216 3700 **F:** +66 2 216 3730
www.HotelClub.com/Hotels/Pathumwan_Princess_Hotel_Bangkok

out over Chulalongkorn campus. European, Thai, Japanese and Korean tastes are individually catered for in the hotel's restaurants. But the hotel's trump card is the string quartet playing a soft welcome in the lobby as you shoulder open the doors with an armful of bags after a hard day flattening the credit card.

Fresh from celebrating its eighth anniversary, the Dusit Group's Pathumwan Princess is as buzzing as ever. Take the side exit from the reception area and you are plunged into that retail Valhalla, Mahboonkrong. Walk across the footbridge and Siam Square is at your feet. Cross the road via the SkyTrain station and you are surrounded by the Siam Centre. Jim Thompson's House is just around the corner. If the message is not clear yet, the should appeal primarily to leisure travellers, and to their primal instincts for shopping. The 462 rooms are comfortable, adequately sized, and many look

Rates from: $
Star rating: ★ ★ ★ ★
Overall rating: ♘♘♘♘

Ambience:	8.28	Cleanliness:	8.53
Value:	8.44	Facilities:	8.32
Staff:	8.40	Restaurants:	8.28
Location:	9.30	Families:	8.34

The Peninsula Bangkok

33 Charoennakorn Road, Klongsan, Bangkok 10600, Thailand
: +66 2 861 2888 **F**: +66 2 861 1112
www.HotelClub.com/Hotels/Peninsula_Bangkok_The

Search in vain for the club floor at the Peninsula on the west bank of the Chao Praya. It does not exist. But it is safe to say that all 39 storeys and 370 river-view rooms of this exceptional, W-shaped building that's blended high-tech with high art are like a club floor to themselves. Rival properties can only dream of emulating the Pen's standards of service and accommodation, which come with a very affordable price tag.

First-time guests should try out the following regimen on their first day, about half an hour before dusk, and repeat it as often as necessary. Broach your duty free, or call room service for a suitable whistle-wetter. Illuminate the "Do Not Disturb" sign. For the sheer hell of it, close the curtains using the electronic control system, then open them again. Fiddle with the mood lighting until it suits. Reach for the CD player and make sure it is playing something that suits both your and the lighting's mood.

Add salts or foam to the marble bathtub, and fill to the brim, ignoring for the present the multi-channelled TV set into the wall. Of course, there is a valet to do all this for you if you are feeling especially pamper-deficient. Should you be lucky (or pecunious) enough to be staying in one of the themed suites, you can look down on the famed regal river and angelic city with the suds up to your neck. The room's outdoor temperature and humidity indicator will show you what the benighted millions below are having to put up with. Sit back, enjoy and just try not to look overly smug.

When the Peninsula opened in 1998, the wiseacres said it was "on the wrong side" and prophesied an early demise. They have since been proved wrong by legions of guests who have been all too happy to catch the shuttle boat across the Chao Praya from the SkyTrain and make free with the hotel's infinite capacity to surprise.

Part of one of Asia's most respected and venerable hotel chains, it is not in the least bit staid or stuffy. Take Jesters, whose Technicolor funk decor and Pacific Rim cuisine are served up in a split-level locale that is off-limits to under-12s. Or the outdoor swimming pool, which is no rectangular watering hole, but rather a 60-metre, triple-tiered channel that is reminiscent of a (clean!) Bangkok klong flanked by sundeck areas and salas.

In the face of such cutting-edge opulence, the Peninsula might not seem to automatically suggest itself to the executive guest, however its rooms come pre-loaded with discreetly placed fax machines with personal numbers, dataports, dual-voltage sockets and double-line telephones. More than 400 guests can be fitted into the pillarless Sakuntala Ballroom, and there are four breakout rooms right next to it. Deep-pocketed CEOs and their ilk, if they do not fancy the trip to the airport in a Rolls-Royce Silver Spur or a Mercedes-Benz S-class 280, can hop into a helicopter via the classic aviation lounge, the Paribatra Lounge, on the 37th floor.

While there are massage and beauty services, there is no full-monty spa here; guests are given automatic access to the upper crust Thai Country Club, south of Bangkok, four days a week, where they can play the 18-hole course or simply indulge in the spacious spa.

Rates from: $$			
Star rating: ★ ★ ★ ★ ★			
Overall rating: ♦ ♦ ♦ ♦ ♦			
Ambience:	9.15	Cleanliness:	9.48
Value:	8.64	Facilities:	8.98
Staff:	9.16	Restaurants:	8.84
Location:	8.32	Families:	8.67

Pimalai Resort & Spa

99 Moo 5, Ba Kan Tiang Beach, Koh Lanta 81150, Krabi, Thailand
T: +66 75 607 999 **F:** +66 75 607 998
www.HotelClub.com/Hotels/Pimalai_Resort_and_Spa_Krabi

Instructed to seek out a Thai island that had gone beyond the palm-shack stage but had yet to reach the watershed of airport, bill-boarded snake/crocodile farm and muzak'd supermarket, you'd be hard pressed to find a better example than Koh Lanta. And tasked to pick a reasonably sized Thai resort that was not just another link in an international chain yet effortlessly met international standards, in a picturesque location yet still blending with the landscape, Pimalai would be elbowing its way to the top of the shortlist.

Much of the west coast along Lanta Yai has been routinely bungalised, but Pimalai stands head and shoulders above its neighbours. All of the 75 rooms, suites and villas - spacious and simply but tastefully furnished - are capped with red tiles and tucked in among the foliage so they appear indistinguishable from village houses. Both the restaurants and the spa are primarily Thai-accented, but can make excursions to other parts of the globe without undue effort. A variety of tastes are catered to by the infinity pool and seaview gym - and it's a rare pleasure to find a hotel library that's actually stocked with relevant and intelligently chosen books.

Perfectly placed for a lengthy, lazy vacation, Pimalai is poised on the edge of a variety of island-wide entertainments. Board an elephant or a mountain bike, try a windsurfer or a boogie board, or head out to sea at sunset and catch some squid for your supper - though of course you'd be hard put to outdo Pimalai's chefs. And the Cousteau element comes to the fore at nearby dive sites like Red Rock, Koh Haa and Hin Muang, all of which Pimalai's English and German instructors know like the backs of their hands.

Strange though it may seem, Pimalai also contains meeting and conference rooms, but it's hard to imagine anyone actually getting any work done once they arrive.

Rates from: $$
Star rating: ★ ★ ★ ★ ★
Overall rating: ♮ ♮ ♮ ♮ ½

Ambience:	9.04	Cleanliness:	8.96
Value:	8.14	Facilities:	8.28
Staff:	8.89	Restaurants:	8.04
Location:	9.21	Families:	8.82

Plaza Athénée Bangkok

Wireless Road, Bangkok 10330, Thailand
T: +66 2 650 8800 **F:** +66 2 650 8500
www.HotelClub.com/Hotels/Hotel_Plaza_Athenee

the gym and the squash court. Very neatly placed to appeal to executives or better-heeled families, the Plaza's trump card is its excellent service, which even by the standards of the Thai capital is really very good. And best of all, you can go beyond merely musing and enjoy every square inch of this hotel for real.

There are few better places to contemplate the pleasures of staying at the five-year-old Plaza Athénée - one of the stars of the Méridien group - than from the comfort of a teak deck chair by the outdoor pool well away from the frantic rush of Wireless Road. Here then is the ideal place to muse on the Plaza's spacious, double-glazed, blackout-curtained regular rooms, the innovatively themed suites, the cosmopolitan offerings of the Rain Tree Café or the more subtle flavours of Utage the Japanese restaurant or the deceptively named Smooth Curry; and of course there's the spa, and

Rates from: $$
Star rating: ★ ★ ★ ★ ★
Overall rating: ♦♦♦♦ ½

Ambience:	8.69	Cleanliness:	9.08
Value:	8.21	Facilities:	8.56
Staff:	8.85	Restaurants:	8.49
Location:	8.76	Families:	8.61

Poppies Samui

28/1 Moo 3, Chaweng, Koh Samui 84320, Suratthani, Thailand
T: +66 77 422 419 **F:** +66 77 422 420
www.HotelClub.com/Hotels/Poppies_Samui

Poppies - Samui's first boutique hotel - is a sister property to its fine namesake in Bali.

Two dozen small but pretty Thai-style cottages have been woven into the scenery at the end of Chaweng Beach, surrounded by colourful and exotic gardens. The layout ensures that each cottage enjoys privacy from the others, and the open bathrooms act as a private sanctum. Teak and the finest Thai cotton and silk lend an intimate feel to the interiors, which are in effect small suites with separate sleeping and living areas as well as an outside terrace.

Poppies has its own spa, a free-form swimming pool surrounded by natural rocks and a jacuzzi overlooking the sea. And between the pool and the beach, Poppies restaurant offers fresh Californian and Thai cuisine, either al fresco or in the shade of an Ayuthya-style teak pavilion. Dining here on the nights when the moon is full is a lovely but popular experience.

Rates from: $$
Star rating: ★ ★ ★ ★
Overall rating: ♦♦♦♦ ½

Ambience:	9.34	Cleanliness:	9.28
Value:	8.76	Facilities:	8.41
Staff:	9.21	Restaurants:	8.59
Location:	8.97	Families:	8.56

The Racha

Muang, Phuket 83000, Thailand
T: +66 76 355 455   **F:** +66 76 355 240
www.HotelClub.com/Hotels/The_Racha_Resort_Phuket

One day, perhaps all hotels will be like this. One day. But for the moment The Racha shines like that elusive good deed in a naughty world, an eco-friendly beacon lighting the way for others to follow.

Like all of the Sanctuary group's path-finding properties, The Racha - on its own beach in its own bay on its own island and reopening after a renovation in August 2005 - aims to go rather beyond a revenue generating "product". First and foremost is the desire to provide a stunning boutique resort with which guests will fall in love the moment they glimpse it from their boat as they round the headland. But equally important is that the staff should go about their jobs with a passion that comes from really enjoying what they do. And similarly, there's the feeling that there would be no point to this hotel if its impact on the environment - be it the local water quality or resident fishing families' lifestyles - was a negative one.

So two trees were planted for every one cut down during construction, waste water is recycled in the gardens, no chemicals go into the pool, and islanders can bring in their rubbish for disposal free of charge.

Guests lucky enough to step ashore here will find themselves staying in one of four sorts of villa, with the most luxurious containing their own pool. All embrace a bold, clean design that harmonises perfectly with the landscape, and each has a rain shower located in an outside courtyard.

There are no jet-skis here, of course, and a marine research facility is being developed alongside other facilities like the garden spa (choose from mind-mapping, homeopathic medicine or fitness evaluation) and the dive shop.

The Earth Café and the Fire Grill lay on a variety of Thai and international dishes, and it is not difficult to while away the hours at the Ice Bar.

In short, this environmentally-conscious hotel is not far short of perfect.

Rates from: **$$**
Star rating: ★ ★ ★ ★ ★
Overall rating: **Editor's Pick**

Ambience:	n/a	Cleanliness:	n/a
Value:	n/a	Facilities:	n/a
Staff:	n/a	Restaurants:	n/a
Location:	n/a	Families:	n/a

Rayavadee

214 Moo 2, Tumbon Ao-Nang, Amphur Muang, Krabi 81000, Thailand
T: +66 75 620 740 **F:** +66 75 620 630
www.HotelClub.com/Hotels/Rayavadee_Resort_Krabi

Myth and modernity meet on Phra Nang Beach, where - legend has it - a princess inhabits the cave at the base of the soaring limestone cliff. But it would not exactly be lèse majesté to wonder if sometimes she does not cast an envious eye from her slightly damp grotto - furnished only with an altar and piles of fisherfolks' offerings - at the Rayavadee next door.

Not that the resort is in any way conspicuous. Designed so that not a single palm tree was cut down during construction, the Rayavadee is barely visible from the sea. Surely the best way to arrive here would be to pitch up on the white and super-soft sand of Railey Beach by longtail and make your way across the strand into the delirious haven of the resort itself. In fact, there is no road here, so a seaborne arrival at the resort's jetty is the most usual way in.

The Rayavadee is not exactly cheap, but you do get the very best for your bucks. Some 103 recently renovated pavilions and villas are scattered about the resort's ten hectares. Each is hexagonal in shape, and the glass walls of the living room create a flowing space to the garden outside; upstairs the high domed ceiling allows the bedroom more breathing space, and there is an ensuite and very romantic bathroom with two-seater bathtub. The more luxurious accommodation comes with jacuzzis or hydropools attached, while the double-bedroomed Rayavadee Villa occupies its own private compound.

The place to eat at Rayavadee is the beachside Krua Phranang, which specialises in Thai and seafood. Jet-skis are banned in Krabi, so there is no noise to interrupt the lingering repasts that the location almost demands. And at low tide, you can walk straight out of the restaurant and wade across to a couple of uninhabited islands in the bay. This is Mother Nature at her best.

Rates from: $$$$$
Star rating: ★ ★ ★ ★ ★
Overall rating: 🐾🐾🐾🐾 ½

Ambience:	9.70	Cleanliness:	9.18
Value:	7.37	Facilities:	8.82
Staff:	9.27	Restaurants:	8.77
Location:	9.20	Families:	8.56

Royal Cliff Beach Resort

√ April 07

353 Phra Tamnuk Road, Pattaya, Cholburi 20150, Thailand
T: +66 38 250 421 **F:** +66 38 250 141
www.HotelClub.com/Hotels/Royal_Cliff_Beach_Resort

A huge swathe of different guests come to enjoy this mini metropolis - four hotels in one with a private beach, three ballrooms, four bars, five swimming pools, six tennis courts, 10 restaurants and 15 meeting rooms - from conventioneers (up to 1,100 at a time) congregating in the adjacent Pattaya Exhibition and Convention Hall (PEACH) to families who are happy just to lap up the water sports. Picking where you stay here is fairly crucial. There are a dozen different room types, from themed suites decorated in different styles, such as Japanese Bonsai or Indian Maharajah, to the mini suites with a step-up lounge area and two-bedroom Family Suites. The

Executive Rooms all have a sea-facing balcony with loungers and walk-in shower, while the Presidential Suites contain three bedrooms with ensuite bath, a private butler and a beach sala. Mounted on its own headland with views over the beach and the city, this hotel is pretty much a microcosm of Pattaya.

Rates from: $
Star rating: ★ ★ ★ ★ ★
Overall rating: ♫ ♫ ♫ ♫ ½

Ambience:	9.03	Cleanliness:	9.06
Value:	8.04	Facilities:	8.85
Staff:	9.00	Restaurants:	8.99
Location:	8.67	Families:	8.88

Royal Orchid Sheraton Hotel & Towers

2 Captain Bush Lane, New Road, Siphya, Bangkok 10500, Thailand
T: +66 2 266 0123 **F:** +66 2 236 8320
www.HotelClub.com/Hotels/Royal_Orchid_Sheraton_Hotel_and_Towers_Bangkok

Consistently praised as one of Bangkok's more remarkable hotels, there is much to appreciate in the 28-storey, dual-lobbied 740-room Royal Orchid Sheraton. Note its brace of ballrooms and pair of swimming pools; remark the dedicated conference area on the second floor with 16 tech-happy function rooms; technophobes will heave a sigh of relief over the specialised staff who are pre-programmed to sort out laptop problems and even to buy IT accessories from nearby malls; and no one has any quarrel with the delicious temptations served up in the eight-room Mandara Spa or the six restaurants and bars. Where this hotel really scores is in its

design. Opened two decades ago, the architects had the forethought and sheer common sense to make the building Y-shaped, so each chic room looks out over the Chao Praya River. Recent renovations have brought the hotel up to date, making it a most charming place to stay in Bangkok.

Rates from: $$
Star rating: ★ ★ ★ ★ ★
Overall rating: ♫ ♫ ♫ ♫ ½

Ambience:	8.72	Cleanliness:	9.07
Value:	8.24	Facilities:	8.56
Staff:	9.02	Restaurants:	8.79
Location:	8.68	Families:	8.70

Shangri-La Hotel Bangkok

89 Soi Wat Suan Plu, New Road, Bangrak, Bangkok 10500, Thailand
T: +66 2 236 7777 **F:** +66 2 236 8579
www.HotelClub.com/Hotels/ShangriLa_Hotel_Bangkok

The Shang issued a clarion wake-up call to Bangkok's hotels when its spa - Chi - opened in 2004. Inspired by the architectural principles of a Tibetan temple, applying the Chinese principles of harmony and balance, and with one tenth of its 1,000 square metres taken up by a single treatment suite, it certainly marked a new beginning in combining luxury and hospitality. The Shangri-La is one of the largest hotels in Bangkok, with 799 rooms split between two separate wings. It is rather less pricey than its neighbour, the Oriental, but much closer to the SkyTrain. If your budget will stretch, grab one of the suites with a river view at the southern end of the Shangri-La Wing which all have an outside terrace to look down on the bustling river and city. Finally, at least one meal at the riverside Salathip restaurant is essential.

Rates from: $$
Star rating: ★ ★ ★ ★ ★
Overall rating: ♦ ♦ ♦ ♦ ½

Ambience:	9.04	Cleanliness:	9.27
Value:	8.39	Facilities:	8.83
Staff:	9.07	Restaurants:	8.90
Location:	8.81	Families:	8.64

Sheraton Grande Sukhumvit

250 Sukhumvit Road, Bangkok 10110, Thailand
T: +66 2 649 8888 **F:** +66 2 649 8000
www.HotelClub.com/Hotels/Sheraton_Grande_Sukhumvit_Bangkok

The 33-storey Sheraton Grande naturally grants the accolade "international hotel" its fullest meaning. Hong Kong Chinese architects took Thai culture and artistic heritage as their inspiration. The 20 executive suites overlook the pretty Lake Rachada, while the business district - and the convention centre - are pretty much on the doorstep. Guests from all over the world come to dine at Rossini's, the signature Italian restaurant, and revel in this thoroughly successful "oasis of tranquillity". As well as the sort of five-star comforts and facilities that are automatic in a 429-room deluxe property, a couple of extras stand out. The first-floor library is exceptionally well stocked, the personal butler service (a UN-style Jeeves if ever there was one) is on hand 24/7, the unduly masochistic can arrange for one-on-one training at the Grande Spa and Fitness Club, the free-form swimming pool and jacuzzi is one of Asia's more exotic, while Riva's brasserie is one of the hottest nightspots on the Sukhumvit strip.

Rates from: $$
Star rating: ★ ★ ★ ★ ★
Overall rating: ♦ ♦ ♦ ♦ ½

Ambience:	8.77	Cleanliness:	9.19
Value:	8.35	Facilities:	8.66
Staff:	8.95	Restaurants:	8.70
Location:	8.85	Families:	8.45

Sheraton Grande Laguna Phuket

10 Moo 4, Srisoonthorn Road, Bang Tao Bay, Cherngtalay, Phuket 83110, Thailand
T: +66 76 324 101 **F:** +66 76 324 108
www.HotelClub.com/Hotels/Sheraton_Grande_Laguna_Phuket

It's essential to savour the thrill of arrival at this resort, one of a quintet of hotels raised on a one-time tin mine and largely surrounded by water. Cross the canal bridge to find two ranks of imposing columns flanking a pool bedecked with lotus flowers that points straight out to the beach and sea beyond. Above is the sky and all around a respectful hush and a feeling of total peace.

The accommodation of choice

here is either one of the two- or three-level Grande Villas accessed by motor launch and where, in what amounts to an enclave within the hotel, the tedious formality of check-in is signed away in seconds flat, or the brand new Golf Villas and Residences. While these represent the acme of opulence - think king-size beds, sunken tubs, free breakfast and cocktails and a mass of other add-ons - the Sheraton's 252 regular rooms are equally appealing. Furnished with local materials, there is a choice of views over pool, lagoon or ocean.

All in all, this is an extremely amenable resort, with a full compliment of recreational facilities catering for couples or families. The shallow end of the 323-metre swimming pool that winds its way throughout the hotel is edged with a mini beach, so you can just stroll into the water. Puccini, the smart Italian restaurant, is about as haute

cuisine as can be found anywhere on Phuket. Or you can don T-shirt and shorts and browse around the Asian delicacies in the open-air Market Place - in all nine restaurants and bars are on offer.

At some stage during your stay climb the observation tower above the main lobby, which affords views over the property and the rest of Laguna, the shimmering waters of lake and sea, and luxuriant trees and lawns. Conclusion? Not bad for a site that UNESCO - with a certain degree of folly - declared unusable for the next 100 years.

Rates from: $$
Star rating: ★ ★ ★ ★ ★
Overall rating: ◗◗◗◗ ½

Ambience:	9.02	Cleanliness:	8.81
Value:	8.12	Facilities:	8.64
Staff:	8.78	Restaurants:	8.53
Location:	8.48	Families:	9.07

Sheraton Krabi Beach Resort

155 Moo 2, Klong Muong Beach, Nong Thale Muang District, Krabi 81000, Thailand
T: +66 75 628 000 **F:** +66 75 628 028
www.HotelClub.com/Hotels/Sheraton_Krabi_Beach_Resort

There are times when the casual observer might be tempted to think many Thai resorts are stamped out by the same cookie cutter with "tropical paradise" written round the outside in coconut-flavoured icing. So full marks to the Sheraton Krabi, not only for thinking outside the envelope, but recycling it too, or at least doing its bit for the environment.

The hotel has gone way beyond lackadaisical "reuse your towels and save the planet" style notices in the bathroom, and made a thorough study of the mangroves that surround the property, passing on its findings to guests. So here is an extensive introduction to the fiddler crab, the mudskipper, the ruddy kingfisher, the butterflies and dragonflies and cicadas and crickets for whom the mangrove is home. And here is something to ponder: it is estimated that some 50 per cent of mangrove areas have been destroyed by industry and pollution, and of those left roughly half have been badly degraded. Sustainable tourism is the way ahead, and here is a delightful spot in which to experience it. Guests are encouraged to report any special findings on their wanderings, particularly animals or birds that have not been previously recorded in the area.

Back in the resort proper, a very respectable welcome awaits. Some 246 rooms and half a dozen suites, an Asian and a Mediterranean restaurant, an extensive spa and two bars are spread around eight hectares. On balmy nights, a movie screen is strung between the trees between the pool and the beach and guests can sit beneath the stars watching a blockbuster, with waiters (keen film buffs themselves) hovering nearby if anyone needs some refreshment. Some 20 minutes' drive out of Krabi town, the Sheraton is a true original eco-haven and an instant favourite with anyone who visits.

Rates from: **$$**
Star rating: ★ ★ ★ ★ ★
Overall rating: ⊘ ⊘ ⊘ ⊘ ½

Ambience:	8.84	Cleanliness:	8.98
Value:	7.96	Facilities:	8.36
Staff:	8.75	Restaurants:	8.13
Location:	8.55	Families:	8.83

Sofitel Central Hua Hin Resort

1 Damnernkasem Road, Hua Hin, Prachuabkhirikhan 77110, Thailand
T: +66 32 512 021 **F:** +66 32 511 014
www.HotelClub.com/Hotels/Sofitel_Central_Hua_Hin_Resort

This perfectly graceful hotel will be instantly recognisable to movie buffs from its inclusion in *The Killing Fields,* which - on celluloid at least - transferred it from the royal seaside resort in Hua Hin to the middle of Cambodia.

It is a fine looking hotel, with a glistening white façade and red-tiled roofs, richly restored using the original 1923 Railway Hotel shell while incorporating the A-Z of mod cons. The main building, made up of three wings (Railway, Colonial and Garden) containing 177 rooms and suites, is shaped like an off-centred "Y", looking out toward the beach over gardens with a weird and wonderful topiary of animals and birds. A further 41

one- and two-bedroomed bungalows (belonging to the cheaper but very cheerful sister Central Hua Hin Village hotel) are set off to one side. Prime accommodation, though, is in the original Railway Wing, where rooms have extra-high ceilings and balconies that are a true reminder of the hotel's glory days in the roaring 20s.

The Sofitel's main swimming pool (there are three) is located down by one of the best beaches in Hua Hin, and the lawns nearby are usually carpeted with sunbathers who fancy being able to hear the waves breaking but do not fancy getting covered in sand.

Naturally, the Sofitel plays up its historical antecedents, but does not overdo it. The rooms are fitted out with polished hardwoods yet softened by warm Thai silks, in a manner reminiscent of pre-war days. A traditional high tea is served in the Museum, which is full

of artefacts from days when the fastest way to get to Hua Hin was by steam train. The Elephant Bar with live pianist is a mass of antiques, sweeping staircases, crystal chandeliers and freshly cut flowers. Spas are almost de rigeur in Thailand's larger hotels, and the Centara at the Sofitel provides an excellent range of on-site treatments and therapies. This is certainly the most atmospheric hotel nestling peacefully right in the heart of Hua Hin town, and all the more successful for its discreet packaging of ancient and modern.

Rates from: $$
Star rating: ★ ★ ★ ★ ★
Overall rating: ♪♪♪♪ ½

Ambience:	9.27	Cleanliness:	9.05
Value:	8.32	Facilities:	8.62
Staff:	9.09	Restaurants:	8.57
Location:	9.04	Families:	8.93

Sofitel Raja Orchid Khon Kaen

8/9 Prachasumran Road, Muang, Khon Kaen 40000, Thailand
T: +66 43 322 218 **F:** +66 43 322 150
www.HotelClub.com/Hotels/Sofitel_Raja_Orchid_Khon_Kaen

Bangkok we know. Phuket we've been to. But where on earth is Khon Kaen? The answer is that it is the heart of Isan, the new northern Thailand that is less rugged than Chiangs Mai or Rai but in easy hail of Laos, some substantial Khmer ruins and surrounded by numerous scenic national parks. Substantial commercial interests in the region attract a large swathe of business travellers too, who make extensive use of the hotels conference facilities, which can accommodate anything from a small board meeting to a full-scale international summit.

And the place to stay in what - surprising to record - is Thailand's fourth-largest city, is the 293-room Sofitel. It may not aspire to the standards of other Thai cities, but it is the best in town so further comparison seems to be superfluous.

Thai silk furnishings and avant garde artwork combine to make the comfortable and extremely spacious rooms more homely, but the Sofitel's real selling point is its diverse food, beverage and entertainment options. The one that springs to mind most readily is the Kronen Braühaus, a sort of mini year-round Oriental Oktoberfest. Even more raucous is the high-tech, basement Gik Club which features international DJs and - as the evening wears on - a predictable amount of love-at-first-sight. Rooms on the upper storeys are recommended for light sleepers.

Other eateries include Vietnamese, Italian, a rather sophisticated Japanese and a brace of Chinese, one of which specialises in Cantonese and Chiu Chow.

The Sofitel also has a small but adequate fitness centre. The outdoor pool is unheated but given Isan's climate this is not too much of a penance.

Finally, the Sofitel could hardly be more neatly located with shopping, recreation and nightlife options all close at hand.

Rates from: $
Star rating: ★★★★★
Overall rating: 4½

Ambience:	8.72	Cleanliness:	9.11
Value:	8.98	Facilities:	8.18
Staff:	8.67	Restaurants:	8.45
Location:	8.02	Families:	8.56

The Sukhothai

13/3 South Sathorn Road, Bangkok 10120, Thailand
T: +66 2 344 8888 **F**:8 +66 2 344 8899
www.HotelClub.com/Hotels/Sukhothai_Hotel_Bangkok

To sidestep the maelstrom of Bangkok, simply slip into the Sukhothai - which means "dawn of happiness" - and is not so much an oasis in "the City of Angels" as completely removed from it.

Low-rise and low-key, the Sukhothai discreetly turns its back on its surrounds to create its own distinctive environment on a 2.4-hectare landscaped plot. A long marbled corridor leads from the minimalist lobby toward the restaurants and rooms, flanked by statuary and reflective pools and scented by gorgeously displayed vases of freshly cut flowers. You do not so much walk down here as glide. The lift lobby, taking its cue from the shrines of the ancient Mon culture, is arranged in an octagon. The corridors leading to the rooms are open-air, lined with heavy wooden lattice panels. And the rooms themselves - inspired by tradition yet with every modern comfort - look out over the water gardens and open courtyards. In short, this is a hotel that takes a different perspective, and wonderfully so.

Complementing the Sukhothai's exceptional architecture are its restaurants. Sunday brunch at the Colonnade has become something of a Bangkok institution - a vast Japanese, Thai and Western buffet overlaid with the aroma of freshly baked bread - that swiftly takes on the hilarity of a wedding reception or birthday party. Dinner at Celadon is more sedate, with classic Thai dishes drawn from all over the country served in air-conditioned salas - or on the terrace outside - which are surrounded by lotus ponds. At a point midway between these two, the Zuk Bar has a lighter menu and is decorated with period artworks and classic antiques, while La Scala is one long aria in praise of classic Italian food.

The Sukhothai takes its name from the 13th-century capital of Siam, an era when art and architecture flourished, the Thai script was invented and Theravada Buddhism was codified. The hotel brings some of that much-needed ethos to millennium Bangkok.

Rates from: $$
Star rating: ★ ★ ★ ★ ★
Overall rating: ♜ ♜ ♜ ♜ ½

Ambience:	9.26	Cleanliness:	9.33
Value:	8.39	Facilities:	8.77
Staff:	8.96	Restaurants:	8.90
Location:	8.05	Families:	8.11

Tongsai Bay Cottages & Hotel

84 Moo 5, Bophut, Koh Samui, Suratthani 84320, Thailand
T: +66 77 245 480 F: +66 77 425 462
www.HotelClub.com/Hotels/Tongsai_Bay_Cottages_Hotel_Samui

It is an old travellers' aphorism: "Ah, but you should have seen this place 30 years ago". But Tongsai Bay retains much of the attraction of Koh Samui of the 1970s - a single and very private 200-metre long beach that is removed both physically and metaphorically from the more built-up parts of the island. That said, the facilities greeting Koh Samui's pioneers rarely went beyond basic bed and board, but the Tongsai Bay resort - neatly slotted onto the hillside easily scaled by humming electric carts - has managed to combine the best of both worlds. Four pool villas now head the accommodation tally; otherwise the 83 seaview rooms are divided between cottages, beachfront suites and grand villas spread over 10 lush hectares; Tongsai retains a very intimate and natural feel, but at the same time one of luxury. One of the swimming pools is saltwater, the covered gym is shrouded in trees and the Prana Spa massage salas lie open to the elements.

The rooms, consistently upgraded over the years, are simple but comfortable with satellite TVs and a private terrace incorporating sunken bathtub.

The other very non-1970s aspect of the Tongsai Bay is the eating options, which go well beyond the old fried rice/banana pancakes of hippie days. Chef Chom's Thai Restaurant stands near the lobby with large open-air terraces overlooking the sea, while Floyd's Beach Bistro (named after the BBC celebrity chef Keith Floyd) offers beachside dining using only the freshest ingredients. Given Floyd's passion for a tipple, there is also a bar named after him. The Butler's Restaurant posts a European-themed menu that is changed daily. Sip, the Internet café, dispenses cocktails, cold beers and fine wines over a computer.

The beach is dotted with shells and umbrellas but not pestered by stray dogs or similarly stray hawkers. Motorised sports are also banned. First-time visitors do not need to be told that the right-hand end is nicknamed Lovers' Corner, for that very soon becomes blindingly obvious.

Rates from: $$$
Star rating: ★ ★ ★ ★ ★
Overall rating: ♙ ♙ ♙ ♙ ½

Ambience:	9.31	Cleanliness:	9.13
Value:	8.03	Facilities:	8.82
Staff:	9.19	Restaurants:	8.88
Location:	8.84	Families:	8.05

Triple Two Silom

22 Silom Road, Suriyawong, Bangrak, Bangkok 10500, Thailand
+66 2 627 2222 **F:** +66 2 627 2300
www.HotelClub.com/Hotels/Triple_Two_Silom_Hotel_Bangkok

Just as Bangkok has produced some amazingly exciting new restaurants in recent years - Bed Supper Club being the prime example - so it's heartening to discover a new home-grown breed of hotels competing with the dreary, shoebox bedroom three-stars and giving the international chains a run for their money. Triple Two was formerly a simple shop-house, and its four storeys have been imaginatively converted into one of the more striking small hotels in Bangkok.

The design is sexy all over, using bright colours and hi-tech materials to impart a fresh and inspirational feeling that's totally Thai without overdoing the tradition. Black and white photos of Chinatown in days gone by contrast with a Zen-like atmosphere, and chrome fittings set off white-washed walls and chocolate-brown furnishings. The decor is by no means conventional, yet it just works perfectly.

Walk-in showers, immense double beds, DVD players and sofas make all 75 rooms into mini suites, while the young and trimly uniformed staff do their utmost to make guests feel very much at home. Triple Two hosts just one restaurant-cum-bar, serving international cuisine at street level so attracting a fair amount of passing trade. While primarily a leisure stop-off - Lumpini Park and Silom Night Market are both within easy walking distance - the hotel could equally serve executives, with five small conference rooms and a fully functioning business centre. The in-room desks, incidentally, are more like a proper work station, with direct access to the Internet.

The only minus mark here is that the hotel does not have its own pool or fitness centre, however guests can use the facilities at the adjoining Narai, which - regrettably to say - are more "two out of ten" than Triple Two. A helpful reminder to steer clear of hotels that regard guests as little more than credit cards on legs, anyway.

Rates from: $
Star rating: ★ ★ ★ ★
Overall rating: 🐾🐾🐾🐾 ½

Ambience:	8.93	Cleanliness:	9.36
Value:	8.64	Facilities:	8.50
Staff:	9.36	Restaurants:	8.07
Location:	8.50	Families:	8.50

VIETNAM

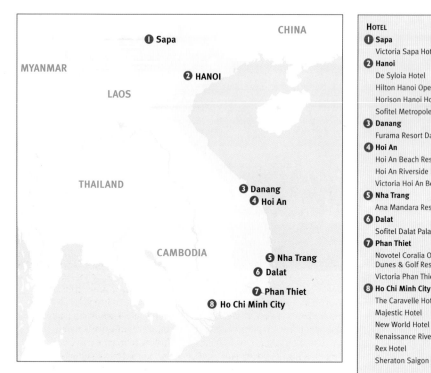

The image of Vietnam as a war is fading fast, with its place being taken by one of the most attractive new destinations in Asia. Beautiful landscapes, a wealth of culture and that feeling of breaking new ground all contribute to make this country extremely alluring.

And despite everything the Vietnamese went through - first under French colonisation and later brutal American invasion - visitors will find them to be a remarkably optimistic and hospitable people with little or no animosity towards foreigners. The smiles and grace of the Vietnamese are among the most lasting impressions of this stunning country.

This patriotic nation's history of fierce resistance goes back a lot further than its battle with the United States. Before ousting the Americans, the Vietnamese repelled French colonial forces and before that, crow-barred out their Chinese rulers, not to mention seeing off the terrifying Mongol hordes.

Having spent a good millennium under the Chinese, the Middle Kingdom's influences have been heavily absorbed and are still very tangible. Much of the culture and historic architecture have strong Chinese foundations. European expansion saw the French colonising Vietnam for a century, ultimately leaving behind a splendidly romantic Gallic footprint. The Americans were to crank up the power struggle that

followed the French exit, and the subsequent division of the country into north and south led to war tearing through the region and years of devastation. Revered national hero Ho Chi Minh lead an ultimately successful effort to reunite the land under communist rule. A landmark offensive took place during the most celebrated national holiday, Tet, the Lunar New Year.

Nowadays, during Tet just about everything stops and it is not the best time to enjoy Vietnam. Weather may also play a part in deciding when to go if you have a particular destination in mind. This is a long gangling country straddling 30 degrees of latitude,

nd tucked just under the Tropic of Cancer. The climate therefore varies notably from north to south. Northern areas experience monsoons from May to September, while the south basks in a typically tropical climate, although it is driest from December through April. With this see-saw of good and bad weather, generally speaking the country is accessible all year round - but be warned, it is prone to sudden and dramatic flooding, especially in the lowlands and river delta regions.

The most attractive section of the capital Hanoi is the charming French Quarter complete with flaking old buildings with charismatic decaying shutters. Hanoi also boasts some proud and opulent efforts such as the exquisite Presidential Palace. The conservative city is usually slow to adapt, but it offers an excellent combination of history and cuisine as well as a more gentle insight into how Vietnam is developing in the 21st century.

Vietnam's narrow central regions have three sites protected by UNESCO for their heritage. The little town of Hoi An is a unique pocket of old French streets especially charming by night when gently lit by colourful lanterns. Beyond Hue's city walls the wooded environs contain dozens of imperial tombs. My Son, a little deeper into the interior, is a crumbling remnant of the fallen Cham civilisation, a pale shadow of the traditional Vietnamese enemy, the neighbouring Khmers. Back up north are the alpine pleasures of Sapa and surrounds, and the poetic rocky limestone outcrops of Halong Bay, another site protected by UNESCO, this time for its stunning natural beauty.

The country has often been polarised into north and south and to balance Hanoi is wild and energetic Ho Chi Minh City, previously known as Saigon.

Vietnam's largest city and economic powerhouse, HCMC has traditionally been viewed as a bit of a rebel by Vietnam's frowning rulers and is certainly that today. The male of the species may have a job fending off unwanted female attentions and vice is rampant. Ho Chi Minh City also has some potent reminders of its recent troubles. Powerful war museums are grippingly absorbing and the infamous Cu Chi tunnel network is within easy day-tripping reach.

Vietnam's infrastructure has quite a way to go and flying is the only practical mode of transport for long distances, unless you have plenty of time and buttocks of steel. It must be said that Vietnamese hotels are improving rapidly. Boring government-run hotels are on the wane, average hotels that tried and failed to be a bit fancy can be safely ignored, and there are numerous new additions that can certainly mix it with Asia's best as well as a select number of heritage properties. And of course the amiable Vietnamese character ensures that service is generally a delight.

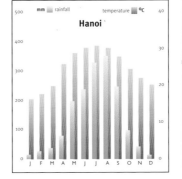

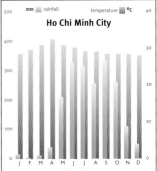

Ana Mandara Evason Resort and Spa

Beachside Tran Phu, Nha Trang, Vietnam
T: +84 58 829 829 **F:** +84 58 829 629
www.HotelClub.com/Hotels/Ana_Mandara_Resort

Ana Mandara's many, many friends around the world will be tickled sunburn pink to hear that its sister "Hideaway" resort - across the bay on its own exquisitely private beach and only accessible by boat - opened for business at the end of last year.

So Nha Trang now offers two top quality resorts to vie with the host of second-raters that line its lovely city-side beach. Most local hotels here cater to the domestic market, especially from Ho Chi Minh City (a 50-minute flight away). They are rather functional and often dated efforts, lagging well behind the appealing and imaginative beach accommodation in more popular countries in the region. But the original Ana Mandara, operated by the classy Six Senses Group, steadfastly bucks this trend - it is a stylish and well-designed four-star resort, capturing that luxury feeling previously rare in Vietnam.

The villas' timber frames and pillars allow sunlight and the sea breeze to flood the interior, along with the gentle sounds of the rolling surf, although guests staying close to the main road might be bothered by passing traffic.

Perhaps the decisive factor is that there are no anonymous corridors or packaged rooms. Its 17 palm-fringed beach villas host the 74 rooms, lending more personality, space and seclusion.

All are tiled-roofed with verandahs the majority with sea views, and al are thoughtfully put together and presented.

The Ana Mandara does not have extensive facilities, but it has brought all of the essential beach amenities to this relatively remote dot on the map. The spa offers comprehensive treatments from highly-trained therapists, rather than the semi-amateur types you often encounter in Vietnamese hotels. Loads of water sports are u for grabs on the beach just paces away, including parasailing, sailing jet-skiing, banana-boating and some reasonable diving. Other activities and tours - such as a river picnic or a trip to the morning market - can be laid on and the seaside Beach Restaurant is one of Nha Trang's most handsome. Note though that none of this comes particularly cheap, and the Ana Mandara is no bargain by local standards.

Rates from: $$
Star rating: ★ ★ ★ ★
Overall rating: ♉♉♉♉ ½

Ambience:	9.16	Cleanliness:	8.93
Value:	7.97	Facilities:	8.30
Staff:	9.02	Restaurants:	8.10
Location:	8.00	Families:	8.54

The Caravelle Hotel

19 Lam Son Square, District 1, Ho Chi Minh City, Vietnam
T: +84 8 823 4999 **F**: +84 8 824 3999
www.HotelClub.com/Hotels/Caravelle_Hotel_Ho_Chi_Minh_City

The pace-setting Caravelle is widely acknowledged as Ho Chi Minh City's best heritage hotel. Everything here is top rate, except the prices, which remain very reasonable. Chiefly the 24-storey towering hotel offers bona fide five-star service, a challenge for a hotel of its size (335 rooms). Professional and welcoming staff are its key asset. Visually it triumphs too, with a sharp, snappy and energetic design throughout and immaculate presentation, which is not bad for a hotel first opened in 1959, although it was given a substantial makeover in 1998. Rooms are well-appointed and warm with caramel-coloured themes, and the hotel has some of Ho Chi Minh City's better business and leisure facilities. Absolutely indulgent dining - especially in the fusion Asian Reflections - could well have you piling on the kilos, and the trendy rooftop bar, Saigon Saigon - a renowned bolthole for foreign correspondents during the war years - now proudly presents a host of live entertainment. The whole property is very hard to knock.

Rates from: $$
Star rating: ★ ★ ★ ★
Overall rating: ♨ ♨ ♨ ♨ ½

Ambience:	8.33	Cleanliness:	8.89
Value:	7.89	Facilities:	8.15
Staff:	8.73	Restaurants:	8.41
Location:	9.21	Families:	7.94

De Syloia Hotel

17A Tran Hung Dao Street, Hanoi, Vietnam
T: +84 4 824 5346 **F**: +84 4 824 1083
www.HotelClub.com/Hotels/De_Syloia_Hotel_Hanoi

Pretty much everything about this cuter-than-boutique hotel conspires to delight and impress. Slotted very neatly into one of Hanoi's signature tube-houses are 33 rooms that are in no way cramped or poky, indeed even the bathrooms all enjoy some sort of natural light. The hotel's single restaurant, Cay Cau, has an outside terrace, is linked to the first floor by a spiral staircase and is staffed by waitresses charmingly dressed in traditional tu than. The business centre and conference room may be tending to the minimalist, but at least they're free. Likewise the roof terrace - capacity perhaps half a dozen - and the fitness centre, which may only host a couple of machines but has floor-

to-ceiling views over the surrounding streets. It's easy to understand that it's not just reasonable rates that make the De Syloia so popular. Mention should also be made of the staff, who go out of their way to succour and assist. More than a few so-called luxury establishments could learn a thing or two here.

Rates from: $
Star rating: ★ ★
Overall rating: ♨ ♨ ♨ ♨ ½

Ambience:	8.70	Cleanliness:	8.90
Value:	8.90	Facilities:	7.82
Staff:	9.15	Restaurants:	8.63
Location:	8.55	Families:	8.63

Furama Resort Danang

68 Ho Xuan Huong Street, Bac My An Ward, Danang, Vietnam
T: +84 511 847 333 F: +84 511 843 666
www.HotelClub.com/Hotels/Furama_Resort_Danang

The beach scene in Vietnam - one of the country's greatest natural assets - is still developing, despite its thousands of kilometres of coastline, much of which remains incredibly pristine. The first of what will probably one day be many international class five-star resorts is the Furama Resort. Representing the future hopes of a new front of Vietnamese tourism, this stunning resort has proved a highly successful experiment. Opened in 1997, the resort is located on the best part of China Beach, famed for providing R&R to American GIs back in the war days. It is somewhat isolated both nationally and locally, though with attractions like the heritage enclave of Hoi An within an hour's drive. Luckily the Furama has been superbly designed and constructed to the extent that those enjoying a stay will not feel the need to leave, and crucially stands in total contrast to the rest of the developing region. It is almost as if the whole thing has been uprooted and teleported in from somewhere else.

Architecturally the experiment is a complete success. The Furama's ambience is luxuriant and tropical, and the facilities truly five-star. It has been conceived with plenty of open space and fresh air in mind and it is set well away from the otherwise dusty industrial town of Danang. This is a most handsome resort - the palm-studded pools are magnificent oases of tropical colour and will have many reaching for their camera for those envy-inducing holiday jpegs. A horizon pool borders the excellent white sand stretch, which has choice water sports on offer, including a diving school, sailing and waterskiing. The powdery beach is cleaned regularly and free of hassling vendors, a big plus in Vietnam. The hotel restaurants are also international, serving a range of excellent cuisines, a real challenge for the area. For those who know central Vietnam, where every meal is a carbon copy of the same Vietnamese buffet, this is a godsend. Instead there is a menu, and not just for show, with choices ranging from Mediterranean to Asian. The quality of the food on offer is the some of the best outside Hanoi or Ho Chi Minh City.

The Furama's standard of service is very high and staff members are a delight. When the sun sets there is a bright, cheerful albeit loud bar to relax in, and a well-equipped gym to ease off any excess pounds which may have somehow accumulated. The 188 rooms flout the usual floor plan and set-up, being unusually spacious and broad with split-levels and generous balconies. Highly polished teak floors and lattice shutters provide a charming French colonial feel. With the inventive rooms and beautiful facilities, the Furama is picturesque resort and a superb escape.

Rates from: $$
Star rating: ★ ★ ★ ★ ★
Overall rating: ♦♦♦♦½

Ambience:	9.02	Cleanliness:	9.00
Value:	7.75	Facilities:	8.56
Staff:	8.86	Restaurants:	8.12
Location:	8.58	Families:	8.52

Hilton Hanoi Opera

, Le Thanh Tongs Street, Hoan Kiem District, Hanoi, Vietnam
T: +84 4 933 0500 **F:** +84 4 933 0530
www.HotelClub.com/Hotels/Hilton_Hanoi_Opera_Hotel

window stretches between the third and fourth floors, making the hotel appear smaller than it actually is.

The 269 rooms and suites enjoy two distinct designs. The executives are decorated in a restful beige and blue, the remainder in a rather sharper green and red and all the floors are distinguished by curving corridors that lend a remarkable, open air to the hotel's interiors. The fifth floor is the only one to come with balconies attached, an essential accessory for admiring the nearby scenery of tiled roofs and leafy boulevards. The rooms are wired with IDD phones and dataports, high-speed Internet access, and the hotel has its own generators to back up any shortfall in the local supply.

The Hilton's "R" floor is devoted to its restaurants - the award-winning Cantonese Turtle's Poem with its quintet of private dining rooms, the contemporary brasserie Chez Manon and JJ's Sports Bar, which offers darts, pool and big-screen events. Just outside is the swimming pool and terrace, both seemingly in touching distance of the Opera House, and the latter an unparalleled location for a party or corporate cocktails. To get the full flavour of this excellent hotel, check in when one of the all-too-infrequent performances is being staged.

Standing at the end of Trang Tien Street overlooking the grand square like mirror images of Hanoi old and new are the Opera House, which is fast approaching its centenary, and the Hilton - opened in 1999 - which happily reflects its neighbour's Belle Epoque exterior.

Strict government guidelines dictated that the Hilton should not be higher than the Opera House, and the architects were presented with an extremely unusual curved site. Design difficulties notwithstanding, the result is a mini triumph, a seven-storeyed, columned crescent that blends perfectly with its historic milieu. As a neat example of its architectural intricacies, a single exterior

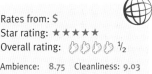

Rates from: $
Star rating: ★ ★ ★ ★ ★
Overall rating: ◐ ◐ ◐ ◐ ½

Ambience:	8.75	Cleanliness:	9.03
Value:	8.46	Facilities:	8.24
Staff:	8.78	Restaurants:	8.22
Location:	8.94	Families:	8.38

Horison Hanoi Hotel

40 Cat Linh Street, Hanoi, Vietnam
T: +84 4 733 0808 **F:** +84 4 733 0888
www.HotelClub.com/Hotels/Hanoi_Horison_Hotel

Of all the larger hotels that are sprouting up around the capital, the Horison has at least made a gesture towards its history by preserving a soaring brick factory chimney on its forecourt. Pretty much everything else in the hotel speaks of the new millennium, with 250 bright if slightly interchangeable rooms, a very presentable array of sports and fitness facilities including an outdoor pool and sundeck, and well-patronised restaurants, of which Le Mayeur's international breakfast, lunch and dinner buffets are probably the most popular. The lobby, echoing and a touch gaudy, is not the best introduction to somewhere most guests would find thoroughly comfortable, although the hotel is not unduly burdened with charm. Gentler souls might find the ground floor - franchised - OV (Overseas Vietnamese) Bar with attendant slot machines anything but entertaining.

Rates from: $
Star rating: ★★★★
Overall rating: 🦋🦋🦋🦋

Ambience:	8.23	Cleanliness:	8.75
Value:	8.57	Facilities:	8.39
Staff:	8.75	Restaurants:	8.10
Location:	8.08	Families:	8.55

Hoi An Beach Resort

Cua Dai Beach, Hoi An, Vietnam
T: +84 510 997 011 **F:** +84 510 997 019
www.HotelClub.com/Hotels/Hoi_An_Beach_Resort

Echoing the design of a traditional Vietnamese village, the relaxed though very modest Hoi An Beach Resort contains 110 suites, villas and rooms (some with quaint Viet-style water jar and ladle bathrooms) - a variety of accommodation that is well in tune with the varied surrounds of the hotel, which is close to Cua Dai beach, 15 minutes out of town. The sleepy De Vong river, the sea, the swimming pools and various water features, to say nothing of nearby paddy fields, all add to an aquatic ambience that make this one of the area's more feng shui-oriented hotels. Musicians strum traditional Vietnamese instruments at the waterside Cua Dai restaurant, where - if your luck's in - you can dine on fresh fish that you caught yourself with rod and line provided by the resort. Sporting types will find a good selection of facilities, however the emphasis is still on chilling out rather than frenetic activity. Some of the rooms close to the road can be a tad noisy - in general the quieter ones are closest to the water.

Rates from: $
Star rating: ★★★★
Overall rating: 🦋🦋🦋🦋

Ambience:	8.38	Cleanliness:	8.57
Value:	8.41	Facilities:	7.56
Staff:	8.41	Restaurants:	7.07
Location:	8.67	Families:	8.07

Hoi An Riverside Resort

Cua Dai Road, Hoi An, Vietnam
T: +84 510 864 800 **F**: +84 510 864 900
www.HotelClub.com/Hotels/Hoi_An_Riverside_Resort

The Hoi An Riverside is a heart-warming property on the verdant banks of the scenic, sleepy De Vong river, a friendly little boutique resort on the fringes of a UNESCO-protected town. The hotel encompasses a series of two- and three-storey apartments loosely sprinkled along the riverbanks and around the chilly but attractive free-form pool. Each apartment block is split into four or six rooms. The rooms are homely and warm with either ethnic Vietnamese or spotless Japanese themes, both

categories are thoughtfully presented with affectionate touches. On opening the curtains, many rooms look out on to the quiet river and lush paddy fields. The photogenic effects of stooping farmers in conical hats and their browsing buffalo cannot be underestimated.

There is little to do at the Hoi An Riverside, and this is surely part of its appeal. Facilities are few and low-key. A relaxing open restaurant in the small timber reception area dishes up some pleasing local food. Central Vietnam is often guilty of a tour-bus factory approach, and nearly all hotel restaurants shy away from à la carte menus,

churning out only monotonous Vietnamese buffets. But not here. Other facilities are few and unspectacular, but the hotel puts on a regular free shuttle to the historic town of Hoi An, which is only a few minutes' drive away. Cua Dai, an agreeable white-sand beach lies only a short distance in the other direction if you would like a break from lazing around the placid pool and a simple spa has been added recently.

Genuinely friendly staff seem to be much more involved with the guests, talking and joking freely. The combination of architecture, location and staff lends a specific warmth to this hotel. If you are not mad on big fancy hotels with reams of facilities, then this will definitely appeal. Certainly one of the most enjoyable small hotels in the area.

Rates from: $
Star rating: ★ ★ ★ ★
Overall rating: ◔◔◔◔ ½

Ambience:	9.20	Cleanliness:	9.02
Value:	8.70	Facilities:	8.34
Staff:	8.84	Restaurants:	8.16
Location:	8.02	Families:	8.31

Majestic Hotel

1 Dong Khoi Street, District 1, Ho Chi Minh City, Vietnam
T: +84 8 829 5517 **F:** +84 8 829 5510
www.HotelClub.com/Hotels/Majestic_Hotel_Ho_Chi_Minh_City

The river bank Majestic's lopsided glamour may not appeal to everybody, but it's pleasing to report that the renovations and additions over the years have not distracted from its very 1925 flavour - the year when it first opened to the public. It's not been over-titivated like some others in the region so there's still plenty of weathered brass knobs and handles, old ticking clocks, and high, regal ceilings and columns. The roof-top bar - a given for many downtown hotels - is relaxing and fun, and the courtyard swimming pool, overlooked by many of the well-appointed guestrooms, is a pleasing "lung" in the middle of a frenetic city. Rather than the ever-so-slightly aggressive style adopted by some of the Majestic's more modern competitors, staff here draw on old-fashioned courtesy and charm. Further discreet expansion and modernisation is planned for the hotel within the coming year.

Rates from: $
Star rating: ★★★★
Overall rating: ♔♔♔♔

Ambience:	8.32	Cleanliness:	8.26
Value:	8.24	Facilities:	7.68
Staff:	8.47	Restaurants:	7.77
Location:	8.71	Families:	7.43

New World Hotel Saigon

76 Le Lai Street, District 1, Ho Chi Minh City, Vietnam
T: +84 8 822 8888 **F:** +84 8 823 0710
www.HotelClub.com/Hotels/New_World_Hotel_Saigon

One of the first of the new wave of hotels to plaster HCMC post doi moi, the New World - at 552 rooms - remains the largest, and as a result is popular with large-scale visiting political delegations and the like. It's slightly remote compared to the competitors that cluster near City Hall, but plunge out of the door and Benh Thanh market is lapping at the hotel's perimeters. The rooms are highly serviceable, if slightly bland, but all are Internet wired. Executive floorites can make use of extensive indoor and outdoor space, with all the standard facilities augmented by excellent views. The health club has been imaginatively put together and golf nuts unable to get out and play for real can head for the outdoor driving net instead. The New World is more attuned to business than leisure accommodation, and large groups rather than individuals. It's very appealing just the same.

Rates from: $
Star rating: ★★★★
Overall rating: ♔♔♔♔½

Ambience:	8.64	Cleanliness:	8.79
Value:	8.66	Facilities:	8.41
Staff:	8.84	Restaurants:	8.59
Location:	8.95	Families:	8.47

Novotel Coralia Ocean Dunes & Golf Resort

1 Ton Duc Thang Street, Phan Thiet, Vietnam
T: +84 62 822 393 **F:** +84 62 825 682
www.HotelClub.com/Hotels/Novotel_Ocean_Dunes_Golf_Resort_Phan_Thiet

The key word here is "golf". When Nick Faldo was commissioned to design this course, he ran a practised eye over the ground, and sensibly decided to let the nearby red sand dunes determine its routing and overall look. The result - a 6,746-yard, par 72, 18 holer - is an engaging and very playable course, and is one of the better ones in Vietnam. This of course is the main reason to come Phan Thiet, a journey made all the more civilised by the Novotel's presence. There are no especial surprises here - all 123 rooms are very comfortable and up to the standard you'd expect from the only international chain in the area, with a brace of reliable restaurants and a couple of bars. If you've brought the family along, there's a club where you can park the kids while you're out on the links. The beach is excellent too, though the sea can be rough at times.

Rates from: $
Star rating: ★ ★ ★ ★
Overall rating: 🌓🌓🌓🌓 ½

Ambience:	7.95	Cleanliness:	9.35
Value:	8.55	Facilities:	7.96
Staff:	8.95	Restaurants:	8.15
Location:	8.55	Families:	8.95

Renaissance Riverside Hotel Saigon

8-15 Ton Duc Thang Street, District 1, Ho Chi Minh City, Vietnam
T: +84 8 822 0033 **F:** +84 8 823 5666
www.HotelClub.com/Hotels/Renaissance_Riverside_Hotel_Saigon

Here is Ho Chi Minh ancient and modern; next door is the plain old Riverside hotel, while the spick and span somewhat newer Renaissance has arguably the best views in the city, stretching across the Saigon River into what is pretty much untouched territory. By contrast, inside the hotel things are thoroughly modern, with 349 rooms and suites crisply if rather anonymously presented, easily adaptable for either business or leisure traveller.

Grab a window seat in the Riverside Café for a full-on perspective of life on Ton Duc Thang Street, which is a constant cavalcade of motorbikes, cyclos, itinerant vendors and more substantial traffic, or - if the carbon monoxide rush is getting to you - retreat to the 22nd floor pool, which although small is very relaxing. The Atrium Lounge, tucked deep within the hotel, is wonderfully calm too. All in all, the Renaissance is a very dependable, if not wildly exciting, choice.

Rates from: $
Star rating: ★ ★ ★ ★
Overall rating: 🌓🌓🌓🌓 ½

Ambience:	8.51	Cleanliness:	9.02
Value:	8.59	Facilities:	8.28
Staff:	8.95	Restaurants:	8.42
Location:	9.04	Families:	8.23

Rex Hotel

141 Nguyen Hue Boulevard, District 1, Ho Chi Minh City, Vietnam
T: +84 8 829 2185 **F:** +84 8 829 6536
www.HotelClub.com/Hotels/Rex_Hotel_Ho_Chi_Minh_City

Rooftop Garden Bar with its tiny pool is a popular place to down a sunset cocktail. The modestly proportioned and equipped rooms are decked out in that unique but slightly unforgettable style, but are great value given the location. Service is patchy for such a friendly nation. Yet despite the holes, when it comes to personality, the Rex is king.

There are few hotels that dare to be as outlandish as the Rex. However, the winds of change are blowing - though they are rather gentle breezes. More time capsule than hotel, it is now making a determined struggle to keep up with flashier local hostelries. The adjoining block has been demolished, and a modern wing is being added. The residual 1970s kitsch either works for you or not - oversized bamboo rattan furniture, gaudy woods and columns, and some interesting trimmings: this is an enjoyable masterpiece of over-the-top. In general facilities are weathered albeit functional. The

Rates from: $
Star rating: ★ ★ ★ ★
Overall rating: 🐾🐾🐾🐾

Ambience:	8.43	Cleanliness:	8.28
Value:	8.30	Facilities:	7.79
Staff:	8.56	Restaurants:	8.33
Location:	9.26	Families:	8.31

Sheraton Saigon Hotel & Towers

88 Dong Khoi Street, District 1, Ho Chi Minh City, Vietnam
T: +84 8 827 2828 **F:** +84 8 827 2929
www.HotelClub.com/Hotels/Sheraton_Saigon_Hotel_and_Towers

facilities - augmented by the Aqua Day Spa whose treatments include hot stone massage and colour therapy - are similarly impressive, and a casino bubbles away on the first floor. This is certainly one of HCMC's best overall hotels, although time's winged chariot hurries near and more competitors are due to open before too long.

The Sheraton - which burst onto the market in May 2003 - brings the cachet of being brand new to the prime city centre location occupied by its older rivals. Walk through the doors here and you're confronted with the Ho Chi Minh City of the future. The bathrooms are floor-to-ceiling marble with massage-style Vichy showers spurting forth, broadband Internet connections hover about the work desk, the ballroom's supersize 759 square metres and there are half a dozen top-flight food and beverage options. The hotel reaches its zenith at Level 23, the highest of the city's iconic rooftop bars, which is swish and sufficiently sheltered to be immune to the weather. Sporting

Rates from: $$
Star rating: ★ ★ ★ ★ ★
Overall rating: 🐾🐾🐾🐾½

Ambience:	8.63	Cleanliness:	8.90
Value:	7.77	Facilities:	8.29
Staff:	8.38	Restaurants:	8.21
Location:	8.99	Families:	8.23

Sofitel Dalat Palace

2 Tran Phu Street, Dalat City, Vietnam
T: +84 63 825 444 **F**: +84 63 825 666
www.HotelClub.com/Hotels/Sofitel_Dalat_Palace

A palace isn't what you'd automatically expect in the rural hill-station of Dalat. The highland town is a national retreat and among the rock-bottom budget hotels, rickety theme park rides and potato patches, this sumptuous residence stands out a mile. Some hotels use the title "palace" rather hopefully, but not the Sofitel Dalat, for palatial it really is.

The restored 1922 colonial mansion is an opulent example of European splendour, not the colonial cottage charm one sometimes finds lingering on, but the sort of indulgence that could have fuelled a very angry peasant revolt. It is easy to engage in brochure waffle when describing the property but, put simply, it feels too personal and too grand to be a hotel and is more like a residence of the aristocracy. Scores of European oil paintings bedeck

the wood-panelled walls, a magnificent chandelier sways above the mosaic-floored lobby, and there are other period pieces such as podgy cherub statuettes. Surrounded by a superb park with grand lawns, the hotel faces out over the picturesque Xuan Huong Lake. It may sound a bit extreme but it is all tastefully done and is a real treat.

This hotel's limited facilities are generally excellent - there's a well-maintained golf course opposite, badminton and tennis courts, petanque and billiards. The cosy watering hole "Larry's Den" is named after Larry Hillblom, one of DHL's founders, and at Le Rabelais, there's some of the most exquisite French fine dining anywhere in Vietnam. After walking up the creaking wooden staircase one enters the quite stunning rooms. More romance awaits, with free-standing baths, honeymooners' beds and, in some of the 43 rooms and suites, crackling fireplaces to keep out the cold on winter nights. There is an absence of air-conditioning due to the altitude, which is usually very temperate. The Dalat Palace has entertained royalty over the years, and is now happily open to anyone ready to hand over the very reasonable price for a night's kip.

Rates from: **$$**
Star rating: ★ ★ ★ ★ ★
Overall rating: ♦ ♦ ♦ ♦ ½

Ambience:	8.96	Cleanliness:	9.18
Value:	8.11	Facilities:	8.17
Staff:	8.61	Restaurants:	8.67
Location:	9.18	Families:	8.61

Sofitel Metropole Hanoi

15 Ngo Quyen Street, Hanoi, Vietnam
T: +84 4 826 6919 F: +84 4 826 6920
www.HotelClub.com/Hotels/Sofitel_Metropole_Hotel_Hanoi

During the past 100 years or so the Metropole has swooped between high-class hostelry and - for a dismal period after Independence - state-run dump. It's now very much back on the crest of a wave, unrivalled when it comes to five-star cuisine, facilities, service and of course heritage.

It's fair to say that much of the capital's new spirit has been captured by the Metropole, which first opened its doors in 1901 and was substantially renovated in 1992. The very best of the original building has been preserved, while a new wing was added at the rear of the property in 1996. The gracious lobby, four-metre-high bedroom ceilings, wide panelled corridors and staircases that greeted the likes of honeymooners

Charlie Chaplin and Paulette Goddard in 1936 are still in situ, but nowadays they are augmented by a Clark Hatch fitness centre and high-speed Internet connections. You can take a tour of Hanoi in one

of the hotel's modern fleet of Mercedes limousines, or climb aboard one of the pedal-powered cyclos whose drivers wait surprisingly patiently outside the front entrance.

This marriage of old and new, traditional and modern, is expressed throughout the hotel. Lunch or dinner at Spices Garden is inspired by the myriad stalls selling pho and other local cuisine on Hanoi's streets. Some 40 dishes - including grilled chicken with lemon leaves, noodles with fried pork and fried rice with lotus seeds - are displayed on low tables and strung from bamboo shoulder poles. At breakfast in the Art Deco-

style Le Beaulieu, crisp French baguettes and croissants take pride of place on the buffet, while tables by the windows look across the street to the ochre walls of the former Governor General's residence, later transformed into an official guesthouse. High tea - delicate pastries and chinaware, pots of Earl Grey and strainers - is served in Le Club Bar to the accompaniment of a grand piano. Evening cocktails at the poolside Bamboo Bar in the central courtyard are shaded by trees that must have been planted at the turn of the last century, and from here you can look around and appreciate the Metropole's classical white facade, stately green shutters and intricate wrought ironwork.

All the hotel's 232 rooms come with modern accoutrements such as satellite TV, and a rolling renovation programme is underway. The 135-room Opera Wing duplicates the hotel's charm, but it is the original rooms that pull in the heritage guest. The timbered walls, the broad polished floorboards that creak ever so gently, and the knowledge that perhaps celebrated guests from the past like Graham Greene, Bill Clinton, Jane Fonda may have occupied the same room all impart a truly unique frisson.

The writer Edgar Snow, visiting the Metropole in 1931, wrote: "It is all very gay and on Saturday nights, when dancing lasts until two o'clock, it even partakes of a breathless abandon". Of course "gay" has a rather different meaning now, but the sentiment that Snow recorded is still very much a part of this thoroughly delightful hotel at the heart of renaissance Hanoi.

Rates from: $$

Star rating: ★ ★ ★ ★ ★

Overall rating: ♨ ♨ ♨ ♨ ½

Ambience:	9.00	Cleanliness:	8.91
Value:	8.02	Facilities:	8.22
Staff:	8.77	Restaurants:	8.70
Location:	9.07	Families:	8.23

Victoria Hoi An Beach Resort

Cua Dai Beach, Hoi An, Vietnam
T: +84 510 927 040 **F**: +84 510 927 041
www.HotelClub.com/Hotels/Victoria_Hoi_An_Beach_Resort

East meets west; the Latin Mediterranean runs up against the Orient, here just a few kilometres from pretty Hoi An. Strung parallel to the beachside is a modern line of bright but pleasant Spanish-style villa-apartments, 105 in all, including 55 bungalows. Upper ones have sloping ceilings and balconies opening out on to the road or sea. Some of these bright and airy rooms depart from the European theme and revel in highly appealing Japanese order. Sporting options are limited, although there are mountain bikes for hire as well as a mini spa. There are few business facilities to speak of, thankfully, but the sharp pool is a hit, and just beyond it lies the extensive though quiet Cua Dai beach. The hotel offers both international and local cuisine, although the food is a litle dominated by a Vietnamese buffet. Still, the resort is original and friendly with an immensely enjoyable ambience.

Rates from: $$
Star rating: ★ ★ ★ ★
Overall rating: 🏠🏠🏠🏠 ½

Ambience:	9.25	Cleanliness:	9.02
Value:	7.98	Facilities:	8.44
Staff:	8.84	Restaurants:	8.04
Location:	8.84	Families:	8.75

Victoria Phan Thiet Resort

Km 9, Phu Hai, Phan Thiet, Vietnam
T: +84 62 813 000 **F**: +84 62 813 007
www.HotelClub.com/Hotels/Victoria_Phan_Thiet_Resort

This is the sort of seaside accommodation that Vietnam really needs, almost a garden with rooms attached, as opposed to larger-than-life concrete and glass monoliths. Once again, the Victoria group provides a lovely low-key haven, with a grand total of 60 seaview rooms built using local materials with private terraces, deck chairs, lazy ceiling fans, comfortable beds and roomy bathrooms. Super for small families, excellent for couples planning on having families. There's a huge amount to occupy you here - a thatched swim-up bar in the centre of the free-form pool (the beach is rocky in parts), a surprisingly extensive and very natural spa, the sophisticated L'Ocean restaurant, tennis, boogie boards and volleyball. There's even a "Cyber Corner", but for a whole host of reasons it doesn't seem to get used very much. The hotel is a little way out of Phan Thiet, but there is so much to get into here, and the service is so charming, there seems to be little reason to want to venture outside.

Rates from: $$
Star rating: ★ ★ ★ ★
Overall rating: 🏠🏠🏠🏠 ½

Ambience:	9.01	Cleanliness:	8.96
Value:	8.43	Facilities:	8.27
Staff:	8.75	Restaurants:	8.33
Location:	8.38	Families:	9.11

Victoria Sapa Hotel

Sapa, Lao Cai, Vietnam
T: +84 20 871 522 **F:** +84 20 871 539
www.HotelClub.com/Hotels/Victoria_Sapa_Hotel_Lao_Cai

Sapa's modern history started with French colonisers seeking out cooler climes in the heat of the summer, and a recreational, holiday air continues to permeate the area. Rattling up here by rail (the Victoria runs its own carriage) or road is a departure to another Vietnam, one populated by colourful hill tribes and with a very different feel from the coast. Built in chalet style, the Victoria's 77 rooms all come with a balcony, and international standard mod cons set off by local handicrafts. Given that trekking - even for as little as a couple of hours - is the main activity here, it's nice to know that at the end of the day you can look forward to relaxing weary muscles in the indoor pool, having a sauna or a massage, and following up with a drink by the fireplace in the bar and perhaps a fondue for supper. Currently this is still far and away the best hotel in the area.

Rates from: $$
Star rating: ★★★★
Overall rating: 🐾🐾🐾🐾

Ambience:	8.32	Cleanliness:	8.04
Value:	7.89	Facilities:	7.69
Staff:	8.32	Restaurants:	8.32
Location:	8.32	Families:	8.23

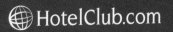

Hotel ratings index

	Area	PAGE	★	👍	Ambience	Value	Staff	Location	Clean...
AUSTRALIA	**Area**								
Burswood InterContinental	Perth	9	5	4.5	8.71	8.07	8.19	8.14	9.
Crown Towers	Melbourne	10	5	4.5	8.90	8.04	8.49	8.85	9.
Four Seasons	Sydney	11	5	4.5	8.68	7.95	8.92	9.41	9.
Grand Hyatt	Melbourne	11	5	4	8.51	7.54	8.10	8.73	8.
Hayman	Great Barrier Reef	12	5	5	9.43	8.05	9.19	9.43	9.5
InterContinental	Sydney	14	5	4.5	8.85	7.98	8.43	9.33	9.2
Langham	Melbourne	14	5	4.5	8.85	8.07	8.44	9.48	9.2
Longitude 131°	Uluru (Ayers Rock)	15	5	n/a	n/a	n/a	n/a	n/a	n/
Observatory	Sydney	16	5	4.5	9.14	7.57	9.00	8.71	9.5
Palazzo Versace	Gold Coast	17	5	4.5	9.17	8.57	8.57	8.48	9.3
Park Hyatt	Melbourne	18	5	4.5	9.25	8.34	8.41	8.97	9.5
Park Hyatt	Sydney	19	5	4.5	9.05	7.52	8.41	9.24	9.0
Shangri-la	Sydney	20	5	4.5	8.76	7.65	8.69	9.35	9.1
Sheraton Mirage	Gold Coast	20	5	4.5	9.24	7.60	8.52	9.04	9.0
Sheraton Mirage	Port Douglas	21	5	4	8.92	7.58	8.21	8.79	8.9
Sheraton On The Park	Sydney	22	5	4.5	8.65	7.89	8.74	9.34	9.1
Sofitel	Brisbane	23	5	4	8.82	7.71	8.41	8.65	8.9
Sofitel	Melbourne	23	5	4.5	8.82	7.59	8.86	9.09	9.3
Marriott	Surfers Paradise	24	5	4	8.33	8.07	8.40	8.67	8.7
W Sydney	Sydney	24	5	4	9.50	7.69	8.48	8.40	9.2
Westin	Melbourne	25	5	4.5	9.13	7.81	8.74	9.36	9.2
Westin	Sydney	25	5	4.5	8.81	7.66	8.53	9.34	9.2
BRUNEI	**Area**								
Empire	Bandar Seri Begawan	27	5	4.5	9.22	8.39	8.42	8.05	9.3
Sheraton Utama	Bandar Seri Begawan	27	5	4	8.33	8.33	8.89	8.11	8.6
CAMBODIA	**Area**								
Amansara	Siem Reap	29	5	5	9.67	8.00	9.00	8.67	9.00
Angkor Village	Siem Reap	30	4	4.5	9.41	8.85	9.21	9.26	9.38
FCC	Phnom Penh	31	2	4.5	9.25	8.50	8.50	9.63	8.88
La Résidence	Siem Reap	31	5	4.5	9.63	8.21	9.11	8.95	9.6
Raffles Grand	Siem Reap	32	5	4.5	9.28	8.07	9.29	9.12	9.16
Raffles Le Royal	Phnom Penh	33	5	4.5	9.48	7.95	8.83	8.58	9.00

Facilities

...ies	Restaurants	Families	🏊	⛷	📈	🧭	♿	🔖	1	✚	🧸	📖	🎵	⭕	☁	✈	CNN	🔑	🏠	🎿	🌀	ℹ	⮡
5	8.69	8.23	•		•	•	•		•	•		•	•		•	•	•		•	•	•	•	•	•
04	8.73	8.22	•		•	•	•		•		•	•			•	•	•		•	•	•		•	•
47	8.29	7.17	•		•		•		•		•	•			•	•	•	•		•	•		•	
19	7.90	7.14	•		•		•		•		•	•	•		•	•	•	•		•	•		•	
94	9.05	7.53	•	•	•			•		•	•	•			•	•	•	•		•		•		
32	8.60	8.17	•		•		•		•		•	•			•	•	•	•		•				
59	8.63	8.41			•		•		•		•	•			•	•	•	•		•			•	
a	n/a	n/a			•		•				•	•			•	•				•			•	
71	8.30	7.10	•		•		•		•		•	•			•	•	•	•		•			•	•
89	8.80	7.47			•		•		•		•	•			•	•	•	•		•	•		•	•
68	8.27	6.83			•		•		•		•	•			•	•				•			•	
42	8.52	7.49	•		•		•		•			•			•	•	•	•		•			•	
67	8.38	7.22	•		•		•		•		•	•			•	•	•	•		•			•	
79	8.32	8.36	•	•	•		•		•			•			•	•	•	•		•			•	•
42	8.13	8.00	•	•	•		•		•		•	•	•		•	•	•	•		•			•	•
51	8.40	8.09					•		•		•	•			•	•	•	•	•					
32	8.50	7.36	•		•				•		•	•	•	•	•	•	•		•			•		
43	8.86	7.27	•		•		•		•		•	•			•	•	•			•			•	
32	7.81	8.59	•	•	•		•		•		•	•			•	•	•	•		•	•	•	•	•
36	8.67	6.13	•		•		•		•		•	•	•		•	•	•	•		•			•	
47	7.97	7.96			•		•		•		•	•			•	•	•	•		•			•	
52	8.42	7.49	•		•		•		•		•	•	•		•	•	•	•	•		•			•	
21	8.82	9.03	•	•	•		•	•	•		•	•	•		•	•	•	•		•	•	•	•	•
08	8.44	8.43	•		•		•		•		•	•			•	•	•	•		•				
00	8.67	9.00			•										•	•				•		•	•	•
19	8.18	8.48	•		•		•								•	•				•		•	•	
89	9.13	6.80			•						•				•	•	•	•				•		
73	7.71	8.33	•		•						•				•	•				•		•		
48	8.64	8.66	•		•				•						•	•	•	•	•	•	•			
40	8.26	8.32	•		•				•						•	•	•	•	•	•	•			

Hotel ratings index

Hotel	Area	PAGE	★	👍	Ambience	Value	Staff	Location	Clean
Sofitel Royal	Siem Reap	34	5	4.5	9.14	8.27	8.94	8.88	9.
CHINA	**Area**								
China World	Beijing	37	5	4.5	8.93	8.29	8.70	8.97	9.
Four Seasons	Shanghai	37	5	4.5	8.85	7.90	8.85	8.41	9.
Garden	Guangzhou	38	5	4	8.33	8.23	8.26	8.47	8.
Grand Hyatt	Beijing	38	5	4.5	8.78	7.97	8.53	8.95	9.
Grand Hyatt	Shanghai	39	5	5	9.52	8.77	9.21	9.07	9.
JW Marriott	Shanghai	41	5	4.5	8.77	8.44	8.71	8.71	9.
Lu Song Yuan	Beijing	42	2	4	9.25	8.69	8.69	8.13	7.
Peace	Shanghai	43	3	4	9.18	8.11	8.16	9.60	8.
Penninsula Palace	Beijing	44	5	5	8.98	8.74	9.19	9.09	9.
Portman Ritz-Carlton	Shanghai	45	5	4.5	8.82	8.15	8.86	8.97	9.
Pudong Shangri-La	Shanghai	46	5	4.5	8.80	8.04	8.54	8.37	9.0
Shangri-La	Hangzhou	46	5	4.5	9.00	8.09	8.79	9.67	9.0
Shangri-La	Shenzhen	47	5	4.5	8.49	8.19	8.58	8.78	8.
Sheraton Great Wall	Beijing	47	5	4.5	8.47	8.20	8.59	8.31	8.
Sheraton	Sanya	48	5	4.5	9.30	8.33	8.85	8.63	9.3
Sheraton	Suzhou	48	5	4.5	9.20	8.53	8.87	8.53	9.2
St Regis	Beijing	49	5	4.5	9.11	8.04	8.94	8.74	9.3
St Regis	Shanghai	50	5	5	8.97	8.81	9.19	7.94	9.4
Westin	Shanghai	51	5	4.5	8.96	8.21	8.58	8.62	9.1
White Swan	Guangzhou	51	5	4.5	8.83	8.17	8.80	8.63	9.0
HONG KONG	**Area**								
Conrad	Hong Kong Island	54	5	4.5	8.85	7.87	8.80	9.13	9.2
Excelsior	Hong Kong Island	54	4	4	8.42	8.12	8.39	9.23	8.7
Gold Coast	New Territories	55	4	4	8.61	8.23	8.29	8.51	8.5
Grand Hyatt	Hong Kong Island	56	5	4.5	9.00	7.85	8.75	8.68	9.2
Harbour Plaza	Kowloon	57	5	4	8.60	8.21	8.40	7.89	9.0
Holiday Inn Golden Mile	Kowloon	57	4	4	8.37	8.00	8.27	9.10	8.7
InterContinental	Kowloon	58	5	4.5	9.01	7.99	8.87	9.08	9.2
Island Shangri-La	Hong Kong Island	59	5	4.5	9.00	7.93	8.76	9.12	9.2
JW Marriott	Hong Kong Island	60	5	4.5	8.85	8.06	8.75	9.28	9.1
Kowloon Hotel	Kowloon	60	4	4	8.03	8.10	8.26	9.33	8.7

Facilities

...ilities	Restaurants	Families	1	2	3	4	5	6	7	8	9	10	11	12	13	14	15	16	17	18	19	20
65	8.40	8.74	•		•		•					•	•	•	•			•			•		•
.81	8.77	8.79			•		•			•		•	•	•	•	•		•			•		•
67	8.61	8.32	•		•		•			•		•	•	•	•	•		•		•	•		
.30	8.24	7.73	•		•		•			•		•	•	•	•	•					•	•	
.58	8.45	8.24			•		•			•		•	•	•	•	•					•	•	
.30	9.33	9.05			•		•			•		•	•	•	•	•	•				•		
.64	8.80	8.49	•		•		•			•		•	•	•	•	•	•				•		
.24	6.67	8.67			•								•	•		•					•		
.66	8.13	8.03	•		•		•			•		•	•	•		•					•		
.00	8.88	8.57	•		•		•			•		•	•	•	•	•					•		
.69	8.59	8.63	•		•		•			•		•	•	•	•	•				•	•		
.50	8.37	8.14	•		•					•		•	•	•	•	•					•	•	
.50	8.45	8.71	•		•		•			•		•	•	•	•	•					•	•	
.47	8.54	8.31			•					•		•		•	•				•				
.63	8.63	8.14	•		•		•			•		•	•	•	•	•		•					
.08	8.22	9.00	•	•	•		•	•		•	•	•	•	•	•	•				•	•	•	
.75	8.84	8.83	•	•	•		•	•		•		•	•	•	•	•				•	•	•	•
.84	8.64	8.33	•		•		•			•		•	•	•	•	•	•				•		
.10	8.86	8.85	•		•		•			•		•	•	•	•	•	•				•		
.67	8.57	8.32	•		•		•			•		•	•	•	•	•		•			•		
.51	8.77	8.64	•		•		•			•	•	•	•	•	•	•			•		•	•	
3.69	8.66	8.40	•		•		•			•		•	•	•	•	•	•				•		
8.16	8.47	8.22	•		•		•			•		•	•	•	•	•				•	•		
8.33	8.26	8.30		•	•		•			•		•	•	•	•				•	•		•	
8.73	8.89	8.39	•		•		•			•		•	•	•	•	•			•				
8.55	8.43	8.31	•		•		•			•	•	•		•	•	•			•		•		
8.24	8.53	8.24	•		•		•			•		•	•	•	•	•			•				
8.86	8.99	8.46	•		•					•		•	•	•	•				•				
8.74	8.91	8.41	•		•		•			•		•	•	•	•				•		•		
8.61	8.65	8.57			•		•			•		•	•	•	•				•				
7.86	8.13	8.18	•		•							•	•	•	•	•	•				•		

Facilities

...ilities	Restaurants	Families	F1	F2	F3	F4	F5	F6	F7	F8	F9	F10	F11	F12	F13	F14	F15	F16	F17	F18	F19	F20	F21
.70	8.83	8.29	•		•		•			•		•		•	•	•	•			•			•	
.46	8.84	8.15	•		•		•			•		•		•	•	•	•				•			
.23	8.50	8.33			•		•			•		•		•	•	•	•				•		•	
.52	9.00	8.25	•		•			•		•		•		•	•	•		•	•				•	
.31	8.28	8.27	•		•			•		•		•		•	•	•					•			
.79	9.08	8.49			•		•			•		•		•		•				•	•			
.59	8.69	8.48	•		•		•		•	•		•		•	•				•		•		•	
.40	8.55	8.28			•			•		•		•		•	•						•			
.52	8.55	8.42	•		•		•			•		•		•	•		•	•			•			
.07	7.60	8.73	•				•			•		•		•	•					•		•	•	
.65	8.46	8.36	•		•		•			•		•		•	•	•	•			•			•	
.32	8.60	9.13	•	•	•		•	•		•			•	•	•	•	•			•			•	•
.67	9.00	7.57	•		•		•				•	•	•	•	•					•		•	•	
.60	9.13	8.64	•		•		•			•			•	•	•	•				•			•	
.42	8.54	8.10			•		•			•			•	•	•	•				•		•	•	
.42	9.07	8.85	•		•		•			•	•	•		•	•	•				•			•	
.69	8.90	8.68	•	•	•		•			•	•	•	•	•	•	•	•			•			•	
.03	8.75	9.17	•	•	•			•			•	•		•	•	•				•	•		•	
.95	9.05	8.96	•		•			•		•	•	•		•	•	•				•			•	
.44	9.11	8.56	•		•		•			•		•	•	•	•	•				•			•	
.35	8.83	8.74	•		•			•		•		•		•	•	•				•			•	
.32	8.67	8.67	•		•		•			•		•		•	•	•				•			•	
.58	8.71	8.67	•		•		•			•		•		•	•	•				•			•	
.33	8.49	7.95	•		•		•			•		•		•	•	•				•			•	
.77	8.40	9.08	•	•	•		•		•	•		•		•	•					•		•	•	•
.83	8.57	8.86	•		•			•	•		•		•	•	•					•		•	•	
9.19	8.75	8.57	•		•			•	•		•		•	•	•			•			•		•	
n/a	n/a	n/a	•		•							•	•	•	•									
.37	9.00	8.31	•		•		•			•		•	•	•	•	•				•			•	
.21	8.49	8.09	•		•		•			•		•		•	•	•	•			•			•	
.45	8.57	8.44	•		•		•			•		•		•	•	•	•			•			•	
.34	8.60	8.32	•		•		•		•	•		•	•	•	•	•	•			•			•	

Facilities

Facilities	Restaurants	Families																					
8.94	8.83	8.50	•		•		•			•		•	•	•	•	•	•	•		•		•	
8.85	8.91	8.16	•		•		•		•	•		•	•	•	•	•	•	•		•		•	
8.95	9.10	8.33	•		•		•			•		•		•	•	•	•	•		•	•	•	
9.05	8.78	8.71	•		•		•			•		•		•	•	•	•	•		•		•	
8.23	8.63	8.00	•		•					•		•		•	•	•	•	•	•	•		•	
8.26	8.49	7.84	•									•		•	•	•		•		•		•	
8.69	8.65	8.14	•		•				•	•				•	•	•		•		•	•	•	•
9.19	9.31	9.22	•		•									•	•			•		•	•	•	
8.76	8.84	8.68	•	•	•			•						•	•			•		•	•	•	
8.67	8.54	8.43	•	•	•			•	•					•	•			•		•	•	•	
9.00	8.75	8.25	•	•	•			•	•					•	•			•		•		•	
n/a	n/a	n/a	•							•				•	•			•		•		•	
7.87	8.00	7.55								•		•		•	•	•	•	•		•		•	
8.98	8.22	9.44	•		•		•				•			•	•	•	•	•		•		•	
8.67	8.50	8.67	•	•	•					•	•			•	•		•	•		•	•	•	•
8.54	8.67	8.89	•	•	•		•	•		•	•			•	•	•	•	•		•		•	•
8.63	8.56	8.93	•	•	•		•				•			•	•		•	•		•		•	
8.48	8.51	8.47	•		•		•			•				•	•		•	•		•		•	
8.81	8.48	9.27	•	•	•		•			•				•	•		•	•		•		•	
8.40	8.19	8.19	•	•					•		•			•	•		•	•		•		•	•
8.45	8.24	7.88	•							•		•		•	•	•	•	•		•		•	•
8.75	8.55	8.47	•		•				•		•			•	•	•	•	•	•	•		•	
8.93	8.42	8.93	•	•	•					•		•	•	•	•	•		•		•		•	
8.83	8.60	8.50	•		•					•		•		•	•	•	•	•		•		•	
8.92	8.51	8.31			•					•		•		•	•	•	•	•		•	•	•	
8.85	8.86	8.80	•		•					•		•		•	•	•	•	•		•	•	•	
8.66	8.62	8.91	•	•	•		•	•		•				•	•			•		•		•	•
8.73	8.64	8.39	•		•			•		•		•	•	•	•		•	•		•	•	•	
8.38	8.57	8.75	•		•			•		•			•	•	•		•	•		•	•	•	
8.32	8.55	8.38			•			•		•			•	•	•			•		•	•	•	
8.32	8.18	8.84	•	•			•	•		•		•		•	•		•	•		•	•	•	•
8.25	8.33	8.71	•		•			•		•	•			•	•	•		•		•	•	•	

Hotel ratings index

		PAGE	★	👍	Ambience	Value	Staff	Location	Cleanliness
JW Marriott	Jakarta	115	5	4	8.47	8.31	8.20	7.86	8.61
JW Marriott	Surabaya	115	5	4	8.48	8.16	8.64	8.28	8.72
Komaneka	Bali	116	4	4.5	9.63	8.50	9.25	8.88	8.63
Le Méridien Nirwana	Bali	117	5	4.5	9.00	8.53	8.93	8.53	9.08
Legian Beach	Bali	117	4	4.5	9.08	8.27	8.91	9.00	9.17
Mandarin Oriental Majapahit	Surabaya	118	5	4.5	9.11	8.56	8.50	8.06	9.00
Mandarin Oriental	Jakarta	119	5	4.5	8.58	8.21	9.13	8.97	9.16
Maya Ubud	Bali	119	5	4.5	9.60	8.33	9.13	8.40	9.13
Melia	Bali	120	5	4.5	8.72	8.36	8.78	8.56	9.03
Mulia Senayan	Jakarta	120	5	4.5	8.94	7.86	8.77	8.23	8.95
Novotel Coralia Benoa	Bali	121	4	4.5	9.26	8.85	8.97	8.26	8.95
Novotel Coralia	Lombok	122	4	4.5	9.36	8.86	8.93	8.57	9.00
Nusa Dua	Bali	122	5	4.5	9.26	8.47	9.00	8.68	8.93
Oberoi	Bali	123	5	4.5	9.41	7.87	9.21	8.97	9.08
Oberoi	Lombok	124	5	4.5	9.78	8.44	9.22	8.56	9.33
Pita Maha	Bali	125	5	4.5	9.47	8.32	9.05	9.00	8.79
Poppies	Bali	125	3	4.5	9.55	8.55	8.85	8.55	8.60
Ritz-Carlton	Bali	126	5	4.5	9.32	8.26	9.22	8.51	9.17
Santika	Bali	127	4	4.5	8.97	8.30	9.03	8.77	9.13
Shangri-La	Jakarta	127	5	4.5	8.71	8.12	8.84	8.02	8.77
Shangri-La	Surabaya	128	5	4.5	9.14	7.57	9.14	8.43	9.57
Sheraton	Bandung	128	5	4.5	8.89	8.89	9.67	7.78	8.33
Sheraton Laguna	Bali	129	5	4.5	9.07	8.44	8.96	8.75	8.94
Sheraton Senggigi	Lombok	130	5	4.5	9.41	8.09	9.05	8.68	9.32
Tugu	Bali	131	5	5	9.44	8.88	9.60	8.72	9.68
Uma Ubud	Bali	132	5	n/a	n/a	n/a	n/a	n/a	n/a
Watergarden	Bali	133	2	n/a	n/a	n/a	n/a	n/a	n/a
JAPAN	**Area**								
ANA	Tokyo	136	5	4.5	8.52	7.57	9.12	8.95	9.36
Century Hyatt	Tokyo	136	5	4	8.42	8.00	8.87	8.07	9.13
Four Seasons Chinzan-so	Tokyo	137	5	4.5	9.11	7.68	9.04	7.79	9.62
Grand Hyatt	Fukuoka	138	5	4	8.61	7.50	8.56	8.17	9.00
Grand Hyatt	Tokyo	139	5	4.5	9.05	7.91	8.80	8.91	9.46

Facilities

Facilities	Restaurants	Families	Facility icons (left → right)
8.33	8.50	8.63	• _ • _ • _ _ • • • • • • • • • • • _
8.48	8.58	8.28	• _ • _ • _ _ • _ • • • • • • _ _ • _
8.89	7.71	6.57	• _ _ _ _ _ _ _ • _ • • • • • _ • _ •
8.66	8.55	8.84	• _ • _ • _ • • • • • • • _ • • _ •
8.38	8.08	8.04	• • _ • • _ _ • • • • • • • •
8.27	8.44	8.27	• _ • _ _ • • • • • • • • •
8.69	8.55	8.21	_ • _ _ _ • _ • • • _ • • •
8.72	8.29	8.45	• _ • _ • _ • • • _ • • •
8.66	8.28	8.70	• • • • • • • • • • • • • •
8.66	8.82	8.49	• _ • • _ • • • • • • • •
8.52	8.54	9.24	• • • • • • • • • •
8.50	8.46	8.85	• • • • • • • • • • •
8.74	8.69	8.84	• • • • • • • • • • • •
8.52	8.13	7.96	• • • • • • • • •
9.00	8.11	7.50	• • • • • • • • •
8.02	7.89	8.50	• • • • •
8.37	8.56	8.44	• • • • •
8.77	8.73	8.73	• • • • • • • • • • • • • • • •
8.21	8.28	8.60	• • • • • •
8.59	8.79	8.44	• • • • • • • •
8.85	8.29	8.50	• • • • • • • • • • •
8.46	8.00	9.00	• • • • • • • • • •
8.62	8.35	8.78	• • • • • • • • • • • •
8.52	8.57	9.36	• • • • • • • • • • •
8.48	8.88	9.33	• • • • • • • • • •
n/a	n/a	n/a	• • • • • •
n/a	n/a	n/a	• • • • •
8.38	8.63	8.00	• • • • • • •
8.18	8.20	8.22	• • • • • • • •
8.74	8.41	8.75	• • • • • • • • •
8.76	8.59	8.36	• • • • • • • •
8.76	8.59	8.18	• • • • • • • •

Hotel ratings index

		PAGE	★	👍	Ambience	Value	Staff	Location	Cleanliness
				Ratings					
Hilton	Osaka	141	4	4.5	8.80	7.73	8.90	8.80	9.47
Hilton	Tokyo	141	4	4	8.30	7.51	8.99	8.58	9.21
Imperial	Tokyo	142	5	4.5	8.99	7.92	9.23	9.27	9.41
Keio Plaza	Tokyo	143	3	4	8.39	7.70	8.86	9.05	9.20
Kobe Bay Sheraton	Kobe	143	4	4	8.08	7.17	8.83	8.92	9.25
New Otani	Tokyo	144	5	4.5	8.95	8.21	8.98	8.98	9.37
Okura	Tokyo	144	5	4.5	9.03	8.05	9.21	8.51	9.46
Park Hyatt	Tokyo	145	5	4.5	9.19	7.77	9.09	8.30	9.51
Prince Akasaka	Tokyo	146	3	4.5	9.03	7.67	8.88	8.73	9.45
Ritz-Carlton	Osaka	146	5	4.5	9.00	8.03	8.59	8.59	9.45
Westin	Kyoto	147	5	4.5	8.92	8.67	9.25	8.33	9.42
Westin	Tokyo	148	5	4	8.73	7.65	8.79	8.29	9.27
Yokohama Grand InterContinental	Yokohama	148	4	4	8.75	7.44	8.56	8.94	9.25
KOREA	**Area**								
COEX InterContinental	Seoul	151	5	4.5	8.43	8.00	8.57	8.85	9.13
Grand Hilton	Seoul	151	5	4.5	8.63	8.13	8.87	8.63	9.24
Grand Hyatt	Seoul	152	5	4.5	8.92	7.86	8.66	8.39	8.94
Grand InterContinental	Seoul	153	5	4.5	8.92	7.50	8.68	9.16	9.13
JW Marriott	Seoul	153	5	4.5	8.83	7.79	8.90	8.33	9.19
Lotte	Seoul	154	5	4.5	8.87	7.98	8.51	9.11	9.15
Marriott	Busan	154	5	4	8.61	7.56	8.78	8.89	9.33
Ritz-Carlton	Seoul	155	5	4	8.56	7.68	8.70	8.32	8.82
Sheraton Walker Hill	Seoul	156	5	4	8.80	7.67	8.80	7.73	8.90
Shilla	Jeju	156	5	4.5	9.11	8.14	9.00	8.68	9.00
Shilla	Seoul	157	5	4.5	8.94	7.94	9.00	7.94	9.21
Westin Chosun	Seoul	158	5	4.5	8.70	7.49	8.85	8.91	9.25
LAOS	**Area**								
Le Calao	Luang Prabang	160	2	n/a	n/a	n/a	n/a	n/a	n/a
La Résidence Phou Vao	Luang Prabang	161	5	4.5	9.75	8.81	9.31	8.88	9.44
Lao Plaza	Vientiane	162	4	4.5	8.75	8.38	9.50	9.25	9.25
Novotel	Vientiane	162	4	4	8.50	8.50	9.50	8.67	8.67
Settha Palace	Vientiane	163	4	4.5	9.53	8.80	9.53	9.00	9.40

Facilities

...ilities	Restaurants	Families	1	2	3	4	5	6	7	8	9	10	11	12	13	14	15	16	17	18	19	20
.49	8.41	8.39			•		•			•		•		•	•	•	•		•				
.37	8.57	8.44			•		•			•		•		•	•	•	•		•		•		
.42	8.67	8.44	•		•		•			•		•		•	•	•	•		•			•	
.28	8.33	7.79	•		•		•			•		•		•	•	•	•			•		•	
.38	8.30	8.22	•		•		•			•		•		•	•	•	•	•	•		•	•	
.64	8.97	8.68	•		•		•			•		•		•	•	•	•		•	•		•	
.37	8.75	8.62	•		•		•			•		•		•	•	•	•		•	•		•	
.77	8.98	8.11	•		•		•			•		•	•	•	•	•	•		•	•		•	
.59	8.50	8.58			•		•			•		•		•	•	•	•			•		•	
.81	8.57	8.32			•		•			•		•		•	•	•	•	•	•				
.50	8.50	8.83			•		•		•	•	•	•	•	•	•	•	•		•	•	•		
.40	8.28	7.98			•		•					•		•	•	•	•						
.22	8.29	7.91			•		•			•				•	•	•	•	•	•	•			
.61	8.38	8.12			•		•			•		•		•	•	•	•			•			
.58	8.36	8.57	•		•		•			•	•	•	•	•	•	•	•		•			•	
.46	8.67	8.44	•		•		•			•		•		•	•	•	•	•	•	•	•		
.67	8.76	8.20			•		•			•		•		•	•	•	•		•	•			
.71	8.46	8.73	•		•		•			•		•		•	•	•	•		•		•	•	•
.63	8.58	8.68	•		•					•		•		•	•	•	•		•			•	
.82	8.88	7.58	•	•	•					•		•	•	•	•	•	•		•				
.47	8.56	7.93			•					•		•	•	•	•	•	•		•				
.53	8.67	8.29	•			•				•		•		•	•	•	•		•	•	•		
.66	8.93	8.77	•	•	•	•		•		•		•		•	•	•	•		•	•	•		
.74	8.77	8.72	•		•	•				•	•	•		•	•	•	•		•	•	•	•	
.60	8.32	7.95	•		•		•		•	•		•		•	•	•	•		•			•	
n/a	n/a	n/a										•										
.67	8.60	9.00	•		•					•		•		•	•	•	•			•		•	
.13	8.63	8.60	•		•			•		•	•	•		•	•	•	•	•		•			
.39	8.17	8.00	•		•			•		•	•	•		•	•	•	•			•	•	•	
.38	8.53	8.20	•		•					•		•		•	•	•	•			•			

Hotel ratings index

Facilities

...ities	Restaurants	Families
...81	8.13	8.90
...14	8.50	8.63
...62	8.79	8.78
...63	8.16	8.77
...58	8.53	8.76
...18	7.79	8.16
...91	8.34	8.04
...28	8.19	8.39
...17	8.16	8.50
n/a	n/a	n/a
...26	8.34	8.96
n/a	n/a	n/a
...53	8.37	8.28
...71	8.64	8.21
...51	8.51	8.32
...68	8.59	8.82
...04	8.16	8.58
...20	8.54	8.21
...90	8.23	7.82
...19	8.37	9.05
...16	8.39	8.33
...52	8.35	8.31
...66	8.62	8.41
...22	8.16	8.92
...70	8.68	8.55
...57	8.57	8.50
...55	8.58	8.41
...55	8.51	8.99
...55	8.56	8.83
...69	7.55	8.33
...34	8.38	8.44

Hotel ratings index

		PAGE	★	👍	Ambience	Value	Staff	Location	Cleanli...
Ratings									
Renaissance	Kuala Lumpur	191	5	4.5	8.66	8.44	8.71	8.71	8.9
Ritz-Carlton	Kuala Lumpur	192	5	4.5	8.96	8.62	9.23	8.76	9.3
Shangri-La	Kuala Lumpur	193	5	4.5	8.85	8.35	8.77	8.76	9.0
Shangri-La's Golden Sands	Penang	194	4	4.5	8.79	8.62	8.51	8.80	8.7
Shangri-La's Rasa Ria	Kota Kinabalu	195	5	4.5	9.00	8.56	8.91	8.77	8.9
Shangri-La's Tanjung Aru	Kota Kinabalu	196	5	4.5	8.97	8.55	9.03	8.93	8.9
Sheraton	Langkawi	197	5	4.5	9.02	8.61	8.86	8.86	8.9
Sheraton Imperial	Kuala Lumpur	198	5	4	8.78	8.29	8.43	7.96	8.9
Sheraton Perdana	Langkawi	198	5	4.5	8.93	8.36	8.72	8.55	8.7
Smokehouse	Cameron Highlands	199	3	n/a	n/a	n/a	n/a	n/a	n/a
Sutera Harbour	Kuala Lumpur	200	5	4.5	8.79	8.48	8.51	8.85	8.9
Sunway Lagoon	Kota Kinabalu	201	5	4.5	8.66	8.17	8.41	8.27	8.8
Swiss Garden	Kuala Lumpur	201	5	4	8.33	8.47	8.56	8.47	8.4
Tanjong Jara	Kuala Terengganu	202	5	4	9.16	7.19	8.63	8.51	8.8
Tanjung Rhu	Langkawi	203	5	5	9.23	8.77	9.14	9.32	8.7
Westin	Kuala Lumpur	204	5	4.5	8.91	8.25	8.52	8.87	9.1
MALDIVES	**Area**								
Angsana	Maldives	206	5	5	9.73	8.07	9.13	9.27	9.0
Banyan Tree	Maldives	207	5	5	9.67	7.96	9.22	9.24	9.2
Four Seasons	Maldives	208	5	5	9.64	7.93	9.38	9.07	9.3
Hilton	Maldives	210	5	4.5	9.67	7.85	8.79	9.24	9.1
Soneva Fushi	Maldives	211	5	4.5	9.94	7.94	8.59	9.06	9.4
Soneva Gili	Maldives	213	5	4.5	9.54	7.46	9.46	9.54	9.6
Taj Exotica	Maldives	214	5	4	9.67	8.00	8.78	8.22	9.0
MYANMAR	**Area**								
Bagan	Bagan	216	3	4.5	9.23	8.77	9.14	9.32	8.77
Grand Plaza Parkroyal	Yangon	216	5	4	7.56	8.72	9.11	8.50	8.6
Governor's Residence	Yangon	217	4	4.5	9.20	8.31	8.76	8.09	8.57
Inle Princess	Inle Lake	218	2	n/a	n/a	n/a	n/a	n/a	n/a
Kandawgyi Palace	Yangon	218	5	4.5	9.00	8.83	8.67	9.17	8.58
Popa Mountain	Mount Popa	219	3	n/a	n/a	n/a	n/a	n/a	n/a
Sandoway	Ngapali	219	4	n/a	n/a	n/a	n/a	n/a	n/a
Sedona	Mandalay	220	5	4	8.20	8.70	8.45	8.10	8.40

Facilities

...lies	Restaurants	Families																						
,6	8.52	8.39	•		•		•			•		•		•	•	•	•	•		•	•		
,2	8.43	8.93			•				•		•	•		•	•	•	•		•	•	•		
,6	8.71	8.52	•		•		•		•	•	•		•	•	•	•		•	•	•			
,7	8.44	8.80	•	•			•		•	•	•		•		•	•	•	•		•		•	
,5	8.50	8.84	•	•	•		•	•	•	•	•		•	•	•	•	•	•		•	•		
,5	8.59	8.89	•	•	•		•		•	•	•	•	•		•	•		•		•	•		•
,6	8.75	8.90	•	•	•	•			•	•		•	•	•	•		•		•		•	
,5	8.38	8.25	•		•		•			•	•		•	•	•		•		•		•	
,4	8.40	8.81	•	•	•		•			•		•	•	•	•		•		•		•	•
,a	n/a	n/a	•							•	•	•								
,4	8.51	8.63	•	•	•		•		•	•	•	•	•		•	•		•		•	•	•
,6	8.59	8.63	•		•		•	•		•	•	•		•	•	•	•		•		•	•
,9	8.24	8.67	•		•					•		•	•	•	•	•	•				•
,9	8.12	8.53	•	•			•			•		•	•	•	•		•		•	•	•
,0	8.14	8.93	•	•	•		•		•	•	•	•	•		•	•		•		•	•	•
,9	8.17	8.06			•			•	•	•	•	•	•		•	•	•		•		
,5	8.67	8.78			•			•				•	•		•		•				•	•
,5	8.58	8.46			•			•	•		•		•		•		•				•	•
,7	8.77	8.41	•	•	•			•		•	•		•	•	•	•		•			•	•
,0	9.00	8.39	•	•				•			•	•		•	•		•			•	•	•	•
,2	7.75	8.58	•	•				•			•		•		•	•		•			•	•	•
,3	8.31	7.25	•	•	•			•		•		•		•	•	•		•		•	•	•	•
,8	8.00	7.50			•			•		•		•		•	•		•			•	•	•
,0	8.14	8.93	•		•	•			•	•		•	•		•		•			•	•	•
,0	7.94	7.76	•		•					•		•	•	•	•	•		•			•	•	•
,2	8.19	8.26	•		•					•	•		•	•						•	•
/a	n/a	n/a			•							•	•			•				
,3	8.42	8.17	•		•				•			•	•	•	•		•		•		•
/a	n/a	n/a			•		•					•	•	•	•	•		•		•
/a	n/a	n/a	•	•			•					•			•			•			•
,7	8.00	8.88	•		•				•			•	•	•	•	•		•	•	•	

Facilities

...ues	Restaurants	Families
31	8.28	8.10
50	8.69	8.86
46	8.65	8.91
25	8.17	8.00
23	8.10	8.15
25	8.27	8.43
50	9.29	8.83
n/a	n/a	n/a
93	8.81	8.36
n/a	n/a	n/a
85	8.80	8.88
13	7.36	8.00
63	8.10	8.67
56	9.43	8.50
39	8.33	7.88
68	8.85	8.55
n/a	n/a	n/a
n/a	n/a	n/a
39	8.35	8.58
.07	8.07	8.37
.48	8.43	8.51
.42	8.55	8.54
.13	7.69	9.04
.51	7.91	9.02
.95	8.37	8.82
.61	8.70	8.57
.18	8.48	8.25
.28	8.45	8.42
.33	8.55	8.53
.68	8.13	8.69

Hotel ratings index

		Ratings						
		PAGE	★	👍	Ambience	Value	Staff	Location	Clea...
Peninsula	Manila	250	5	4.5	8.66	7.99	8.41	8.84	8.
Plantation Bay	Cebu	251	5	4.5	9.00	8.07	8.68	8.03	8.
Shangri-La's Mactan Island	Cebu	252	5	4.5	8.94	8.09	8.58	8.45	8.
SINGAPORE	**Area**								
Conrad Centennial	Singapore	255	5	4.5	8.95	8.35	8.96	8.83	9.
Four Seasons	Singapore	255	5	4.5	9.13	8.17	8.99	8.86	9.
Fullerton	Singapore	256	5	4.5	9.02	8.05	8.57	8.85	9.
Goodwood Park	Singapore	257	5	4	8.86	8.11	8.57	8.84	8.
Grand Hyatt	Singapore	257	5	4.5	8.62	7.88	8.48	9.27	8.
Hotel 1929	Singapore	258	2	4	8.62	8.54	8.08	8.23	9.
InterContinental	Singapore	259	5	4.5	8.79	8.25	8.65	8.82	9.
Keong Saik	Singapore	260	1	4	7.57	9.21	8.64	8.43	8.8
Marriott	Singapore	260	5	4.5	8.63	8.02	8.53	9.24	8.
Orchard	Singapore	261	4	4.5	8.58	8.24	8.61	9.15	9.
Oriental	Singapore	261	5	4.5	8.71	8.20	8.72	8.75	9.
Pan Pacific	Singapore	262	5	4.5	8.60	8.21	8.41	8.84	8.
Raffles The Plaza	Singapore	262	5	4.5	8.64	8.24	8.73	9.15	9.2
Raffles	Singapore	263	5	4.5	9.26	7.90	8.98	9.01	9.3
Ritz-Carlton Millenia	Singapore	264	5	4.5	9.09	8.21	8.98	8.48	9.3
Sentosa	Singapore	266	5	4.5	9.07	8.14	8.51	8.32	8.9
Shangri-La	Singapore	267	5	4.5	9.12	8.22	9.02	8.47	9.3
Shangri-La's Rasa Sentosa	Singapore	268	5	4.5	9.12	8.22	9.02	8.47	9.3
Sheraton	Singapore	269	5	4.5	8.69	8.04	8.91	8.13	9.
Swissôtel Merchant Court	Singapore	269	5	4.5	8.62	8.33	8.63	9.04	9.
Swissôtel The Stamford	Singapore	270	5	4.5	8.74	8.30	8.53	9.22	8.9
SRI LANKA	**Area**								
Apa Colombo House	Colombo	273	2	n/a	n/a	n/a	n/a	n/a	n/a
Apa Villa Thalpe	Galle	273	3	4.5	9.46	8.18	8.98	8.46	8.7
Club Villa	Bentota	274	3	4	9.42	7.75	8.42	8.08	9.0
Colombo Hilton	Colombo	274	5	4	8.30	7.69	8.47	8.32	8.6
Elephant Corridor	Sigiriya	275	5	n/a	n/a	n/a	n/a	n/a	n/a
Galle Face	Colombo	276	4	4	9.13	8.65	8.46	9.08	8.1
Helga's Folly	Kandy	276	2	n/a	n/a	n/a	n/a	n/a	n/a

Facilities

...ilities	Restaurants	Families	F1	F2	F3	F4	F5	F6	F7	F8	F9	F10	F11	F12	F13	F14	F15	F16	F17	F18	F19	F20
.28	8.48	8.29	•		•		•		•		•		•	•	•	•	•	•		•		•	
.43	8.10	8.73	•	•	•		•	•	•	•	•		•	•	•	•		•		•		•	•
55	8.49	8.78	•	•	•		•	•	•	•	•	•	•	•	•	•		•		•		•	•
73	8.63	8.59			•		•		•		•		•	•	•	•		•		•			
.71	8.57	8.54	•		•		•		•		•		•	•	•	•		•		•		•	
.61	8.52	8.23	•		•		•		•		•		•	•	•	•		•		•			
.19	8.44	8.11	•		•		•		•		•		•	•	•	•		•			•		
.45	8.48	8.39	•		•		•		•	•	•	•	•	•	•	•		•		•	•		
.59	8.00	6.90	•										•		•							
.50	8.42	8.37	•		•		•		•		•		•	•	•	•	•	•		•			
.04	7.75	8.44					•							•								
.35	8.40	8.37	•		•		•		•	•	•	•	•	•	•	•		•		•		•	
.40	8.59	8.65			•		•		•		•		•	•	•	•		•		•		•	
.54	8.48	8.36	•		•		•		•		•		•	•	•	•		•		•			
.50	8.58	8.31	•		•		•		•		•		•	•	•	•		•		•		•	
.67	8.54	8.46	•		•		•		•		•		•	•	•	•		•		•			
.66	8.86	8.53	•		•		•		•		•		•	•	•	•		•		•			
.86	8.70	8.47	•		•		•		•		•		•	•	•	•		•		•	•		
.52	8.43	8.52	•	•	•		•		•		•		•	•	•	•		•		•			•
.78	8.72	8.71	•		•		•		•		•		•	•	•	•		•		•		•	
.78	8.72	8.71	•		•		•		•	•	•	•	•	•	•	•		•		•	•	•	•
.45	8.49	8.42	•		•		•		•		•		•	•	•	•		•		•			
.48	8.34	8.41	•		•		•		•		•		•	•	•	•		•		•			
.60	8.60	8.43	•		•		•		•	•	•		•	•	•	•		•		•	•		
n/a	n/a	n/a	•											•	•							
7.81	9.15	9.15	•	•										•				•		•		
7.75	7.25	8.75	•	•									•	•				•		•		
3.23	8.65	8.70	•		•		•		•		•	•	•	•	•	•		•		•	•	•
n/a	n/a	n/a	•				•						•	•	•	•	•	•		•		
7.01	7.55	7.75	•	•	•		•		•				•	•	•	•		•		•		
n/a	n/a	n/a	•										•	•				•		•		

Hotel ratings index

		PAGE	★	👍	Ambience	Value	Staff	Location	Cleanli...
					Ratings				
Kandalama	Dambulla	277	5	4.5	9.39	8.82	8.75	8.86	8.6
Lighthouse	Galle	279	5	4	8.95	8.05	8.45	8.85	8.7
Mount Lavinia	Colombo	280	5	4.5	8.92	9.08	8.83	8.92	8.9
Sigiriya Village	Sigiriya	281	2	4	8.75	7.95	8.75	7.95	7.9
Sun House	Galle	281	4	n/a	n/a	n/a	n/a	n/a	n/a
Taj Exotica	Bentota	282	5	4.5	8.64	7.97	9.08	9.31	8.7
Tea Factory	Nuwara Eliya	282	4	4	8.25	8.25	8.75	8.75	7.7
TAIWAN	**Area**								
Far Eastern Plaza	Taipei	285	5	4.5	8.99	8.20	8.62	8.61	9.2
Grand Formosa Regent	Taipei	285	5	4.5	8.86	8.10	8.84	8.73	9.1
Grand Hotel	Taipei	286	5	4.5	9.00	8.34	8.69	8.47	9.0
Grand Hyatt	Taipei	287	5	4.5	8.66	7.92	8.67	8.68	9.0
Lalu Sun Moon Lake	Nantao	288	5	4.5	9.43	7.57	9.00	9.29	9.1
Landis	Taipei	289	5	4.5	9.18	8.68	9.18	8.35	9.2
Les Suites	Taipei	289	4	4	9.00	8.00	8.83	8.83	9.1
Sherwood	Taipei	290	5	4.5	8.75	8.09	8.77	8.48	9.0
Westin	Taipei	290	5	4	8.62	7.85	8.46	8.27	8.9
THAILAND	**Area**								
Allamanda Laguna	Phuket	293	4	4.5	8.38	8.60	8.40	8.60	8.4
Amanpuri	Phuket	294	5	5	9.62	8.26	9.35	8.94	9.4
Amari Palm Reef	Koh Samui	295	4	4.5	9.22	8.26	9.00	8.67	8.78
Amari Watergate	Bangkok	295	5	4.5	8.60	8.40	8.70	8.73	8.8
Anantara	Chiang Rai	296	5	5	9.29	8.59	9.12	9.18	9.47
Anantara	Hua Hin	296	5	4.5	9.31	8.55	9.14	8.58	9.42
Marriott	Bangkok	297	5	4.5	9.07	8.61	8.90	8.36	9.15
Banyan Tree	Bangkok	298	5	4.5	8.91	8.25	8.98	7.85	9.28
Banyan Tree	Phuket	299	5	4.5	9.23	7.86	9.09	8.46	9.20
Central Samui	Koh Samui	301	5	4.5	9.03	8.55	8.68	9.02	8.87
Chedi	Phuket	302	4	4.5	9.00	8.51	9.25	8.89	9.05
Chiva-Som	Hua Hin	303	5	4.5	9.16	8.72	9.40	7.96	9.08
Conrad	Bangkok	304	5	4.5	8.91	8.41	8.87	8.37	9.38
Dusit Laguna	Phuket	305	5	5	9.32	8.62	9.16	8.94	9.13
Dusit Resort	Hua Hin	306	5	4.5	9.13	8.55	9.06	8.62	9.28

Facilities

…ilities	Restaurants	Families	🏈	🏔	📈	🌐	♿	🔄	1	✚	🧸	💻	🎵	📷	☁	✗	CNN	🐚	📞	🐟	👕	🔵	ⓘ	⤵
.23	8.68	8.80	•		•					•				•	•	•				•		•	•	•	
.04	8.00	7.62	•	•	•					•				•	•	•	•	•		•		•	•	•	•
.17	8.50	8.58	•	•	•					•		•	•	•	•	•	•			•		•	•	•	
.68	8.75	8.55	•											•	•	•				•		•			
n/a	n/a	n/a	•											•	•					•					
.35	8.64	8.86	•	•	•					•		•	•	•	•	•	•			•		•		•	
.35	7.50	7.42	•											•	•	•			•				•		
.71	8.76	8.41			•					•		•		•	•	•				•		•		•	
.79	8.90	8.49	•		•		•			•	•			•	•	•				•		•		•	
.37	8.55	8.37	•		•					•		•	•	•	•	•				•		•		•	
.48	8.46	8.16	•		•		•			•		•	•	•	•	•				•		•		•	
.00	8.43	7.43			•		•			•		•	•	•	•	•	•			•		•		•	
.72	8.85	8.23	•		•					•		•		•	•	•								•	
.42	7.50	7.93			•					•		•		•	•									•	
.49	8.53	8.09	•		•		•			•		•		•	•	•		•						•	
.30	8.39	8.27	•		•		•			•	•	•		•	•	•				•					
.27	7.84	8.90	•	•				•	•		•			•	•					•		•	•	•	•
.87	8.93	8.47	•	•	•			•		•				•	•					•		•	•	•	•
.50	8.42	8.86	•	•				•						•	•					•		•		•	•
.42	8.57	8.46	•		•		•			•				•	•					•		•		•	
.74	8.59	8.65	•		•					•				•	•					•		•	•	•	
.77	8.78	8.71	•	•	•					•	•			•	•	•	•			•		•	•	•	
8.71	8.87	8.72	•		•		•			•	•	•		•	•					•		•	•	•	
.73	8.60	8.23	•		•					•	•	•		•	•					•		•			
.86	8.45	8.62		•				•	•					•	•					•		•		•	•
.36	8.47	8.90		•	•			•		•	•		•	•	•					•		•		•	•
.38	8.22	8.51	•											•	•					•		•	•	•	•
.23	8.48	7.59		•			•	•	•	•			•	•	•				•	•		•		•	•
.82	8.74	8.46	•		•					•		•	•	•	•	•				•		•	•		
.54	8.52	9.21	•	•	•				•	•	•	•		•	•	•				•		•	•	•	•
.82	8.89	9.14	•	•	•					•	•			•	•	•				•		•	•	•	•

Hotel ratings index

		PAGE	★	👍	Ambience	Value	Staff	Location	Cleanliness
Dusit	Pattaya	307	5	4.5	9.21	8.51	8.72	8.77	9.02
Dusit Thani	Bangkok	307	5	4.5	8.96	8.63	9.09	8.97	9.12
Evason	Hua Hin	308	5	4.5	9.19	8.47	8.77	7.74	9.19
Evason	Phuket	308	5	4.5	9.13	8.64	8.54	7.90	8.93
Four Seasons	Bangkok	309	5	4.5	8.97	8.36	9.13	8.93	9.24
Four Seasons	Chiang Mai	310	5	5	9.57	8.06	9.31	8.55	9.55
Grand Hyatt Erawan	Bangkok	312	5	4.5	8.93	8.15	8.93	9.14	9.07
Hard Rock	Pattaya	313	4	4	8.43	8.16	8.59	8.27	8.65
Hilton	Hua Hin	313	5	4.5	8.98	8.77	8.88	9.00	9.12
Holiday Inn	Phuket	314	4	4.5	8.78	8.69	9.02	9.06	8.97
Hyatt Regency	Hua Hin	315	5	4.5	9.21	8.64	9.02	8.48	9.05
JW Marriott	Bangkok	315	5	4.5	8.88	8.40	8.98	8.80	9.17
JW Marriott	Phuket	316	5	4.5	9.27	8.47	9.00	7.92	9.31
Laguna Beach	Phuket	317	5	4.5	9.03	8.38	9.04	8.78	8.94
Landmark	Bangkok	317	5	4.5	8.46	8.48	8.86	9.28	9.03
Le Méridien Beach	Phuket	318	5	4.5	9.03	8.50	8.96	8.91	9.01
Le Royal Méridien	Koh Samui	319	5	4.5	9.30	7.73	9.03	8.47	9.23
Le Royal Méridien Yacht Club	Phuket	320	5	4.5	9.00	8.21	9.15	9.10	9.13
Marriott	Hua Hin	320	5	4.5	9.11	8.23	8.81	8.72	9.02
Novotel On Siam Square	Bangkok	321	4	4	8.12	8.31	8.46	9.02	8.52
Novotel Coralia	Phuket	321	4	4	8.54	8.37	8.56	8.34	8.51
Oriental	Bangkok	322	5	5	9.27	8.30	9.36	8.71	9.46
Pathumwan Princess	Bangkok	324	4	4	8.28	8.44	8.40	9.30	8.53
Peninsula	Bangkok	325	5	5	9.15	8.64	9.16	8.32	9.48
Pimalai	Koh Lanta	327	5	4.5	9.04	8.14	8.89	9.21	8.96
Plaza Athénée	Bangkok	328	5	4.5	8.69	8.21	8.85	8.76	9.08
Poppies	Koh Samui	328	5	4.5	9.34	8.76	9.21	8.97	9.28
Racha	Phuket	329	5	n/a	n/a	n/a	n/a	n/a	n/a
Rayavadee	Krabi	330	5	4.5	9.70	7.37	9.27	9.20	9.18
Royal Cliff	Bangkok	331	5	4.5	9.03	8.04	9.00	8.67	9.06
Royal Orchid Sheraton	Pattaya	331	5	4.5	8.72	8.24	9.02	8.68	9.07
Shangri-La	Bangkok	332	5	4.5	9.04	8.39	9.07	8.81	9.27
Sheraton Grande Sukhumvit	Bangkok	332	5	4.5	8.77	8.35	8.95	8.85	9.19

Facilities

Facilities	Restaurants	Families	Facilities (icon columns)
8.75	8.83	8.78	• • • ⚬ ⚬ • ⚬ ⚬ • • • • • • ⚬ • • •
8.72	8.89	8.74	• ⚬ • ⚬ • ⚬ • • • • • • • ⚬ • •
8.53	8.42	8.77	• • • ⚬ • • • • • • • • • • • • • • •
8.55	8.22	8.55	⚬ • • • • • • • • • • ⚬ • • • • •
8.61	8.91	8.51	• ⚬ • • • • • • • • • • •
8.71	8.57	8.43	• ⚬ • • • • • • • • •
8.62	8.83	8.49	• ⚬ • • • • • • • • • • • •
8.43	8.35	8.84	• ⚬ • • • • • • • • • • • •
8.72	8.76	9.16	• • ⚬ • • • • • • • • •
8.55	8.54	9.02	• ⚬ • • • • • • • • • • •
8.69	8.46	9.28	• • • • • • • • • • • •
8.62	8.81	8.61	• ⚬ • • • • • • • • •
8.85	8.70	9.04	• • • • • • • • • • • • • •
8.74	8.34	9.23	• • • • • • • • • • • •
8.56	8.71	8.74	• ⚬ • • • • • • • • •
8.71	8.81	9.01	• • • • • • • • • • • • •
8.61	8.27	8.57	• • • • • • • • • • •
8.57	8.60	8.57	• • • • • • • • • •
8.44	8.71	9.00	• • • • • • • • • • •
7.98	8.12	8.09	• ⚬ • • • • • • • •
8.32	8.50	8.70	• ⚬ • • • • • • • •
8.89	9.14	8.85	• ⚬ • • • • • • • • •
8.32	8.28	8.34	• ⚬ • • • • • • •
8.98	8.84	8.67	• ⚬ • • • • • • • • •
8.28	8.04	8.82	• • • • • • • • • •
8.56	8.49	8.61	• ⚬ • • • • • •
8.41	8.59	8.56	• • • • • •
n/a	n/a	n/a	• • • • • • • • •
8.82	8.77	8.56	• • • • • • • • •
8.85	8.99	8.88	• • • • • • • • • • • • •
8.56	8.79	8.70	• • • • • • • •
8.83	8.90	8.64	• ⚬ • • • • • • • •
8.66	8.70	8.45	• ⚬ • • • • • • •

Hotel ratings index

		PAGE	★	👍	Ambience	Value	Staff	Location	Cleanliness
Sheraton Grande Laguna	Phuket	333	5	4.5	9.02	8.12	8.78	8.48	8.81
Sheraton	Krabi	334	5	4.5	8.84	7.96	8.75	8.55	8.98
Sofitel Central	Hua Hin	335	5	4.5	9.27	8.32	9.09	9.04	9.05
Sofitel Raja Orchid	Khon Kaen	336	5	4.5	8.72	8.98	8.67	8.02	9.11
Sukhothai	Bangkok	337	5	4.5	9.26	8.39	8.96	8.05	9.33
Tongsai Bay	Koh Samui	338	5	4.5	9.31	8.03	9.19	8.84	9.13
Triple Two	Bangkok	339	4	4.5	8.93	8.64	9.36	8.50	9.36
VIETNAM	**Area**								
Ana Mandara	Nha Trang	342	4	4.5	9.16	7.97	9.02	8.00	8.93
Caravelle	Ho Chi Minh City	343	5	4.5	8.33	7.89	8.73	9.21	8.89
De Syloia	Hanoi	343	2	4.5	8.70	8.90	9.15	8.55	8.90
Furama	Danang	344	5	4.5	9.02	7.75	8.86	8.58	9.00
Hilton Opera	Hanoi	345	5	4.5	8.75	8.46	8.78	8.94	9.03
Horison	Hanoi	346	4	4	8.23	8.57	8.75	8.08	8.75
Hoi An Beach	Hoi An	346	4	4	8.38	8.41	8.41	8.67	8.57
Hoi An Riverside	Hoi An	347	4	4.5	9.20	8.70	8.84	8.02	9.02
Majestic	Ho Chi Minh City	348	4	4	8.32	8.24	8.47	8.71	8.26
New World	Ho Chi Minh City	348	4	4.5	8.64	8.66	8.84	8.95	8.79
Novotel Coralia Ocean Dunes	Phan Thiet	349	4	4.5	7.95	8.55	8.95	8.55	9.35
Renaissance Riverside	Ho Chi Minh City	349	4	4.5	8.51	8.59	8.95	9.04	9.02
Rex	Ho Chi Minh City	350	4	4	8.43	8.30	8.56	9.26	8.28
Sheraton Saigon	Ho Chi Minh City	350	5	4.5	8.63	7.77	8.38	8.99	8.90
Sofitel Dalat Palace	Dalat	351	5	4.5	8.96	8.11	8.61	9.18	9.18
Sofitel Metropole	Hanoi	352	5	4.5	9.00	8.02	8.77	9.07	8.91
Victoria	Hoi An	354	4	4.5	9.25	7.98	8.84	8.84	9.02
Victoria	Phan Thiet	354	4	4.5	9.01	8.43	8.75	8.38	8.96
Victoria	Sapa	355	4	5	8.32	7.89	8.32	8.32	8.04

Facilities

Facilities	Restaurants	Families																					
8.64	8.53	9.07	•	•	•		•	•	•	•	•	•		•	•	•	•	•		•	•	•	•
8.36	8.13	8.83	•	•	•		•	•		•	•	•	•	•	•	•	•			•	•	•	•
8.62	8.57	8.93	•	•			•	•		•		•		•	•	•	•	•		•	•	•	
8.18	8.45	8.56	•		•		•			•		•	•	•			•			•		•	
8.77	8.90	8.11	•		•					•		•		•	•		•			•	•	•	
8.82	8.88	8.05		•						•		•		•	•		•				•		•
8.50	8.07	8.50			•							•		•	•	•	•	•					
8.30	8.10	8.54	•	•	•			•		•		•		•	•	•	•			•	•	•	•
8.15	8.41	7.94	•		•	•	•			•		•	•	•	•	•	•			•		•	
7.82	8.63	8.63			•			•	•		•	•	•										
8.56	8.12	8.52	•	•	•		•	•	•	•		•		•	•	•	•			•	•	•	•
8.24	8.22	8.38	•		•		•			•		•		•	•	•	•			•		•	
8.39	8.10	8.55	•		•		•		•	•	•	•		•	•	•	•			•	•	•	
7.56	7.57	8.07	•	•	•		•	•		•				•	•	•	•			•		•	•
8.34	8.16	8.31	•	•	•			•		•		•		•	•	•	•			•		•	
7.68	7.77	7.43	•		•		•			•		•		•	•	•	•				•	•	
8.41	8.59	8.47	•		•	•				•		•		•	•	•	•			•	•		
7.96	8.15	8.95	•	•		•	•		•	•	•	•		•	•	•	•			•	•	•	•
8.28	8.42	8.23	•		•		•			•		•		•	•		•			•		•	
7.79	8.33	8.31		•	•	•			•	•		•		•	•	•				•		•	
8.29	8.21	8.23	•		•	•	•		•	•	•	•	•	•	•	•	•			•	•	•	
8.17	8.67	8.61	•		•			•		•		•		•	•	•	•				•	•	
8.22	8.70	8.23	•		•			•		•			•	•	•	•				•		•	
8.44	8.04	8.75	•	•	•		•			•		•	•	•	•	•	•			•	•	•	•
8.27	8.33	9.11	•	•	•			•		•		•		•	•	•	•			•	•	•	•
7.69	8.32	8.23	•		•				•	•			•		•	•		•		•	•		

Hotel index